LOOKING BEYOND

LOOKING BEYOND

by Lin Yutang

New York
Prentice-Hall, Inc.

PRINTED IN THE UNITED STATES OF AMERICA

LIBRARY OF CONGRESS CATALOG NUMBER 55-5859

To

L. C. W.

B.C./I.T.W.

LOOKING
BEYOND

Chapter I

EURYDICE felt a floating sensation. Without fever of any sort, she felt like being in a dream, which she knew she was not.

She would like to convince herself that it was all a dream. She would have been less miserable. The scratch on the base of her palm from the fall on the beach that day, now hardened and turned purplish black, told her that she was not resurrected in some empyreal region—the garden of the Hesperides, for example. No, she was down on earth, on the island which she and Paul, only a fortnight ago, had, by what they thought was a pure stroke of luck, discovered while on routine duty. They had popped champagne to celebrate their discovery—the crowning touch of their otherwise dull and monotonous work for the Geodetic Survey.

Fondly she looked at her watch. It was a complicated piece of mechanism, with four dials and five hands, a gift of the Democratic World Commonwealth, of which the Geodetic Survey was a section, given in appreciation of her signal, meritorious services over the Andes. On the inside of its back cover was an engraving: "To Miss Barbara Maverick, For Her Brave Pioneering Work in Geodetic Survey, Division of World Food and Health, Democratic World Commonwealth. May 22, *Anno Domini*, 2003." (Shortly after her recovery from her illness on the island, her name was changed to Eurydice, for the convenience of the inhabitants who were principally of Greek extraction.) The calendar

watch was a most useful gift in her travels. It said now definitely
Monday, September 18, '04. She needed no other assurance of
her connection with the outside world and of its very present
reality. She needed that assurance.

Sober and sane, she reassured herself repeatedly that she was
landed on this strange island of the mid-Pacific, which her generation had never heard of. She could recall vividly the events
of the past days, their leaving San Felipe on the Chilean coast,
the smooth flight, the landing at night, the death of Paul, her
co-worker and fiancé, the funeral pyre the next day—and the
blank which followed. She went over these events, tried to
absorb them in her memory. She disliked dramatizing her situation; it wasn't in her Ohioan blood. She hated pursuing the
thought that she was alone, a permanent captive, cut off from
the world, with a slim chance of return. Only a preposterous
change of circumstances could make her return possible.

She had fainted on the summit of the hillock where Paul's
remains were consigned to the flames, and had remained unconscious for twenty-four hours. In the days of somnolent weak-
ness which followed, a sense of the unreality of her situation had
constantly assailed her. Thainos on the South Pacific—Paul's discovery and hers. Yet it could be equally true—the thought haunted
her—that she had very likely died in the crash, that this life she
saw now on the island was the world into which she had been
reborn. Nobody could say what life after death was like; perhaps it was just like the world she had left, only a little better,
more gay-colored, more peaceful. Peaceful, that was the word.
But if it was a peaceful world, it was heaven, anyway good
enough for heaven. To found a world of peace was the sole object
of the Democratic World Commonwealth, the reason for which
she had thrown her heart into its work. Was she dreaming now,
or was she bodily, physically alive? Then her head cleared when
she had taken soup, and those wild fears and imaginings of hers
vanished. Her sensuous contacts registered. Unquestionably, she
was alive. Only the life around her was so novel, so unexpected,
so strange.

It was not so strange that the sky was bluer, the bougainvillea creeping over the walls of her cottage a brighter, more intense, almost insulting purple, if the yellow citrons in the garden, thick-rinded and ending in strips like half-clasped fingers, were monstrous in shape and size. From her bed she could see the milky sheen of the morning sea, flecked by a few fishing boats, standing out against it in sharp outline, so calm and placid without movement of any sort that the view stood still like a picture captured at some moment by an artist, and held immobile for eternity. At this moment, the sea appeared like a body of whey, or like some pale blue, heavy molten liquid, firm with a silvery radiance which a light breeze had no power to wrinkle. Against it, the dark silhouettes of the boats and the black heavy lines they traced on the water's surface stood, bold and strong, like daubs of black and sepia laid by a master. Beyond, it became bands of opal glistening in the sun, disappearing into a misty, hazy white indistinguishable from the distant frozen clouds on the horizon.

She perspired, more from the tepid warmth of the air than from bodily fever. The air was astir with the faint, unrecognizable buzz of insects, drowsily repetitious, now and then broken by the short, sharp notes of a passing whippoorwill or the liquid song of white-throats. She occupied a room on the lower level of a house situated on the northerly ridge of the island overlooking a deep gully below, where a rivulet separated the row of straggling houses on the ridge from the generous incline sloping downward toward the sea half a mile away. The room on the lower level was perceptibly cooler during the day; its double exposure permitted an enticing view of the rocky brook coming down from above, whose merry babble, sounding like the voices of playing schoolchildren in the distance, increased noticeably in volume after an afternoon thunderstorm. These brief showers, lasting perhaps a quarter of an hour or half an hour, were a regular feature of the island climate, sweeping all dust from the air and off the roads. After the shower, waking up from an afternoon nap, she would listen, with some amusement, to a different strain of music. From the high tree tops, the leaves trembled and shook down the rain water in showers of driplets, falling into a pool somewhere in the yard below. This whirl of sounds gradually slowed down, and then usually two or three streams of regular, rhythmic beats remained, each with its own intervals, one faster than the other, now meeting and synchronizing, and now lengthening out and catching each other up again.

Half raising herself on the bed, she could see the hawthorn underbrush, lying in the shadow, lining the banks of the rivulet. Bowena, the native maid, would often go down the brook for a mid-afternoon swim; her tawny limbs, her long hair, her flashing eyes and the complete naturalness with which she exposed herself naked in the open, the simplicity of it all fascinated her. Occasionally, too, other women appeared like sylvan nymphs on the upper reaches of the rivulet, similarly devoid of appropriate coverage. Her experience on the Chilean coast and on the Peruvian border had accustomed her to strange manners and ways of different people. She should have expected them, as well as the tropical forests and the giant cedars and the olives around the town.

No, she should make an exception of the olives. That was the disturbing note, and not the only one. In her more somnolent states, brought about by the shock and exhaustion, she fought against the impression that she was on some island of classical Greece, or perhaps Arcadia, or somewhere on the plains of Attica. Those olive groves and square white shepherds' cottages on the uplands below the giant rocky peaks, with sheep pasturing on them, visible from her back window, gave a definitely Greek impression; they made her think that the island had gone crazy, or she had. Such impossible names, too! Emma-Emma, the American woman with whom she shared the cottage, presumably an anthropologist, with a head of white hair buried in her voluminous notes. Why should an American woman call herself Emma-Emma? That should be M.M. in Greek; everything here had a Greek touch about it.

There was Dr. Lysippus, who had come to see her every morn-

ing since her illness, a short, stumpy figure, bringing always a
bunch of marigolds and a bottle of pale orange liquid for her
to drink. Remonstrations with this transplanted version of a
modern physician were of no avail. Eurydice profoundly dis-
trusted him. One would hardly trust a doctor with a bare chest,
rustic looking, wearing an eternally half-idiotic smile and speaking in a half-archaic idiom. There was no compassion in his
eyes, no trace of solicitude for his patient's welfare. He came
in with that alleged medicine, never inquired about her progress,
and to all her questions gave a thoughtless, cavalierly abrupt
"Drink it!" Then he talked to Emma-Emma about the variety
of sparrows and thrashers which were passing through the island—
the doctor was an ornithologist. He took his ornithology more
seriously than his patient. "Drink it!" he said. He simply had no
clinical manners. Quite possibly, he did not even believe in his
profession. He simply had no use for patients.

Illness, Eurydice learned from Emma-Emma, cured itself, with
or without medicine, on this island. Or so Dr. Lysippus said.

She grew suspicious of the liquid—horrible stuff prescribed by
a horrible doctor. Either take that, she was told, or he would
perform phlebotomy on her. Dr. Lysippus said he would not
phlebotomize anybody if he could help it, least of all such a
pretty young lady. "The Americanithá—so pretty—like Diana,
is it not so?" he said in his broken English. It sounded so wonderful; the Greek intonation was always soft and leisurely and euphonious, with the graceful habit of ending a statement with a
is-it-not-so? like someone carrying out, or about to plunge into,
a long philosophic inquiry into the truth of things or the nature
of our ideas. The very mysterious word enchanted her; any
lady would be glad to walk out of a hospital and tell her friends
that she had been "phlebotomized" by her doctor.

"What is phlebotomy?" she asked Emma-Emma after Lysippus
left.

"It means having your *phleps* cut."

"My *phleps?*"

"Yes, your *phleps*—vein."

"Oh, I see," Eurydice said with a sharp intake of breath. The idea penetrated her head—fuzzy and never quite sure of itself— that the doctor might let her blood. No, she would, like a good child, take that nasty medicine.

The orange liquid, Eurydice suspected, was a kind of philter, because she had caught the word distinctly in Dr. Lysippus' talk with Emma-Emma. Devoutly, she hoped it was not an aphro- disiac, to make her fall in love with the doctor, that squat, bare- chested, curly-bearded gentleman! Anywhere she turned, she saw or heard or was reminded of something Greek. The Greeks seemed to have a monopoly of *phils*—from philter to philosophy. And aphrodisiac! Did the Greeks love so much? The liquid, of indescribable odor, had a definite effect on her, she observed. It calmed her nerves, and restored her good cheer. Her head usually felt clearer after a drink.

Frankly, she had been delirious. She wouldn't be surprised to find savages, or even cannibals here, but why should she find a colony of Europeans, happy, contented, with a high degree of culture, apparently free from worry about war? The thought struck her that perhaps this, the opportunity to live a happy, carefree, simple life, might be a way of life enjoyed by the modern man, might be a possible development of an ideal human society, away from the self-imposed complexities and conflicts of modern civilization, if the shadow of war did not fall so heavily on it. Ever since she was born, in the 1970's, she had heard of nothing but wars and the threats of war. Where did this colony come from? Who had planned it? And what was this American woman, Emma-Emma, doing here? Everything did not add up right. When she became stronger, this sense of unreality left her; then she felt normal again. But in the middle of the night, these doubts assailed her once more.

She had read about a colony of Germans and Austrians some- where in the jungles of Venezuela and Colombia, completely for- gotten by the world, discovered by some flier after the First World War; they had been so isolated that they had never heard of the great war at all, and what the women wanted most, when asked, was a meat grinder to replace the old one fast wearing out. A colony of Chinese had been discovered in the jungles of Malaya in 1953, when the British authorities were resettling the inhabitants, who had been cut off from the world for over two hundred years; they had heard their ancestors speak of the sea and were still reading Confucius by copying manuscripts. After the defeat of Hitler, a German submarine had disappeared with its crew; after fifteen years they were discovered to have founded a colony on a remote Pacific island, having married native women and raised families, knowing nothing about the outside world and caring not a whit about it. Perhaps this was one of those strange settlements, created by the circumstances of war and completely forgotten by the world.

Yes, she knew there was nothing wrong with her. She was physically and mentally intact. It was just that the shock of the recent happenings, the sights and costumes and manners of the men and women on the island, plus the death of Paul, had been too much for her. An arrangement of life, so different from what she was used to, could not but produce a quaint, unsettling impression upon her mind; one might say, its very order and peace were confusing to her. She needed just a little time to recover herself and find her bearings again.

Perhaps in her discovery of Thainos she had stumbled upon something exciting and new.

Chapter II

SHE HAD NOT quite gotten over it. Lying in bed, she tried to piece together the impressions of the past few days.

"Keimai, keisai, keitai," she had been repeating in bed when she was quite ill, she remembered. The impression of the funeral procession, of the music and song and dance, of those beautiful girls in white tunics, breasts and one shoulder bare, with a white veil over their heads—the weird music of the lyre, Orphean, of the netherworld, and the lutes and violins—those images passed vaguely through her mind, invested with a dreamlike insubstantiality. Why the violins? Who had brought them here? Certainly not storm-wrecked sailors; not war refugees who suddenly had found it necessary to pack up and escape atom bombs. She had learned, unlearned and properly buried her Greek since she left college. Now bits of it came back to her from her submerged consciousness. Of all the Greek she had learned at college, this stuck—*keimai, keisai, keitai.* She loved it. I lie still—you lie still—he lies still. It sounded so lazy, invitingly so. She used to lie in bed on Sunday mornings, till eleven, and recite those words with a feeling of positive luxury. That was the time when she and her classmates loved to say, "I feel comatose," when they meant "sleepy."

Only four or five days ago she was Barbara Maverick. She and Paul had been working in a lonely outpost in a Chilean village. Their work required surveying by plane, on a gridiron pattern, all areas of land and sea in that corner of the world. The work was becoming monotonous, mechanical and getting to look foolish. Of course, there were no islands in that area—just thousands upon thousands of square miles of water. On one of the trips, they were flying at 3,000 feet. The sea below was covered by a bank of foamy clouds, rendering visibility difficult. Through rifts between the clouds they could see only dark shadowy patches of indigo water. Paul insisted on maintaining the altitude as a principle of safety. Mechanically, they took a few photographs. On return to San Felipe, they found that one of the photographs showed, between the clouds, extremely dark patches that could be thick timberland as well as water, fringed by what seemed to be a section of shoreline, represented by circles of lighter shades. In the dark areas, there were tiny, straight, white lines, at three or four different spots, that could be some kind of masonry. If this was an island, perhaps even inhabitable and inhabited, it would be the most exciting discovery of their work, which was getting to be a bore. They would be able to report something new to the WFH Division. Of course they would not say anything to anybody until the discovery was confirmed.

Eurydice remembered vividly the excitement when they took off in the night, to be sure to pass the island, if there was one, before the sun set the next day. They arrived when the subtropical sun was sinking low into the sea, directly in their face. The excitement at the confirmation was followed by confusion and fear. There could be cannibals. Eurydice remembered seeing Paul adjusting his belt and clicking his pistol. It made him look ridiculous. Paul was not a soldier; he was a scientist. For three-quarters of an hour, he flew low, encircling the island again and again. From the airplane, the island looked like a sprawling, maimed octopus which had lost some of its legs, marking a zigzag shore outline, with parts of the outer extremities forming little isles around it. Coral reefs had grown around the periphery on the west and again on the south. The island itself was a mass of timberland and pastures, dominated by a smooth, round, rocky peak of considerable height which now glowed a reddish purple in the westering sun.

Unquestionably the island was inhabited; they had spotted white cottages and a few bigger square, columned structures built of tufa. They were amazed. They could not make up their minds. The island had no right to be there, much less houses that spoke of a certain degree of human civilization, a civilization unheard of by anybody. Then, on the second run, they discovered a few fishing boats lying off shore. Yet for all these signs, the island seemed to be dead. The center of the town, heavily clouded by the vegetation, did not attract their attention. Paul decided to "buzz" the island and expected to see people running out and screaming into the open. No one seemed to be alive.

They decided to land on the lagoon side. To their horror, they saw groups of corpses strewn around the beach. Their engine whirred in a slow descent, skimming the shore tentatively, ready to fly off in case of a shot or a spear issuing from the wooded shore. Silently, they made the landing, their eyes looking about, their ears alert. A dead quiet, while they remained in the cockpit, waiting momentarily for anything to happen. The silence was inexplicable. Surely the inhabitants had seen them. Were eyes peering from behind those wild thickets dark with foliage? Paul was tired and Eurydice's heart was thumping like a village pump. To all appearances, they were ignored.

Darkness was coming over the island, giving a false sense of security. Anyway they were glad to be under the benevolent cover of the night. They had to do something, and they were really too tired. Who could tell? Perhaps the inhabitants would be friendly. Gradually they got up enough courage to come out and breathe the fresh air of the island. They could not explore; there was nothing to explore in the dark. No lights on the island as far as they could see. This alone was singular. Alone together, silent in a deserted universe, Paul suddenly broke out into a laugh, and Eurydice laughed, too, overcome by a sense of the madness of the whole situation. Then Paul let out, deliberately, a laugh which was a succession of howls. Paul was afraid. Anybody would be afraid. Why didn't those inhabitants shoot a gun or something? At least they would then know what to do—clamber back to the cockpit, and fly away into the black immensity of the night.

But there was just nothing. The surface of the lagoon glowed a metallic gray in the warm, fragrant half-light that was sub-tropical night. They slept under the plane that night.

It was a mistake for Paul to have carried a pistol along. Eury-dice remembered only they were standing near the entrance to the town the next morning, some hundred yards away from the fountain, under a mangrove whose twisted and interlaced beards touched the ground, Paul swishing his gun around in a horizontal circle. It made him look ridiculous. In front of them, in a semi-circle, was a group of bearded and semi-naked men, and even a few women. Paul was tense. Eurydice, standing by his side, could hear his heavy short breaths. The faces of the inhabi-tants were sullen and coldly resentful.

A man, arms folded across his chest, glowered at Paul.

"Put that toy down!" the man said in good English.

Paul should have been glad. He wasn't. Perhaps he was stunned by the strange sight of these curious-looking inhabitants, some in tunics and sandals, some in open shirts and shorts. He still pointed his gun around.

"Put that toy down!" repeated the man.

Eurydice, standing close, lightly tipped the gun down in his hand. Paul relaxed, his lethal weapon slowly finding its way to its holster.

But gun or no gun, it would have made no difference. The man stepped forward and they shook hands. The man said he was Groucho, an American. The inhabitants were certainly polite, even friendly, as friendly as they could be to an unwelcome guest. An exchange of questions and answers followed. Paul explained to Groucho who they were and what they were doing.

The man who was known as Laos now stepped forward. He could speak fluent, if a little professorial English, with a trace of Greek accent. They were ushered to the square and entertained at a restaurant. They had lunch with Laos and Groucho, Laos asking many questions about their work. A red local wine was served. A large group of men, women and children clustered around the square in evident excitement. They felt like a pair from another planet.

Paul and Eurydice were now relaxed, in fact quite enthusiastic and happy at the discovery of this colony. And Groucho had become very friendly. He said his name was Marx, son of the famous comedian. Nobody could tell whether he was playing a hoax upon them, and anyway it did not matter. Groucho had been a navigator-pilot, the only survivor of a crew which had crash-landed into the island. And here he was. Was he happy? Very happy. Didn't they see the many pretty girls around the place?

Groucho, heavy-shouldered and a big chunk of a man, was a swaggering, talkative, friendly, vain sort, who loved to parade himself in front of ladies. He offered them his humble services; he would show them the town. No, they must not think of leaving. What was a few days' stop in this God's paradise? Why, the Allah's own paradise had no better-looking dark-eyed houris. Laos had spoken to Chiron, the tavern keeper; there was a room upstairs in the inn where they could take an hour's nap—they should, in fact, after such a long flight. After the nap, he would take them to the inland lake. Had Paul even seen public bathing? He meant public bathing, Mediterranean style. Well, he hadn't seen anything yet.

Eurydice thought of her first arrival at the lake shore. It might have been a picture of water nymphs by some Renaissance painter come to life. She could not believe her eyes. Considering the fact that the young girls of the island were customarily stripped to the waist anyway, she shouldn't be surprised. Six or seven girls were playing in various depths of the water, completely naked. Groucho was a great swimmer.

"Come on down!" he shouted from the water.

The sultry heat of the afternoon made the water inviting.

Paul took off his clothes and plunged in after him. Eurydice was terribly amused.

After a while they came up. Two or three girls had come up, too, and were winding their skirts in the open under the tall pines.

"Don't you think you should take a look at the plane?" Eurydice asked.

"Yes, I think I should."

Chapter III

WHAT FOLLOWED was tragic, but inevitable. It happened only within the space of a few minutes.

Paul and Eurydice could never have gotten out of the island anyway. The friendly luncheon, the rest and the bathing in the inland lake were designed for the men to inspect the plane and carry out their orders. But Paul need not have been killed.

Eurydice followed him to the shore where their plane stood. They had heard the noise of hacking and chopping as they approached. For a few seconds, they stood and watched aghast from behind the thicket. There was no doubt the islanders were trying to put the plane out of commission, dismantling parts for their own amusement and destroying the rest. The gleaming silver body glittered in the broiling heat on the sand. How much had they destroyed? It was reckless of Paul to try to save what he could.

"You wait here."

Paul dashed out of the thicket, crying like a madman for them to stop. He opened a shot, felling one man immediately. Two others ducked under the fusillage and scurried to the other side.

"Come back, Paul! Don't!"

Eurydice ran after him. She saw only shuffling and scuffling legs on the other side. Another shot and a man tumbled to the sand. A third man scampered around to the near side, screaming frantically. Suddenly the shape of a huge dark figure sprang out of the cockpit, axe in hand, and took a flying jump on the other side. Bare feet and Paul's boots closed in in a quick, bewildering, blinding scuffle. Then silence, and Paul's limp body dropped beside the other prostrate body. Eurydice's knees buckled as she ran, trying to reach Paul. She tripped and fell on the sand, face downward. She tried to sit up, but could only raise herself on one elbow. She saw the pair of bronze feet kicking up, maliciously, a cloud of sand over Paul's body. The sand was burning to the touch, but luckily her head was in the shadow. The other man who had dropped first began to sit up.

Eurydice lay motionless, careless of what had happened. A smell of gasoline stained the sea air. Her head was perfectly clear. As she looked up, she saw the gas streaming down from the wing, forming a rivulet in the sand. From the distance came noises of men and women, a confusion of distinct if unintelligible words, swelling nearer and nearer. Paul's body was lying on the sand, motionless. Blood was spurting down his temples, forming a pool on the sand, joined by the rivulet of leaking gasoline which now ran toward his body, drenching his pants, then his jacket. Paul dead, dead as a rock by the seashore.

The crowd, attracted by the shots, had gathered around. Eurydice sat up in a blank stupor. She saw the tall man coming up from the water, where he had gone to clean the axe of blood. The inhabitants were helping the wounded man up and questioning him about what had happened. Eurydice looked up at the eyes of pity and eyes of resentment around her.

At this moment, a slim old woman with white hair stepped forward and helped Eurydice to get on her feet.

"Don't be afraid. They won't do anything to you." It was Emma-Emma. "You are an American, aren't you? I am, too."

"Is he dead?"

"Yes. I am awfully sorry this has happened. He shouldn't have killed one of our men."

"What are you people trying to do? We mean no harm."

"Come on. You won't understand. We don't want anybody to get away from here. I will explain it to you."

In Emma-Emma's cottage, Eurydice lay dazed, unable to think. It looked as if she could never get out of this place. The island, as far as she knew, lay at least a thousand miles out of the routes of the South Pacific tramp steamers. There was a bare chance the WFH would learn about their disappearance and send some-one in search of them. The San Felipe station was a temporary outpost, manned by Paul and herself. The WFH probably did not even know where they were, as they had been working their way down an ancient Inca trail along the west side of the Andes. They might have given them up for lost in the Andes, for they had been moving, gathering data, and were required to send reports only once every quarter. As for the villagers, they had seen these two mad tourists about the town a great deal, but had shown no profound interest in them. The head of police was more interested in his own fishing junks than in the tourists. No, he did not inspire confidence. It would be weeks before they suddenly remembered that the tourists had not returned, rent unpaid. What could you expect of those crazy American tourists? Probably another month would elapse before a departmental re-port was drawn up and reached Valparaiso, in its leisurely course of time. The Department of Valparaiso might want a confirmation for more details. . . . The WFH would hear about the disap-pearance of its field workers some months later, and when it did, would find it too late and give them up for lost. There was not one chance in a hundred they would find her on this island.

She remembered the funeral procession the next day. She might have seen the whole thing in a dream, so unaccustomed was she to the costumes and customs of the islanders. It was out of this world. She was told Paul's body was to be cremated to-gether with that of the man he had killed. She forced herself to get out of bed and join the procession.

A tinkling sound came from the distance. The whole village had turned out, converging from the alleys and the straggling houses on top, and gathered in the olive grove a short distance from the square. The women were in white, their heads covered by veils; men in long tunics, others in open shirts, all wearing sandals. There was a good sprinkling of natives with dark tanned limbs, almost naked, their skin showing a healthy metallic sheen like well-fed horses. Some were evidently assigned to carry the two bodies which lay covered on stretchers.

The white robes began to come together and form a line. The women pressed their hands against their chests, their heads bowed. Sounds of flutes floated across the glen in tentative, preparatory snatches; clay pipes made a few desultory piercing notes. Eurydice moved mechanically along with them. Light filtered through the foliage overhead, submerging everything in a pool of greenish shade. Aristotimus, in his tall miter and his lavish priestly garments and sandals, was seen moving slowly and pontifically among the crowd, whispering answers to questions. Out of nowhere, it seemed, an orchestra of flutes and guitars came together and stood behind this tall Greek priest, chattering noisily. Just in front of the stretchers stood a group of some twenty girl dancers, dressed in billowy white with a clear blue piping, their black hair let down in flouncing locks, unlike the other women who had theirs done up in sharp comely coils at the back. Many of them turned their heads to look at Eurydice, as curious about her alien dress, her blouse and slim fitting breeches as she was about theirs. "The Americanitha," as they called her, was a being of the "Old World" they had only heard spoken of in gossip and read about in story-books, who had shot down like a meteor into their midst. But every one of the girls bore herself with a carriage worthy of Athena herself; they had evidently been put through a course in beauty training. Civilized? Decidedly, yet in a strange, gracious way. She was not accustomed to seeing a friendly, cheerful, sunny character beaming from young faces. Perhaps if men were truly civilized, they should look exactly that way.

This jumble of impressions was heightened when the procession of men and women began to move, with Aristotimus at the head, followed by two boys holding bells in their hands. They followed a trail for an even hundred yards and then led through broader paths shaded by tall, slim palms, continuously up the

country, which consisted of slopes and ledges that toppled down-
wards from the mountain toward the sea. The flutes and the
guitars started and the dancers sang a plaintive melody in a
rolling, repetitious rhythm, sad yet pleasing to the ears, intoxi-
cating, hypnotic, somber and timeless, like a song from the
underworld.

They came to a hillcrest. A funeral pyre had been made ready.
The bodies, borne on stretchers, were placed on top. The men
and women lined up in a circle some thirty feet away. The wood
was kindled. While the logs crackled and a blue column of smoke
rose from the pyre and ascended into the incredibly blue sky,
the dancers began a slow, rhythmic dance, symbolizing the joining of the body and the spirit and the madness and yearnings of
life; and finally the departure of the spirit, represented by a chief
dancer casting her veil into the fire.

Eurydice was under a spell. She had hidden her face when
the flame leaped up and licked Paul's stretcher. Then her attention was sharply called back to the scene. She forgot where she
was. Whence came this music and this dance? Who were these
people?

Eurydice's nerves were dazed, shattered, but she tried to hold
herself together. A tall old man with a long beard and foamy
white hair stepped forward and read a prayer, joined by everybody present, his voice coming calm and clear through his beard.
The ceremony over, the men and women returned. Eurydice remained sitting on a rock, watching some men putting out the
fire and clearing the ashes. Wisps of blue smoke curled up into
the sky. Down below lay spread the island with its circle of
white sand, fringing the pea-green offshore waters. Far toward
the lagoon side, she caught a glimpse of the wrecked airplane,
still gleaming in the sun.

Death was not ugly, she thought as she watched the last
faint traces of smoke disappearing into the exhilarating island air.
It was good-by, then, Paul. Good-by while she remained on earth.

Then she passed out. Laos ordered the attendants to have her
carried to Emma-Emma's cottage.

Chapter IV

HOW DO YOU FEEL? asked Emma-Emma. Her pen-
etrating eyes, her sharp, straight nose—said to indicate straight
thinking—her very sensitive, if rather wide, mouth spoke of a
highly intelligent, cultivated mind, gifted with normal emotions.
Somehow intellectual women have to insist that they have the
normal emotions of a woman. Eurydice could see that this middle-
aged woman—well in her seventies or eighties, it was anybody's
guess—this woman was worried about her. Because she had caught
her furtive, but well-concealed, glances at her.

"I am feeling better. Thanks."

"You have been very ill."

"Have I?"

"Yes. I am sure you will be up and about in a day or two."

"You are an angel." Her eyes opened for a fleeting second,
to see if wings did not suddenly appear on the woman's shoulders.
Then she added, "Why is Dr. Lysippus not here?"

"Oh, he will be here—before noon, I am sure." That added
"I am sure" meant she was not sure. "Perhaps he has to see other
patients. The Countess has been unwell. She threw a fit when
your plane was discovered."

"The Countess?"

"Yes, Countess Cordelia della Castiglioni. An Italian who came
with us, one of the original colonists. She lives on the other side
of the town, in her own villa, toward the southern promontory.
I bet you he is having breakfast with her; she does not get up till
eleven."

19

"I thought the people here were all Greeks."

"No, there is quite an Italian colony here. They contribute a great deal to the gaiety and color of the place. She was a friend of Athanopoulos, our founder, and jumped in at the last minute when our ship was sailing, all decked up in her jewels and finery. Then she made us wait another two hours for her confessor, Father Donatello. He didn't come aboard; he literally rolled over, like a pork barrel. It was very funny; I remember it very vividly, though this happened thirty years ago. Don't worry. Dr. Lysippus will come around to see you. He is all about the town, a very energetic person, very, in spite of his slight limp . . . ah, there's Bowena!"

Bowena's dark, girlish figure, with smooth brown limbs and flashing white eyes, was visible outside the reed screens on the porch, on which the door opened.

"The ewe is here. How many bowls of milk do you want?" she asked in the Thainian language.

Bowena was a native Thainian girl. She had been adopted by Emma-Emma when she was a child of five. The native Thainians were, according to Emma's theory, probably of Inca race, having settled here centuries ago; certainly they were considerably taller than the natives of the South Seas. To the north lay a Thainian village of some hundred inhabitants, principally those who had come to work for the European colonists. Emma-Emma had chosen the location of the house, to be close to them, to be able to watch from her veranda all the doings of the villagers.

The Thainians were her special hobby. Case history after case history had been written about the Thainian girls and boys and men and women, their customs, religious rites, communal living, the relation of in-laws, puberty, time of first menstruation, etc., etc. What was the effect of interracial marriage upon the arrival of puberty? That was the great question which formed part of her great opus, *On the Effects on Patterns of Culture Arising out of Racial Mingling between the Irenikis and the Thainians.* The term Ireniki was the name given themselves by the European colony, which included the Greeks, Italians, Thracians, Phrygians

and others from the islands of the Aegean Sea, of which the
Delian shepherds and wine-growers living on the middle heights
were the most numerous. There had been considerable race
mingling between the Irenikis and the Thainians, which was what
made the subject fascinating, and practically inexhaustible for
Emma-Emma. The learned lady actually encouraged it for her
own benefit. Her presence was felt at all the christening parties
and teething of babies. She was mad, as far as the others were
concerned, but was adjudged completely harmless. The crossing
of cultures, the blending of local divinities, the mutual borrow-
ing of favorite goddesses and the resulting confusion, the unrav-
eling of the rich store of mythology, and, on the physical side,
the effect of race mixture on jawbones and teeth formation, and
the humid climate on tooth decay, the change of height and stature from change of climate and habitat—all these formed a vast
realm of studies, any one of which would occupy the lifetime of
a dozen Emma-Emmas madder than herself.

In Bowena's case, Emma-Emma was able to record from first-
hand knowledge that her first menstruation began when she was
thirteen years, seven months, and seven days. The learned lady
felt affectionate toward this young girl with the feeling of a
gardener toward a cucumber plant planted by his own hands,
particularly toward the first cucumber grown on it.

The question of the quantity of milk wanted from the ewe
having been settled, Emma-Emma asked casually whether she
had seen Dr. Lysippus. Bowena should know. A girl of twenty
couldn't stay around the house. She brought all kinds of gossip
from the market place every morning.

Bowena said something in quick syllables, in a voice that was
rich, and not without a certain femininity. Her long black hair
and her lithe, brown young body made her handsome. Yes, Dr.
Lysippus had been at Chiron's tavern for over an hour, and was
still there.

Dr. Lysippus had been on his way to see Eurydice. Emma-
Emma's prognosis was at fault; he had not been breakfasting
with the Countess. The doctor had a theory of his own. You

must not encourage patients by making too regular visits. It leads them to expect you at a regular hour, and then a doctor's life is ruined. Freedom of sick members of the community must not be construed to permit impinging upon the freedom of doctors. The success of the theory was made possible by the untimely demise of Dr. Cadmos, the only other doctor on the island. Dr. Lysippus enjoyed his work; it enabled him to make the round of the island, called for by his profession, between sunrise and sunset. What was golf for anyway, but making the pretext of putting a tiny ball into a hole, or series of holes, an excuse for a good day out in the country? He had no illusions about the importance of his visits. But he knew he was welcome as a postman is welcome; all doors were open to him, and some mothers were bound to interrupt him on his daily round and ask his advice on an ailing child. He spread comfort everywhere he went. He loved nothing more than making the rounds; unquestionably the right man in the right job.

Today, however, he was the target of many inquiries, mainly about the young American woman who had arrived less than a week ago, now confined to his professional care. Eurydice had no idea of the excitement and confusion caused by her unwilling descent upon the island. Not since the colony came here in 1974, a year before World War III broke out, had they seen a stranger upon this island, outside Groucho, who had already become completely assimilated by this queer, exotic and most extraordinary community of Europeans.

Dr. Lysippus knew he was in possession of great and important secrets. Laos, philosopher and the one-man brain trust of the colony, had told them, when Eurydice was ordered carried to Emma-Emma's house, that they were to show complete respect and courtesy to this young woman, whose fiancé's body they had just cremated; above all, to allow her complete rest and relaxation. Laos' word was law on this island; without him there would not be this settlement today; they owed their lives and the lives of their children to him; they probably could not have survived the holocaust of World Wars III and IV, and even if they had, they would be living in a world of ruins. Hence his word was associated in the minds of local people with prescient wisdom.

Groups formed around the curly-bearded doctor as he approached the square, the center of the town, with a fountain in the center where Hermes was continuously performing a certain physiological function. He brushed the questioners aside, with the air of a diplomat making for his airplane on the way to attend an international conference. He headed straight for Chiron's tavern. The crowd surged after him, the men in an odd assortment of open shirts and tunics, and the women in convenient skirts wound high up to the waist, otherwise bare. It goes without saying that the thin, wiry Chiron stood a glass of *retsina* in front of him, with a plate of *meze* — olives and cheese and what looked like potato-chips.

Dr. Lysippus was not at all anxious to talk. He knew the art of suspense. The community of interest in the subject was so international that Joanna, the loud-voiced wife of Giovanni, owner of the Italian restaurant across the square, actually crossed the threshold of the Greek's tavern — a circumstance considered most unusual by those who knew the verbal vendetta which had been going on from day to day across the figure of Hermes, drowning the gurgle of the fountain itself. Joanna considered it her professional duty to know all that was happening on the island, professional in that she should be well-informed so that she would be able to answer in case her customers asked questions, and volunteer bits of stimulating information in case they did not. Joanna's tongue was compared to the river of Cephisus; it never ceased to flow. A faithful transcription of her words should be rendered without commas and periods. She was the authority on all the love affairs, imminent engagements, anticipated pregnancies, alienations of affection, desertions, wife-beatings which were going on on the island. Her speech was florid, her vocabulary colorful, her technique that of a storyteller who has seen everything on the spot. This extraordinary accumulation of facts, necessarily complex and uncertain, sometimes threw her memory out of gear, but was readily supplemented by surmises, conjectures and her gift of imagination and outright invention. Between her flow of speech, her son Alberto's accordion and the occasional descent of Galli the violinist, she was able to keep Giovanni's restaurant noisy and full most of the evenings, and to Chiron's sorrow, even attracted the Greek customers.

On this particular occasion, she had been able, by offer of a pizza pie, to induce Bowena, Emma-Emma's servant, to tell all she knew about the Americanitha. Eurydice had slept well; had liked the native goat-cheese; she had no false teeth; she smoked, instead of a pipe as the Ireniki women did, a white paper roll which went by the name of cigarette. Yes, she wore what must be unmistakably interpreted as a slip; inexplicably for a young woman, she never would take her blouse off, which was to say she kept her torso carefully concealed, a circumstance very puzzling to Bowena. Bowena took a charitable view of the new American; Eurydice could not possibly be over twenty-five, and she refused to believe she had anything to hide. Yes, she remembered, Eurydice was twenty-five, unmarried and had no children, a most horrendous state of things in the Thainian girl's eye . . . the Fourth World War had ended. There was peace in the Old World. There Bowena got a little mixed up . . .

Joanna had now stepped inside Chiron's tavern door under the cover of the black cluster of men, women and children. Unnoticed, she approached, arms akimbo, nearer and nearer. Her nerves were on edge, her neck craned forward (for she was underheight) and her ears sharply focused to catch every whisper of Dr. Lysippus' low voice.

"The scarlet tanager is still around. I saw it this morning in the outskirts. Its bright scarlet — absolutely fantastic. It comes a little earlier this year than usual." It was a nasty trick of the doctor — the ominous pause of the accomplished orator before a telling phrase, or a dramatic disclosure of a matter of great consequence.

"Never mind about the scarlet tanager. Tell us about the Americanitha!" someone said.

"Yes, tell us."

Dr. Lysippus' eyes surveyed his audience. He was satisfied. Slowly, in most casual tones, he began:

"You know, she tells Emma-Emma that World War IV was ended years ago. The people in the Old World call it the Ten Years' War, the most uninteresting war of all. Nothing sensational. World War III was the thing. A little pinching here, squashing a revolt there. That wore out the American taxpayers. They got tired of ruling the world. The forty-first President of the United States was assassinated. The people had had enough of him. Remember that when Groucho came the Ten Years' War was still going on? Well, it was ended six years ago. They have a kind of Democratic World Commonwealth now. This American woman is working for that organization."

"Pish!" someone interrupted. "It will never work. Groucho told us they had one before that between World Wars III and IV. They just changed the name once again. It will never work."

"She is constantly asking about her radio. Emma-Emma does not want to tell her. You know what happened to the radio." The radio was one of the things they had smashed, as they had smashed what remained of Groucho's wrecked plane.

"Will her people come for her?" someone suggested.

"Don't know. Laos is worried; has been looking that way these days. He doesn't want strangers to come here. We all don't. Why don't they leave us alone here?"

A stumpy figure in black appeared in the outer circle. It was that of Father Sebastian Donatello. He had the knack of making his presence felt by his unmistakable wobble in the distance and, when close by, by the peculiar noises issuing from his nostrils, resembling a zephyr sousing through an olive grove. Shepherd of his small flock of the faithful, he was friend of everybody. There was no more ubiquitous body on this island than Father Donatello. He knew everybody; everybody knew him. He loved the Greeks even, because, though Greek Catholics, they were also God's children, and besides, they were in the majority. He loved all of them except the Orthodox priest Aristotimus. He called him Aristotimus the Apostate. Friend of children, helper to the distressed, companion to the widows — Father Donatello could sit out a whole evening with widows — his was the cheerful kind of religion. His pocket, hidden under his black coat, was seldom without sweetmeats for children. He spread light and good cheer around, as Dr. Lysippus spread a more material kind of comfort.

"I have shifted the corpses about," he announced in his noted baritone. In spite of the prosaic tone of his announcement, he was heard all right. The listeners turned their heads. The chapel of St. Thomas where he preached was very small. Sometimes an old Italian woman would go up after the service and say to him, "Father, I was so inspired by your sermon. But would you mind speaking a little softer next Sunday?" To this the good-natured priest would reply, "Oh, I am so sorry. I didn't mean to shout."

"I have shifted the corpses about, arranged them in a more effective, more realistic formation," he continued. "Don't know if it will work. Some of the spears have fallen. I've stuck them up again, right through the chest. I wish there were more corpses to be spread around, and made attractive-looking, no matter from what end the strangers may approach."

This mysterious discourse did not frighten his listeners. The "corpses" were only dummies, smeared with goat blood, spread along the beach on the lagoon side to discourage intruders upon the island. The assumption was that the sight of these dummies, lying by the hundreds in fantastic positions, would scare away any unwitting visitor, savage or civilized. It was an old, old practice, long discontinued until recently, when they had dragged out the corpses again for fear of a visit by representatives of the Democratic World Commonwealth. It put "teeth" into the system of island defense, the strength of which had better not be told to an invading enemy. It was nil.

Father Donatello's brief speech had the effect of dampening the company's spirits. The best testimony to the success of the colony was the fact that no one wished to have anything to do

with what they called the Old World, the world they had left
behind them some thirty years ago. The possibility of another
visit by somebody from the outside world was far from attractive.
At the same time, short of an invasion by a navy, the islanders
were well able to take care of small groups of intruders by cutting off their means of escape, as they had done with Eurydice
and with Groucho previously. They would make them welcome
guests, or involuntary captives — that was the choice of the intruders themselves. Groucho had adapted himself admirably,
so probably would Eurydice.

"How is the Countess?" asked Dr. Lysippus of the Italian priest
as he stood up. "I shall get there some time this afternoon. I
started my round today from the south, for a variation. Variation
is the spice of life, don't you think?"

"Certainly. I was there yesterday. The Countess said she liked
her medicine a little sweeter. She is a dear. Perhaps you may be
of service . . ."

With a knowing blink, the father took Dr. Lysippus by the arm
and walked out of Chiron's, past the square, into a narrow, serpen-
tine, pebbled alley. Having escaped out of the hearing of the
listeners, the father said to Dr. Lysippus, "There's nothing really
the matter with the Countess. Just weak nerves. When you go
to see her, do not mention anything to suggest in any way the
state of anxiety of the island. What I was going to suggest was
this: a good drink of stiff brandy will do her an enormous amount
of good. And nobody has that precious stuff except Iolanthe.
But, in the first place, she lives so far up. A trip up there would
be a bit strenuous for a man of my age. In the second place, a
prescription from you would make the request so much more
proper, businesslike, as it were. I do not want Iolanthe ever to
think that the Countess covets that liquid merely to satisfy her
carnal longings. You will be kind enough? Wonderful. That
settles it. A note from you will do. I can have someone sent up
for it. It is so unfair, preposterously unfair. Nobody else has it,
and she has a whole cellar . . ."

The slight tone of disapproval in his reference to Iolanthe was unusual in the good father, who, as has been mentioned before, was a friend of everybody. At other times, Father Sebastian Donatello, slightly under the influence of liquor, had been heard to refer to Iolanthe in the Countess' hearing, as "quite a bit of a bitch."

The fact was, behind it there was a long story, and Iolanthe never wanted to see the Catholic priest. He would probably be thrown out if he dared to touch her for a bottle of brandy. As for the proper justification for that bottle, the primary reason was the Countess' weak nerves, the secondary one being that she often required him to stay for a game of chess.

"I shall be glad to oblige," said Lysippus.

"There, I knew you would." The father gave the doctor a friendly pat on the shoulder.

Dr. Lysippus scratched his head. "I made such a prescription for the Countess about three months ago. But I will do it. What is the matter with the delicious Delian wine, or Thrasymachus' brew?"

Father Donatello laughed affably. "Oh, Doctor, you don't mean it! Thrasymachus' brew! Bah! Iolanthe's cellar would be highly appreciated in Rome or Athens itself. Forty or fifty years old, and only *grand cru*. Its punch, its graceful, mellifluous smoothness, its bouquet! Why, it is a poem. It will cure any sickness. I know the Countess will be glad to do something for you in return."

"I shall be there, then, this afternoon."

"Are you on your way to see the Americanitha?"

Dr. Lysippus signified yes by lifting the bottle of orange liquid in his hand. The liquid's acrid taste was due principally to the juice of a wild species of persimmon in it, plus a dash of pine resin, which gave it a bitterish flavor. It certainly waked up anyone who tasted it.

"Then be kind enough to do this. Tell her that Countess Cordelia della Castiglioni sends her compliments and begs for the first opportunity to have the pleasure of having her to dinner as soon as her condition permits. And as soon as she is able to see anybody — you are the judge — I shall be most happy to be among the first received by her. I consider it my duty to befriend her and minister to her spiritual needs. Is she a Catholic? Well, you find out. I shall be most happy if she is, and equally happy if she isn't. In the latter case, she will have more need of me. You see what I mean. I don't want to see such a pure, young soul fall under the influence of the Apostate. Well, so long!"

"So long!"

Dr. Lysippus smiled a wan smile to himself as he turned north toward Emma-Emma's cottage. Father Donatello's concern for the spiritual welfare of the new arrival was obvious, understandable; he had been fighting a losing fight against the wave of paganism that had swept over the island. A small band of Catholic followers, principally Italians, remained faithful to the Church, and he had been able to make a few converts among the Thainian natives. But the Greek community, by and large, had reverted to paganism, with the connivance of their priest Aristotimus. Emma-Emma thought that was because they were now living closer to nature; a "pagan" after all meant only a man living in the country. The term "pagan" was thrown upon them, when the Roman Christians were confirmed urbanites. By some strange twist of usage, or some unwritten convention based upon mutual respect and courtesy among the major religions, neither a Jew, nor a Mohammedan was considered a pagan, but a man who believed in Greek and Roman gods was. Emma-Emma held that the insolent beauty of the island, the openness of sky and sea, the comparatively primitive aspects of life, where man was daily subject to the influences of sea and wind and the southern sun, acted as a liberalizing influence upon the colonists, made them closer to the fountain of the religious spirit, and on the whole made religion simpler. Out there sitting under the canopy of a cloudless sky, it was difficult to contemplate sin, or even think of eternal damnation. The Greek blood in them once more came back to its own, open, imaginative, unashamed of God's universe. There was no great desire to escape from this earthly life when heaven was all around them and the sunsets superb. Aristotimus

had compromised; he was a Greek himself. He said frankly that
he was "liberal." He based himself on the authority of one no
less than St. Paul — of this anon. And Laos, who started this
colony as a social philosopher aiming at a grand simplification
of all things, included religion among the first things he wished
to simplify.

But, Emma-Emma had concluded, with great, feminine intuition and perspicacity, if also with a somewhat professorial ponder-
ousness, Laos' influence and Aristotimus' return to Hellenism
were extraneous factors. Fundamentally, it was the influence of
the southern climate, the plenitude of sun and air and space, the
weightless light of the sunny sky, responsible for the extraordinary clarity of objects and their colors, plus their geographical
isolation from the Old World and the lifting of the incubus of
the past, which furnished the mainspring for the sudden upsurge
of paganism recalling ancient Greece. You take any group of intelligent people uncorrupted by civilization, throw them back
upon nature, and the result would be the creation of pagan gods
and goddesses. If the elements were turbulent and destructive,
you would have fearful, malevolent gods and demons; if the
aspects of nature were beautiful and benign and the air voluptu-
ous, you would see Venus rising from the waves; and provided
these inventors of tales of gods kept their balance and sense of
humor, you would not idealize them, but make them an amorous, faithless, polygamous, even incestuous lot, as the Greeks did.
The Greeks kept their senses regarding their gods; that was
what was so wonderful about them.

Anyway, Father Sebastian Donatello was fighting a lonely,
heroic, if losing battle. But he never gave up. He was so anxious
not to have Aristotimus approach, ahead of him, the new, raw,
pliable, tempting material for conversion in the person of Eurydice.

Chapter V

EURYDICE was open-minded. Why shouldn't she be? A girl who had been willing to risk her life surveying the sources of the Amazon for the cause of world peace — for which she received that beautiful calendar watch in recognition of her service — why shouldn't she be open-minded? Travel broadens one's mind. The World Food and Health Division under the DWC held, in her view, the key to world peace. She thought like the others of her times. To put it very briefly, world peace must be based upon the equal distribution of food and population. Men must not be allowed to starve, or they will start wars. A rising standard of living was equivalent to a guarantee for world peace. That was a thesis to which everybody in the Old World subscribed, a very convenient view in that it took the source of wars and international troubles outside their own country, and put them comfortably in some remote, underdeveloped areas. That men were willing to fight, and did fight, for other things, and that some of the best-fed nations were at the bottom of all world wars were completely ignored.

By the 1990's, the world was running into an acute food shortage. Partly owing to the advance of medicine, the elimination of tuberculosis, cholera, malaria and other factors decimating the population, the decrease of infant mortality — largely the work of the WFH itself — and owing to the irresponsible breeding of Asian mothers, the population of Asia alone had grown to 1,900,-000,000. World War III had decimated the population of the

31

United States by 10,000,000, but the American mothers kept working. In the last decade of the twentieth century, the U.S. population had gone up to 195,000,000. Only France, a Catholic country and presumably ignorant of birth control, remained a population of 40,000,000; this in spite of state subsidies to large families. In this situation, Brazil attracted the attention of the WFH as the largest undeveloped area for future food supplies.

This much must be said for Eurydice. Born in Cincinnati, Ohio, she had grown up in a self-consciously sober and sophisticated generation, against whose demoralizing influence she had rebelled. Cincinnati was the big, midwestern metropolis after the complete destruction of Chicago and of Manhattan during World War III (Manhattan had disappeared, together with a good slice of New Jersey and Brooklyn, but this is hardly important in the general picture). A cynically wise generation, the people's pride in sheer material progress had been rudely shattered by four world wars. As culmination of two full centuries of materialistic thinking, in which the economist was the high priest of society, a mechanistic cynicism and hedonist abandon had gripped the younger generation. Asa De Witt, an imitator of Ambrose Bierce, flourished in that decade of the Ten Years' War (1989-1998), and was greatly admired for his twisted, wry humor. A species of mordant wit had grown up in American literature since the shutting down of the *New York Times* by the forty-first President of the United States, who was then *de facto* dictator of the world. (The cause of this development will be explained later.) Side by side with the vogue for mordant wit on account of the closing of the normal channels of opinion, there grew up in certain young circles a cult which might be described as a combination of Zsazsaism and Sartrism, a mixture of exaggerated sophistication and effete intellectualism, an assertion of the will to live and enjoy the day, whatever was happening to the world.

Modern Art, too, had progressed so far that a blank canvas, containing nothing at all, entitled "Loneliness of Infinity," received the first award for originality and imaginative power by the American Society of Art Critics for the year 1995. As a matter of fact, the paint brush had been discovered to be not needed at all, by a school of painters known as New Instrumentalists. Crumpled-up Kleenex balls, tips of bananas, squirt guns usually produced more expressive results than the paint brush. The great advantage of the New Instrumentalist school, its votaries held, was the abolition of the distinction between oil and water color, and further between water color and plain black-and-white.

Eurydice, coming temporarily under such influence, had the good sense to break loose and join the DWC. The UN had died a smooth, silent death with the breaking out of World War III in 1975, and had been succeeded by DWA (Democratic World Alliance), an alliance of the victorious powers, with a more frank recognition of the importance of fire-power, replacing the UN belief in word-power. It was believed and consistently argued that world peace could and should be maintained by force, and America, as the leading power, had the necessary force to maintain it; had in fact the moral obligation to do so. The UN floundered by having too little power; the DWA by relying too much on it. Then came the Ten Years' War, which was no war at all, but a series of trouble-shooting expeditions. After the Ten Years' War, the DWA was succeeded by the DWC (Democratic World Commonwealth), which had a more democratic conception. Eurydice was willing to give it a trial.

The American people were thoroughly aroused. The Pax Americana during the life of the DWA had been a pain in the neck. Of course the most foolish thing the United States did after the defeat of the Union of Soviet Socialist Republics in World War III was for them to undertake, in their great nobility of heart, to feed the 200,000,000 Russians. It had started of course as psychological warfare; the Voice of America thundered, "We will undertake to feed you and give every Russian man, woman and child a pair of brand new shoes." The USSR could not stand under this cannonade; it just cracked up as Tsarist Russia had cracked up, in spite of its secret police. And America of course made good her promise; Uncle Sam never went back on his word. But it just broke the camel's back. Minimum income tax had risen to fifty per cent for the wage worker. It meant that every worker was working twenty hours a week to give the Russians those shoes without which civilization presumably could not exist. This Ormann Plan to feed 200,000,000 Russians by the labor of 195,-000,000 Americans was an astute move by the American President. It began by winning for him the support of the American workers and ended by making them hate the very thought of Russians; it thus saved democracy for the world, as the American President claimed, and it led straight to his dictatorial powers, as he had foreseen. Under the economic strain, when class revolts were rampant, the forty-first President wrung from the Congress practically dictatorial powers. The *New York Times* protested vigorously against the folly of this whole trend of things; it was charged by the President with willful, deliberate sabotage of the peace and national security — and was shut down.

After the assassination in 1998 of this president who had kept himself in the White House for four terms, the people of the United States were very tired. They wanted to make a clean start. That there should have been a truly democratic world government, an association of the peace-loving states, joined together to establish a rule of world law and law enforcement, had been long apparent. Nothing novel, just the usual tried-and-true democratic principles and machinery of representation and justice for all, found in any democratic schoolhouse, or county government. But the great stumbling block had been national sovereignty. No, nobody was going to tell the Big Powers what they should do; they could do what they damn please. That, and that only, was what national sovereignty meant. As far back as sixty years ago, an American, Emery Reeves, had pointed this out; all specious arguments for dilly-dallying and putting off world government had been answered with great force and clarity. The world, however, had preferred to learn it the hard way; mental inertia was the greatest force in human history. Now they *had* learned it the hard way by two more costly wars. An American senator had stood up in the year 1999, and called the attention of the American people to the fact that they had chosen to spend

$850,000,000,000, raise the national debt to astronomical proportions, suffer the bombing out of two dozen of their fair and prosperous cities and the snuffing out of 10,000,000 lives of their women and children — rather than partially give up their "sovereignty." No word had cost more in world history.

All this was done with, there was no point crying over it. The point was that the DWC had come into being, and was auspiciously started at the turn of the millennium, on Jan. 1, 2000. It was just rudimentary common sense. But if the United States had waked up, the other nations were cynical, sullen and indifferent. The ominous roll of the Juggernaut was too recent, still echoing in their ears. Because of the Pax Americana, the other nations looked upon U.S. leadership with distrust and suspicion. After burning her fingers, the United States cared not to offer to feed the Russians any more. Why the lethargy, the indifference of everybody else? The DWC was born and christened without much enthusiasm.

Great Britain had muddled through famously, though London was destroyed; King Charles III was still on his throne, worshiped by the labor unionists. That was where Karl Marx was wrong; human nature never changes. With great luck, England survived; she possessed that mysterious factor "X" for sizing up a situation correctly without the benefit of logic, which was the key to her success and the despair of other nations. Subjected to bombing and devastation, the English, to a man, gritted their teeth, tightened their belts and said nothing, and in remarkably few years rehabilitated their country to prewar level.

France was still the "cultured" nation of Europe, very cultured and very tired. Members of the Chamber of Deputies were still gesticulating, haranguing in fine Corneillian French, and occasionally taking one another by the scruff of the neck, which gave birth to an old Louis XIV social institution, the shielding of the scruff of the neck by a shrug of the shoulders.

Italy had gone Communist, which worried nobody because Soviet Russia had already cracked up in World War III. Communism was merely a luxurious label they gave themselves; their chief intent being nationalization of natural resources and key industries.

As for Red Russia itself, there was not a single Communist alive in the USSR as early as the 1950's, since Vishinski as the State Prosecutor under Stalin had murdered all the old Bolsheviks. The character of the USSR had so changed that by 1980 the Central Political Committee of the USSR decided to discard the old, antiquated and misleading slogan, "dictatorship of the proletariat." Henceforth the Soviet regime decided to call itself, quite accurately, the "dictatorship of the bureaucariat." The evolution of society in the Soviet Union had gone so far that bourgeois and capitalist had disappeared, and only two social classes remained, viz., (a) those that sat behind desks, and (b) all the rest. An Oxford professor of economics pronounced this new classification as a great gain in clarity. Of these two great social classes, postbureausky and probureausky, the former was decidedly in public favor because every doctor, every musician, every novelist, every plowman, every cowherd and every veterinary surgeon and every blacksmith aspired to sit behind desks. In consonance with this dialectically necessary stage of evolution, therefore, and in recognition of the new economic class system, the Soviet flag had been changed. Instead of the sickle and the hammer, it showed against a red background, an office desk with two legs, four drawers on each side — a testimony to the remarkable good taste and intellectual honesty of the Soviet rulers. The deciding Marxist "environment" or environmental influence, which was supposed to change human nature, was now the direction in which you face the office desk, from behind or in front. That was the determinant factor; all the rest did not matter. If you are safely behind it, you stand for socialistic progress; if you stand in front of it, you are most likely of a warped mind and character, you love to commit acts of sabotage as an emotional outlet, and are frequently subject to attacks of a most unholy desire to act as imperialist agent. It was all a matter of psychology, the *Pravda* oracle explained, what the environment could do to men's minds.

All this Eurydice knew. She had been able to tell Emma-Emma much about it. There was a curious point which Emma-Emma did not know, being too absorbed in her notes on anthropology. This was what actually happened during the last years of Stalin's regime. In accordance with the cardinal tenet of Stalinist biology, the theory of the preponderant influence of environment, over against heredity, the Central Political Committee had given directives to the agricultural bureaus in the various regions that all the American talk about improved wheat seeds and apple seeds was bourgeois and unscientific. The soil and fertilizers and sunlight — the environment — were the determinant factors. To hell with wheat seeds! Any expert submitting a report recommending the importation of better seeds was accused of reactionary tendencies, even of ungodliness, so far as this reflected upon his attitude toward orthodox biology. It did not work of course. Wheat crop after wheat crop failed. In the first years of Malenkov's regime, after Stalin's death, agricultural bureaus dared to make factual reports analyzing the causes for the failure of agricultural production. This particular Stalinist biology therefore was temporarily discarded. But as to the significant influence of environmental direction vis-à-vis the office desk upon human attitudes and psychology in general, the main Marxist tenet still held its ground.

All in all, a very sad story. The vanquished weeping in defeat, and the conquerors groaning under the burden of victory. What a picture!

Chapter VI

HAVING DEPOSITED the bottle of medicine and conveyed the message of the Countess, Dr. Lysippus stood up to leave.

"I am going up to see Iolanthe. It's getting hot, is it not so?" Dr. Lysippus took out a bright-tinted handkerchief large enough for a scarf and wiped his perspiring forehead.

"Not at this hour!" Emma-Emma protested. "Quite a climb."

"Yes, but on the other hand, it is cooler at the crest. Shall I tell the Countess that Eurydice accepts? I shall be there about teatime this afternoon."

Emma-Emma had translated the question, or rather had mended the doctor's English in places so that it became understandable.

"But when am I allowed to go out?" asked Eurydice.

"Why, Eurydice, you decide, not me. You are the patient. You like to go, you go, tomorrow, or a week from tomorrow. That means you are well. You don't like to go, you sleep tomorrow, and tomorrow and tomorrow. That means you are ill. How do I know?"

What a doctor!

"And I say this unto you," continued Lysippus who had learned his English from the Bible; the Bible, the Countess had told him, is the best model for English prose. "And I say this unto you: Beware of Father Donatello, he that cometh among you and maketh you feel sinful and afraid. Be unafraid, Eurydice; let not your heart be troubled by the Italianos. He the stumbling

38

block. I spake these words to comfort you. Be unafraid of him."

"I see what you mean," stammered Eurydice.

"Receive him that speaketh unto you, but be unafraid. Father Donatello is not bad. Much charity in his heart. Much charity. I forget — which your church?"

Eurydice had not been to church for five years. After a momentary pause, she said:

"Episcopalian."

"Ah! Episcopalian! Good church! I am Greek Orthodox. I still am. No difference. All churches good, saith Father Aristotimus. No bad church. But Aristotimus don't like Father Donatello, the Italianos. The Italianos baptize; Aristotimus no baptize. Jesus no baptized; he that believeth in me is saved. *Baptisma*, no *baptisma*, no difference. *Baptismos* not necessary. St. Paul no baptized, saith Father Aristotimus; St. Paul thanked God he baptized only two Corinthians. Only two, and he stopped. He didn't want people to misunderstand. First chapter, I Corinthians. St. Paul liberal. Aristotimus liberal. Not important, saith St. Paul, saith Aristotimus. All churches good. No bad church."

"About the Countess — does she speak good English?"

"Oh, yes, the Countess is very intelligent, very intellectual. She patron art, literature. She patron everything. She patron Eunice."

"Oh, Doctor! Don't be wicked!"

"That's what everybody say. He that hath ears hear. Good day, Emma-Emma. Good day, Eurydice. I must see Iolanthe on account of a prescription for the Countess."

Dr. Lysippus left.

"You like him?" asked Emma-Emma.

"Yes, I like him. He seems to talk a lot of sense."

"Well, when are you going to see the Countess?"

"That is the funniest doctor I've ever seen. I sleep, or I go out as I like. The patient himself is the best judge. Not a bad idea. I think I like to rest for a few more days. They are so nice about it."

"Yes, they are. Laos told them to leave you absolutely alone."

"Who is Laos?"

"The leader of the Irenikis — the philosopher who planned all this. The man, with a long white beard, his beautiful white hair swept back from his forehead — the man you saw reading the prayer at the funeral ceremony — dressed in a white tunic, remember?"

Eurydice said she remembered. She had to learn about everybody from Emma-Emma. That the Greek Orthodox and the Italian Catholic priest didn't get along together she sensed clearly enough. Father Sebastian Donatello was not at all a bad man, far from it, had "much charity" as Dr. Lysippus had put it. But he wanted to convert everybody. She could expect a visit from him any day so soon as Dr. Lysippus permitted him. The doctor could be counted upon to keep him away as long as he could. Father Donatello was the Countess' confessor. The Countess, it was rumored, was the *grande passion* of Athanopoulos, the Greek financier who made the establishment of this colony possible. She was well-educated and one of the intellectual women of the colony, having come from the ancient family of the Cionis, and been educated in Paris, Florence and Lausanne, a protector of art and artists. The ball she gave annually at her villa was something that caused the tongues of the Ireniki peasants to wag.

"It's a rich field for anthropology, very rich," said Emma-Emma. "Human psychology is fascinating. Anthropology used to be a classification of brachycephalic and dolicocephalic races, like Linnaean botany. We have gone far beyond that, to the study of men's customs and institutions and beliefs, and from there on to the interplay of social forces that make men what they are. We begin to study men's minds, taboos, inhibitions, motivations. And don't think only savages have taboos; the modern man is full of them. That is what makes anthropology so interesting. The Countess' relation to Eunice, for instance. Simply fascinating. You'll see Eunice when you go to the Countess'."

"What about Iolanthe? Who is she? I love the sound of that name."

"Yes, the Greeks have charming names. She was at first the

mistress of Athanopoulos — mistress in modern English, concu-
bine in the Orient, courtesan in eighteenth-century France,
hetaera in ancient Greece. We anthropologists are apt to be
broad-minded; we disregard the terms and go back to what you
may call the *Ding an sich,* thing-in-itself, the residue common
to all races. A concession to man's polygamous nature, providing
a social, emotional and esthetic answer to man's need for admiring
a perfectly charming and accomplished woman. You are not
squeamish, I hope?"

"No," protested Eurydice rather vocally.

"I don't mean brute prostitution. The hetaera type, you know,
like Aspasia who taught Socrates the art of eloquence. Or charming Phryne, or Theodota. I cannot help thinking what a charming courtesan Theodota must have been, quite intellectual perhaps, to make Socrates seek her company from time to time. A
temporary vision of the charm of feminine beauty, grace, and
intelligence, a realization of the feminine ideal. A mature, eman-
cipated, and sometimes very intelligent woman at her prime.
Man pursues that image of a perfectly fashioned woman and
woman pursues that image of a perfectly fashioned man. Some
find it among the movie stars in modern days. It's all a temporary
illusion, of course; man projects that image from his own head
and associates it with some particular woman. But the illusion
is satisfying while it lasts. There is really no difference. The
modern man worships that image on celluloid, or in a pin-up, a
photograph at best; the ancient man worships that image in the
flesh."

"What about Iolanthe?"

"She is a princess, one of those white Russians. Her father is
Prince Andreyev Somovarvitch, a friend of Athanopoulos, too.
He did a great deal for the community when we first came. A
humbug, but a very useful humbug. I mean whatever people
say about him, he looks princely, tall, colossal — very impressive
when all his ribbons and decorations are on. We needed an offi-
cious humbug of that kind at the beginning, especially in our
subjugation of the Thainians. Iolanthe, however, prefers to be

known by her name only. This speaks for her intelligence. She
does not care for titles. She displaced Athanopoulos' affection
for the Countess; you know what men are, though Athanopoulos
remained a close friend of the Countess to the end of his days.
He died six or seven years ago, a most extraordinary person, and
left Iolanthe all his wealth. She lives up at the crest, a spacious
bungalow of stone, very elegant, if not palatial in size. Her son,
Stephan, an idiot, and her daughter, Chloe, live with her. In a
way it was tragic for Athanopoulos — the idiotic son, I mean.
They were as a matter of fact later married by the Greek priest.
Father Donatello created a lot of trouble at the time, stirred up
the whole Italian Catholic community against the immorality of
Athanopoulos' example. As a diplomatic gesture, following an
adroit suggestion by Iolanthe, Athanopoulos proposed to have a
Roman Catholic wedding performed by Father Donatello himself.
But the good Italian father was adamant. He declared that
Athanopoulos was already married, and his wife presumably
still living, that short of a special dispensation by the Pope, he
could not and would not marry them, and the Pope was incom-
municable of course under the circumstances. He refused to
marry the couple and tried his best to prevent their being married by Aristotimus. For two successive Sundays preceding the
wedding, he thundered from the pulpit with more than his usual
fervor about the holy tie of marriage and fornication and the
Seventh Commandment, with copious references to Delilah and
the woman of Babylon. Aristotimus found it necessary to reply
from his pulpit, too; he knew his Old Testament just as well.
Abraham had two wives, so had Isaac, and Jacob had the sisters
Leah and Rachel — Solomon had three thousand — all this dropped
casually in establishing his point that God, in His infinite wisdom,
did change His Commandments for His chosen children, according to His great mercy for them that love Him. St. Paul, who
was Aristotimus' favorite, said it is better to marry than to
burn. . . . The whole community enjoyed the learning of the
rival priests tremendously. Opinions were divided. Some thought
that Athanopoulos, being a leader, should set a better example

of God-fearing conduct; others were more sympathetic. It was true that Athanopoulos' legal wife was still living, but any husband so cut off from her for life should be free to take a woman he liked. They were married. But Iolanthe has never forgiven the Italian priest since. I do admire Donatello for his principles, though."

"But you say she was a princess. How come she was a hetaera?"

"I say she was the mistress of Athanopoulos. Before that she was a girl trained in our Institute of Comforters of Men's Souls, a most peculiar institution, conceived by Laos. Wife-beaters go there and get cured. It is not *that* profession modern Europeans are apt to think it is. The girls, selected from among the prettiest and the most talented on the island, are sent there to learn song and dance and poetry. They marry husbands afterwards and make better wives. The purpose of the Institute is to teach girls, before they marry, something about the darker side of men and the art of handling the male sex. It is our most high-class finishing school. You admit the proper study of woman is man . . ."

Just then Bowena came in to announce Sister Teresa. Sister Teresa was an apparition of youth and virginal sweetness. Unlike the lay woman, she was dressed in a robe of white, and a white veil came over her head. The rosary and the belt with long-hanging tassels made her look like the Goddess of Mercy; in Goddess of Mercy fashion, too, she put her palms together to greet them.

Emma-Emma asked her to sit down.

"Dr. Lysippus gave me special permission to come and visit you," she said sweetly in tolerable English. She asked how Eurydice was feeling, and lightly referred to her sympathy for what had happened. She hoped she was comfortable and happy here. She was sure it was God's will.

Eurydice expressed her surprise that there were sisters on the island. She was told that there were only six, including the Mother Superior, four Greeks and two Italians. Their nationality made no difference whatsoever in the convent. They studied and they planted their garden.

"You must come and visit us when you are well. Stay a few days if you like, and enjoy the peace and quiet of the convent."

"Are you happy?" Eurydice inquired, somewhat incredulously.

"Very happy." The sister's smile was genuine, showing a row of white, even teeth.

"Eurydice," said Emma-Emma, "you are very lucky to have come here. You don't know how lucky you are. We don't have everything here; on the other hand, we have much."

Eurydice was continually amazed. She reflected that indeed the life on the island on which she was stranded was better than she had imagined, or dared hope. At least, there were no cannibals. They were Europeans, of a queer sort, unlike any people she had known, but Europeans all the same, with a high degree of culture, a reflowering of the arts, of sculpture and music and song. She was even thankful for the rustic delicacies, goat-milk and cheese and good meat, and such a comfortable cottage. Set back a few centuries perhaps, in the calendar of the world's scientific progress, but comparatively comfortable. Walking through the streets of Thainos was not so different from walking in some quaint Italian town of the sixteenth century. And the landscape was superb; the climate, except for the heat in the middle of the day, quite pleasant and agreeable. Against her wishes, she liked its ease, its sense of peace, its serenity. Already she felt something was happening inside her.

"I am lucky, I guess," she said, without too much conviction. "If I could believe that you people are quite real. I suppose I am just not used to it."

Sister Teresa stood up to leave. She extended her invitation again and said she would be glad to show Eurydice around, or do anything for her.

"You are very kind."

Eurydice was very happy to have a young woman, and such a gentle one, for her friend.

"Can you come out when you like?"

"We can, when there is duty to be done. We are busier this week. There are about six wives in the place. Dr. Lysippus said one or two more may be coming in a day or two. It is not good when too many women are together."

Eurydice saw her to the porch, and watched the young nun's figure disappear around the corner.

"She is very pretty," said Eurydice, turning to Emma-Emma. "What does she mean by saying that wives are staying with them?"

Emma-Emma smiled. "I know this will surprise you. The convent is a public institution, supported by the taxpayers' money. Most of the public things, as a matter of fact, are of a religious nature. A stay of ten days or a fortnight in the convent gives the wives a rest and a change. They may stay longer if the place is not full, perhaps three or four weeks."

"What about their husbands, the meals and the babies?"

"They have to get along the best they can. Laos insists on this. The wives have the right to get away from home, strictly by themselves, without their husbands and babies for half a month or a month in the year. It is good for them. Of course it is. And it is good for the husbands too; they learn to appreciate their wives more when they come back. It is quite a sensible idea, I think."

"Laos must be a remarkable man."

"You will find out."

Chapter VII

EURYDICE was already feeling better. The crinkles in her mind had begun to smooth off.

Her senses registered. The Old World she had left behind her and this island community she had stumbled upon began to connect up. Plainly, she had discovered a European colony in mid-Pacific which, by some cunning plan and purpose, had escaped the last two World Wars. Perhaps it was like the colony established by the crew of the German submarine which she had read about. This one in which she found herself was obviously the result of a plan conceived by a man who, so far as she was able to observe, was a kind of new social philosopher determined upon a course of contrariness to all she had known and believed to be sacred to the world. Compelling wives to leave their husbands and babies for a short period every year! And the Institute of Comforters of Men's Souls — evidently its counterpart for curing men's psychic ills! Quite novel, delightful ideas! The Museion, the Athenaeum, of which she had only heard, but not seen — what was the fellow Laos trying to do? Return to the Hellenistic way of life, a re-examination of all values of civilization, ancient and modern?

"Tell me about Laos. How did you people come here? What is all this — a Utopia?"

Emma-Emma looked up from her spectacles, her lips dipped in a smile of satisfaction like a person about to recall something pleasant, something odd and extraordinary and adventurous in the remote past.

"No," she said, "don't use that word. Not in the presence of

46

Laos. It savors of a pipe dream dreamed up by somebody, some fantastic scheme of life conjured up by a visionary who wishes life to be different and proceeds to reshuffle it in any way he likes. Laos will be offended if you call this Ireniki colony a Utopia. All socialistic experiments have failed; some were never meant to be put into practice. Plato's community of wives and children, his eugenics and his philosopher-king. His *Republic* was an inquiry written down for his own pleasure as to what an ideal country should be; I don't think he ever entertained the idea of seeing his Republic brought into existence. As you know, he had no luck with Dionysius of Sicily, and went back to teach in Athens. Laos is an intensely practical man. All utopias, he says, presume too much upon human nature, and therefore must fail. It's very easy for a man to write a book and say, I don't like human nature this way — all right, I'll change it. Karl Marx is one of them. A classless society in which the state withers! We have seen in practice how his followers found it necessary to erect the most despotic state known to history — just to enable those in authority to remain in power. A classless society united in brotherly love and devoted to the public good! Parent-child affection will be replaced by a higher kind of loyalty! Men will work for the love of the state, not for profit! That is where Marx went completely nutty. Any time man plays a trick on Nature, Nature plays a nasty trick in return, and exacts payment with double interest. No, Laos prides himself rather on being conservative. If there is one thing he understands and respects, it is human nature. He never wants to change it, just because he knows it can never be changed. The first duty of a philosopher, he says, is to face human nature resolutely and make the best of it. He has got Chinese blood in him. He does not want it changed. You haven't seen some of the people here, or you won't call it an ideal society. Far from it. Father Donatello, Lysippus and others. I have told you about the Countess, and Iolanthe and Aristotimus. We haven't changed a bit, have we? You let Bowena tell you about Joanna, Giovanni's wife, and you'll imagine you're back in Naples again. That is what makes life colorful, charming."

"I certainly think it colorful here."

"And you haven't seen Prince Andreyev Somovarvitch yet. That is a romantic figure, stranger than fiction. If I didn't know this man in person, I would say he walked right out of the pages of some novel. No, life is with us still; human nature is still with us, very much."

"Then what is the point of founding a colony? I thought it was meant to be something new."

"Quite the contrary. It is meant to be something old, ancient. Human society put back a few centuries. You see we have lost something during the progress of human society. Since industrialization man has changed a great deal. That is what interests Laos. Human nature isn't whole any more. Something is lacking. His original and full nature is cramped, desiccated, dehydrated and badly creased in the corners. Laos wants to recapture what we have lost. A little more life, a little more imagination, and a little more poetry and sunshine and the original liberty and individuality of man. That is what Laos tries to put back. This community impresses you as very Greek?"

"Very."

"What, for instance?"

"Well, nudity, for instance. I was shocked."

"There is no reason to be. Modern man pretends to admire nudity in stone or oil, but is ashamed of it in the flesh. It makes no sense. Be a good Christian, or be a good Hellene; the mixture of Hellenism and Christianity has played havoc with modern civilization. It makes man neurotic. It is an unresolved conflict of our heritage, like an unresolved chord. It's bad for one's moral health. Am I boring you?"

"Not at all. Go on."

"Speaking as an anthropologist — student of man — I am deeply interested in man's mental habits and psychic reactions and outlets. This nudity — you think it is erotic?"

"I am not used to it."

"It is in a way symbolic of a different kind of philosophy, of a way of life. We should have more respect for the human frame.

It is frankly pagan, I admit. I have seen enough of life in Samoa, Tahiti, the Pago Pago Island. The first thing the missionaries inject into the natives' minds is a dirty conception of the human frame. It is not erotic to them. Speaking of eroticism, do they still have movies in America which are advertised 'For Adults Only'? I used to imagine all kinds of things as a child, and I thought the word 'adult' was connected with 'adultery,' which is etymologically correct. What the adults do is called adultery. As a matter of fact, all those pictures should have been labeled 'For Children Only, Adults Not Permitted.' The harm came only when the children got the adults' adulterous notions. You should let Laos talk to you about human psychology."

"You were going to tell me about Laos, and how he got this colony started."

"I can only tell you how we started it. I was one of those who signed up to come, attracted by a few things Laos said to me. We had met casually, at a *tavernas* in Athens. As for the ideas behind it, and what he meant to do, you should go to Laos himself. He is a fascinating talker, has a way of making you share his thinking, leading you step by step, to a conclusion known only to himself. A thorough devil with ideas, goes to the bottom of things; a strong streak of the heathen in him. He questions everything, takes nothing for granted, turns ancient truths into new paradoxes. He says there is nothing new under the sun, quoting Ecclesiastes. Everything has been said before. A man of considerable daring. He and Athanopoulos were both extraordinary characters. They had to be, to conceive such a daring scheme."

It was way back in 1974, the year before World War III broke out, Emma-Emma went on to explain the origin of the colony. She was then sojourning in Greece, trying to study the folk psychology of the Ionian shepherds and see how much of the ancient mythology had persisted, and how much of it had been eradicated or transplanted to Christianity. She got deeper and deeper, as she became aware of the literature on the subject of mutual borrowings of gods and goddesses and rites and mysteries around the Mediterranean Basin. She stayed two years. There she met Laos, a man of about forty, still in his prime, but already a retired diplomat with an extraordinary career behind him. A face that was distinguished by black bushy eyebrows, broad cheekbones, powerful eyes, and unusually long ears. Not handsome, but unforgettable. A silent, detached observer of humanity, he spoke with eloquence and conviction when he was drawn into a subject, beneath a tone of suave imperturbability, as befitting a philosopher. If his ideas were ruthless, his tone was quiet, contemplative, enlivened here and there with a witticism. Emma-Emma had known of him; his self-obliteration from the diplomatic picture and ten years of retirement helped to build up his reputation as a singular, original and wayward genius. Emma-Emma, then a professor and author of many volumes, had not talked with him for more than ten minutes before she fell under the spell of his ideas, which she shared by some original independent thinking of her own.

Retired at the age of thirty-two as a Greek delegate to the United Nations, Laos had gone into hiding as far as the public was concerned, communing with himself and reading rare ancient authors usually difficult to find in public libraries. He was born of a Chinese grandfather on the mother's side, a Syracuse merchant in Sicily, his father a Greek. His grandfather was practically illiterate, one of those ubiquitous Chinese merchants who had trekked across Siberia and seeped like water into every nook and cranny of the world — Dresden, Berlin, Paris, Sicily, Algiers, the Belgian Congo — without the shadow of a consulate's protection. Some of these businessmen were in St. Helena when Napoleon was there. His father died when he was still quite young, and his mother married again a farmer of Crete. Here the boy grew up, his imagination stimulated by the old ruins and stories of Minotaurs his neighbors told him. This had something to do with his incomplete acceptance of the civilization of western Europe. To grow up as a barefooted boy among the shepherds was to be imbued with a rugged independence of spirit, to reach self-sufficiency and self-reliance, to retain for

life in one's inner consciousness a store of imagery of the fields
and streams and beauties of nature, to have the strength of simplicity which recoils, in a mind like Laos', from all the artificiali-
ties of fashionable society.

The boy grew up illiterate. He said he had practically wasted
his boyhood, and was glad of it. At the age of fifteen he suddenly
felt impelled by a mad craving for knowledge. He taught himself
to read, with the help of a village priest. At the age of seventeen
he boarded a fishing boat and went to Athens. Rapidly he made
progress, and in spite of his deficiency in mathematics which he
hated, he was soon enrolled in the University of Athens, where
he developed a propensity to question his professors, but was
aloof from his fellow students. Meanwhile, he was studying English, German and French, and his curiosity about his grandfather
led him to study Chinese. To this knowledge of languages he
added Turkish. He never played a game or shot a gun. While
working in the office of a small local paper, he continued to read
voraciously. At the age of twenty-three, he was able to induce
an Athens publisher to publish an original work, *A Study of
Brahmin Influence on Pythagoras,* drawing many parallels of
ideas, particularly the idea of metempsychosis, or transmigration
of souls. This work attracted the attention of scholars, but otherwise secured neither public acclaim nor money for him. There
followed his next book, *The Comedy of Gods,* a satirical novel
about the statesmen of his days. His reputation was established.
At the age of twenty-seven, he was appointed Chargé d'affaires
of the Greek Embassy at Cairo, then promoted to minister, becoming known as one of the youngest persons ever to hold such
a post. However, he was more interested in the antiquities, in the
history of the Pharaohs and the cult of Isis and Osiris and Mithras,
than in current politics. At the age of thirty-one, he was appointed
Greek delegate to the United Nations, where he made the internationally famous opening remark, "Here lie the hopes of the
world."

He should have known that the United Nations was conceived
merely as a forum of world opinion, and all that it implied. Being

a sort of accomplished orator himself, he snored through the speeches of the other orators. He knew exactly what the Polish delegate was going to say, the Soviet delegate had said it already, and the Pole would take another hour and half to say it again. Every one of the delegates tried to be a little professorial, to love peace and justice and the international amity of mankind. He got very bored. He had a rather low opinion of diplomatic speeches, which he associated with cocktail sausages and martinis; he had scant respect for adroit maneuvers, whispering caucuses, deals for mutual support, and watering down of resolutions. The UN was avowedly designed to stop wars and did a splendid job in stopping skirmishes and border conflicts, such as the wounding of a few highway policemen, among the small fry of the nations. This gave the delegates some satisfaction, a sense of accomplishment, with much wringing of hands. Its many activities in the field of health and sanitation and controlling white-slave traffic gave an illusion that something was being done, progress being made. As for stopping the big war, *the* war, it was powerless to do anything. It was not designed for that. It was none of the UN's business. The UN, Laos thought, could stop narcotic trade, plagues, famines — it could stop everything including sewers, except The War. It was not a world government, it had no body of enacted world law, and no means of law enforcement. It was just a splendid opportunity for the powers to come together and chatter over their differences of point of view. Some nations had to abide by the will of the majority, the bigger powers didn't. That was class, a very flattering feeling. You surrendered not a whit of your rights or dignity. The world was moving on. The only useful value of the UN, Laos discovered, was as a moral force, but moral force was not enough. It deceived many people; it did not deceive the perspicacious Laos.

Sadly disillusioned, he resigned and went into hiding. Technically, it is correct to say that he resigned, for resign he did. It was whispered, however, at the time of his resignation that the Greek government had recalled him, or had suggested his resignation as a desirable course of action. It was after he had made a speech at one of New York's most exclusive club meetings, with a glittering array of socialites and diplomats' wives present. His delivery was flawless, his ideas were stimulating — as they always were — and he went into a philosophical examination of human progress. He denied it. He said that before talking about progress, man had better find out where he was going. So far so good. Then he committed a social *faux pas,* discreditable for a diplomat and a representative of the Athenian government. He said, "Man is steadily going somewhere without knowing where he is going. Civilization is gripped by a new disease, called *men-no-pause.*" The atrocious pun was considered in bad taste; the younger diplomats' wives tittered, the older ones frowned. Laos was recalled.

While at Cairo, he had married a young Greek girl whom he loved passionately but who died within a year after the marriage. He never married again. He became a kind of anchorite, following Pythagorean example. He tried everything, including keeping fast and vegetarianism. Then he traveled to the Orient, and unable to penetrate Communist China, studied for two years in a monastery near Kyoto, where he became fascinated by Zen Buddhism. The place that impressed him most, however, was Bali. It lived up to its tradition, except that the westernized Indonesian government had got infected with the Christians' dirty conception of the human body and compelled its innocent girls and women to cover their breasts. Otherwise the creative, artistic genius was still there, very much alive. Bali strongly influenced his thought.

Aften ten years of wandering and hibernation, his idea for a colony slowly formed and matured. He was not against material progress as such, he was against having too much of it, to the detriment of man himself. He studied carefully the history of the last two centuries since the industrial revolution, and was sure that man had lost as much as he had gained. What exactly had he lost? Few scholars, he found, ever went into the problem deeply. Of one thing he was sure: as more and more progress was made in the study of matter, less and less attention was given to man. Man's character had changed; his beliefs had changed; his relation to nature had changed; his individual role in society had changed. Spiritually, man was poorer off. He was less of himself. It would not be a bad idea to call a temporary moratorium on mechanical progress; what there was was good, but quite enough. He was going to take time to think if nobody else did. What had happened to philosophy as concerned with the conduct of life? He discovered that all that was left of philosophy was history of philosophy. Should the true philosopher pick up again where the eighteenth-century man had left off? He needed time to think, to retrace lost values, and an opportunity to see what man should be ideally, in a new setting, if given a chance. He wanted a colony far distant from the world.

One day he walked into the office of Athanopoulos and told him his idea. Athanopoulos was the logical man for him to see; he and nobody else could finance such an expedition and make a graceful exit from the modern world immediately threatened with another world war. Athanopoulos was then only forty-five, a few years his senior, well-dressed, polished, keen, jovial, practical, decisive, with a flair for doing the unusual things, still exuberant in spirit and body. Only a man of daring would receive hospitably Laos' original idea, of writing off the whole mess and starting off a new life afresh, perhaps a new type of civilization, somewhere quite remote and undiscoverable by the rest of the world.

Athanopoulos was the man. He had left Greece at the age of fifteen or sixteen and landed penniless in South America. He said he wanted to make a million before he was thirty, and he made it before he was twenty-eight. He was then the owner of a large fleet — in fact several fleets — of freighters plowing the seven seas all over the world. What he wanted he got. A multi-millionaire, collector of Greek antiques and Stradivarius violins, owner of mansions and yachts, he had achieved his life ambition at the age of forty. He had even bought up an internationally known casino, and supported a ballet corps. And he had conceived the idea of retiring at forty-five to enjoy himself. Such was the man Laos approached.

"Would you like to scrap all that you have, forget your fleets and villas and everything and hide yourself in some corner of the world — South Pacific, for example — and start something new?" Laos began.

"What a brilliant idea!" Athanopoulos knew Laos by reputation, had admired him and met him a few times. "The war is coming. Anybody who has eyes can see. You are a philosopher, but I am a practical man. I suppose it won't be difficult for me to pick up another hundred million dollars in shipping when war breaks out. On the other hand, I may become radioactive dust before I know it. It's a practical choice. I like the idea of prolonging my life for a few more years and spending the rest of my days in some more restful place. A hidden paradise perhaps. As a matter of fact, I've been wanting to retire — I do very much — and take up something else, something nobody else has done before." He added with a manly, robust laugh: "If you have something fantastic, tell me. Or I am not interested. If men cannot think their way out of this coming war, we two will do it."

They went into the plan of a new colony, not a temporary retreat, but a permanent settlement where they could start something new. Laos furnished the ideas. Call a moratorium on scientific progress. Athanopoulos agreed. It would have to be something youthful and new and fresh, like ancient Greece. Athanopoulos was enthusiastic. Yes, he knew exactly one such island way out of freighter routes, being of no commercial value. Subjugation of the inhabitants would be no great problem. They would have to have a couple of hundred people join them, preferably married couples with children, and preferably Greeks. They would have to have tools, motors, materials, mechanics, a few scientists, doctors. They would have to have wheat seeds, corn, sugar cane, tobacco — he was sure tobacco could be grown there. And yes, wine. In that subtropical climate, not much different from Greece, he was sure they could grow grapes. And of course cattle and sheep.

Silently and without much fanfare the word spread around that Athanopoulos the merchant prince was recruiting a group of men and women for a distant settlement. For six months, they worked to get the expedition ready. The problems were appallingly complex and many; like preparing Noah's Ark, but exciting. Both of them were inspired with Platonic madness. They almost thought of themselves as buccaneers drawn by a sense of high adventure. The S.S. *Arcadia* was chartered. A large number of shepherds, farmers and fishermen signed up. No young rebels. No long-haired artists and red shirts. Laos insisted that life would not be worth living without good cooks and musicians. The hunting and securing of good cooks to carry on a fine culinary tradition on the island received Laos' personal attention. It was not a casual item; wine, song and good food, and women, constituted nine-tenths of any passable way of living. Laos headed for the arts; they were very much on his mind. He was trying to cut life down to its essentials, and he could not cut out good food, or a good bed, or violin music. Laos was a complex man.

Athanopoulos went as far as to secure a violin-maker from Verona. When his firm in Naples leaked out the news, it was swamped with applicants. Athanopoulos had always liked Italians, their gaiety and their friendly hospitality. Laos liked the Italians for his own reason: they disliked wars and loved their families. But they had to reject twenty barbers from Messina; they couldn't possibly need so many haircuts. About fifty Italians in all were taken. A rumor even sprang up that they were on a treasure hunt. Laos himself busied about selecting 12,000 volumes to go with them. He induced Dr. Artemos, head of the College of Science of Athens University to make the exit with them. So along with turtle doves and sheep and olives, they shipped large crates of books, scientific instruments and four pianos.

At the last moment, Athanopoulos was appalled by the thought of the unavailability of modern medicine. He had a quarrel with the economic system — which had made him a rich man — but he had unqualified admiration for modern medicine. They could not possibly carry enough medical supplies to last forever. On this subject, he was reassured by Dr. Cadmos who was going with them. Laxatives, quinine, penicillin and some kind of anesthetic to dull pains were all they needed.

Dr. Cadmos was a first-class doctor. He had readily consented to come with Athanopoulos, who had heard of his reputation as a research doctor rather than a practitioner.

"You mean those pills?" said Cadmos when Athanopoulos asked him. "You are an intelligent man. I must confess to you that pills are concessions of the medical profession to the ailing patients. They are not happy unless they are given something to take. They all ask the physician, 'Doctor, do something.' What can we do except give them pills? All that a doctor can do is to put the patient in the best position for the body to recover itself. Pills usually relieve symptoms only. Corrective food, rest, a healthy way of life — that is what cures the patient. The first thing we say to a patient is, get in bed and lie down — right? We never tell a patient to jump about. Lie down, we say, lie down."

"But surely medicine helps?"

"I am amazed at you, Athanopoulos. At least eighty per cent of the diseases cure themselves, and the doctor has nothing to do with it."

"You say eighty per cent?"

"Yes, eighty per cent. You love figures, so I give you the figures. Another fifteen per cent receive great help from medicines, specific medicines. Another five per cent are incurable, with or without pills. For the large majority of cases, pills only help the body to fight back. The body fights back if given a chance. The incurables remain uncured. Patients get better after a lapse of time anyway, without any apparent cause, or application of medicine. That is the scientific basis for all miracle cures, Buddhist or Christian. Credit is given to prayers or to pills — that is the way the patients will have it. Besides, half of the diseases in modern life come from crowded city living and from the tenseness of modern business life. Thus fifty per cent of the illnesses and ailments of modern man are automatically eliminated. There is nothing like sunshine and fresh air and a healthy, restful way of living, of which we shall have plenty on the island. A healthy way of life is a better guarantee of life than all the medicines known to men put together. How do you suppose Caucasian peasants often live to a hundred? No, plenty of sunshine and castor oil would take care of most medical troubles on the island."

Athanopoulos felt much relieved.

It was about this time that the newspapers of the world carried the story that the fabulous merchant prince, Athanopoulos the Greek, had sailed on an expedition to the South Pacific, on the S.S. *Arcadia*, destination undisclosed. When the war broke out in the beginning of the following year, everybody had forgotten about him and about the group of men and women who had sailed with him.

Chapter VIII

ATHANOPOULOS' wife refused to come with her husband," concluded Emma-Emma. "She thought he was crazy. Don't blame her. A woman of her age, with her security, used to her villas, servants, ease and comfort, was not going to abandon them for a primitive existence on some bare island. Besides, Countess Cordelia della Castiglioni was going; a much younger woman whose intellectual assets her husband appreciated; she not only shared his love of Martel and Greek antiquities, she was full-bosomed. That was how Father Donatello came into the picture, for the Countess was an ardent Catholic. Athanopoulos never cared for priests, he was a kind of agnostic; he yielded, however, when the Countess said the father, her confessor, was to go with her or she would not go at all. Women need religion, he thought, but the Countess told him frankly that there were certain verities, obvious truths of life, which a woman's more sensitive soul could feel, but which he, with all his masculine intellect, was congenitally incapable of feeling. He just had no tentacles, no antennae, for them. Athanopoulos liked her for saying so. Because all that she said was incomprehensible, and being incomprehensible, it made her also incomprehensible and mysterious and therefore charming.

"We sailed from the port of Piraeus on August 15, 1974," continued Emma-Emma. "By this time, most of the people on the boat thought that we were going to some treasure island, a rumor actively promoted by Thrasymachus, one of the passengers, once we were on our way. Laos discountenanced this rumor, told them

59

that all the gold they were going to find would be found by the sweat of their brows, by their hard work, in their flocks, harvests and their fruityards. He promised them hard work, low taxes, a beautiful climate, and peace. It was fair enough. So there we were, five or six of us, in the close company of Athanopoulos — Laos, Dr. Artemos the scientist, Dr. Cadmos, the Countess, and Prince Andreyev Somovarvitch, a very special friend of Athanopoulos, and his very young daughter, Iolanthe. They thought I might be useful because I knew some words of the South Pacific languages and their laws and customs. We headed out past Gibraltar, toward Trinidad, through the Panama Canal — temporarily destroyed a year later in the Third World War — and worked our way down the South American coast.

"So far it had been a smooth, pleasant sunny voyage. There had been only one desertion, at Trinidad where we stopped for water and fresh supplies. A young mechanic got scared with all this talk about going off to some unknown island for years, never to return; he went on shore and never came back. Life was easy on board. It was like an ordinary cruise, with card parties and deck games and cocktails, excellent wines and nightly music. Galli was one of the best violinists, picked by Athanopoulos himself. Sometimes we made believe that we were just on a cruise to the Pacific, that we would never find the island, or Athanopoulos might change his mind and we would all be back in a year. There was just as much life on the lower deck; the peasants and the fishermen took out their violins and some thrummed their guitars and the men and women danced on the moonlit deck; the music and the laughter mingled now and then with the mooing of cows and bleating of sheep — all just like one big, happy family. Everything very pleasant except for the goaty smell that was all over the place. We were lucky, for this was the end of August, but the sea was a white sheet of limitless expanse by day and a limpid deep in indigo by night, glowing phosphorescent as the ship's hull cut through it.

"We were well down the Peruvian coast when we discovered we had a Greek Orthodox priest with us, stowed away as one of the shepherds. It was Aristotimus. The mildly anti-clerical tendencies of Athanopoulos were well known. Some priests had registered to accompany the expedition, to look after the spiritual welfare of the colonists, but he had firmly turned them down. Besides, one priest was enough. However, the Greek peasants were Orthodox; they were horrified at the thought of having no one to baptize their babies. Aristotimus was then a young prelate, stationed near Mount Olympus. The peasants conspired to have him register as one of the shepherds. He was a regular Orthodox priest there. That was before he came under the influence of Laos.

"We ran into a storm along the Peruvian coast. For two days the ship rolled and tossed amidst pelting rains and an angry sea. She shivered and creaked and made an ominous rattle every time her stern was tossed up into the sky. She was like a shuttlecock kicked about the dark sea by some demon spirits. After the storm ceased, a ground swell kept the ship rolling from side to side, rhythmically, in slow, rocking movements. A number of the peasants who had never been out to sea fell sick. On the third day, an old shepherd gave up his ghost. This was reported to Dr. Cadmos. A bright sun was shining overhead now and the ship's crazy, temperamental movements had stopped. Father Donatello was sent for. With prayer-book in hand, he came down, ready to give the dead man his blessing before they threw the body overboard. There stood Aristotimus, in his black skullcap and his full priestly robe, also with a prayer-book in sheepskin. Their glances met. The Italian father scanned the tall figure of the stowaway priest from head to foot in stunned astonishment. He was sure from what the Countess had told him that he was the only priest permitted in this group of settlers, the only spiritual shepherd of this flock. Whence came this intruder, this wolf in sheep's clothing? Father Aristotimus was a tall man, standing six feet two, without the benefit of his skullcap. Father Donatello hated all tall men, because of the necessity of looking up when talking to them. He loved to look down and pat short peasant women and little children on the shoulder — much the more becoming posture for a spiritual father. However, they shook hands. Father Donatello was by nature frank and warm and friendly, and he had an open smile; if he bared his teeth a little more than usual, it was also natural under the circumstances.

" 'Well, where's the body?' he said, straightening up a little.

" 'It's over there,' replied the taller priest. 'This is very embarrassing, but the family desire that I attend to the last rites of their beloved kin. My name is Aristotimus, prelate of Mount Olympus.'

"Father Donatello was inwardly pleased to find that this strange, unaccounted-for priest's voice was soft, even self-effacing. He was not unconscious of his own good baritone, the kind of voice that found its noble qualities reflected to best advantage in the Cathedral of Milan, filling every crevice in the upsweeping dome and setting the stones to reverberate with a clear, resounding, celestial echo, to the glory of God.

"This momentary confusion was finally settled when, Athanopoulos arriving upon the scene, the Olympian villagers begged him to have their priest officiate for them, saying that it was the wish of the deceased. Father Aristotimus had in fact given extreme unction to the old man before he expired. Athanopoulos very kindly gave his consent, seeing that this was a thing in which the wish of the family must be respected. Afterward, Athanopoulos took Aristotimus to the upper deck and questioned him. Athanopoulos had as much concern in such affairs as Pontius Pilate over the private quarrels of the Jews. He didn't care at all. Furthermore, he found the tall priest to his liking; he liked tall men — the reason why he liked Prince Andreyev — and Aristotimus talked both learning and sense. After that, Aristotimus was much seen on the upper deck with us, and he struck up quite a friendship with the Russian Prince. The Russian Prince, Aristotimus, Athanopoulos and Laos looked very much like the 'Apostles' of El Greco. The Countess did her best to make Father Aristotimus welcome and cheer up Father Donatello again. Devout Catholic as she was, she was too intelligent not to see that Aristotimus and Donatello worshiped the same God."

This very edifying account of their voyage was interrupted by the sudden appearance of two or three bronze, naked figures in the garden, asking for Bowena in a stream of rapid-firing, high-pitched voices.

Emma-Emma and Eurydice rushed to the porch.

Bowena was out, somewhere around the square, and Emma-Emma told them to find her there. For the first time since her arrival, Eurydice saw her happy face clouded in trouble.

"What is it?" she asked Emma-Emma.

"Her father wounded a man, knocked his teeth out while drunk."

"Too bad."

"I hate this, but it's the Thainian custom. I would like to stop it if I could. It is a semi-religious custom. It dies hard."

Bowena came, her head bent in silence. They saw her tawny, erect figure follow the Thainians out of the gate. She looked back and threw a smile at them.

"My heart aches for that girl. She is going to take it. A brave girl."

"Take what? What has it got to do with her?"

Emma-Emma answered in a voice of resignation, almost a drawl. "It's their custom," she said. "She is going to expiate her father's crime."

"I don't understand."

"Of course you don't. She's going to be whipped for her old father's offense. But she will take it like a good girl. I would like to stop this, but she is still her father's child and she has to follow their tribal customs."

"What exactly do you mean?"

Emma-Emma showed considerable emotion. "I will tell you in a minute. I am going to heat up some water and prepare a poultice. I think she will be able to get back this evening. She won't talk about it — just accepts it as part of a daughter's duty. I hope they will not whip her too hard. That girl is as tough as a weed."

Emma-Emma was clearly fidgety. She ran about the house looking for some clean rags and boric acid powder. Eurydice had never seen her so agitated. Bowena had taken it before; she would

come back smiling with bruised marks on her back, and insist it
was not so bad. But it took some time for Emma-Emma to calm
down.

For hours they sat on the porch, gazing into the Thainian village on the north shore about a mile below them, and beyond to
the blue water, flecked by a few fishing boats. The bluff mud
houses the Thainians built themselves looked like a serrated
rabbit warren in the distance, clustered closely together, broken
by patches of greenery. It looked so idyllically peaceful.

"If the wind blows this way, we might hear her screams."

"No, that girl does not scream. Thainians don't scream when
flogged. There is wonderful strength in their native character."

"Why don't they whip the man himself who committed a
crime?"

Emma-Emma said at last, relapsing into her objective, professorial manner: "The Thainians, like all primitive people, have a
logical and stern, if somewhat barbarous, sense of justice. If a
man strikes his neighbor in anger, one of his sons receives spank-
ings on his buttocks. In Thainian law, this is known as the
'transfer of guilt.' The essential idea that sin can and should be
absolved by punishment received by someone other than the
offender equates with the primitive sense of justice, basically at
the back of human and animal sacrifices. Sin must be paid for,
but as it was undesirable for themselves to receive the punishment,
they invented the idea that someone must die for their sins, either
a lamb, or in earlier stages, another human being. That made it
even in the eyes of their gods. You surely have heard of throwing
a pretty maiden into the sea to save a village from a plague, or
a drought."

"I wouldn't like to be that maiden."

"But she had no choice. Even in civil life, it is perfectly all
right to punish someone for his father's irregularities, and of
course when the father's authority is great, it is not difficult to
persuade themselves that the son must take the punishment in
place of his old parent. Laos, however, has put through an
Ireniki law, which is the reverse of this and which seems socio-

logically sound. It works. The Ireniki punish the parents if the children misbehave. If a boy steals, we shut up his parents — his father, or mother, or both — for three days. Usually it does not come to that, but the theory is there. Whose fault is it if the children misbehave? It is a matter of the honor of the family. Very Confucian. And it works. The parents feel disgraced if their children steal, or otherwise break the law. The responsibility is squarely put on the shoulders of the parents. They are considered as having been derelict in their duties. This, I believe, is why we practically have no cases of juvenile delinquency on this island. We let the parents punish their own children, if they see fit. That is the time to stop them before they become confirmed lawbreakers."

"It sounds sensible. But what about the Thainians?"

"They have a perverted sense of justice. They do the reverse. If a woman is caught in adultery, they stone her daughter. You can't quite see the point, but they do. Of course, they don't stone the poor girl to death, but punishment must be meted out somewhere or a plague will descend upon the island. It's the whole familiar idea of vicarious sacrifice and expiation. Prince Andreyev once saved a child of four from being stoned to death. His grandfather had been caught stealing a neighbor's sheep to kill it for food. We saw the villagers gathered around that naked child. The child was confused, frightened; even a child of four could sense that the whole world was against him, that he was in danger. He screamed and ran. Somebody started throwing a pebble which grazed the boy's head. Prince Andreyev walked out, his face a burning flame. Without a word, he raised his whip and lashed a man with a stone in his hand, then the next man, then another and another. The others let the little rocks drop out of their hands as he advanced. The Prince was a sight to behold; six feet four, a fiery forehead and auburn hair flaming in the sunlight, and decked out with medals — he was never without them when he left his house. They knew he was the Prince. He demanded to know who had cast the first stone. A boy of sixteen or eighteen was seen scampering away. He was brought back and the Prince cut him up so thoroughly with his leather whip that the boy whined and howled for mercy. The little child had been watching all this time from behind a bush. The Prince had great difficulty in stopping his crying, and after succeeding in bringing him back to his mother, bade them never let this happen again.

"It was entirely logical," continued Emma-Emma. "For if it was justice to visit a man's sin upon his son, it was but a logical extension to let his grandchildren pay, even for three or four generations. It is religion with them; the gods don't like to see sin go unpunished. Their theory is that the baby had 'sin' in him when he was born by the mere fact that the grandfather carried the sin, mystically, in his seed, and it would be an act of mercy if the baby were spared the trouble of living. You wouldn't believe it, would you? The theory works to the detriment of the young of course, a heinous doctrine, accusing an innocent baby of guilt and sin before it knows its right hand from its left. But the Thainian priest is sure of it, dogmatic about it. The baby was born with sin. On the other hand, if the family is rich enough to be able to kill a lamb, the baby's sin is 'taken over' by the lamb which has died in the baby's place. You put sin in, then you take it out, which keeps the priests busy. This may sound complicated to us, but it is perfectly logical to the savage mind. The animal sacrifice in place of human sacrifice was already a great advance in human civilization; then burned sacrifice replaced blood sacrifice, in a much later stage. God was at first a blood-drinking being, a cannibal like themselves; as the savages discovered the art of roasting, their gods correspondingly developed a taste for roast meat."

"It's gruesome. Shocking!"

"That is what makes anthropology interesting. You try to place yourself in the position of the savages and follow the workings of their minds. They don't hate the baby, or the sacrificial lamb, or Bowena whom they are probably whipping now. They are just so absurdly logical about it. Nobody can shake their belief that sin must be paid for, either by the guilty party, or by somebody else. So long as someone pays for it in the sinner's place, it will do."

What puzzled Eurydice still more was the story Emma-Emma had been able to get out of them. This may sound like an amusing tale, for it is characteristic of the imagination and terrific sense of justice of the Thainians. It was somewhat difficult for Laos and Athanopoulos to follow when she told it to them. The story was told that an ancient king lived in a grand palace, surrounded by a royal park. (Emma-Emma imagined that it might be an ancient king of the Incas, living on the top of the Andes; she had a theory that the original inhabitants came from there, rather than from the jumping-off islands of the mid-Pacific.) The king forbade his subjects to pick fruits, or in any way trespass upon the royal preserves. One day some children of a nearby village went picking berries, innocently finding themselves inside the royal park. They were arrested by the royal guards. The great king was so angry that he banished the entire population of the village to a distant land. The villagers were very unhappy, for the soil was arid and difficult to grow things on. They blamed their children for bringing them to this plight. And their hearts were rebellious and there was much grumbling against the cruel king. The king had one son, who one day passed through the new village on one of his hunting trips. The villagers recognized him, fell upon him and clubbed him to death. And here was the amazing sequel. Upon hearing of his son's death, the king was so delighted that he forgave them all, for his sense of justice was satisfied. He sent his royal messengers, who said to them, "His Majesty has forgiven all of you because you killed his only begotten son. He is dead. All your sins are forgiven. You can all come back." A little stretched as this reasoning seemed to Emma-Emma and Eurydice, it illustrated very well the idea of the Thainians that sin must be expiated.

As Emma-Emma interpreted the story, the king promised them forgiveness of future crimes, too — robbing or stealing, even adultery — because their sins had already been paid for. This was so delightfully easy that the laws of the land almost broke down, for every time a thief was caught, he had only to remind the king of the prince's death to be acquitted. The primitive naïveté of their belief was irresistible, for it relieved them of the much harder and more odious duty of moral regeneration. The shift of character, in terms of the storyteller's art, from the king's unreasonable severity in the beginning to his unbridled generosity in the end, did not seem to bother the simple minds of the Thainians. To them, it was logical, consistent, wholly in character and satisfactory.

The discovery of the story of the killed prince greatly delighted Emma-Emma, for it formed one of the pieces of evidence for her theory of the Inca origin of the Thainians. While traveling in Peru, she had heard a similar story told of the Incas, with minor variations. The villagers had thrown the prince over a cliff instead of clubbing him to death. One important detail caught her attention. In the Peruvian story, the king's name was Yahuno, whereas in the Thainian legend, the name was Gajunta, evidently the earlier word. If she could collect examples of the phonetic change from g to y, and from j to h, the connection could be established beyond a doubt. One thing was clear — g was an earlier sound, as is well known to students of phonetic history. It would make her very happy if she could establish the "breaking" of the hard guttural into a palatal sound in the Inca language; it might help her to date approximately the migration of the Thainians in the dim past. For it is generally true that colonies do not share the phonetic changes occurring in the mother country, so that their migration must have antedated the change from g to y.

Chapter IX

LATE, TOWARD SUNDOWN, they could see Bowena's dark figure limping up the incline, supported by a young man, now and then blocked from view by a sugar-cane plantation at the foot of the hill. The valley below lay in the shadow, while the blue sea glistened still in the evening sun. From the porch they watched the young man assisting Bowena up the rocky path, which wound up toward the center of the town, some fifty yards from the house. Emma-Emma stood up and waved to her. Bowena waved back and smiled.

"Who is that young man?" asked Eurydice.

"Tihualco, her boy friend."

Passing through the square of the town, Bowena attracted much attention. People gathered to ask her questions and survey the marks of chastisement on her back. Joanna had told them what was happening, and the idle citizens with nothing to do had been hanging around, waiting to see her return.

"How bad is it?" Emma-Emma asked, when they came in the front door.

"I've had a good rest already," replied the girl, instinctively turning sidewise to show her back. Her dark-tinted face showed a smile, suggestive even of pride, of duty well done. Running across her back and extending below her waist, disappearing beneath her short red skirts, were a series of dark red crisscross patterns, and green leaves applied on the severe injuries. The blood marks had already darkened. She limped noticeably; every step she took must have caused intense pain, but she made the best of it. Tihualco was holding her arm, muttering soft, unintelligible words while the girl smiled.

"Come in. You must lie in bed. I will have the wounds treated."

She was escorted to her room on the west. A primitive bamboo bed filled about half the room. Tihualco and Eurydice bustled about to help bring the water and the compress. The girl's fine body lay on one side, smooth and sinewy like a black leopard. Eurydice and the young man stood and watched through the porch window, while Emma-Emma washed the wounds and applied the poultice. The climb up the rocky path had caused some blood to break out afresh, staining her skirt. It was a miracle that she could walk at all. But the girl was chattering on. Bowena was the one "case history" Emma-Emma the anthropologist could not be objective about. She had seen this Thainian girl grow from childhood into a buxom, independent-minded, always helpful maid of twenty. She could not do without her silvery laughter and even her occasional willfulness.

"Oh, dear, what have they done to you?" she remarked as she peeled off the green leaves.

"If they didn't do it to me, they would have done it to my younger brother. He is too young. When he is sixteen, I will let him take my place. I left instructions at home that they are to send for me if my father gets into a fight again."

"Didnt' your father see the whipping?"

"He did. After the whipping I turned my back toward him and told him to behave. I think he felt ashamed."

The strange thing about it, Eurydice thought, when she was told what the girl said — the strange thing was that the punishment worked after all on the committer of a crime. Unless he was a thorough unregenerate scoundrel, he wouldn't like to see his child whipped for his own sake; he would think twice before he got drunk and hit a man again. Eurydice did think, however, that Laos' way was better; if a child was caught stealing, his father should be locked up for three days. Let every family take care of its own growing children. This idea should have been applied in the United States. There should be no juvenile delin-

quents at all. This question of juvenile delinquency had occupied her labors and thoughts for some years, and she had been
unable to accept any solution — least of all the solution of shutting up the young offenders in state reform institutions together
with older confirmed toughs and rowdies. The Thainians, on the
other hand, seemed to have hit upon the perverse idea of educat-
ing the parents by punishing their children. The wisdom of the
savages. . . . Travel did broaden one's mind.

Tihualco, having left the girl in Emma-Emma's tender care,
returned to the village. He said he would come to see her the
next day.

The next morning, Eurydice was lying awake in bed. She felt
perfectly strong and well. She had been at Thainos a week. She
thought she ought to get up and take a good look at the island.
She would like to have a morning swim, which she had enjoyed
with Paul at San Felipe. They used to work at night to the tune
of four or five cups of black coffee, take a morning swim, then go
to bed. A week here, and she had put so much behind her.
Bowena, still limping, was already up at the kitchen. Emma-Emma
enjoyed lying in bed, reading or working at her manuscripts, and
usually got up around ten. Time meant nothing on this island.

She thought of all those people she had heard about — Laos,
the Countess, Iolanthe, the Prince. Fate had thrown her into
this strange company — her work abruptly terminated. Statistics,
papers, reports, her trips for the Geodetic Survey — all lay behind her, safely, irrevocably. She was going to be here for a long,
long time, in a strange community of men whose ways, as in
some ideal republic, threatened to shatter all her beliefs. She
could mentally picture its place upon the map, a jewel upon the
vast Pacific body of water, secluded, self-sufficient, a settlement
not without the amenities of culture, of a genial way of life —
there were 20,000 volumes of books (the first 12,000, having been

found inadequate, had been supplemented by further shipments on the S.S. *Arcadia*) somewhere, perhaps in the Athenaeum, she had been told — far removed from the vexatious and incredibly complex problems of a civilization grown too big for human intelligence to cope with. Food problems, population pressures, the incurable jealousies and contentions of warring nations — all these seemed to be separated from her by the wide gulf of centuries. Then it seemed that all these complexities need not be at all, that mankind had, in its unthinking and unplanned evolution, merely stumbled into an incredible mess of its own making. Nobody had pondered, or foretold, the effects upon man of industrial progress. She was gaining a certain perspective.

Altogether, she thought it would be no misfortune if the Geodetic Survey people did not come for her for a year or so. She would learn something fresh and new.

Emma-Emma was serenely lying in her bed. No morning papers, no office hours, no telephone calls. Where had she heard the phrase, splendid isolation? Emma-Emma told her that she was lucky to have landed here. The serenity of the place was almost Byzantine. She heard noises in the kitchen, and her thought turned to that Thainian girl — her courage, her sense of duty, her love for that young man, the incredible simplicity of her ideas. Twice now, she had seen that girl go down by herself in mid-afternoon, to have a dip in the rocky brook below, with nothing but a towel around her. And she had thought enameled bath-tubs were indispensable to civilization! She was reminded of a saying that the best things in life cost nothing.

As she lay in bed, Eurydice felt and knew that she was going to come to close grips with the fundamentals of human life, with problems of human society and psychology, seen in an unaccustomed light. Her waiting upon this island, her extended captivity, if forced upon her, at least did not entail the agonies of suspense. She was there. And Paul was dead. It relieved her mind of the duty of making decisions.

She got up and threw on a frock Emma-Emma had given her.

"Where is that lake?" she asked as she walked in to Emma-Emma's room.

Emma-Emma took her spectacles down.

"Good morning, Eurydice. Tell me, when did your first menstruation period arrive?"

Now this was too much. Eurydice flushed, visibly discomfited. Byzantine serenity indeed! She shouldn't have roomed with an anthropologist.

Perceiving the young woman's reaction, Emma-Emma explained. "I hope you don't mind. I have been trying to take some notes about you . . ."

"Am I one of your case histories? Or is it a Kinsey report?" Eurydice had certain Episcopalian sensibilities; the question struck her as bordering on vulgarity.

"Tell me — you don't mind — I am not compiling a police dossier — it's all for science."

"I don't know. Do you remember when yours first arrived?"

"Unfortunately I have forgotten. But I assure you that the information has scientific significance. I have the records of one hundred and thirty-five girls here on this island — Greeks, Italians, Thainians, the mixed-bloods." She pointed to the piles of folders on her shelves. "It has great significance."

"And what is that, may I ask?"

"I am trying to establish the sex cycles of men and women. Laos himself is interested."

"And that's what keeps you busy all these years?"

"It's what keeps me happy. Not that alone, of course. I am trying to penetrate into all the forces, internal and external, which make men and women what they are, their customs, their beliefs, their prejudices."

"You said Laos?"

"Yes. He has an amazing theory. He has run across an ancient Chinese author of the second century A.D. This Chinese author . . ."

Bowena knocked on the door, tea and breakfast on a tray in

hand. Emma-Emma winked a smile at her. "How is the wound? Doesn't it hurt? You are a good girl. Just put it down there."

As the girl went out of the door, Emma-Emma's eyes followed her. "What a wonderful girl," she resumed. "I wouldn't take such a beating for my father, not for Jove's sake." (Emma-Emma swore a little.) "This Chinese author, I was saying, gave a mystic number for the sex cycles, seven for women, and eight for men. It seems to work out. There is something mystic about it. Girls' puberty begins at two times seven, or fourteen. Boys begin at two times eight, which is sixteen. Then women's menopause begins at forty-nine, while men's begins at sixty-four. This basic cycle seems correct. It certainly has important social implications. Men mature more slowly and their cycle lasts longer. It is like the seventeen-year locust, or the wisdom tooth; a mysterious factor 'X' in the human body determines the clockwork . . . hand me that tea, will you? Much obliged."

Emma-Emma sipped her tea. On the tray lay Greek pastries. "Laos infers also that the full adolescent period ought to be seven years for girls and eight years for men. The girl is fully mature at twenty-one, and the man at twenty-four. That is the period they ought to get married and have children. What do you think?"

"I wouldn't know. It certainly sounds interesting. Where is the lake?"

"What lake?"

"Where I saw some girls bathing the first day I arrived. I have a good mind to go for a morning swim."

"Not a bad idea. You are well now. Bowena will show you — no, I will come with you. You ought to see the island a bit, you really haven't seen it."

Chapter X

THEY HAD FOLLOWED the road, paved with coarse tuff slabs, up the slope, along which straggling houses stood embowered in tropical greenery on the northern ridge, parallel to the stream which ran some thirty feet below, lined with tumbling rocks and luxuriant underbrush. Below, to their left, lay the sea in its velvety morning calm. Nobody seemed to be about. The rocky pavement, a deep, rusty brown, looked clean because the frequent afternoon thunderstorms, acting as a general scavenger, had washed the leaves and débris down the swift slope.

Some hundred yards above, they turned into a dirt path. Following around a copse of yews, the road disappeared into an open ground, covered with pine needles, lying in the half shade of sparse tall pines. Directly in front of them lay the limpid blue lake, some three hundred feet above sea level. Here the timber thickened; bird cries were heard seventy or eighty feet overhead. Eurydice recognized with a start the landing where on that fateful day, Paul came up from the swim, water dripping from his head and face, while two or three girls were dressing in the open under the trees. The past week had been like a dream.

"Jump in, and come up quickly. The water is cold in the morning," said Emma-Emma.

"Aren't you coming in?"

"No, not at my age."

Eurydice had a rapid swim halfway down the lake and turned back in swift, graceful strokes. The dip did her good. Her skin felt atingle. Quickly drying herself, shivering, she gave herself a hard rubdown with her towel. She felt good again.

"Come on," said Emma-Emma. "I will take you to the crest on the further side beyond this timber. There you will have a good view of the island."

They went along the reddish sand, then picked their way through a trail, leading through the heavy forest, sweet with a resinous fragrance. A short climb, and they were standing on a ledge overlooking the town, sleeping below under a cloudless sky. A thick line of green bordered the town and sea, and then beyond stretched the lagoon like a sheet of pale blue silk with a few dark spots marking bars of coral growth. The undulating country ran leisurely in a succession of cornfields and terraces and small rocky ridges toward the sea. All around, the land was covered with pale, ashen-blue patches which marked the olive groves. The shoreline curved playfully toward a vast flat promontory jutting far out to the south. It wasn't at all like what she had seen from the sky, a rugged octopus-shaped island, inhabited by cannibals and wild beasts. There was something bland and human about the island, full of graceful curves and soft tints, warm, inviting, peaceful.

The shepherds on the highlands were already out. Emma-Emma told her that this was called the Delian Heights, the shepherds and wine-growers coming chiefly from the island of Delos. Toward the south on about the same level as where they were; perched on top of a headland, was the villa of Athanopoulos, known as the Residence, where Iolanthe and her father lived. A heavy coppice of cypresses and a white line of balustrades marked the approach to the house. Behind the house lay a curious structure of stone, open in front, where Athanopoulos had kept his black goats. Goats, bearded and thick with hair, were his special hobby. It was more than a hobby; it was an obsession with him. The entire house had reeked with the smell, Emma-Emma said. But Athanopoulos could not live without it. Quite a psychological study, Emma-Emma said; it was rumored that he had a preference for women with plenty of hair. The dark-eyed Iolanthe might be a case in point . . .

Toward the east, the plateau on which they were standing dropped gently in an endless series of vineyards, and then rose in ever-ascending slopes toward the majestic craggy top, which the Irenikis called Mount Ida, following the custom of colonists in naming places after those of their mother country. There was nothing feminine about Mount Ida, except that its broad flanks and the rich fertile plains on its slopes, coming down toward the valley in generous curves and folds, might make her a symbol of motherhood. A curious rampart of granite, with many fissures, but seemingly of one piece, rose to form a crown upon the mount, remarkably resembling a shuttle, or the tip of a giant peony bud just about to burst into flower, its smooth, round petals gently sloping upward. The lines were soft and harmonious; nothing awesome or sinister about it. The strange thing about the whole area was the bright magic hues of the entire mountainside, which wallowed in a medley of opalescent colors — the peculiar tawny blue of the crags, daubs of green and glistening purple which were the vineyards, and patches of red standing against the bright enamel of the grasslands. The clarity of the air no doubt accounted for this; even the white sheep on the distant slope stood out in clear detail. Between the slope and the plateau ran a glistening band of water, coming down from a dam above, now gleaming in the sun, racing mirthfully across four or five small, picturesque cascades toward the sea. There was a playful, frolicsome character about the landscape.

"What is beyond that peak?" Eurydice asked.

"On the other side, it drops rather sharply into the bay in unscalable cliffs. But toward the south, it extends for miles into a primitive timberland where some of the natives live. We don't live there because the water is slightly salty. But there is good grassland for the sheep and cattle."

Toward the town side in the foreground below them, the red spire of a small church, marked by a cross, rose a short distance from the square, imbedded in green foliage. Emma-Emma pointed out to her the roof of the Museion and the Athenaeum standing midway up the incline above the town.

"What is that?" Eurydice asked, pointing to an open semicircular space to the left.

"That's the amphitheater. The Greeks are great at plays. Once a year, they celebrate a big festival, the Irenicia. The girls from the Institute of Comforters of Men's Souls give a play, and there are recitals of poetry and gymnastic contests. The whole colony goes mad for three days, with wining and feasting and song and dance. Let's go down. I will show you the way; we will go back through the town."

"Where is the library? Can we take a look?"

"You will have plenty of time for that. It's in the Athenaeum."

They went south by a narrow path. A narrow flight of rocky steps, between pinkish walls, led straight down. Eurydice found her high heels almost impossible for the descent. It was torture going down, and she could not take them off. Once she stumbled and almost fell, but caught herself against the wall.

Down on the ground level, and emerging out of an olive grove, they entered the amphitheater from the back. The stage, opposite them, was entirely open, built of big slabs of stone. Eurydice seized the chance to take off her shoes and rub her ankles.

"Does it hurt?"

"A little."

"You shouldn't put on those high-heeled shoes."

"I have nothing else."

She surveyed the empty tiers. "You people built all this?"

"Yes. With the help of the native tribesmen, of course."

"Tell me, what happened when you first arrived? Didn't you have to fight them?"

Emma-Emma was particularly proud of this episode. "No, dear, no," she said in a slightly gloating tone. "Laos didn't want any bloodshed. We were going to need them, their labor and their friendship. What do you think? We call them savages, and ourselves civilized. I have seen everywhere, in the South Pacific, Australia, New Zealand, Africa, the white man going about with his guns. We are the aggressive, warlike type. The native tribesmen are usually honest souls, simple-minded like children. Some of the tribes are warlike, but they are seldom aggressive. They don't want fighting any more than we do."

"What did you do?"

"Strategy. A strategy to win them over and overcome them. By a few lambs and some violins and a painted white cow. It was a confounded trick. To the last moment, we could never be sure whether it would work or not. We had to risk it. The painted cow and Prince Somovarvitch."

Eurydice giggled every time she heard that name.

"What are you laughing at?"

"Nothing."

"Athanopoulos was for landing fully armed. Laos and I persuaded him not to. We were going to make this our home. Between Laos and Prince Andreyev and myself we won him over. We had worked out a plan before sailing. I was sure it would work; I knew the tribesmen pretty well. The simple-minded natives were easy to overawe, and they were peaceful people if my experience with the Tahitans and Samoans were any guide.

"We planned to arrive in the dark. The first night we arrived, we put on the searchlights, and let them crisscross the sky above the island in a weird, playful pattern. We spotted some of the native huts, and focused on them for some time. We could see dark figures running about in the white glare. Then we sailed off, without landing. The next night we came again, and put on the same show, fired a few rockets. Again we pulled out of sight before dawn. The third night we prepared to land. We thought the natives had been sufficiently confused and awed. We had to do something spectacular. We had come inside the lagoon, and could see the island, a vague mass, with an overhanging bank of mist. The sub-tropical night was never completely dark, as you know. When all was ready, we put on a beautiful display of fireworks, a succession of blue, green and purple rockets, showers, shooting stars. The crackle of the fireworks awakened the whole island. It was about nine o'clock. Then searchlights played. Hundreds of men, women and children had come to the shore. We kept them entertained. As they were getting tired, the music started. Horns blared, drums rattled, and then the soft music of flutes and violins followed. You have no idea of the magic influence of music on savages. Prince Andreyev was all dressed up, a golden star on his cap, and a selected group of us who were going up first were dressed in white. I had a hunch that with the prince and the white cow and the music, they might mistake us for gods. They did.

"We got into the small boats, just about two dozen of us. I had a star, too, on my head and a golden staff. I was the goddess. Me riding on that painted cow. The band followed us. Just as we were about to land, the ship sent off a white glare which hung suspended in the sky for five minutes, transforming the night into day. The natives were utterly bewildered.

"It was an act of extravaganza, superbly timed and played. The effect was devastating. There I was, mounted on the white cow, a golden staff in one hand, a bag of beads in the other. We advanced, Prince Andreyev on my right, leading a lamb, the violinists behind us. We were superhuman, supernatural beings. The natives prostrated themselves. A few ran away into the dark, but most were spellbound. I don't know which produced the greater effect.

"But it was of course the lamb." Emma-Emma laughed; she seemed still to enjoy the joke. "The little lamb ran forward a few steps and bounced back. I could not help laughing. They had never seen such an animal. If they came from the Incas, they must have heard their ancestors talk about the llamas in the Andes. Anyway, their chief came toward me. I attempted a few words. He didn't seem to understand. All of a sudden, he fell on his knees, as before a goddess. I laughed gently, and touched his head with my golden staff, and motioned for him to rise. Graciously, I got down from my cow and presented the king with a string of beads. It wasn't difficult for me at all. I knew the natives well. I put the string of beads across his neck, and said as sweetly as I could, 'There!' Then I stepped forward, picking out the young women and gave them each some baubles. Sure enough, it worked. They were mystified, but friendly. Prince Andreyev went on distributing his baubles, rings, bracelets. I was sure there was a queen. It was not difficult to spot her. A dark, middle-aged woman was shouting and gesticulating to the chief. I had reserved the biggest necklace, studded with glittering stones, with a gold-plated circle in the center, for her.

"After that, we knew we were in no immediate danger. The skipper, Telemachus, had been ordered to keep the searchlights ready, so that in case of a sudden attack, the light would blink directly against their faces and blind them. However, that was not necessary. We signaled back for more people to come on land, while the band played and we danced and made merry and laughed. We really laughed; we had landed after a voyage lasting seventy-five days. It was the end of October. 'Do you think they are impressed?' Prince Andreyev whispered to me. 'It's safe,' I said, 'The natives have never been so entertained as tonight. You go. Hypnotize them with your size and your golden star, show you are friendly. Touch them on the head. Keep up the spell. And make them obey you. Speak like a god.' He did. After a while, he gave a kingly shout and made a gesture for them to go home. They ran off like little children.

"That night many of us camped on the shore, some keeping watch to make sure that nothing happened.

"The next morning, we invaded the village, having given orders to everybody to be friendly to the natives and do absolutely nothing to provoke them. To make sure of their fear of us we gave a display of shooting clay pigeons. Athanopoulos and a few of us who were good shots gave an impressive show, which remained in their minds forever.

"Then it happened, Dr. Artemos informed us, that there was to be a full eclipse of the moon when the next full moon was due. The eclipse of the moon came in very handy. With much adroitness, Laos arranged for a meeting of our leaders and the Thainian king over questions of the settlement on the day the eclipse was due. We had given them liberal presents, and the king had been disposed to be friendly, and given us the site of the town. But now Prince Andreyev demanded further that the slopes of Mount Ida should be made available for our pasture. We knew the king would resist. Prince Andreyev was to grow very angry and cut off the discussion, saying, 'Go away! I shall shadow the moon tonight, at half past nine.' This was carefully explained, with the help of many gestures, to the Thainian king. We took care to make a show of it, and made sure the tribesmen come to see it. Dr. Artemos had the watch in hand. Five minutes before the eclipse was due, drums were beaten. At the dramatic 9:35, Prince Andreyev brandished his golden staff and commanded the moon to grow dim. After that we had no more trouble with the Thainians."

"What happened to the ship? Did they destroy it?' 'Eurydice asked.

"No. Telemachus went back. Athanopoulos gave the ship to the skipper. During the two months on the voyage, we realized what we were going to miss. However carefully we had planned, we were going to need more metal tools, supplies, paper, cloth, medicine. The skipper had been bound to secrecy; none of the sailors knew exactly where we were. Athanopoulos had a horror, a most uncomfortable feeling that the crops of grapes might fail, that the supplies of wine and tobacco might be cut off. It is a funny thing. When you come to chalk up the progress of human civilization, you suddenly realize that tobacco and wine and the lyre are among the very few important permanent discoveries of mankind, the real, definite gains for human comfort and wise, genial living. You could do without railways and motor cars and the radio, as we do here, and be still quite comfortable, but without tobacco and wine and the flute and the lyre, the accent of living would be lost. Mankind would be infinitely the poorer for it. You would think Athanopoulos would have regarded the sixty cases of wine he had brought as sufficient. But he felt uncomfortable. He wanted to be sure that the island could produce its own wine, and it had to be good. That was why he had brought those expert wine-growers from Delos. Anyway, he told the skipper not to whisper a word about the island. He was to come after a year with the supplies, according to the list we gave him. Athanopoulos promised to give him one of his tankers as a present for each trip. Telemachus came the next year, and the year after that, for three years. The wine-growers had been successful, and we had all the tools and supplies we needed. Athanopoulos told him to stop coming. Telemachus was very happy. He was now the owner of three tankers. Years elapsed before he turned up once more, for old friendship's sake, to inquire how we were faring. He had really kept his word, had not told a soul about it. That was some eight or nine years ago."

A glimmer crept into Eurydice's eyes. "Is he never coming back again? Was it good-by forever?"

"It was supposed to be. Who can tell? Sheer curiosity may drive him to come for a visit again, or perhaps to retire here himself. Or he may be dead."

"How old was he when he came last?"

"Fifty or sixty. What are you thinking?"

"I don't know."

Chapter XI

COMING OUT of the amphitheater, and following the maple lane around the gymnastic ground, they were approaching the street of shops leading to the square. Eurydice's presence had been noticed; the villagers had not seen her since the day of the funeral. Her white blouse and black breeches tied below the knees, her blond hair, stylishly done, singled her out among the inhabitants. This was the young American woman, engaged on some fool's errand, who had landed in their midst. They all wanted to be friendly. Children with lingering smiles, fingers on their lips, surrounded her. Girls, some with blue eyes, stared at her with a dreamy curiosity. The narrow street, lying in the shade, was delightfully cool in the morning hours. Some had shawls. It was remarkable what the young girls did with their shawls — some over their heads, some over the right shoulder, or left shoulder, or tied around their neck or just swung across the bare shoulders, the two ends hanging over their backs — in a bewildering variety of positions. The shawl was not an article of clothing: it was an infinitely flexible instrument of feminine coquetry. These girls studied Eurydice's hairdo and shoes and the color of her lipstick as minutely, as lovingly, as a scientist ever pores over a tertiary fish specimen. Give a woman a pin, a bauble of some sort, a ribbon, a red napkin, and she will experiment with it, with a delightful feminine sense of color and fitness, be she a New York socialite or a grandmother of Tasmania. They remembered seeing Iolanthe's golden slippers and the Countess' platform shoes with butterfly pompons, and thought Eurydice's

ultra-modern flesh-colored shoes with intercrossing ankle straps
of black compared favorably with them. Many of them would
give an eye to own such a pair. Such dignity, such high fancy,
such design! There was nothing so structurally unique, and so
flattering to a woman's vanity as a pair of shoes. And these
girls were for the most part barefooted.

They passed into the square. The houses were closely packed,
some three-storied, faced with stucco, others two-storied. Potted
flowers lined the windows. Eurydice stopped to admire the
statue of Hermes in the center of the fountain, made of bronze,
specked with green, his lower parts wet with the spray trickling
down a stone base coated with lichen. It was a first-class object
of art, Hermes' face invested with a Puckish humor, head tilted
so slightly, looking into the cloudless sky.

Eurydice became aware that a plump young woman, in white
blouse showing a wide open bosom, and a heavily embroidered
black skirt, was standing close to them, jabbering with Emma-
Emma. She was Joanna, mistress of Giovanni's restaurant. Joanna
directed a frank, gracious, friendly glance at Eurydice. She was
saying she would be honored if Emma-Emma and Eurydice would
condescend to have a Neapolitan dinner one evening as their
guest. It would be a supreme pleasure. Her husband was the best
cook in Naples.

"Giovanni, come out and meet our guest," Joanna shouted in
the direction of the restaurant.

From the dark cavern of the building emerged an apron,
greased and stained, then a stumpy figure with a bald head
fringed with a circle of spotted gray hair, and a face manifestly
born round, but now sallow and sunken below the protruding
cheekbones displaying a full, stiff mustache, curled upward, almost Stalinesque. It was such a manly mustache. Giovanni knew
that this was the most important feature of his face, the index
of his masculinity. He always twisted it when he was summoned
from within to appear before his guests, or when Joanna was
particularly loving and demonstrative, or pouring out a torrent
of words, to which he had nothing in particular to say. It was

a conscious, cultivated gesture. He was Giovanni Francesco Salvellini, reputed the best cook of Naples, in other words, an artist
in flavors, as a painter is an artist in colors. A man must have his
dignity before his customers. Let no man say that he was henpecked. It was most unfortunate that Joanna had not only such
a big rasping voice, but had such a decided opinion about things,
was so sure of herself, particularly about what she wanted him
to do at a particular moment. He was an artist, and an artist was
perceptive, liked to take time to think things over and look at
both sides. He always ended, however, after sufficient twisting
and curling of his mustache, in seeing Joanna's side, and acted
accordingly. The rumor, persistently promoted by the gossip of
the village, that he was henpecked was due, he reflected, to the
fact that Joanna outweighed him physically, in terms of kilograms.
Joanna grew heavier, plumper and softer as he grew thinner,
lighter and wirier. All the fat in him had burned out, but the
wick of his flame still burned bright, that artistic awareness and
masterly witchery which could turn a common eggplant into a
dish fit for kings. Athanopoulos had come himself for his hot
antipasto of black olives, prepared by himself, capers, and eggplant slices sautéed in oil and rolled with anchovies, mushrooms
and pimiento. It was useless to give the cold formula, the master's
touch was the thing. He baked his own bread, too. His baked
clams, his *calamare*, his sensational sea bass, with a sprinkle of
mushrooms and garlic and oregano, saturated in olive oil, his
chicken arregante and shrimp marinara were creations out of this
world. The secret lay probably in his seasoning, mixed in right
proportions. A dinner like that, rounded out with coffee Napoli-
tana would make any exiled Italian reconciled to this island.

Seeing the new American woman at the fountain, he knew
what he had been sent for. Once more, his wife was right. It
was annoying to have a wife who was always right, who thought
ahead of him. It wasn't that he didn't see the point; his masculine
intelligence was merely slower in matters of mundane business.
Here was the American woman, a being from the outside world,
a God-sent opportunity to increase the restaurant's business if

they made her their steady customer. Any outlay, such as a free, friendly dinner of introduction, would be amply covered by the customers she attracted. It would make their place popular; it would give the right touch of novelty. Why, she had done the same with Pietro Galli; she was full of attentions when Galli came; the food served was superb and charges cheap, and Galli inevitably ended up by taking out his violin and giving a concert free for the public. Chiron the Greek in the tavern opposite was just asleep. Giovanni had to admit that the prosperity of his business was due very largely to the forethought and machinations of Joanna. Joanna was not a miracle, but she was God's blessing to him.

"*Benvenuto*," said Giovanni, extending his hand to Eurydice. "We like you take dinner with us, any evening you like. You and Emma-Emma. Any evening. I am Giovanni Francesco Salvellini of Napoli. Just call me Giovanni. *Ospitalità Italiana*. I will give you something very special — a dream — Bvwah!" He pulled his earlobe, jerked it lovingly, and made a smack of gastronomic appreciation. "Giovanni cook for you special. You will come?"

"You are irresistible," said Eurydice.

"Ever saw Napoli? Well, you should know, then. This place not bad. But Napoli and our calamare, the metropolis of the gastronomic empire! Not all the ashes of Vesuvius could cover up the proud tradition of ancient culinary art. Ha, ha! *Benvenuto*, three times *benvenuto!* Giovanni himself cook for you. And I get Pietro here with his violin, and we are in Napoli again. Bvwah!"

They shook hands and parted in smiles.

"Well," said Emma-Emma to her companion. "You see you are welcomed by everybody. There's Theodota and her children. I don't think we should favor one side."

Theodota, Chiron's wife, had been standing at her restaurant door with her two little children, silently watching the procedure of the last five minutes. She was a quiet woman, about forty, a little aged before her years. A strong peasant face, hooded with a black scarf, square and heavy-chinned, but kindly looking. Emma-Emma and Eurydice walked toward them.

"Come in for a drink," the woman said with true Spartan brevity.

Emma-Emma spoke for them, while Eurydice smiled. "Thank you. We must be on our way."

"Your friend is completely well, I hope."

The woman put her hands on her chest and smiled. They passed. It was nice. Everybody was so friendly.

Back at home, they found a note from the Countess lying on Emma-Emma's desk, inviting them to dinner.

"You are popular," said Emma-Emma.

Eurydice studied the note. It was in English, written with a very broad pen in large letters, three or four words to the line, in swift, generous strokes, suggestive of the expansive character of the writer, dated "Late-autumn, 24, Saturday, 2004," and signed Countess Cordelia della Castiglioni.

Bowena came in to say that Dr. Lysippus had brought the note. They had seen it already.

"Tihualco is here," she said with a happy, proud smile. "He has come to see me."

"That's fine."

"If you want to send an answer, he can bring it to the Countess for you. You are going, I hope?"

"I will tell you," answered Emma-Emma abruptly.

The girl went back happily to her room.

"When is it for?"

"For Saturday," said Eurydice. "She invites both of us."

"You must go of course. Everybody will be anxious to meet you and be introduced to you, properly, in a social way."

"Who else will be going? It doesn't say."

"Oh, the usual crowd. Father Donatello, of course. Wriggs, the Englishman — Alcibiades Wriggs. His mother is English. He has taken his mother's name, to remind himself that he is English. A fine, sensitive young man. I don't know about the Prince and his daughter, Iolanthe. But Laos, I am sure, will come."

"The philosopher?"

"Of course. Don't be afraid of him. A most genial, human, de-lightful talker, mellow and witty. Very relaxing company, in fact.

A good observer of human nature, and a bit too tolerant, I am afraid. Can talk on any topic with you, from frogs to philosophy, from poetry to filet mignon. Not at all an ascetic, or disciplinarian, nothing doctrinaire about him. He has only one fear, one hatred: dogmatism. Only stagnant water stinks, fresh water doesn't, and he says dogmatism is the stagnation of the mind. It means the mind has shut up, refuses to do more thinking. There is something uncanny about this man's thoughts, strikingly realistic, soft and fluid. Softness outlasts strength, he says. I don't know where he got all this. Once one of us asked him how he survived to his age — he must be about seventy now. Softness, my dear friend, he says, softness is strength. He opened his mouth and asked if his teeth were still there. He had lost all his molars. And is my tongue still there? he asked. We said it was. So, he says, my dear friend, the tongue outlasts the teeth because it yields and rolls and twists and avoids obstacles; it does not bite. You see the point? We all said we saw the point. . . . I think you had better write a note to accept."

Eurydice took a pen in hand, and was prepared to write a graciously worded reply. She consulted her wrist watch. It read September 24, Sunday. Something was wrong. She looked up the Countess' note.

"What is this 'Late-autumn' on the date?" she asked. "And it should be Sunday today."

"No, it can't be. September 24 is always a Saturday. The Sundays are always 4, 11, 18, 25 for September and all the last months of the seasons."

"What kind of a calendar is this?"

"We have no need of a calendar. Every year the Sundays fall on the same days. A wonderful thing, a great saving of energy. It was offered as the world calendar, but the Jews, the Protestants and the Catholics fouled it up. It was worked out by an Italian astronomer more than a century ago. It would save our manufacturers and businessmen and statisticians a lot of confusion and helpless rage. The old Gregorian calendar was a heritage of the past. Wouldn't it be a wonderful thing if we never had to consult

a calendar or carry one in our pocketbook? Well, here the
Irenikis don't."

"How do you do it?"

"All quarters contain 13 weeks, or 91 days. Therefore all the
quarters begin with a Sunday, the first of spring, of summer, of
autumn and winter. It's a neat division. It never changes, never
varies, from year to year. The first two months of each quarter
have 30 days, and the last 31 days; 0-0-1; 0-0-1; 0-0-1; 0-0-1. Simplicity itself. Only we call it Firstspring, Midspring, Latespring,
instead of January, February, March, etc. Spring begins from the
shortest day of the year, and the days grow longer until the end
of summer, the longest day, and grow shorter again until the
New Year's Eve is reached. New Year's Eve coincides with winter
solstice — December 23. New Year's Day is December 24, and
Christmas December 25. We have a grand holiday of New Year
and Christmas combined."

Eurydice was not good at mathematics. "Why did the churches
foul it up?"

"You forget," said Emma-Emma. "The four quarters of 91 days
make only 364 days, one day less than the year. If the year had
364 days, it would have exactly 52 weeks, and the Sundays would
never vary from year to year. By making the New Year's day
an extra day, a sort of world holiday, outside the weekly cycle,
the year is equated. But the churches would have none of it,
neither the Jews, nor the Gentiles. The Gentiles are of course
Christians. The loudest protests came from the Seventh-Day
Adventists of course and other fundamentalists. According to
them, our Sundays are wrong anyway; our Saturdays are the his-
toric, divinely appointed Sundays. Does it really matter? Those
people take the Bible by the throat and believe they are honoring
God by doing so. According to them, the earth is still regarded
as five or six thousand years old. Their faith is admirable, but
their geology is execrable. As a matter of fact, if we want to be
historically correct, Jesus was not born in the year one A.D. Christ
was born probably four years "before Christ." Why? Because
Herod died in 4 B.C. Does it really matter?"

"So September becomes Late-autumn?"

"Yes. Here in the south hemisphere, it is actually late-spring. But Laos thought, we might as well make it uniform with the northern hemisphere."

Eurydice wrote her note and then had it sent to the Countess by Tihualco. Then she suddenly exclaimed:

"Oh, dear, what am I going to wear?"

Chapter XII

OH, DARLING, we don't want to appear frivolous to our new guest, but at the same time we don't want to be squeamish or anything, you know. You are charming in that black organza, but you might have more respect for your bust," said the Countess, her soft fingers holding a lady's pipe. The person to whom she spoke was her friend Eunice.

Eunice did not know how to dress, never cared much for it. In that black frock, laced up to the neck, she might have passed for a sixteenth-century Florentine. The bust, it was the Countess' firm conviction, was a woman's glory. Eunice was thin, she thought the frock was becoming to her, and she had besides a rather aristocratic taste for antique flavor. Woman was all spirit, she thought; the interplay at wit and intelligence and charm was the thing. She abhorred modernity. In accordance with that notion, she had her hair done in what might be called a not entirely successful pompadour. She couldn't do anything of course with her suggestion of a mustache. The swift play and penetration of her ideas was her distinctive gift. She did not propose to trade on her young charms. The more antiquely she dressed, the more harmoniously, she felt, would it fit with the spirituality of her intercourse. She had the intelligence to turn her disadvantage into a *forte*. She knew she had certain disadvantages to overcome; her voice, for instance, an octave lower than a woman's. Yet she had been successful, she knew; men had liked her talk and her company. She was usually able to carry through an evening triumphantly. In fact, she need have no body at all. And she was well-tanned, being a confirmed sun-bather, practically and theoretically. Theoretically, she loved to lie on the terrace and receive the subtle emanations from the sun and feel herself in the bosom

of Mother Universe. She believed the entire universe was spiritual, rather than physical, consisting entirely of radiations of one
sort or another. Our thoughts, our emotions, are a form of spiritual
exhalations from our ego, our soul. She was inclined to be Diony-
sian. Force, emanations, exhalations, were what constituted the
universe. Hence, our emotions were as important as our intellect;
our intellectual emanations were by necessity too thin.

The Countess, on the other hand, was a good old Mediterranean,
born near Sorrento, of a sunny, Apollonian temperament, with a
characteristic gurgle, which was her way of laughter. Her Italian
was mellifluous, ringing and pleasant to the ear. God was in a
cheerful mood when He created the Italian language, reminding
one of the laughter of sunny brooks and spring freshets. In those
waters glided only round, smooth boulders, no jagged rocks, no
coughing, splashing cataracts as in German, for instance. She
said when she had studied German she could talk it only when
standing up, heels together. She used up twice as much energy;
it allowed no slurring, no indecent, wobbling consonants or smothered vowels. On the other hand, she found it perfectly easy to
talk French in bed; the best French was spoken in bed anyhow.
Italian again was the golden mean; she talked Italian best in a
chaise longue, easy, at home, but acceptable in company. It was
as if the French words had suddenly sat up and assumed shape
and form. What was *beurre* became *burro*, *l'heure* became *la ora*,
pain became *pane*. As for speaking English, all she needed was
a muffler tightly tucked below the neck to emulate the most approved Oxonian brand. Of course, an accidental catarrhal condition of the pharynx would help. . . . Why didn't someone write
a doctorate dissertation on the relation between climate and language, between the English fog and the care with which they
protected their vocal passages?

That pipe in her mouth, twelve inches long, slender, graceful
with a miniature bowl, was a visible mark of the Countess' aristocratic leanings, of her contempt for conventions; or it might
be ascribed to the influence of the Thainians on the Hellene im-
migrants — a sociologically interesting phenomenon. The ex-

change and interplay of cultures is a fruitful field for speculation. American music, for instance, bears the unmistakable stamp of the Negro spirit, with its peculiar jerks, hops and jaunty, feverish rhythm. Christian influence had affected the Tahitians; why shouldn't the Thainians have influenced the Irenikis? All Oriental women, Arabs and Chinese, are permitted to smoke pipes. It is a matter of convention. Why shouldn't women smoke cigarettes in the streets? The answer is simply that they don't. Eunice could enlighten you on the irrationality of human conduct and of all human customs, yes, even on the fascinating subject of eroticism. But in this matter of pipes for women, Laos had systematically encouraged it, out of a noble desire to open the realm of imagination and as a great source of spiritual comfort to the fair sex. Laos used to joke that he owed his peace of mind to his pipe. For the Countess, however, she owed it to *lagrima Christi,* a wine produced on the slopes of Vesuvius which the Italian winegrowers on the island had been able to produce. It also agreed with her Catholic faith; it helped her in her devotions to the things of the spirit and generated, if taken in sufficient quantity, great faith, which is defined as the power to believe things that are unseen.

The *lagrima Christi* stood now prominently on the table amidst silver and sparkling glass. The Countess surveyed the plates and mentally scanned the seating arrangement. She would be at one end, and Laos at the other. On her right of course would be the Prince; it was not merely a matter of protocol, not exclusively. She knew Prince Andreyev would be badly put out if not accorded the seat of prominence in any group. He was jovial, entertaining, full of anecdotes of Soviet internal intrigues and hair-raising murders. But he lacked tact; he was liable to grow objectionably sentimental in her proximity in public . . . Yes, Eurydice would be at the other end, on the right of Laos. And Eunice would be opposite her. In honor of things spiritual, she would place her confessor on her left, opposite the Prince, the symbol of things temporal. Emma-Emma, Philemon and Alcibiades Wriggs would be in the middle. She had invited Galli to come in after dinner with his Stradivarius, a gift of Athanopoulos on his deathbed. Athanopoulos had expired listening to Galli playing for him Schubert's "Ave Maria," his hand touching his favorite goat to his last breath. Chloe, Iolanthe's daughter, one of the girls from the Institute of Comforters of Men's Souls, had also been invited to recite some poetry.

The dining room looked out through French windows on the sea. Immediately in front was the stone terrace, a spacious area, good for forty or fifty people, bound by a series of balustrades. Below the terrace, the sea line was cut by a grove of umbrella pines which grew on the sand, framing a view of the sea and a few outlying islets of the lagoon — just at this moment a sheet of flaming orange reflecting the sky aglow with tropical sunset. The fine figure of Timalpo, dark and handsome, was seen watering rambler roses growing along the pergola and the hedgerows to the right. The Countess was imaginative; she called Timalpo her "Moor," for she thought life unbearable or unromantic without a husky Moor around the house. She was perfectly innocent, though gossip had it that the tall Timalpo was too handsome a chunk of flesh, too finely featured a human male specimen to be just a gardener. It was true that the Countess was indulgent, was in a way even quite democratic with her domestic; she wanted her manly Timalpo to walk and talk like a noble Moor. The tall dark figure lent enchantment to her landscape, along with the umbrella pines and the palms in the distance and the heavenly shore view. The Countess was by nature of a cheerful disposition. Between the intellectual company of Eunice, and the spiritual comfort of Father Donatello, who was a source of strength to her in moments of nervousness, and surrounded by the physical environment of her house on the sea, the garden and the Moorish addition to the landscape, she was completely happy.

Father Donatello and the Countess were chattering away in Italian.

"I do wish, Countess, that you would help to give a good impression of me to the new American woman. You might even induce her to come to church with you. Make her feel the comfort, the security, the all-embracing peace, that can be found only in the Catholic Church. Who knows? God may have sent this American woman here to be saved, that, abandoned and alone on this island, she may yet find a new life, a new peace and a new strength of soul. How should we otherwise explain her coming into our midst — a miracle in itself?"

"I will, darling," replied the Countess. It was a habit of hers to call everybody a darling, a habit which she had picked up from the circle of artists and theatrical people she had once associated with.

"His Royal Highness is harmless. In spite of his buffoonery and his occasional vulgarities, he stands for God and order in the universe. Were it not for you and the Prince, the whole island would have gone pagan. Eunice"— he turned to her —"you are not much of a help, you with your pride of intellect."

"Maybe I am not." Eunice, tall and thin in her black frock and semi-pompadour, had just come to the French window. "But don't you see, the place oozes with paganism. It oozes from every pore of my being. Look, Father, if you can convert that fine, healthy Moor, it will be to your credit."

"Your pride is your stumbling block. You have no meekness in your soul. Blessed are the meek, for they shall inherit the earth. Be ye like the little children . . ."

"I have read somewhere," replied Eunice, "of course, the meek shall inherit the earth, but they will no longer be meek when they have come into the inheritance."

The father's belly shook in spite of himself. Personally, as a matter of fact, Father Donatello was very tolerant, and enjoyed a good joke. "It's delightful, but I still say that it's your intellectual fireworks that keeps you from seeing the truth. It vitiates nothing of the teachings of the Bible; they shall have lost their inheritance again when they are no longer meek. The fact remains . . ."

Prince Andreyev Somovarvitch, six foot four of a figure, had appeared around the steps to the terrace unannounced, erect as an oak. The Countess waved gracefully from her cane-bottomed chair. The Prince was nothing, if not chivalrous. His greeting always had the manner of a happy surprise.

"Ah, my dear Countess!" he exclaimed, stretching both his arms high up, as if his eyes had accidentally and by a happy chance lighted upon the blond Countess. He bowed gracefully and with royal dignity to the ecclesiastic, who had stood up, and then walked straight up to the Countess and kissed her hand.

"How are you, darling?"

"Fine, fine!" His eyes roved around the beautiful shoreline beneath the glorious sky. "This is colossal. *Entzückend,* what?" He began to flap his arms around his tremendous body in a hugging motion, to work off his surplus energy. "Is the Americanitha here yet? No?"

"Not yet, she will be here. Why can't Iolanthe come? I am deeply disappointed."

"She sends her profound regrets. Will come to see you another time."

Father Donatello breathed an audible relief and quickly covered it up. "Indisposed?"

"Yes."

The Countess giggled, as she always did. "She is afraid of my confessor," she said, casting a smiling glance at the father. The latter was twiddling his thumbs complacently, trying to appear amiable. The Countess, like a true-born aristocrat, was able nobly to forgive her lover's sweethearts. Besides, it was so long ago. She and Iolanthe got along very well, as soon as it was decided that Athanopoulos was going to marry her. They had remained friends. The Countess could not hate anybody for long; it was not in her nature, and Father Donatello, observing this perfectly cordial relationship between the two women, once said she was more of a Christian than himself. The fact of the matter was, the Countess had too much human understanding not to appreciate Athanopoulos' fascination for that dark-haired Russian. She was an admirer of her beauty herself, being an artist, which meant merely that she had a passion for art and artistic people, and Iolanthe was a flamboyant beauty, with such soft lashes! Everybody said the Countess had a beautiful disposition and a sense of humor. It was true.

"Me compete with that dark-eyed Venus? No." She smiled happily.

Besides, she was at least ten years older than that Muscovite Venus. Such profound self-knowledge! That was why Iolanthe also could not help liking her. It was only on the issue of religion, in particular of Father Sebastian Donatello, that the two women split. Iolanthe, brought up in Smyrna and Athens, where she took her Greek name, was a hundred per cent pagan. More Greek than the Greeks, if ever there was one.

The Prince strode about the terrace, inhaling the resinous fragrance of the pines and the sea air. His long bearded chin tilted out, he was always lord of all that his eye surveyed. He could not help it. An aristocrat to his fingertips, his high-born nature was unmistakable in every inch of his body and his carriage. Seeing him, you were not likely to argue that men were born equal; besides, he would not admit it. "Why aren't you six foot four?" he would say if anybody dared breathe a word about human equality in his presence. Consciously, deliberately, he had adopted up here on this island a pair of sandals with Roman leggings, supporting his long, flowing purple toga. It was a most unfortunate circumstance that the *Purpura Lapillus* shellfish, common in the Mediterranean, could not be found in the sea around here. A wonderful sepia dye, however, was produced in plenty from the juice of the cuttlefish. It gave the walls of the houses such a mellow tone, agreeing with the bluish green of the olives. By mixing the juice of freshly picked red grapes with this dye, Prince Andreyev was able to find the purple he wanted for his toga — not perfect, but good enough. What was lacking in that royal tint was supplied by the rest of his physiognomy.

It was recalled by Emma-Emma when they came home that evening, that the Prince's face glowed a royal purple in the proximity of the Countess toward the end of the dinner. Why, he had never taken his eyes off her as he drank glass after glass of *lagrima Christi*. And the Countess was really jolly that night.

Chapter XIII

THE DINNER had been superb; the wine delicious, the baked clams a dream and the sea bass, soaked in olive oil, filled with finely chopped ham, mushroom, flavored with thyme and red piquant peperichino was a prayer for heavenly happiness come true.

Laos had been the last to arrive, in a homely and not too well pressed tunic of white. Eurydice, all keyed up to meet this man, observed him keenly. She saw his prominent forehead, his enormous ears; but his eyes were soft with an inner light. Laos was so casual. Eurydice, sitting on his right, thought at first he did not want to talk. But she was so excited that even his temporary silence meant something to her, suggested profundity of mind. She thought that in his severe reticence he saw all, understood all. It was nothing of the kind, she soon discovered. He had been suffering from a swelling of his throat. After a few glasses of Chianti, his favorite, the tenseness of his throat had completely disappeared. It was the old Laos again; the hostess relaxed.

In a tone almost of an old acquaintance, he said to the American guest, "Eurydice dear, you must drink."

Eurydice dear!

"I really don't." But she held her glass, as he poured the red liquid into it.

"Taste it . . . how's that?"

"Fine," she gasped.

"There's a good girl."

Eurydice was not offended. His tone was not condescending,

just familiar, as if he were talking to a niece of his, now grown up.
"You'll like it."

Now he spoke in his measured, philosophic undertone. "It
will put you in harmony with the universe — and with this island.
I am sorry for what happened, but we have our own way of doing
things. I heard you were unwell and told the people to leave you
alone."

"It was very kind of you. Emma-Emma told me I am lucky
to have come here."

"Yes, that was what I said," confirmed Emma-Emma, diagonally
opposite.

"You don't have to agree, you know."

Eurydice thought a compliment was due. She did not want
to say she agreed and she did not want to say she disagreed.
"I am open-minded. Everything seems so fresh, novel. I haven't
had time to take in and digest all this. What is this? An eternal
holiday? Or a Utopia planned by you?" The word had slipped
out of her mouth against Emma-Emma's caution. Young Wriggs,
sitting next to Philemon, was uneasy. His small talk with the
sculptor suddenly stopped. Eurydice noticed she was the center
of attention. From the other end of the table came the Prince's
stentorian voice:

"A New Jerusalem, where men are men, and women are women.
Princes are princes, and plebeians are plebeians. The only draw-
back is that we have no king here. Laos, why don't you make
me the king? I have told you so many times; don't I look like one?"

Everybody laughed and Laos broke into a smile. "I don't
want to see you murdered. You should remember history. Caesar
murdered Pompey, Brutus murdered Caesar, and Antony murdered Brutus and killed himself."

"What is death?" The Prince's voice carried easily across the
table. "Make me Antony, and I will make Countess Cordelia
della Castiglioni my Cleopatra."

"Shame on you!" said the Countess.

Eunice interposed and said to the Countess: "It will give you
the right to slap him with your sandals, as Cleopatra did."

"Frankly, I wouldn't mind," said the Prince. "What is death? The important thing is what happens before that."

The Countess flushed a little. That was what she didn't like about the Prince; beneath his majestic exterior there was a grain of coarseness, of sheer love of debauchery.

Laos was tolerant. He knew the Prince was a buffoon, and left him alone.

"You see what happens?" he said, turning to Eurydice. "Here's our beloved Prince, with the brains of a chicken. He wants to be a king. That's what happens in Utopia. Human nature, my dear Eurydice, human nature never leaves us. You can plan everything, measure everything, predict everything scientifically, except human nature. Athanopoulos, for instance. He had the right to be king here, if anybody. But look at his son, Stephan. He's a half-wit. What would have happened if we had to make the idiot succeed to the throne? As a matter of fact, the courts of Europe were full of such idiots in the eighteenth century. You might as well make the chair for mathematics hereditary in a college. That's what your Thomas Jefferson said."

"He did?"

"No, Eurydice dear, no kings and no Utopias mapped out by half-witted visionaries trying to beat human nature. We are extremely conservative here. We don't repudiate progress — but are rather trying to stop in this midstream of progress and find our bearings, like standing on a rock in mid-river while the swift tide rushes past us. Call it a haven — if you like. A haven, a point to rest and think and live in peace. You will admit that thinking became impossible in the headlong progress of the twentieth century. Men were moving too fast. Vast changes, material discoveries affecting our lives, shortening of communications, obliteration of national frontiers through aviation — these changes happened so fast that men were dragged along . . . ah, here come the baked clams!"

There was evident gusto in Laos' voice. Eurydice thought she spotted a sensualist in him.

"They are not to be despised," he added.

"And put you in harmony with the universe," broke in Eunice.

"You don't really mean it," said Alcibiades Wriggs.

"I do," said Eunice emphatically.

The conversation drifted to inconsequential topics. A Thainian woman passed the clams around in a basket and asked if people wanted a second helping. Eurydice was struck with the comic situation, everybody eating clams and everybody so silent while they had been so intellectual a minute ago. Actually, she was feeling guilty. The day before they arrived, she had heard on the radio that the Milwaukee Braves were three games ahead in the National League and her favorite pitcher Angelo Reese had been taken out of the game after yielding two walks, filling the bases in the ninth inning. The commentator said it was due to an attack of flu he had suffered a week ago. Had he got well? Perhaps he was there pitching again, for the glorious Braves, and she was out here eating baked clams! She did miss the baseball series; otherwise she was quite willing to admit life was quite perfect, anyway better than she had the right to expect in mid-Pacific.

"Don't you have a radio?" she asked.

Eunice looked up while Laos answered diplomatically: "What's the use of a radio? We are so far from the Old World." A glint passed over the old philosopher's eyes, as he added quickly, "We destroyed yours."

"Why did you do it?"

"We don't like what happened to Paul any more than you do. I suppose you know we resent intruders, who may leak out the news of the colony to the world. Then we'll have tourists and diplomatic busybodies on our shoulders. No doubt it will make front-page news. But we prefer to be left alone. As a matter of fact, I've been worried about you. Do you think your people, I mean people of your organization, will come after you?"

"They have no idea where I am, I'm sure."

"I am glad." Laos lapsed into silence.

Galli the violinist and Chloe had joined them for coffee on the terrace under the starlit sky. Chloe had brought a note from her mother Iolanthe, addressed to Eurydice, and another one to Laos, inviting Eurydice to come over and stay with her; if she found the place to her liking, she could stay as long as she wished. She begged Laos to intervene and persuade the young American to come. She had plenty of rooms and would be delighted to have her company. She thought Emma-Emma, while a fellow American, was a hard-working scholar loving solitude. She didn't want to rob Emma-Emma of her guest, but admitted great selfishness in desiring her company. Charmingly put! Eurydice was to decide for herself. It was really very good of Iolanthe to think of it.

"I heard my daughter talking about it," said the Prince. "In fact she told me to extend the invitation personally. My daughter knows me. She knew I would forget; she didn't trust me with this note. You must come, Eurydice. We have a fine view to the south."

"What do you think?" Laos asked Eurydice. "It is a delightful place. We want you to be as happy as possible, as we feel responsible for keeping you here."

"What shall I say?" said Eurydice, feeling pleased that the people here were so hospitable.

"You decide for yourself," said Emma-Emma. "You know you are welcome to stay with me as long as you like. You don't disturb me a bit."

Chapter XIV

CHLOE, A YOUNG GIRL of seventeen, danced to the divine music of Galli's violin, a dance to the honor of Isis, the Egyptian goddess. She was still in her novitiate at the Institute of Comforters of Men's Souls, her best friend Berenice being with her, now in the third year, and ready to marry. The training at the Institute was so much valued — men placed value on girls who had made "a study of man" at the Institute — that many applied. They all loved to study man. Men sought such girls for wives, mature, sophisticated, who knew how to "handle" men in their tired hours, dispirited, downcast, sometimes drunk, and frequently in short tempers. There the treating of men's psychic ills was taught; men wanted to be babied, patted, adored, lied to, coaxed out of their childish moods, allowed to cry if they wanted to, and withal looked up to. The girls understood them; all understood them, because "all men are alike," the girls were taught. They had to listen patiently to their complaints about their wives, were apt to take the husbands' side. Sometimes they felt very angry, like the Catholic confessors, at men's and women's wickedness; but like the priests, they must restrain themselves, must never lose their temper. It was extraordinary how a cup of sweet tea, offered with a smile by a young demure virgin, could obliterate the depth of men's woes and bring a smile to their lips, how the gentle touch of a girl's hand upon an irate husband's shoulder could reconcile him to this earthly existence, how his frame relaxed and the ominous scowl, the conviction that all the world was set against him, disappeared from his face, how the cloud of worries and perplexities on his brow could be kissed away by a gentle touch of her lips, a whisper in his ears. Man recovered his equilibrium again.

It stands to reason that a girl receiving such training in the art of entertaining, cajoling and bedeviling men, should by the time she graduated, become a pretty knowing woman. It stands also to reason that such girls of the hetaera type were much sought after by bachelors prepared to enter the holy state of matrimony. And the girls knew it; that was why so many applied.

"The proper study of woman is man," so runs the Institute's motto. A very laudable and sound foundation, somewhat on the realistic side, was thus laid for a happy marriage in the school for wives. Of course, Laos always pointed out to them at the commencement exercises, the study of man can never be ended. The graduates had just learned the ropes. It was an endless quest. Man the unknown, the elusive, the ever-changeful, the unpredictable, the infinitely variable factor in God's universe. The possibilities of man, particularly of the male sex, could never be exhausted through the eternities to come. Above all, the art of deception, of some appropriate, benevolent "white-lying" at some given moments, of tact and silence, of guiding the dear beloved to do the thing you want him to do, like all other arts, must be cultivated with infinite patience. Life is short and art is long, he quoted Goethe. You have been taught the difficult art of navigation in matrimonial waters, with some field practice. Now go forth, through the Scylla and Charybdis, unafraid, confident in yourselves, chins up, hands on the helm of the rocking ship, looking to the great future before you. . . .

Between the snatches of liquor, and the playing of selections by the violinist, a drifting, aimless, but restless conversation went on on the terrace. Prince Somovarvitch would never sit down; he paced the yard interminably, his bare head silhouetted against the myriad clustering stars of the night, while the music floated and dissolved upon the waters of the lagoon. Chloe was such a perfect dancer; though a novice, she had the inborn grace and swing, a sense of rhythmic movement. Most girls on the island

were. It was a general atmosphere; every movement a graceful
gesture, every posture a model's delight. The habit of carrying
pitchers on their heads no doubt had to do with the erect figure
of the girls on the island; their hips learned a modulating, balancing movement as subtle as the seal's. Of course the absence
of brassieres and other encumbrances of any kind of textile fabric
around their shoulders and chests permitted a complete freedom
of movement. Anyway, training or no training, the Ireniki girls
were natural dancers. At times, it seemed Chloe's dancing was
really inspired as she swung and leaped and whirled on that starlit
terrace. And Pietro Galli's violin swelled in intensity or dimin-
ished to a beguiling softness in perfect sympathetic response.

Someone called for a recitation. Chloe had just learned the
invocation of Venus, at the beginning of Lucretius' great poem.
Lucretius was no less sonorous in Greek translation than in Latin.
Her voice had a virginal ring and purity as she declaimed:

"Mother of Aeneas' sons, joy of men and gods, Venus the Life-
giver, who beneath the gliding stars of heaven fillest with life the
sea that carries the ships and the land that bears the crops; for
thanks to thee every tribe of living things is conceived, and comes
forth to look upon the light of the sun. Thou, Goddess, thou
dost turn to flight the winds and the clouds of heaven, thou at
thy coming; for thee earth, the quaint artificer, puts forth her
sweet-scented flowers; for thee the levels of ocean smile, and
the sky, its anger past, gleams with spreading light. For when
once the face of the spring day is revealed and the teeming
breeze of the west wind is loosed from prison and blows strong,
first the birds in high heaven herald thee, Goddess, and at thine
approach, their hearts thrilled with thy might. Then the tame
beasts grow wild and bounce over the fat pastures, and swim
the racing rivers; so surely enchained by thy charm each follows
thee in hot desire whither thou goest before to lead him on. Yea,
through seas and mountains and tearing rivers and the leafy
haunts of birds and verdant plains, thou dost strike fond love
into the hearts of all, and makest them in hot desire to renew the
stock of their races, each after his own kind . . ."

Father Donatello sat up. He had been charmed by the girl's ringing accents, the smooth flow of the words of the poet. Now a cloud came over his face; he thought, "Is this proper reading for young girls?" Something in his whole training prevented him from the wholehearted enjoyment of the poetry. Why, the whole passage dripped with paganism, pagan addiction to the flesh. Was it possible to believe that such reading was conducive to the purity of a girl's soul and elevation of her character? He had held his breath during the first part; as soon as the trend of the passage became evident, he did not. The sousing from his nostrils started again, the air had to go through a difficult passage. Besides, he had been unhappy ever since he learned of the possibility of Eurydice going to stay with Iolanthe, in whose house he knew his presence was not welcome. Would the new, pliable creature for conversion slip out of his hand into the depths of the demon's lair that was Athanopoulos' villa on the peak?

Meanwhile, the conversation turned upon the poet's enjoinment upon overcoming the fear of death, and upon a sane restraint in pleasures of the senses. Lucretius was a masculine poet; there was no cloying sentimentality about him.

"Lucretius is incredibly complex," said Laos. "Like his master Epicurus, he is liable to be misunderstood. He is sane and strong. He is worth pondering upon. I like his passage where he says, 'Even as children tremble and fear everything in blinding darkness, so we sometimes dread in the light things that are no whit more to be feared than what children shudder at in the dark, and imagine will come to pass. This terror, then, this darkness of the mind, must seeds be scattered not by the rays of the sun and the gleaming shafts of day, but by the outer view and the inner law of things.' *The outer view and the inner law of things.* Who knows that has a philosophy that will help him through life. Chloe, have you studied the Second Book yet? No. Then Philemon, will you recite that passage — you know what I mean, about the heights of philosophy. It contains a whole philosophy of living. *For the body's nature, but few things are needful.* You can read it in English for our American friend. Eunice, I remember you have a copy in English of your favorite."

Eunice rose, found her copy and gave it to Philemon.

Eurydice listened carefully. Perhaps it was intended by Laos for her.

"Sweet it is, when on the great sea the winds are buffeting the waters, to gaze from the land on another's great struggles; not because it is pleasure or joy that anyone should be distressed, but because it is sweet to perceive from what misfortune you yourself are free. Sweet is it too, to behold great contests of war in full array over the plains, when you have no part in the danger. But nothing is more gladdening than to dwell in the calm high places, firmly embattled on the heights by the teaching of the wise, whence you can look down on the others, and see them wandering hither and thither, going astray as they seek the way of life, in strife matching their wits or rival classes of birth, struggling night and day by surpassing efforts to rise up to the height of power and gain possession of the world. Ah! miserable minds of men, blind hearts! in what darkness of life, in what great dangers ye spend this little span of years! to think that ye should not see that nature cries aloud for nothing else but that pain may be kept far sundered from the body, and that, withdrawn from care and fear, she may enjoy in mind the sense of pleasure. And so we see that for the body's nature but few things at all are needful, even such as can take away pain. Yet, though pleasantly enough from time to time they can prepare for us in many ways a lap of luxury, yet nature herself feels no loss, if there are not golden images of youths about the halls, grasping fiery torches in their right hands, that light may be supplied to banquets at night, if the house does not glow with silver or gleam with gold, nor do fretted and gilded ceilings re-echo to the lute. And yet, for all this, men lie in friendly groups on the soft grass near some stream of water under the branches of a tall tree, and at no great cost delightfully refresh their bodies, above all when the weather smiles on them, and the season of the year bestrews the grass with flowers. . . ."

Philemon's voice stopped. "I can never do it properly. I am not gifted at this kind of thing." As a matter of fact, he had not done it badly at all. The touch of Greek accent made it more charming, Eurydice thought. He had read it with true feeling. The dim light from the candelabra coming through the French window fell on his head of tousled hair, his handsome, classical profile, and the bright glimmer of his eyes, the eyes of a sensitive sculptor. All sculptors have a way with their eyes; they seem to see things with greater concentration and seize at a glance the shape and form and meaning of things. With a modest cough, he retired to his seat.

Chloe, with a shawl thrown around her tunic, cast him a glance of unfeigned pleasure and approval. She had looked up, wild-eyed, while he was reciting the poetry, though she understood very little of the gibberish of sounds.

"How perfectly charming!" remarked the Countess from her cane-bottomed chair, her earrings glistening in the dim light of the terrace.

"I prefer it in Greek, or Latin," said Eunice. "Something is lost in the translation, don't you think? The sounds are so important, in prose as well as in poetry. The sounds are the body, the external dress; a translation gives it meaning; its spirit, if successful. The body, the external sensuous appeal, is just as important as the content. I believe there is a chemistry of sounds, in which there is a definite interplay of sound and meaning, not to be rudely torn apart without loss of its external beauty. What do you think, Laos?"

"I think all literature should be read aloud. Literature is charming chatter, to be heard through the ear to be enjoyed. A combination of sense and sound, which plays upon the mind and the spirit of the listeners. However, I don't share your view. There is music in every language. I admit that Greek is more euphonious; it is the language of the gods, permeated with the light of the Ionian Sea. But there is music in every language, especially when spoken by sweet young women. I would say it is the speakers, their ways of expression, that make a language charming. It is a living thing, delightful when modulated by a woman's voice, molded by sweet young lips. The written language is at best a poor substitute for the oral. That is why I am so happy that we have revived the art of recital at the Institute. Chloe does it very well indeed."

This last remark made the young girl very happy. Philemon turned his head and beamed a smile upon her.

"Clams have souls." These ringing syllables wafted across from the outer dark corner of the terrace and startled Eurydice. Unmistakably it was Prince Andreyev's voice.

"They have not." Father Donatello's baritone dropped still more distinctly upon Eurydice's ears. Alcibiades' young white face was seen among them, keenly interested in their discussion. Silence fell upon the company.

"The Bible never says clams have no souls," retorted the Prince. "With all deference to your priestly learning — allow me to say — clams have souls. They probably shut up and pray all day for the blessing of the sea water. Why shouldn't they? They are God's creatures."

"But the church of God teaches that animals have no souls, only man has. The creatures of the sea and the land are created for man's enjoyment. I simply can't imagine a heaven filled with the souls of clams and crayfish. What would they be doing in heaven, those myriads and myriads of crawling creatures? It is to man alone that God gives the intelligence to know his Creator and adore Him . . ."

"The Prince is drunk," remarked the Countess.

"They are arguing about who has a soul and who has not without agreeing upon what they mean by a soul," said Eunice. "The soul is only a function, a label for the emanations from consciousness."

From the outer darkness the majestic shape of Prince Andreyev was seen to rise abruptly. "I still say clams have souls," he protested. Somewhat unceremoniously, it seemed to the company, the Prince left the father and Wriggs and disappeared below the terrace. The Countess knew this Muscovite prince well; his grandfather was an Alexandrovitch, son of Alexander III. There was a strong streak of mysticism in him. He had a curious nocturnal habit of strolling about the island in the dark, walking through forests, wrestling with his conscience, which he conceived to be a tormenting black beast. Anyway, he was very close to the stars. Some shepherd had once found him in the twilit hour of dawn way upon the other side of Mount Ida. He would surprise nobody if he reported he had conversed with the angels on top of Mount Ida. Such nocturnal strolls seemed to have a definite religious effect upon him. What he had wrestled with was not clear. But he always returned a contrite, even a humble, person. "I am a small man. I am a sinner," he used to report to his astonished daughter.

The Countess sniffed the coming fog.

"It is getting chilly, don't you think?" she said to her guests. "We had better go inside."

The Italian father had joined them. With the consummate tact of a hostess, she guided him toward Eurydice. They went into the brilliantly lit parlor, illuminated by two candelabra. On the mantelpiece stood a few exquisite statuettes, coated with a patina, green with age, and several opalescent ancient Egyptian glasses, probably two thousand years old. They were the gifts of Athanopoulos. On the walls were portraits of the Count's family, of the grand uncle and uncle of her husband, Count Guiseppe Andrea di Michele della Castiglioni, the great Alpine climber, a contemporary of Edward VII; of Vittorio Ferdinande della Castiglioni, a saintly man who devoted his entire life to restoring ancient chapels and the service of the peasants; and portraits of her own family, her father and mother, the Cionis. These the Countess had thoughtfully brought with her when she decided to come with Athanopoulos, together with an extremely valuable golden crucifix, framed in a three-paneled case, gilt on a green background. But undoubtedly, the most precious piece was the Greek statuette of Hermaphrodite, barely eighteen inches high, said to have been found in Crete. By its sheer perfection that marble figure seemed to dominate the entire room. Roving eyes were inevitably arrested by its perfect harmony, its living breath of beauty — a joy to look at and a vision of the form divine. It made one think of ancient Hellas, of the age of Praxiteles and Lysippus and Phidias, when man's spirit was free and serene, when concurrent with the wars on sea and land, man had learned the art of serenity and ease.

The Countess was a devout Catholic at heart. These pagan symbols did not detract from her religious devotion or in any way conflict with it. She adored these statuettes, these things of the spirit, these durable records of the sunny Mediterranean soul. She was at home in it. Christian asceticism or denial of the beauty of the flesh found no harbor in her thoughts. She experienced no conflict. In her home, in this parlor reminiscent of ancient glories, art and religion had blended together in the joy of existence. She was too sunny-tempered to be bothered by questions of theology, and in spite of her nervousness at times — she had unnatural horrors of mice and bats, of which a huge-sized variety existed on the island — she was usually of equitable temper. To her, what was ancient was good; Hellas, the Christian Church, her family were all ancient and all had meaning for her.

Chapter XV

ARE YOU GOING to accept Iolanthe's invitation?" said Father Donatello, who had appropriately seated himself in a chair beside Eurydice.

"Perhaps I will. I have to think about it. You people have been uncommonly kind."

"Just Christian hospitality. I am sure a divine purpose has guided your steps to this island. Don't you think it is strange — it is almost inexplicable — that of all the 190,000,000 Americans, you should be the one selected to come among us?"

"Selected? You flatter me."

"I hope you are enjoying your stay on this island. And I hope you will drop in often to see Countess della Castiglioni. She comes from a very ancient, devout family. I am sure you will find her a very sincere and companionable friend."

"I am sure I shall," replied Eurydice, failing to catch the drift of his intercourse.

"I am not saying anything against Prince Andreyev. He is a strong supporter of the Christian Church. I do feel, however, that he is not exactly the kind of person to associate too closely with. I am not trying to influence you one way or the other, but . . ."

Philemon entered the room at this moment, hand in hand with Chloe. They were laughing, and the girl's eyes beamed a smile. Young Wriggs was now seated in another corner with Eunice, the Countess and Laos.

"What are you people laughing about?" queried Emma-Emma.

"Oh, just gossip," replied Philemon.

"Some more coffee?" asked the ever-attentive hostess.

"No, thanks."

"Then come, Chloe, sit by Eurydice."

Philemon, his young, carefree face graced with a well-trimmed mustache, led the young girl toward Eurydice on the sofa where the Italian father's conversation had just been interrupted. Chloe sat in the center, while Philemon stood before Eurydice.

"You must come to see the Museion. I work there, you know."

"I am told you are a sculptor."

"Trying to be." Philemon's tone, sincere and unaffected, was pleasantly buoyant. "I am working on a frieze at present."

"You ought to see the 'Athanopoulos' he has done at the square of the Athenaeum. It is just next to it," added the priest.

"If you will do me the honor, I shall be happy to come and accompany you there. I only hope you will not be too critical; judge us by too high standards. The greats must be forever beyond our reach. The standards we have before us are high, make one feel humble and small. Look at that Hermaphrodite! It can't be done nowadays. We haven't that feeling for form and spirit, because we do not see with the eye of the ancients. It must come from within."

"You must be happy with your work."

"I am. To have the opportunity to work at ease. Nobody tells me what to do, or when to complete a statue. Laos tells me to take five years or ten years if I like. It's a wonderful feeling. I am profoundly grateful. But of course it is the only way any great work of art can be done. I would gladly give ten years of my life if I could produce a piece with half the witchery of that Hermaphrodite, its beauty of spirit and sensibility."

"Don't you have to make a living?"

"I am maintained by the republic, at public expense."

"That's wonderful."

"Then I may have the pleasure? Perhaps tomorrow, or day after tomorrow, any day you like. If you move in with Iolanthe, just let me know through Chloe."

"I'll be delighted. I am so confused, rather overwhelmed as a matter of fact, to hear of a Museion and an Athenaeum out here in mid-Pacific. What are you people here trying to do?"

"You will find out," answered Philemon gaily. "A fulfillment of a human dream, perhaps. The opportunity to work and live a good, simple life. That is the most difficult thing in the Old World, I am told. I was born here. A simple life, the opportunity to be yourself — that's about the way Laos puts it. You ask him."

Philemon turned to the other groups. A very animated chatter was going on, amidst which might be heard the rather low-pitched, quick voice of Eunice.

"What are you people discussing?"

"You tell us first the gossip you heard," said the Countess, taking her pipe from her lips.

"What gossip? Oh, Chloe was telling me that Oaxus has beaten his wife again, and she has gone to the convent, this time taking the baby with her."

"I heard it from Berenice," said Chloe.

"Is she thinking of leaving him?" asked Laos in a concerned voice. "These wife-beaters! When will they grow up?"

"Berenice told me he turned up at the Institute, quite drunk. No one in the Institute likes him. Berenice says she had to take care of him. After all, when husbands and wives quarrel, it is possible to listen to both sides, and we girls find it easy to take a lenient, sympathetic view of the man's case. The women are as often at fault as the men. In Oaxus' case, we just had to endure and humor him. Berenice gave him a strong admonition that if he did not reform his presence was not welcome."

"What was the provocation?"

"Provocation enough. He had an affair with the Thainian maid at home, Oona. He was carrying on shamelessly. Oona didn't mind. What has she to worry about? And she flaunts it in Clymene's face, is rather proud of it. A girl is naturally happy, conscious of her power over a man. The wife remonstrated with him, and he beat her. She said she would not return unless Oona leaves. The poor fool! I don't think he will ever reform. Berenice

has given him a piece of her mind, and he takes it quietly from
her. What he needs is a wife to put her foot down on him. Clymene is too good, too gentle with him."

Laos laughed. "You see Chloe is already learning a lot about
life. About handling men. Chloe, you tell Berenice to tell him
to go to church. And Father Donatello, you'd better scare the
devil out of him. Tell him there is a demon in him. Tell him
he will be damned, that he will burn in eternal fire. Frighten
him. He is mentally only a child. I don't think you need be particular about the forms of divine punishment. Eternal fire, gnaw-
ing worms, ground covered with wriggling centipedes and
scorpions, a seething cauldron of boiling oil to boil him alive —
anything will do. Make it as gruesome as you wish. He is a fat man;
tell him his fat will light up and splutter. Scare the hell out
of him. Flagellate his soul. That's the kind of religion he needs,
and he needs no other kind."

"I would love to do a head of Oaxus," said Philemon. "Bald
head, a thin tuft of hair, his enormous shoulders, and a face
which is a combination of owlishness and assininity — perhaps
with the body of an ass — the ancient Greeks would know how
to do it. It would be absolutely fascinating, a useful reminder of
the stage of evolution of the human soul."

"And I will make the Prince flagellate him physically," said
Laos, "if you don't succeed in flagellating him spiritually. Where's
His Royal Highness?"

"Oh, he is somewhere in the fog," drawled the Countess.

The priest spoke. "You people are somewhat hard on the poor
fellow. There's never a creature so low that he is without a divine spark in him. God, in His infinite mercy, has put a soul in
every man."

"A soul in that semi-chimpanzee?" interrupted Philemon.

"Yes, even in that semi-chimpanzee, as you call him. He is a
son of God, like any of us."

"You are being very generous, father," said the Countess indulgently.

"And noble," remarked Eunice.

The priest was happily surprised at the turn of the conversation. The company — or many members present, Laos, Eunice, Philemon, all except the Countess — had been suspected of anti-clerical tendencies, pagans at heart and in thinking. The father didn't tipple; he was amenable, however, to the relaxing influence of a few cups of *lagrima Christi*. His face oozed at the moment a beatific satisfaction.

"I say he is a son of God, although a weak brother, we may say perhaps even contemptible in his conduct. But we must recognize there is evil in all of us. The Devil is still with us, even in Thainos."

"Say the problem of evil is still with us," interposed Laos.

"Well, say human evil, the heart of evil, is still with us. You planned, Laos — didn't you? — that the island was to be all order and beauty and reason and peace, a model society of classical perfection. Wasn't that the idea?"

Laos' dark eyes glimmered for a second in protest. "I planned nothing of the kind. I am not trying to escape anything, least of all human nature. We are only a company of poor mortals, struggling to live, as far as our understanding permits, a simple, happy, and creatively useful life. I expected troubles. You put two girls and a boy, or two boys and a girl on an island, and immediately the human problem arises, to say nothing of a whole community of men and women. You have seen those spick-and-span hospitals of the Old World — the discipline, order, cleanliness. You would think such a place was an acme of human reason and order. I assure you it is deceptive; it practically seethes with love, hatred, jealousy, ambition inside. Throw a pretty nurse in and see what happens. Or austere science, objective, coldly analytical and unemotional — you have no idea of the intense professional competitions and jealousies that make for scientific progress. Fact is, you can plan everything in human society — production, distribution, food, population — but you cannot plan human nature. You confess to a little dislike to Aristotimus, perhaps?"

"There is nothing personal about it. I am against his principles, his compromise with paganism. It is a rather serious conflict of principles, where the Church is concerned. I have searched my heart at night. I confess to a slight antipathy toward his smirk of satisfaction, his complacency with things on the island."

"You don't like him."

"I don't dislike him, not in a personal sense."

Emma-Emma sat silent, watching the byplay of verbiage and sentiments, humorously observing that the father was human, too.

Chapter XVI

You WERE TALKING about the worship of Isis," said Eunice to Emma-Emma. "We would love to hear you continue."

Chloe sat up. Philemon wanted to say something, but she pressed him gently with her hand.

"I was saying that Jupiter was like any modern banker who falls in love with his wife's pretty nurse. I was talking about the confusion of the Greek Io with the Egyptian Isis — how the Egyptian, Sicilian, Greek and Roman gods got all mixed up. Io was Juno's priestess. The poor girl, transformed into a cow by Jupiter to escape Juno's jealousy, mooing, wandering alone all over the world, and stung by gadflies sent by Juno to persecute her, after she had suspected her identity — until she ended up in Egypt and she prayed to Jupiter to have her human shape restored, and became a good and much beloved queen. So the goddess Isis was represented as a cow, and her husband Osiris as an ox. Isis, as a matter of fact, was a combination of Venus of Cyprus, Athena of Athens, Proserpine of Sicily, and Diana of Crete. The Greek gods were all over the place; Hermes was Isis' son, Hercules, her great warrior, and an army of satyrs conquered Ethiopia. Quite possibly the Greeks, in coming under the influence of the cult of Isis and Osiris, had to tell the Egyptian legend in terms the Greeks could understand. Roman soldiers conquered Greece, but Greek gods and goddesses invaded Rome, particularly the Roman army in the provinces. The Persian

Mithraic cult was popular, too. Some of this found its way into Christianity. St. Paul might have read the prayer to the Egyptian Osiris. 'As truly as Osiris lives, shall he live; as truly as Osiris is not dead, shall he not die.' Osiris, Isis' half-brother, you remember, was butchered by Typhon. And the prayer to Isis, strikingly reminiscent of St. John: 'Glorify me, as I have glorified the name of thy son Horus.' It was all very dramatic and very confusing. The heroic role played by Isis' son. Then the worship of phallus, credited to the invention of Isis, in memory of the unrecovered part of her husband when his dismembered body was thrown into the sea off Phoenicia — the worship was carried back to Greece and became an Athenian institution. In Rome, Priapus became the god of fruit orchards, holding a scythe to prune fruit trees, nothing lascivious about him — a perfectly natural transition as the emblem of fecundity. I believe it was all very innocent."

"Does it matter?" said Laos. "The gods were created in the folk mind by the believers themselves, in imagery that the people's minds can understand. The people demand an explanation for fecundity — in men, or in fruit trees. Such nature forces are personified. Why the annual floods of the Nile? They came of course from the prolific tears of Isis, grieving for the death of Osiris. Which will you have — the melting snows of Ethiopia and the mountains of Khartoum, or the tears of Isis? Which is more beautiful?"

Father Donatello was feeling uncomfortable.

"My dear Laos, I must credit you with a romantic imagination."

"On the other hand, I believe our modern religions are a little leaden-hued because they have been divorced from poetry. The spirit of religion withers and becomes desiccated in the dark subterranean vaults of theology. I wish you would come up to the sunny surface of the garden and worship God with the poetry and fancy and the lively imagination of the ancient Greeks."

"No, I disagree with you there. You will never make me say, 'Thou hast almost made me a pagan.' After all, myths are myths, illusions of the popular mind. The tears of Isis, indeed!"

"Illusions are necessary to human life. They are what make life endurable. Strip the world of illusions, and we have nothing to live for. The Buddhists believe that if you contemplate a pretty young woman as consisting of perishable flesh, liable to putrefaction, containing a grim skeleton within, only masked in a skinbag to give a deceptive illusion of beauty, you will overcome your desire of woman. What do they do that for? As a matter of fact, the world cannot exist without illusions. All men think of women better than women think of themselves. That is illusion; but that is what puts romanticism and chivalry into human life. Suppose beauty is an ephemeral illusion, is it not good to look at? All life is illusion, *maya,* as a matter of fact. The question is what to do with it? Deny it? No, illusions are necessary to human life. I am willing to go with Plato and reduce everything to ideas — images given the temporary attributes of material existence. It would be clearer perhaps to call them ideals — ideas existing in our minds, never quite corresponding to reality. The idea of a tree, for instance, which is not a chestnut, nor an elm, nor a maple, nor an oak, nor any of these concrete species we know. Just the concept of a tree. Plato thought that the concept of a tree was there — an eternal image — antedating, as it were, the material forms such as a maple or a pine. Unfortunately such pure concepts are difficult to establish; the concept of a tree merges imperceptibly into that of cactus, and cane and bamboo and grass, and finally fungus. But we all work with myths, illusions, ideals. Democracy is a myth, too. Anything the people believe in, they straightway make a god of it. The true Christian is a myth also. But it would be manifestly foolish to give up the ideals of democracy, and of a true Christian because they do not yet exist, and probably will never exist in the ideal Platonic sense. We need such myths, illusions, every day of our life. Without illusions, there would be no love, no art, no religion."

"You mean we must deceive ourselves," remarked the Countess.

"I mean we cannot afford to live with raw, naked facts. That was where the Old World philosophy was wrong in its overstraining after objectivity. We must clothe life with a beauty of

our own making. It would help beautify life if we had a more
plastic imagination, a more lively fancy, a more intimate contact
with nature, if we had the freshness and the poetic fancies which
distinguished the Greeks in the morning of man's youth. It is
not unimportant; it is a question of method, of how we choose
to stand vis-à-vis the world of phenomena, leaving the question
of the ultimate reality aside."

"You were talking about myths."

"Myths are a form of language, the language of symbols, poetic
and fanciful, to explain the forces of the universe, to record by
delightful fiction a momentary glimpse of certain divine truths.
Modern man has lost that gift for imaginative fancy, for delightful fiction. He loves to live with raw, naked facts, and prefers
to strip them of all color and emotion. He will not call a young
offender and lawbreaker an ill-bred brat, but a juvenile delinquent,
or a maladjusted individual with a warped pattern of behavior
during the secondary period of adolescence. The 'ill-bred brat'
did not exist for the scientific social workers of the Old World.
Now philosophy, which is an inquiry into the art of living
well . . ."

Eurydice involuntarily started.

Laos' brow puckered slightly. "Does it surprise you?" he said.

"No. Well, I never heard it put that way."

Laos paused a moment, and added, "Oh, it's my mistake.
When I say 'living well,' I don't mean living in the lap of luxury.
It has undeniably that connotation in English. And yet I wouldn't
know how else to put it. To live well — to live simply, beautifully,
with ease and amplitude of power, as I believe God intended
us to do."

"I am sorry to have interrupted you. I didn't mean to."

"I like interruptions — this sharing of the minds which is called
conversation. What was I saying? I was saying that philosophy
is, or should be, an inquiring into the art of living well. You agree
that to know how to live well should be the object and goal of
philosophy?"

"I think I do," said Eurydice. "Philosophy wasn't that you

know — the kind I learned at college. Principally a study of the theories of knowledge, of the *possibility* of knowledge, rather, and its relation to reality."

"Don't you think it is all rather idle and unnecessary?"

"Perhaps."

"That was where philosophy got lost. You'll never exhaust that problem, or get anywhere with it. That is why I say the approach, the method, even the goal of philosophic inquiry was all wrong. I was merely saying that philosophy, being an inquiry — a fearless search — for the art of living well, should take good account, as a prior matter of method, of certain human illusions."

"Love, of course," said Eunice.

"It will be well to start with love, since no man or woman I know but admits to a quickened heartbeat when the subject of Eros is mentioned. Even those cold, gray-plastered souls of quasi-scientific philosophers do. Even Descartes, who doubted everything, had to start with a psychological fact, had to assume that he did think. He never questioned that he was thinking. Why didn't he? All that tomfoolery about the derivative nature of phenomena and knowledge. We know that we think, and feel and do. We can safely start with that. Chapter on Epistemology closed. Now the man who falls in love and believes or makes himself believe that the girl he loves is all beauty and all excellence is of course creating an illusion. The fact that the girl in the bloom of youth is exactly like most other girls does not matter. The truth of his feeling or his illusion, however, cannot be denied. And here the Platonic concept comes in. The man has created within him an image of the ideal woman, of a particular color of hair and pitch of voice and manner of smile and light of eyes, and when he sees a girl answering more or less to that inner ideal within him, he projects that image and identifies the girl with his own ideal. The same is true of the girl meeting the man embodying her unconscious or subconscious ideal. Is that not so?"

"True," said Philemon.

"And we must further grant that it would be deplorable to destroy that illusion, to take away from the young man or the girl that gift of seeing perfection. The world would be infinitely poorer for it, would it not?"

"That seems to be the case."

"We can take art next. Art is also the projection of a subjective idea upon a material object. Art idealizes reality, and in doing so, falsifies it. It is art's function to make it truer than life, seize its invisible essence, as it were. Frankly, it is a falsification of life. It is a momentary glimpse at truth — at harmony, proportion, color, which are all subjective — while the world of reality rushes on. It is the distillation of the quintessence of a material object — a face, a scene in the street — as the artist sees it. Now I don't mean the distortionists of the mid-twentieth century. Art is not a grimace. Nor is it an intellectual analysis. Unable to feel, the artists of those days just hacked away at reality, like bad children hacking away at a piano. In a portrait of a human being, they wanted to take it to pieces; like Picasso's masterpiece of the 'Girl Before the Mirror,' to look inside her, her breasts and her womb — the critics called it internal vision; or to look around the girl from the right and left and front and behind, all at the same time. Certainly, they took the girl to pieces all right. I tell you what; these artists were mad, mad at their impotence to feel externally. Certainly, they were in a fury. They were not satisfied till they had seen the world tumbling down, after their successful taking it apart, in a jumble of squares, triangles, surfaces and lines. I don't mean they did a bad job of it. They successfully took the world to pieces, as a child takes a watch and reduces it to a jumble of wheels and pinions and springs. Don't you feel the esthetic satisfaction of the child when he does that, when he gazes upon what he has done, the analytical pleasure it confers? That child got an internal vision all right. But is it art? Others tried to run away — they were all trying to run away from something, never *toward* something. Some preferred to admire an African head, its force, its strength, its simplicity and imaginative daring. The plain fact is, the African savages never knew better, never had very good, sharp tools to do a finer job. No, that generation of artists were striving laboriously to be simple, methodically to be spontaneous, with calculated self-conscious purpose to appear naïve. What was the trouble of it all? They didn't see and didn't feel, as the classicists did. They were not simple, they were ingenious. You came away from an exhibition, your senses mildly tickled, and said, '*C'est amusant, n'est-ce pas?*' exactly as you would feel when you left a novelty shop, having seen some ingenious set of cocktail glasses or cigarette lighters. Greek art is never just *amusant;* it touches the heart. The Greeks never ran away from anything, never hacked away at anything; they faced nature resolutely, to seek within themselves what there was, to invest it with beauty. They felt and saw because their vision was whole. You cannot produce great art when the man within is not serene. Unfortunately, I have a rather serious quarrel with the men of those days of three score and ten years ago. Man had changed, because his relation to Nature had changed. That was the key to the whole trouble."

"What was the whole trouble?" asked Eurydice, thinking that she was coming to Laos' idea of the colony.

"That man had grown apart from Nature, that he wanted to take Nature by the throat, tear it apart, analyze — never to live in harmony with it. Always man versus Nature, never man with Nature. A Prometheus, unreconciled to his fate. He, not Nature, was the lord of the universe. Whenever man gets too clever and tries to turn away from Nature, Nature plays a nasty trick in return, and destroys or blinds or cripples him."

"Your ideas seem Wordsworthian."

"Very akin to it. The whole problem of modern civilization is to keep man whole, be himself. I, too, am projecting an idea now. I assume that there is a whole man, a man with physical and psychical needs which must be fulfilled, spiritual resources which must be developed, powers which must be expressed. Modern society has grown too complex for him to do that; he is an infinitesimal cog in a gigantic wheel of machinery, lost, labeled, pigeonholed in a giant social and political machine."

"May I interrupt?" asked Eurydice, who had burned with a question uppermost in her mind all evening.

"Certainly you may."

"Why did you found this colony? To escape from the coming wars?"

"There was that. I wanted to have time to think. And I knew I could not think when I became radioactive dust. All I would be able to do would be to poison Indian corn or fish in the sea. My radioactive life would go on, perhaps energizing the legs of a grasshopper, or the shoulders of a cricket. It wasn't good enough for me."

"But you had a fundamental idea — what you wanted to do and see established here."

"A question easier to ask than answer. Man had reached a stage of civilization when simple life was no longer possible. Too many problems impinge upon your consciousness. I don't say that industrial progress was bad; it just grew; nobody had planned it or measured its consequences. Human life had become incredibly complex. Fine, you say, that is the natural result of progress. You are in it, you take your part in it. I happen to be different. I inquire into the basic questions, in a quite detached manner. I ask whether that which is is the best. I count the score of the net gain and loss in its effect upon man himself. Has he gained or lost more? Nobody seemed ever to enter into that fundamental question. You fuss around with the questions brought about by the modern industrial civilization, and you get deeper and deeper into it. You can't see the forest for the trees. You tackle each problem by itself. Everybody was talking about the high standard of living, and everybody was involved in the high cost of living. So you jacked up the wages to increase the purchasing power to meet the high prices; then you jacked up the prices again to cover the increasing high costs of wages; and then jacked up the taxes and the wages again to cover the high prices, in an endless upward spiral of rising cost of living. The high cost of living could mean only one thing, the low value of savings. You lost your security. The economic pressure increased. So you worked and worked. So you paid security taxes to provide for your old-age security, and jacked up still higher the cost of living on account of the security taxes accounted for in the cost of manufacture. You ended up in a planned economy. You got rationed — your energy, your working hours, your old-age security, your sick leaves, your hospital allowances, your holidays and number of days at a summer resort. Everybody was dependent upon somebody else. Ninety per cent of the population become employees of some public or private or governmental organization, finding therein the wherewithal to raise their families and feed their children. You were trapped. You knew that if you saved ten thousand dollars, in ten or twenty years the purchasing power would be exactly reduced by half. You couldn't retire on ten thousand, or on a hundred thousand, because the purchasing power would fall to five, fifty thousand. You were cheated out of your savings. By whom? Nobody knew. By that never-ending spiral of increasing prices. Wonderful! The eternal wheel goes on. Then you pay the police to raid the gamblers, then you pay the police not to raid the gamblers, then you pay the police to make a show of raiding the gamblers. It is all too darn complicated — excuse the slang. Then you pay taxes to keep the peace in Tasmania, or Mesopotamia. . . . Why? Because what happens in Tasmania affects your life intimately. No, human life was too well organized.

"You ask me what do I want? I want less organization, not more. Your social organizers, your visionary socialists, your planned economists, who want to ration your raw material, your time, your labor, your holidays, are all communists as far as I am concerned. I want, first of all, a society where man can recover some of the individuality and independence he has lost. A simpler life. Why not? I wanted a grand, complete simplification of human life, to find out what man wants in this earthly life, that man may live in harmony with nature. In the words of the Chinese philosopher Chuangtse, that man may live out the peaceful tenor of his life, fulfilling his nature. *The universe gives me this form, this toil in manhood, this repose in old age, this rest in death.* To appreciate this universal harmony, the beauty of this cycle, and let our nature be fulfilled in it. And secondly, a society where the excellences of his being can be brought out, where man may develop himself along the lines of his excellence in ease and in freedom."

"You believe there are excellences in man's being? I am glad to hear that. I was so sick of the pose of cynicism of my days, the 1990's when I grew up. I am sorry I interrupted. What about religion?"

The Countess said, "Certainly you don't mean that religion is an illusion."

"It is not. But it can't work without it."

"Why not?" asked the Countess.

"You have to visualize your god, don't you? When you make images of God, or gods, of course you are creating an illusion. Icons are illusions, are they not?"

"You mean idols."

"Don't fool yourself. No major religion is without them. The true religious spirit, an appreciation of the greatness and mystery of God, as seen in the harmony of the heavens and the mysteries of life on earth, is for the scientist and the philosopher. As soon as Moses came down from Mount Sinai, he found the Israelites worshiping the golden calf. A universal God, monotheistic, abstract, existing alone, is too much of an effort for the popular imagination. You must fragmentize your gods, individualize them. And you want a lively, material heaven and hell. All illusions, of course, mythic ways of expressing a spiritual truth. Buddha, according to the Pali scripts, was an agnostic. Prince Sakyamuni was an intellectual, a spiritual philosopher of the first order. Yet look at the Buddhist temples, filled with this god and that god, a whole hierarchy of buddhas and boddhisatvas and interceding saints — they call them arahats. One God isn't enough. You want two, three, a trinity, a whole galaxy of them. Then you want what I call the petty gods; I refer to the patron saints. Each locality and each individual wants a patron god, personally assigned to him, to look after his own welfare, a deity who whispers across your shoulder and tells you where to find your wrist watch, lost while bicycling. It is comfortable, a personal attendant of that sort who guides you at every step. If this is not polytheism, I'd like to know what is. The process of God-fragmentation goes on. It cannot be helped. The Holy Mother, for instance. There cannot be one Lady of Lourdes, another of Fatima. Of course, they are the same person. But popular imagination will not have it that way; the Lady of Lourdes is a particular individual associated with a particular locality, more efficacious than this, that or the other Lady in a different locality. The fragmentizing process goes on, you see, with the same God. No doubt the early Greek Christians were happy to find God had a family; in their imagination, Joseph and Mary were like gods dwelling on Mount Olympus. A Chinese Christian, leader of the Taiping Rebellion who wanted to set up the Kingdom of God on earth, invented even a 'heavenly sister-in-law,' since he was the younger son of God and Jesus, very logically, was his 'elder brother.' You want, besides the several persons of God, an archangel, a heavenly host, and heaven and purgatory and hell. The Arabs living in the desert could think of nothing better than fresh, gurgling streams, plenty of shady grass and cool springs everywhere, luscious grapes and superb wines and a bevy of dark-eyed houris. So they have them in their paradise. The Christian heaven consists of pearly gates, walls studded with diamonds, rubies, agates and amethysts — why, it is a pawnbroker's dream. Lots of people who have never entered the door of Tiffany's in this earthly life hope to do so in the next. The Greek Olympus was filled with incredibly amorous gods and goddesses, and clear streams and nectar of the gods; they came considerably closer to earth, with nymphs and fauns and oreads and nereids. These things are neither true, nor untrue. They are efforts of the human imagination to visualize what is essentially an immaterial life. Such illusions are necessary to man's belief. An image, an icon, is certainly a help to devotion."

"You are not by any chance defending the necessity of idolatry, I hope," said the Countess.

"But I am. And what about the atheistic communists? They carry huge portraits of Stalin about the streets, hang them in all public halls. Don't tell me they have no idols. Made of paper, cellophane, wood, stone — what does it matter? No, you don't get away from idols in any human society. We must either make gods like men, or make gods of men. The public must have something to worship. The worst thing is to have nothing to worship — to gaze perhaps at the steam radiator which you put your tired foot on. That is where the modern economic man has come to, why he is so sad, so uprooted, so scientific and so worried. Any idolatry is better than that."

This smooth and illuminating discourse was interrupted by a grunting, rhythmic noise coming from the left side of the Countess. A very rhythmic noise, something between an unholy snore and a more pious snuffle, certainly produced by obstructions in some generous air passage. Father Donatello was happy, and happiness induced a state of drowsiness. He had followed along, in the first stage, enchanted particularly by that reference to the illusions of love. When the discourse went on to art, he felt very peaceful. Laos' words maintained an even pace. Oh, dear, he thought to himself. I must have taken too many clams. It will do no harm to snooze a bit. In such a state of alert drowsiness, he listened quietly, with complete relaxation of mind. It was then that a perceptible, rhythmic sound began. Very vaguely, he heard him move on to religion, a subject of which he was not unfamiliar. He knew Laos' heresies very well. Deliberately, he shut his mind off. He might or might not have heard the rest. Then something interfered with his respiratory functions, and he choked, readjusted the passage to order by a series of nose twitchings and lip smackings, all in somnolent fashion — and choked again.

"Oh, dear," he said as he sat up. "This chair is too comfortable, too indulgent to the flesh. I must have missed some delightful bits of your conversation."

He began to take out his pipe, chuckling to himself.

Chapter XVII

THE COUNTESS, reclining in her chaise longue, was at her best now. Nothing made her happier than to be in the company of Laos, Philemon, Eunice, Emma-Emma — friends who elevated her mind and spirit by their philosophic chatter. They gave her parlor an intellectual atmosphere, worthy of the Cionis. This was her salon, a salon, she felt, of whom Madame Récamier would be proud. Her own father, Marchese Giuliano de Paula, was an architect and classical scholar, who was suspected of atheism; her mother, a devout Catholic, of a very old Spanish family of Sevilla, was the youngest of three sisters, an extremely beautiful woman with whom her father fell madly in love when traveling in Spain. The marquis gratified every whim of his young wife, summering in Tyrol and skiing in St. Moritz in winter. Their daughter Cordelia was sent to Paris and Lausanne to study, but spent her vacations largely in southern Italy — Capri and Sorrento where they had a villa. After the death of her brother Antonio from an accident in the Alps — he was a daredevil ski champion — her mother grew more and more religious. Her father had been disappointed in the son who went in exclusively for sports, and concentrated his love on the young daughter. The conflict between the atheistic father and the devout mother was calculated to stimulate the mind of the perceptive young girl. The marquis, without being a believer himself, was tolerant toward his wife's religion; he loved to see her go to church and even joined her at Easter and Christmas. Cordelia, through early association and affection for her mother, and by a healthy instinct of adolescent girlhood, had been inclined to be religious. Her father was good enough to attend her confirmation, though he often horrified her mother by what he said at table about the village priest. The village was in an isolated area, and there were usually under a dozen men and women who attended the sacrament; he accused the priest, unjustly, perhaps, of consecrating twice more wine than he knew his congregation could possibly consume, which, by ecclesiastic practice, had to be quaffed to the last drop during the ceremony by the priest himself. The priest's gulps were quite audible in that small chapel. The little child saw her father's silent smirk. It was his way of expressing his spiritual and intellectual independence of the Church.

However, when she grew up, she flew into the bosom of the Church. Nothing made her mother happier than to see Cordelia married to a strong Church supporter, Count Valentino Jose della Castiglioni. The Count, however, made an indifferent husband; he loved to break the Seventh Commandment, preferably with peasant girls. To her horror, she found that his conscience was clear; he had let the Church take care of all the problems of his soul. He felt that, by his generous contributions to churches and charities, he had laid up enough treasure in heaven to cover the multitudinous sins to which his body was prone. He had faith in the infinite mercy of God; that was the wonderful thing about the Church, he told her; it gave you peace of soul and an iron-clad guarantee of a reserved seat in heaven. The Countess left him pretty much alone in his travels. This attitude of the Count toward the Church, as an agent entrusted to take care of his soul's welfare, much as his bank was entrusted to take care of his finances, shocked Cordelia more than anything else, and contributed to generate some doubts in her mind about the function of the Church.

She accused herself of feeling no great sorrow when the Count died in a car accident speeding on the Dolomite Pass. She passed into her Greek period; she loved Athanopoulos with the passion

and the grace and the mature charm of a Spanish señora. Athanopoulos had such dark lustrous hair. Athanopoulos was a man,
with the dash and daring she had found so sadly lacking in the
deceased Count. And now the Athanopoulos episode was over.
With much good sense and a touch of humor, she had bowed
graciously out of competition with Iolanthe. She was approaching forty then. Yet after Athanopoulos' marriage, they had been
able to preserve a friendship based on a deep respect and appreciation for each other's qualities.

The Countess usually came alive toward eleven in the evening,
and grew brighter and brighter toward midnight. The day for
her began. Her graying hair was becoming to her, and her white
bosom, half lying in the direct light of the candelabrum, showed
against her black lace frock, a fitting subject for Tintoretto. She
had a fair comprehension of what was going on, though she could-
n't say that she followed very closely the progression of Laos'
ideas. She loved Laos' saltiness, his iconoclastic shafts which
she felt were like spice to the imagination. Sometimes in a tilt
about logic between Eunice and Laos, the conversation got beyond her depths. But Laos always got out of the depths first;
he always returned to the earth, and she loved it. It was the part
of woman to listen, to appreciate what was wise and true, to lend
the milieu of understanding of the things of the spirit. And she
always had a sense of humor. That was why, without being exactly an intellectual herself, her place was popular. And she
made such divine Italian coffee.

Timalpo brought in some more coffee. She had no use for
maids; they spoiled the intellectual atmosphere of the place. To
make him look more like a Moor, she had given him a large silver
bangle, which Timalpo wore on his arm.

The evening was perfect.

"Alcibiades, come and sit by my side."

The Countess took a protective attitude toward young Wriggs.
She had always associated with artists, and liked to encourage
young writers, poets, painters. Alcibiades, more English (by his
mother) than Greek, was a serious, sensitive novelist. At least,

he was trying to write, and the Countess believed in his talent. "Let go," she often said to him. "Let yourself go. Fight against your English breeding. Don't be afraid of your instincts. And don't be afraid of grammar. You can polish that later. Store up things to say, ideas, feelings, observations of life. Pour yourself out. Then lop off later; you have to have things to lop off from. There are no rules to follow in art, the theater, the novel. You have to find yourself first and everything else follows."

Alcibiades was in the throes of a young man of twenty-four, intelligent enough to see everything around him, not mature enough to reduce his impressions to order, to some sort of perspective. He was extremely shy; he held himself aloof, usually silent in company. He alone, of all the Irenikis, had scaled the peak of Mount Ida, to the consternation of his East-End mother. It was a hazardous undertaking. In doing so, he had merely followed an irrational impulse; he couldn't quite explain it, and no Alpine climber could.

"Mountains are to be gazed upon, looked up to, not to be conquered," Laos had said to him. What was he to think of that? Laos was always too much for him; an alien spirit whose words he could hear, but not understand. According to Laos, mountain climbing was symbolic of a Nordic disease, a spiritual restlessness at the back of all modern discontent. "Don't conquer Nature, merge yourself with it. Nature is not hostile to man; she is your friend. Don't match yourself against the mountain; feel humble and admire it. It is symptomatic. The Nordic people want to grapple with Nature, to take her by the throat and harness her, break her into service as you break a horse. A very worthy object, of course, provided you don't forget Nature has other uses as well. They want to take a mountain by the throat, too. I know. People speak of the 'challenge' of Everest, of Jungfrau. Jungfrau never challenges anybody; she is just there, content, eternal, a mother in her peaceful sleep. I can hear the Alpinist say to himself, subconsciously of course, 'I won't have you look down upon me, laugh at me. I will get as high as you are, and get even with you, establish myself as your equal.' And he would come

down and announce his 'conquest.' Jungfrau is not even aware
of her defeat; she would not lift an eyelid in her peaceful sleep.
But it is in your blood. The Christian missionaries have to speak
of the 'challenge of heathenism' to get their blood boiling sufficiently to preach the gospel of forgiveness and peace. The Greek
hills are never very high. Perhaps that was why the Hellenes felt
and thought differently. The gods walked upon Mount Olympus,
and the Hellenes walked with gods. As Enoch did. There was
a period in Hebrew history, too briefly passed over, when the
gods and men met socially on a friendly footing, like the Greek
gods. Jehovah did not get really angry, filled with wrath and
vengeance, till after the Exodus. Down to the time of Abraham,
God was still a friendly being. He came knocking at your tent
door. Abraham was able to converse with God, questioned Him
and extracted promises from Him. Jacob even wrestled with
Him. All on friendly terms. But for the Greeks, what was Par-
nassus but a little friendly hill? What the Greeks lost in elevation of spirit they gained in zest of life. Their gods went whoring
in a friendly world, as the Greeks themselves did. The Gothic
and the Mediterranean spirits must ever be at variance with each
other."

This was typical of the confusion bred in young Alcibiades'
mind by Laos' set of ideas. He understood it, but was not in
sympathy with it. He couldn't quite wrestle with Laos' ideas,
although he was enormously receptive, remarkably intelligent.
But he was laboring under a great disadvantage. He loved,
craved, yearned to see the Old World. How could he write a
novel, when his experience was confined to the island? He would
not wear a tunic; he insisted on wearing a tie, which his mother
made for him, true to his blood. He was proud of being half
English; that was why he took the name of Wriggs, his mother's,
rather than that of his deceased Greek father. He knew England
only from his mother; her stories of the East End did not inspire
him. But he had read enormously, of Waterloo and Duke Welling-
ton, of the Battle of Trafalgar, of the Charge of the Light Brigade.
How was he to write a novel, if he had never seen a castle, a

fort, an old-fashioned cannon, a Swiss mountaineer? He had seen pictures of the Lake District, of rose-covered cottages, of winding country paths and milkmaids under bonnets and the London policemen and Westminster Abbey. He even adored King Charles III whom he thought he would never be able to see in his lifetime unless something happened. He developed an intense nostalgia for England, Ye Olde England. He wanted to break out of this island if he could. Knowing that he could not, he felt very sad. This tinge of contemplative sorrow and the habitual furrows on his brow, which he had cultivated from Edward-to-be-the-VIII's example, lent him a special charm. He looked serious, contemplative, as a young author usually looks.

"Don't think of Westminster Abbey, darling," said the Countess. "It isn't there. It was blown to smithereens — evaporated early in 1975."

He felt he could cry, to be deprived of the excitement and the tumult of war and struggle and the rough tumble of a big city life, the adventures, the hazards of a moderately civilized world, even though it was not as peaceful as Thainos. That was why he had to climb Mount Ida, since he could not climb the steeple at Oxford. He wanted to cry. But of course he didn't. He kept a stiff upper lip, suppressed everything downward. He would not even mention to others his feelings on top of Mount Ida. There, on top of the highest point of the island, he surveyed the encircling ocean, forming a hopeless girdle around it, extending hundreds of miles. And England, dear old England, and the entire Old World, lay below the arc of the horizon on the other side. He was determined to break out of this island paradise.

There must come a chance, sooner or later, before he grew old. Of all the heroes, he admired most Sir Francis Drake. Why, at his age, he ought to be a buccaneer, sailing the Seven Seas. And he was a captive, an exile, about as happy as a bird in a golden cage. Only when swimming in the sea did he feel better, reconciled with himself. He loved to row out to the sandbars on the outer side of the lagoon and spend his days alone.

Frustration, only frustration.

"Have some coffee," said the Countess now. "Cheer up. You haven't spoken a word all evening."

"Thanks a lot. You mustn't think I am rude. I don't mean to be." He lapsed into silence again.

There was a general shifting of positions, while coffee was served. Philemon had stood up, stretching himself. With a smiling wink, and an inviting bent finger, the Countess beckoned to Chloe to come over. She loved to surround herself with young people. Eurydice had left her seat, holding a cup in hand and listening to Pietro Galli talking with Laos. People all called him Pietro. He was not only a violinist, but also a fiddle-maker, and a very thoughtful, well-read man. He was talking about the externalizing of religion, about religion as a socialized institution and as a direct experience of God.

"Faith in God is one thing, knowledge of God another," said Eunice.

Laos looked up. "I hope I have not bored you," he said to Eurydice.

"Come, sit with us," Eunice said as she stood up to make room.

"I really shouldn't," protested Eurydice, feeling very happy.

"You are the guest of honor tonight."

"Sit down," said Laos. "You might tell us some news of the outside world."

"What about the space ships? Have they been able to reach the moon?" Pietro asked.

"There were three attempted voyages, the first when I was a child of ten. They went off all right, and they were able to send back messages after they started. But none of them has come back." Inevitably eyes turned to her; she was occupying the center of attention. How was she ever to begin? "We have pocket phones that we carry about; we can talk with anybody on the continent we like by contacting the telephone stations."

"Has cancer been conquered?" asked the Countess.

"Long ago. Back in 1980. That was the trouble. It was a blessing of course for the individual; the expectation of life was increased ten years between 1950 and 1980. But from the world's point of view, population was growing too big. That was what I was working on. How do you do it here?"

"Very simple. We have a system of proportionate taxation. The larger the family, the higher the tax. That stops it all right. Normal tax for every family a flat 10 per cent. A man is permitted, even encouraged, to have three children. If they want more, it is their lookout. The fourth child raises it to 12½ per cent; the fifth to 15 per cent, etc. It works."

Emma-Emma interposed. "And the mothers are happy about it. They are through with motherhood by thirty-five. As I told you, the girls are supposed not to marry before twenty-one; they have all the courtship they want before that. They space their children, too. They can have their children between twenty-one and thirty-five. After that they are relieved of the fear of maternity. A simple operation does it. Of course, we have the advantage over the Old World; we have no religious prejudice against birth control. It works a hardship on the big families; but you know we have this limited area, and drastic measures have to be taken. We've managed. But tell us . . ."

"I don't know what to say."

"Are the people happier?"

"It is hard to say. Of course, after about 1950 the outward appearance changed. Fine throughways, crossing at different levels, planned cities, with space for trees, real boulevards in the midst of a city. Faster travel, and of course higher death rates on the highways. We killed people, or people killed themselves on the highways at the rate of over a hundred a day, annual rate 38,000 in the 1950's, at the time of the Korean War. I remember reading that more people were killed on the road in one year in the United States than during the entire Korean War. Now it has gone up to 78,000 per year. About three-quarter million people casually kill others or themselves in ten years. It cannot be helped of course. Better roads, faster travel, more deaths. Car insurance has gone up to five hundred dollars a year. This is not as frightening as it sounds. Everything has gone up. A beef steak is $7.50. That is considered cheap. The average worker earns about $1,000 per month, and requires about $1,200. Nobody benefits by it. The trouble is, taxes have gone up to fifty per cent because of the world situation, the threat of war. You have no idea how much war, the mere shadow of war, costs. In comparison, peace is dirt cheap. That is why we are working for it. Why should a man slave half a week to pay the costs of maintaining peace? Of course, there are many conveniences. We shoot the garbage down a sink, which eats it up. Little things like that. But these are merely conveniences. They touch only the surface of things. I wouldn't say people are less worried, less discontented. We work harder, faster, and save less. The crux of the whole thing is the international situation. We can't let the nations alone, and we can't let the individuals alone."

"Tell us about the Democratic World Commonwealth," asked Philemon. "Is it any different from the previous world organizations?"

"The DWC. It is just common sense. It should have been that long ago. The first two, League of Nations and United Nations, were of course speaking forums only, were never intended for anything else. Alliances, counter-alliances, peace treaties, commercial treaties, all took place outside these debating societies. They took away all power from the truly democratic, representative body, the General Assembly, all except recommendatory powers, and concentrated it in the Security Council, then strangled the Security Council by veto of the big brothers. It was designed not to work. And if it made decisions, it had no power to carry them out. Here we were, a tight world economic community, separated by nationalities, trying to live together without a world law, without wanting a world law, and orderly processes to enforce respect for that law. What alternative was there but war? Where law and respect for law do not exist, the pistol must rule. It is like any lawless society anywhere, big or small. We hadn't come to that stage of development yet where we wanted the orderly processes of law governing nations. The people of those days did not think, or did not think clearly enough to realize the consequences of what they were doing.

It is just that the idea was so new, people had never heard of a sovereign nation taking orders from a supra-national body and abiding, like civilized persons, by the law and the majority. It was thought a disgrace to do so; every nation was sovereign, supreme. Particularly the Big Powers. It was as if a New York senator had the veto power over all the votes of the majority of the states; of course such a federal congress would never work.

"After the Third World War," continued Eurydice, "we realized our mistakes. We realized the world organization had to be given power — naked force, in fact — to enforce peace. It had worked before, of course. The Pax Romana effectively enforced abstention from war in states subject to the Roman Empire. The victorious nations got together. But every nation was tired, devastated, ruined economically. The U.S. foolishly stuck its head up as the leader of the Democratic World Alliance. If it was not Pax Americana, it was at least world oligarchy, rule of the few rich powerful nations. We called it democratic; of course we meant nothing of the kind. The U.S. did, with the nominal help of other victorious powers, enforce peace. But that was what pushed the taxes up and gave the chance for a dictator to come into power. Why were we so foolish? Sentimental nobility, I suppose. We did it, paid for it, and got hated for it everywhere. Why should the U.S. go it alone? The Ten Years' War dragged on, small revolts flaming up here, squashed, and flaring up elsewhere again, undramatically, but very annoyingly. It wore the world oligarchs out. There was peace all right, but somehow it looked very militaristic, martial. The world was being ruled by dreadnoughts, carriers, atomic submarines on sea and monstrous jet squadrons in the air. It did not look comfortable. A sewing woman, member of the Garment Workers' Union, wrote a letter to the New York Times, then published in Poughkeepsie, after the American President was assassinated by an Arab, of Saudi Arabia. She asked, 'Why shouldn't we let the world share the common responsibility, and let the nations govern themselves? Why should we do the governing for them, and invite universal hatred? Why don't we let the schoolhouse democratic principles and practices prevail in a new world organization? Just that. No vetoes. No Big and Small Powers. Equal justice and equal responsibility.' It started the whole movement. The fact is, the world in general was at last ready. That woman merely expressed what everybody else was feeling. So the DWC was born in 2000 A.D."

"Wasn't there quite a celebration?"

"Not comparable with the religious one. A religious fanaticism had broken out as early as 1995. A prophet appeared to heal the sick and founded a sect called the Second Adventists, which numbered three million followers. The followers gave away their property, clothed themselves in white, and sang all day. They expected Jesus to appear in glory in person, bodily, to establish the New Kingdom. The prophet scared a lot of people by saying He was coming to judge those who did not believe in Him. They went up to the Poconos, and the Adirondacks and the Rockies and the Blue Ridge, for the Bible said He would be seen by all. There they sat all day, and all night, and all day and all night for five days from January 1 to January 4, working themselves into a frenzy; some of them professed they were speaking Russian, Chinese, Greek, Tasmanian. They thought that God who worked with hundreds of millions of years had respect for a paltry 2000, or for any round number of human arithmetic. It is rather pitiable to watch men and women like that in the year 2000. On the fifth day came the inevitable anticlimax. The squatters began to have doubts, but more important, got very hungry. After they came down, they felt very foolish. Some sharp real estate man had bought up a lot of houses and made a tremendous profit. The Prophet, it was whispered, ended up as a multimillionaire, changed his identity and sailed off in a private Diesel yacht to some unknown destination."

Eurydice's voice was softly feminine. Naturally shy, she had never been at home in society, would rather avoid talking. She admired the poise and ease of women who had the ability to carry on small talk, swimming on a current of words. She hated giving lectures. Tonight she thought she was expected to say something. The people had been so friendly, and she was carried away by the subject.

She stopped abruptly. Heavy footsteps were heard across the stone terrace, scraping sand off sandals. They couldn't see the individual from the drawing room.

"His Royal Highness has come back, I am sure," said the Countess. "Is that you, darling?"

The Prince's steps were heard in the next room, measured, majestic. His head appeared at the door. He exuberated, his eyes glittering.

"Well, well! A cozy company, heh? It was wonderful. The night air . . . the stars!"

"You didn't see the stars. Don't fool me. Not in this fog."

"What's the difference? They are there, all the same . . . The night air, the stars, the salty sprays that come with the breeze. It is stuffy in here."

"We are comfortable," said the Countess smiling. "Don't you blow in all that salty breath from the sea."

"Why not put on some music?"

"Alcibiades dear, will you be so good. Put on the *Air for G String*. It is right in the bottom shelf."

Alcibiades went to the albums, picked out the record and put it on.

"What time is it?" asked Emma-Emma.

"You mustn't think of leaving yet," said the hostess. "The Prince has just come back."

"I really must," insisted the anthropologist. "Eurydice, you can stay if you like. Philemon or Chloe will accompany you home when you are ready."

Eurydice said to the Countess, rolling her words easily, "You have been very kind, Countess. I think it is late. I'll go back with Emma-Emma. I really envy you people, having music and all that."

"Well, we are well provided. You must come again then, now that you know the place. I hope you enjoyed the evening."

"I did tremendously."

"Then perhaps we may have another evening like this."

"I would love to."

Eurydice had stood up. Turning to Laos, she asked a question she had been wanting to ask.

"Tell me why did you smash the radio in our plane?"

Laos laughed. "Why? Eurydice, you will understand, I am sure. Of course we smashed it! We love you too truly to want you ever to get out of here."

"Don't you ever want to receive news of the world?"

"Why should we?"

Philemon had come up. He repeated his invitation to Eurydice to go to the Museion.

"I'd love to."

"Show her the solar motor, too," said Laos.

"Solar motor?"

"Yes," said Philemon. "That's something we have developed on this island. I don't think they have harnessed the sun's energy yet, have they?"

"They haven't."

Now Eurydice said good-by to everybody. Father Donatello offered to take her up to see the winepress at the uplands and visit the vineyards. Young Wriggs offered to row her out to the sandbars. Eurydice was perfectly delighted with it all.

Chapter XVIII

ᴮOWENA was crying in bed when they returned at about one o'clock in the morning. It had been over a mile and a half's walk, and they felt rather tired. Eurydice stumbled in the dark several times on account of her shoes. It was remarkable to see the older woman going in firm, agile strides, day or night.

"I can never guess how old you are," said Eurydice.

"Does it matter?"

"I am just curious. You walk so much faster than I."

"Thank you. I had written a dozen books before I came here thirty years ago. You can draw your own conclusions."

"You must have a good constitution."

"It is the quiet and relaxation here, I believe, the absence of nervous tension. And my work keeps me happy."

They asked for water when they arrived.

"Bowena!"

Bowena took some time to appear, her eyes swollen. Emma-Emma was stunned.

"What's the matter?"

Bowena was silent.

"Your father again?"

She shook her head.

"Anybody in your family ill?"

Emma-Emma sensed something much deeper. Bowena never looked that way, so utterly miserable. She was like her own child.

144

"Tell me what happened. Has Tihualco been here?"

The Thainian girl's eyes suddenly gleamed, enormous in the candlelight.

"No, no. You must not tell him. Please, I beg you."

Puzzled, Emma-Emma sensed a deep trouble; a young girl's trouble, she was sure — love or sex.

"Sit down. Calm yourself."

Bowena sat on Emma-Emma's bed, her beautiful full-grown figure and her powerful olive thighs against the white sheet, her eyes dilated in fright.

"Now tell me, my child."

"It's Oaxus. He's been here. He bothered me. He took me by force. I slapped him. I fought. But he took me. But you mustn't tell Tihualco. You mustn't. He will kill me, and he will go and kill him. I don't want him to get into trouble."

"Don't worry. He does not have to know."

"You promise?"

"I promise you. I shall never tell him. Don't worry, my child."

Bowena suddenly let out a string of expletives, which Emma-Emma could not understand.

"Yes, he is a bad man," she agreed. "Very bad. But you don't have to worry. Go back to bed. I will never tell Tihualco."

A smile returned to the girl's face. She got up and prepared water for them. Her problem appeared quite simple. It was Tihualco's knowledge she was worried about.

It did not appear quite that simple when Emma-Emma lay abed thinking about it. If the offender who had assaulted her had been a Thainian tribesman, he would be dealt with according to their tribal customs. Oaxus was one of the Irenikis. Apparently taking advantage of his wife's absence, he had come to violate the girl. He could be brought to trial according to Ireniki law. Usually, among the Greeks and Italians, it was fairly simple, owing to a very special form of *noblesse oblige* on the part of the injured girl. The law prescribed a severe penalty for rape — ten years' imprisonment, including three years' hard labor. But it seldom came to that. Usually it was settled out of court between the families; if the young man was respectable and solid, he might be compelled to marry her. Once it went through the processes of law, the girl was beseeched by the young man's parents and lavished with presents, begging her to have mercy on the young man. They would do anything, make him marry her, build her a new house, stagger her with honey and olives and costly quilts — anything to save their son from a hard sentence. The law was strict on rape, but entirely absolved the man if the girl admitted it was fornication. Unless the girl strongly resented the young man, for personal reasons, moved by uncontrollable venom of hatred, she usually relented. After all, the man who did her the honor of overpowering her, the parents argued, was paying a tribute to her charms. The deed was execrable, the cause nothing but her own irresistible beauty.

The legal farce was put on. (Laos thought that all legal actions were farces.) After the necessary questionings, the girl usually stood up and answered:

"My Lord, I was so carried away by his soft entreaties that I consented for him to violate me."

"You did this of your free will?"

"Yes. He was so handsome. I could not resist his attentions."

Nobody was surprised. This usually brought such gratitude to the young man and his parents that, even if they did not marry each other, the girl was looked upon as a great benefactor of the family, having thus placed it under an eternal obligation. Nobody thought this unusual. Like all social customs, it was liable to abuse. Some girls made a profession of being raped. By the time one of these had been ravished by five young men, whom she generously absolved by settlement in court or out of court, she usually had two houses, three vineyards, and perhaps fifty sheep to her credit. Man makes the law, and man is always able to beat it, Laos always said. He was an antinomian. Quoting Anacharsis, he said, the law is like a cobweb which catches the small flies, but the larger insects are usually able to break through it. He was undoubtedly influenced by Confucius, an antinomian, who fought shy of placing too much faith in laws and punishments. The laws should be simple, and the punishment light. This was in consonance with his general basic idea of simplifying life.

Of course, the girl's generosity in publicly admitting fornication was made possible by the Ireniki attitude toward motherhood. The girl did not have to marry the man if she did not want to. Motherhood was motherhood, wed or unwed. All children were "natural," and all were legitimate. Many unwed mothers had brought up their children in honor and respect; no social stigma attended to the "natural" child. This strange social attitude stemmed from Laos' belief that every woman had the right to become a mother, that motherhood was a divine, unalienable right of woman, and that she who violated this violated one of the first laws of nature. Consequently, it was better to be an unwed mother than no mother at all. Laos was a little facetious about it; he said goslings could do without the gander, but not without the mother goose. But he was also serious. "What is God-given is nature; to fulfill nature is the [moral] law; to cultivate the law is culture," he quoted Confucius' grandson. He had given this matter careful thought. The whole psychology of his social philosophy may be stated in the cardinal Chuang-tsean tenet that man must be free and able to pursue the even tenor of his span of life, and that his nature must be fulfilled. In terms of Greek philosophy, man should be free to develop along the line of his excellence. That was the true meaning of freedom. All social happiness depended on it. Just as it was the talent of fruit trees to bear fruit, so it was the particular talent of women to become mothers. No woman could be completely happy until she was a mother, until that part of her nature was fulfilled. No woman looked more beautiful than when she stood over the cradle of her baby, or was nursing him. Nordic pruriency had made El Greco's "Virgin of Pure Milk" obscene.

In the case of Bowena, Emma-Emma decided the best thing was to keep quiet and tell nobody about it. Bowena had begged her, and she had promised.

Chloe came late the next morning with Philemon. It was clear they were very much in love with each other. She was only seventeen: blond hair, blue eyes set in a face that was light olive, a little darker than her mother, with a noble Grecian profile. Mentally, she was still very much a child, naïve and free with laughter. Hearing that Philemon was coming for Eurydice, she asked to come along, too. Eurydice was much older than herself, and an American, completely mysterious to her. She was not jealous of her. She just wanted to be sure. She knew how her whole insides vibrated when she beheld Philemon's blond hair, blue eyes, his well-trimmed mustache, the very subtle, clear, classical line of his nose beginning slightly lower below the brow. Philemon was so white, fair-skinned. His head sat nobly upon his shapely, manly neck and shoulders, no matter how carelessly he wore his working frock.

Chloe surveyed Eurydice's white blouse, fitted pants and high heels, with a proper woman's respect for another woman's attire. It was so unfair, she thought, those shoes. They had something bewitching about them. And the color of her lipstick. Most of all, she thought of her blouse, the unfairest of all. It wasn't the custom. A mother of three children, yes; let her cover her breasts. But Eurydice was not even married. It made her feel highly uncomfortable. It was as if every girl had laid her cards down on the table, and she was concealing hers in her hands. A girl like that might be up to anything.

Chloe's look made Eurydice uncomfortable, too.

When Eurydice stumbled on the pebbly path up to the Museion, Chloe couldn't help laughing.

"Why don't you take them off?" Chloe asked.

Eurydice thought she would rather die than go barefoot like Chloe.

The Museion was a single-gabled rectangular edifice, tinted very faint pink, standing on a high ledge, some two hundred feet above the town. A series of short stone steps and a porch with Grecian columns led to the massive portal. It was a structure entirely out of proportion to the town in size and material splen-

dor; it was built with public money and labor, taking ten years
to complete, and occupying a great deal of the thought of Athanopoulos and Laos. Strategically, too, it occupied the dominant
position on the island, like the cathedral in a European town.
Tall stone columns and sculptures graced the sides. Some of
these were imported, while others were copies made by Ireniki
artists. Delicate friezes ran around the walls, picturing the ancient gods. The very size of the place, the cool dimness inside,
the massive, tall pillars of stone receding into the semi-darkness,
and the slanting light from above created the impression of
the inside of a Grecian temple.

Philemon translated some of the mottoes inscribed in stone
panels for her. Eurydice thought they would contain some stern,
philosophic precepts; she found on the other hand, they were
familiarly human, relaxing in fact. They were largely ethical,
of course, but more epigrammatic than moralistic, homely-wise
with a Montaigne flavor. "Do not be perfect, be reasonable"— so
ran one of them. "Commit mistakes, but confess and rectify
them." Eurydice felt very comfortable.

"These were carefully selected by Laos," Philemon commented.
"In a way, they embody his whole philosophy of living. He is
against mankind striving after divinity, imitating God's perfection. It makes no sense whatsoever, like a toad aspiring to be a
peacock. It is an impossible job. No man should be fairly asked
to imitate the gods. Be ye as perfect . . . We are *not* gods.
Suppose you are not a Galli-Curci, or a Paderewski, and you
strive to be such a one, you will kill yourself in the attempt,
won't you? You will hate yourself, your audience, your critics,
and society in general. It creates a psychic tension, a feeling of
inadequacy and guilt, that you are not what you should be.
You become neurotic so long as the conflict, the disparity between
the ideal and the real, cannot be resolved, and you generate certain destructive tendencies, such as love for war-making and
the desire to annihilate somebody. You've got to shift the blame
somewhere."

Another one which attracted her attention was "Excess of

virtue is a vice." Of course, Philemon pointed out, this was the same old counsel, moderation in all things, including virtue. That was where moral purity became puritanism. Laos probably wrote this himself.

"Do not try to appear better than you are, nor worse than is really necessary."

"Always admire the good in others, and forget not sometimes to admire the good in yourself."

This last bit, Eurydice thought, was superb. She became thoroughly enamored of such a style of philosophy.

The statues, Philemon pointed out to her, were those of the nine Muses, daughters of Jupiter and Mnemosyne: Clio, goddess of history, Euterpe, inventor of the flute and wind instruments, Thalia, goddess of comic poetry, Melpomene, of tragedy, Erato, of lyric and love poetry, Polyhymnia, of song and rhetoric, etc.

They went on to Philemon's workshop in a back wing of the building. The gigantic Poseidon in reclining position, twenty feet wide, intended later to be placed outside the Museion, on which he had been working for three years, stood on a wooden base in the lighted corner of a room covered with clay, plaster, wooden boards and casts. A head of a young girl, Chloe herself, in white plaster, stood beaming at them from a wall bracket, smiling an impish smile. Eurydice could see the unfeigned pride of the young girl as she stood beneath her sculptured likeness.

In the right wing of the Museion was a back room, heavily locked. Philemon said the lock was the biggest they had taken out of the S.S. *Arcadia* and Laos kept the key himself. It was never opened to the public.

"What's in it?" Eurydice asked.

"Nobody knows. Only Laos and Athanopoulos had access to the place. Perhaps a hoard of gold, or evidently something they did not want anybody to know about."

The left-wing gate opened on a spacious square fronting the Athenaeum, set some fifty feet further back than the Museion. Opposite them, fringing the square on the south, was a covered colonnade, designed as a broad shaded walk commanding a superb view of the south shore. Eurydice could not help being overtaken by a feeling of surprise at the magnificence of the layout, the fine masonry, the cut-stone benches lying in the shade of rows of graceful, small olive trees, the fine-grained slab pavement, drenched with sunlight, the harmonious line of the sheltered corridor, overhung by the incredibly blue sky. Whence came all the money and the labor, in such a small island community? Perhaps any community would be able to build such a place dedicated to the arts and learning if the taxes all went to such purposes. This little place compared favorably with many public buildings and squares and parks in her own country; she had seen better, grander things, the temple to Jupiter in Baalbek, for example, but there was an element of balance and proportion which made this peculiarly soothing to the spirit, an inner harmony of plaster and stone and form and color. Perhaps the setting had much to do with it, its location on a jeweled island of the Pacific Ocean, its air and sky and sun.

Inevitably their steps led toward the bronze statue of Athanopoulos and his goat. It was Philemon's work, an inspired piece, a happy creation which the artist probably could not duplicate again. It had taken him no more than a year to do it. So that was Athanopoulos, Eurydice thought as she gazed up at its head of shaggy hair, eyes looking down paternally on the town below with a suggestion of a mysterious smile, his body slanting slightly sidewise, a pipe in his right hand, his left hand in his trouser pocket — definitely an attitude of happy relaxation and contentment, of work accomplished. His left leg was solidly planted on the rough-hewn base, his right leg bent forward. This unusual inclination of the body and arrangement of legs seemed to suggest at the same time rest and movement. There was a witchery of line about it, too, so that the whole suggested amplitude of power and life.

"He did this," said Chloe proudly.

"How did you do it?" Eurydice asked.

"A happy fluke, I suppose," said the sculptor.

Chloe said, "He was inspired." She added something in Greek, which was translated as the inner vision. They walked around the statue.

"No," said Philemon. "It is a philosophy of art, taught me by Laos. I am profoundly grateful to him. I did not know a thing, was concerned chiefly with the technique. He opened my eyes, as it were, gave me the key."

"A key?"

"Yes, a key to all beauty, not sculpture alone. Just two words, grace and strength. Anything of beauty, in human character, in politics even, must have these two elements in proper proportion. Even a literary essay. It must have meat, substance, power of ideas, and this meat, this substance must be clothed with a peripheral beauty of style and language. An essay with all the peripheral style and grace without strength of ideas is not esthetically satisfying. So with human character, with a husband for example; kindness and consideration are not enough, the man must have strength of purpose. A too 'graceful' husband can drive a wife mad. A loving, clinging wife may hang like a limp wet rag on her husband's neck. It can be too much of a good thing. We can drop in to see him. His house is just there."

He pointed to a small vine-covered wall, behind which the low roof of a cottage was visible.

"What do you think of Laos? What is your impression of him?" he asked.

"I don't know. I heard of him from Emma-Emma, and I had pictured him as a kind of supra-mind, rather austere, remote, unapproachable. I was impressed by him last night, but he was certainly not austere."

"Not at close range. Of course, he is a remarkable man, to have done the things he did, founding this colony, and all that. The very idea was an audacious one. He was fond of using the expression, cut the Gordian knot. A swift, sure mind, a mind pretty sure about its ideas."

"I saw him last night," said Eurydice. "He is like any of the others. Don't you think there's — I don't know how to phrase it — a plebeian streak about him?"

"Yes, if you mean he is not aristocratic-looking, like Prince Somovarvitch, or one of those lonely, towering intellects, aloof and sufficient unto themselves. He mixes with everybody, is tolerant of everybody. I have seen all phases of him, in different moods. When he is annoyed by something he is very glum. He can remain silent for a whole half-day. You can see then he is nervous about something. Then after a good dinner he forgets all his troubles and is himself again."

"Has he ever lost his temper?"

"Oh, yes. When the City Council refuses to do what he tells them to, things like taxes, etc. Then he goes down to Giovanni's, hugs a bottle of Chianti under his armpit and goes silently to his house. The people feel so sorry for him that they generally end up by following his idea. They love him."

"I think I understand that man now, when I read that motto he writes, 'Do not try to appear better than you are, or worse than is really necessary.' So human, isn't it?"

"Yes, then after you know him well, after you have lived with him at close range, you get a new kind of respect — for the integrity of his ideas."

"What's the idea of that goat?"

Philemon smiled. "The goat is sacred to Athanopoulos, as we might say; the animal was his favorite. The Hellenic gods all have an animal sacred to them respectively — a hawk, or a dove, or a grasshopper, or some particular tree. I put it there because he had a kind of fascination, almost an obsession, for the animal. He told us that he was suckled by a goat when a baby. It may be true. Romulus was supposed to have been suckled by a wolf, according to the Roman legend. Anyway, Athanopoulos could not live without goats — or hairy women."

The Athenaeum was of the same pattern as the Museion, only smaller. It was what one might call a library, with a hall for meetings, paneled and furnished with heavy carved tables and chairs. Shelves lined the walls. There was no note of antiquity about the place. Eurydice was amused to find a row of card-catalogue cabinets. She hastily went through the index cards.

The books were mostly in Greek, but a fair proportion of English, German and French volumes were there. She even found Marlowe and Maupassant, close to Marcus on the radio. The interior was extremely cool, in spite of the hot sun outside, the walls being built of stones over two feet deep. The library, more than anything else, reconciled Eurydice to her captivity on this island.

She met Wriggs pouring over a volume on a heavy board table, pencil in hand. Wriggs had seen them coming in, but he was too much absorbed, or he was too shy. He stood up at last when they approached.

"Hullo," he said, offering his hand. "Seeing the Museion?"

"I am showing her around," said Philemon.

"What are you working on?" asked Eurydice.

"Oh, it's nothing important. Just fooling around a bit."

A fine specimen of a young man, Eurydice thought, reticent, modest, reserved. A young man trying to keep up his good manners in this Pacific outpost, wearing a trim bow-tie.

Up above across the inner end of the building ran an inscription, deeply engraved in stone. Eurydice asked what it said. It was a quotation from a fragment by Euripides: *Happy is he who has learned the value of research.*

"There is a film library, too, in the inside room."

Eurydice was amazed. Certainly the colony was well-planned, on a better scale than a group of ordinary adventurers would be able to do. Books, long-playing tape recordings, films — safekeeping the progress of knowledge, forestalling an abrupt return to savagery.

Emerging into the sunlit outdoors, Philemon pointed out to her an inscription near the entrance done in beautiful Greek letters in sharp relief.

"That is the Ireniki prayer, like the Lord's Prayer, which every member of the community knows by heart. It gives the essence of the articles we believe in."

"A creed, I see."

"No, not a creed. There's a great difference between a prayer and a creed. A prayer is the expressing of a wish, a striving toward an ideal; a creed is a formulation of intellectual beliefs, usually encased, embalmed, I might almost say, for good. A creed has something dogmatic about it, permitting no discussion, or only a discussion limited to agreement and a predetermined conclusion, which is the same thing. That is the prayer Laos read at the funeral ceremony."

Eurydice begged him to translate it for her. He did, carefully, with much searching and groping for the right word. The strange thing was that it was not addressed to God. It said:

"O friends, let us take time to think about life and be unafraid, that we may see life with simplicity and clarity, without confusion and without artifices of the mind, neither looking backward, nor straining after the unattainable Beyond. Let us try to believe that life is good, and that without further waiting, the opportunity to live the good life is here, if we will it should be so. The earth is ours as we make it, society is ours as we create and improve it. Let us strive to live with our fellow men in peace and civility, that we may work fruitfully, endure nobly and live happily. Let us further take time, when our hands are freed from the toil of labor, to admire and wonder, in reverence and humility, and enjoy in beauty and in wisdom, this great spiritual universe, of which we are a part, partaking of its harmony. And when it is time for us to depart, let us leave content and grateful for having enjoyed this short, but precious gift of life. Amen."

"I should like to make a copy of it, if you will write it down for me," said Eurydice. "It is so simple, and well expressed. Does everybody know it by heart here?"

"Yes, everybody, as I told you. Like the Lord's Prayer, it is simple, but there's more in it than is at first apparent. Come on. Let's go over and see Laos. It's only next door."

Chapter XIX

A PERGOLA ENTRANCE, lying in the shadow of the Athenaeum, opened into a small, unpretentious, pebbled yard, with a bird-bath in the center. The place smelled of ferns and lichens which grew at the foot of the walls, where enormous tiger lilies from the shade beckoned a homely greeting to the visitors. A door, reached by two steps, stood ajar.

"Where's Laos?" asked Philemon, as they went in through the corridor.

Eugénie, a fat French woman, reputed to be a fabulous cook Laos had discovered on the Riviera and pressed into his service, had met them in the corridor. She pointed with her stubby fingers to the garden and said, "He is out there."

From the corridor they could see straight through to the garden on the other side. It was a three-room house, with a longish chamber facing the garden which was the combination living-dining room. Here and there stood cane-bottomed chairs. To the right, the living room opened into a library, Laos' retreat, provided with a lounge and a divan. Pipes, a wide leather jar, a pair of library scissors, an assortment of papers in not-too-good order, lay on the big, low desk. On the desk stood an old, faded photograph of Laos' wife, a sweet young thing with flaming red hair. The chairs were low, the desk was low, the divan and everything suggested a man who had no desire to overcome gravity. The walls, except where covered by bookshelves, were bare.

The large banana leaves outside the window shed a greenish light into the living room, which lay in subdued luminence, suggesting quiet. The furniture might be adjudged on the bare, rustic side, but the room was nevertheless pleasant and cozy, and had an atmosphere of extraordinary ease and seclusion like a mountain lodge. A few pewter cannisters lined the windowsill.

Laos came in from the garden, in his tunic and sandals, his broad forehead well-tanned in the sun. Eurydice always thought his mouth and his white goatee the most beautiful part of his physiognomy. It made him look alien and gentle and refined. He extended a leisurely hand of welcome.

"You got home safely last night?" he said. "I hope the evening was not too dull for you."

"I enjoyed it tremendously. Philemon came to take me to see the Athenaeum and the Museion."

Philemon said, "I thought she would love to see your house. So we've dropped in. When did you get home?"

"We didn't come home till three o'clock. With Prince Andreyev and the rest, you know. After you left, Pietro played some more music for us."

He invited them to sit down. Philemon thought they should not intrude upon his time.

"Since you are here," he said to Eurydice, "you must take a look at the garden."

The back terrace, paved with large flags, with grass growing along the fissures, was bounded on the south by tall bamboos, casting long shadows over half the place. Close by, large banana leaves, transparent green in the sun, waved lazily in the morning breeze. Though this was the back of the house, it commanded by far the better view of the open country to the east with the advantage of a sense of privacy. Mount Ida, its craggy top now submerged in misty, vapory indistinctness, towered in the distance, while its great slopes studded with cottages and vineyards and pasture land lay spread in the sunlight, making a pretty picture from the elevated terrace. Directly below the terrace, fifty feet down, fringed by a number of stone seats and potted flowers, was a flower and fruit garden, and beyond it tall coconut palms and cedars rose to meet eye level.

Looking up at the superb view of Mount Ida, partly hidden by straying clouds driven by the mountain wind, Eurydice accidentally stumbled upon one of the fissures of the stone pavement. These suedes were her only pair. They had been subjected to some rough treatment in the last few days, walking up and down those hilly, rocky paths. One of the heels had come loose and was hopelessly scuffed and streaked, besides.

Laos caught her just in time, and pulled her up.

"Why don't you go barefooted like Chloe? Or change into sandals?" he said with characteristic frankness. "They are kinder to your toes. You can have a pair made at the shoemaker's in town."

"Certainly not."

There was an overtone of stubbornness in Eurydice's reply. Shoes happened to be a touchy topic with her. She was not without a woman's vanity. It was more than that, too. While working at San Felipe, she had been accustomed to order her shoes from a firm, Laufer & Laufer, in New York. She felt a little apostolic about it. Shoes, to her, represented civilization. Working for DWC, she had been severe with herself, feeling she should set an example to the natives, and of course, she told herself, she must not stint on shoes, whatever else she might sacrifice. The first index of a rising standard of living was the number of shoes manufactured, paid for and worn by the men, women and children in a given population. Her heart went out to the poor Chilean children who went about barefooted. It was only necessary to send a report of the percentage of men, shod and unshod, included in the sociological data for the Geodetic Survey, to convince the DWC that Chile was practically living in a state of dire economic misery, of a sub-standard of living. How the native women's eyes glittered whenever she appeared with a new pair of shoes from New York! She would save on her pull-overs and hats, but on shoes she determined to be extravagant. And justifiably so. She had good ankles to match them.

"No, I'd rather die than go barefoot," she added.

"What's wrong with bare feet?" replied Laos.

"Like a bunch of . . ."

This touched off a most curious and energetic discussion on the human foot between the old philosopher and the young American woman. A discussion entirely unintended. She had hoped to ask him about the meaning of the Ireniki prayer. Now she was caught. Laos meant well, she knew. She did not want to be unkind.

The classification of human civilizations, she had maintained, following the general trend of thinking of her civilization about the "rising standard of living," etc.—the classification of human civilizations fell conveniently into three categories:

shoes = civilization
sandals = semi-barbarism
bare feet = savagery

Consequently, more shoes meant more civilization and economic prosperity. Every man has his prejudices, and Eurydice had hers. The unimaginable misery of the Indians, Indonesians, Africans, and of peoples in all the underdeveloped areas, as evidenced by the general prevalence of bare feet, especially around the equator, was in fact the reason for her throwing herself into the work of economic rehabilitation of the world. If she could make the Java boys and Bali girls wear shoes, she would feel happy. It was a new kind of economic evangelism, bringing the good tidings of a general economic uplift, and presumably of happiness. First food, then shoes. The absence of shoes among the people living near the equator meant that they were living on the level of bare subsistence. On the other hand, the wearing of shoes was a clear index that the local inhabitants had emerged from the struggle for food with an economic surplus.

But she did not have the heart to say, "like a bunch of savages."

Laos felt the rebuke in her eyes. He launched forth with

some evident emotion on a semi-metaphysical and semi-practical disquisition of human iniquity, beginning with the encasement and ending with the deformation of the human foot. The human foot, to begin with, was a noble work of God, a work of wonder, designed perfectly by Nature to deal with every possible situation — for balance, grace, comfort, mobility, flexibility, evaporation, yes, even evaporation. Why, barefootedness was a positive luxury, as every husband and every wife who dared to walk barefoot in their apartment could testify. In a machine civilization, infected with a pathopsychic disease called *philophthoggia* (love of noise in general), one might even discover and appreciate the velvety silence of the barefooted step.

"As for your balancing acts," said Laos, "I cannot profess much admiration. I never liked the circus, or the ballet. There is a beauty of natural rhythm of men walking barefooted, far subtler and more varied."

Who was Laos anyway? A half-Greek, a Cretan boy or a Sicilian who ran barefooted on the hills until he was fifteen or sixteen. No doubt this accounted for his deep-seated prejudice against shoes, tuxedos, neckties. To him these were shackles of the spirit, visible symbols of his bondage. He wore them when he had to. Wasn't that the hidden reason why he had created a situation making it necessary for the Greek government to request firmly his resignation from the diplomatic service? He had, while living in North Europe, abjured two things, belts and suspenders. He was original: he wore short tabs hanging from the inside of his waistcoat which fitted into the buttons on his trousers, in place of suspenders, thus eliminating both suspenders and belt and ensuring a more logical, more equitable distribution of the weight of his lower garments over his shoulders.

Eurydice was visibly weakening. Moreover, she was in despair. The Ireniki shoemakers, she was sure, would never be able to repair her shoes or make any quite as comfortable. The art of making ladies' shoes requires a highly developed and specialized technique; the professional has to take the bull by the horn and produce beauty with comfort, a contradictory and impos-

sible proposition. In other words, he has to develop the know-
how of squeezing the toes, naturally spread out like a phalanx,
into an enthralling, narrow symmetrical point, bend the lady's
metatarsis at a sharp angle, throwing the body weight entirely
upon the ball of the foot, establish a precarious balance by re-
ducing, if not entirely eliminating, the heel to a vanishing point,
and yet have the lady customer pronounce it as entirely comfortable. The Ireniki cobbler could never make it, she was sure.
Her heart sank as she realized that from now on her connection
with the firm of Laufer & Laufer of New York, ladies' shoemakers
since 1962, was severed and there was no chance of replenishing
her supplies.

With much persistence, Laos persuaded her to go to the village cobbler's and have a pair of sandals made. He offered to
accompany her.

"I would never think of it," protested Eurydice.

"I am going down to Giovanni's anyway. Philemon and Chloe,
you are going home, aren't you? It is a shorter way for Chloe
to go straight from here without having to climb up again."

"Are you sure you are going down?" Eurydice repeated.

"Of course."

Philemon and Chloe turned south as they left, and Laos and
Eurydice went down.

"You have no idea how comfortable you will be in sandals.
It will take time. You may not get used to it at first. Take your
time. A foot so long shackled and maladjusted from childhood
will take some months of gradual rehabilitation." Eurydice's
face felt hot. "Maladjusted" and "rehabilitation"! He had taken
the very words out of her mouth. She had been interested in
juvenile delinquency. Was she a maladjusted child to be morally
rehabilitated?

"Re-educate your toes. Give them freedom, they will gradually
recover their mobility and straighten out. Leave the rest to
Nature. I won't urge you to go barefooted at first, until your
toes have been sufficiently educated to hold their own."

Was this to be the beginning of her degradation — the first sign of her abandonment of all that civilization stood for and cherished? Fatalistically, she followed him into the cobbler's shop. She was forced to reveal her feet in Laos' presence.

Slightly abashed, she took off her shoes and socks. It was a point of feminine modesty with her.

"See what you have done to your toes!" Laos flashed at her. "Misshapen! Deformed!" His tone was playful, but certainly he meant it.

She flushed red. It wasn't feminine modesty any more. The impudence of that old man! She would have liked to slap his face, if he were some other man. But not Laos.

"You!" that was all she managed to say.

Strange to say, the little episode gave her the first feeling of intimacy with Laos. She felt vanquished and liked it. They became closer friends from then on.

The question about the Ireniki prayer was left unasked.

Chapter XX

EURYDICE got the impression that Philemon and Chloe had taken her to Laos' house and then left by prearrangement.

"The delicacy of the shrimp marinara is unmatched here," said Laos as he led Eurydice into Giovanni's. "French cuisine for steaks and game; Italian and Basque for sea food. That seems to be the conclusion I have arrived at."

Coming out of the cobbler's, Eurydice had experienced a curious emotion. She was being assimilated by the colonists. The cobbler had treated her with such courtesy; he had with laudable professional care and pride taken out a piece of leather from a top shelf, the best and finest he had, and had bent it to show its fine, flexible quality. "That is the best piece of leather you can find anywhere in the world. I will make the best pair of sandals I ever made in my life — for the Americanitha. *Ba-la-la-la.*"

"What does he say?" Eurydice had asked.

"He says it will be a pair of shoes worthy of your adorable ankles."

She had stepped forth with a feeling of walking out of the best house of women's outfitters on Fifth Avenue in Cincinnati. And then Laos had said, most casually, "Let's go to Giovanni's for lunch." Eurydice could not resist the idea of a *tête-à-tête* with Laos.

Of course Joanna was on her feet, keen with excitement. "Why! You had not told me you were coming!"

She had got down from her cashier's post, where perched on high she could preside over her customers and, through a wide horizontal opening in the door leading to the kitchen, supervise Giovanni's activities, culinary or otherwise. There was a wide wall-mirror, too, on her right; without turning her head, she knew all that was going on in the kitchen. She told Giovanni, at the time of cutting the wide opening, that it was to enable him to peep out from the kitchen and survey his customers. Giovanni said work was work, that he had neither time nor inclination to survey his customers. He agreed, however, that the opening was useful for her to supervise the kitchen maid and see whether she was attending to her chores, such as pouring garbage, flushing the floor, shelling peas, as she was supposed to do.

"To run a business and make it bring in profit," she often said to her husband, "you have to keep your eye on every detail."

"Of course, my sweet."

Now Joanna did not shout across the opening. She said to Laos, "You should have told me," and without waiting for an answer she moved as fast as her feet could carry her to the opening and said, "Pss-t! See who is here!"

Giovanni's head appeared above the opening. Immediately he came out, and wiping his wet hands on his apron, shook Laos' hand and then Eurydice's.

"We are honored. What will you have? Antipasto, of course. I will make it fresh for you. Clams, always fresh of course."

"No clams. We had them last evening."

"Mutton pizziola cooked in olive oil with garlic, marinara sauce with fresh peppers and mushrooms. Or we have good fish—merluzzo fried crisp, or with sauce Veneziana, with onions and white wine — any style you like. Or perhaps chicken arregante."

"What is chicken arregante?"

"Sautéed in hot oil, with garlic and parsley and oregano. And green noodles to go with it!"

"This is for lunch. Don't make it too elaborate. It sounds heavy, doesn't it!"

"The midday meal is the heavy meal here. They have their siestas after dinner."

"Here!" said Joanna, as she sweetly put a newly laundered cook's cap on Giovanni's head and adjusted it. "And here!" she handed him a new apron. She turned to the guests. "It is a great pleasure. The dinner is on the house. Giovanni will cook the best meal for you. Would you like to bring some other guests, or would you rather be alone?"

"Alone," said Laos.

Meanwhile she was helping to tie the apron on her husband. Giovanni said something in Italian, which probably meant he could do it very well himself, that she had better attend to the wine, and then beamed a big smile on them.

"I would not know what to do without my Joanna, a wonderful help, so devoted!"

Joanna flashed a smile at her husband for their benefit.

She went to the front door and shouted, "Alberto! Alberto!"

Alberto, her sixteen-year-old son, was sitting on the steps of one of the houses on the square, talking with other boys. He dashed up.

"Go downstairs, and fetch the *grand cru*, 1985."

Meanwhile they had settled on chicken and green noodles. And *caffè diavolo*. After the wine was brought, Laos sent Alberto to tell Emma-Emma that Eurydice would not be home for lunch.

While they picked at the black olives and eggplant slices, hot and freshly made, rolled and filled with anchovy, chopped mushrooms and pimiento, Laos asked,

"Did you see our film library?"

"No."

"I should like you to see it — educational films, travel films and others — when you have time."

"I was greatly impressed by the Athenaeum and the Museion. And the beautiful statue of Athanopoulos. You must have spent a lot of thought on all this."

"We have. The arts are a necessity in human life, don't you think? They minister to the pleasures of the mind as food and wine minister to the pleasures of the palate. . . . Taste that egg-plant. A good chef is an artist, too. It is all a matter of divining and bringing out the essence of the eggplant — that individual piquant, aromatic flavor. It is like any other art, trying to record a subtle, evanescent, almost imperceptible flavor which the hustling world passes over without ever noticing, and giving it form and expression. Poetry is no more than that. It is surprising how men have learned to live without art, feel no need for it at all, let their sensibilities atrophy as it were. Then men become coarse and vulgar."

And then with characteristic frankness Laos said, "I've been worried about you since your arrival."

"About me? What for?"

"In the first place, we want you to be happy here. If your friend were here — Paul was his name? — you would probably marry and have children. As it is, the matter is on our conscience. I do hope that you will not find it too difficult to adjust yourself to a permanent captivity on this island. In the second place, frankly I do not want your people ever to come in search of you. Thainos, Paradise on the Pacific — I can visualize the screaming headlines in American newspapers. Then a swarm of tourists. Then your DWC may want to take us in hand, order us to do this and do that. The whole place will be corrupted, vitiated. Tell me, will they ever find out — such a big world organization?"

Eurydice told him she did not think there was much chance of that. They had left no signs, nothing in writing about their discovery of the island. Of course it was possible their papers and photographs at San Felipe might be sealed up by the police authorities and eventually find their way to the DWC authorities. They would then have some idea of the area they had covered and follow up. On the other hand, they would certainly give them up for dead when several months had passed.

"I feel much relieved after hearing you say that."

Chicken was being served. Joanna stood guard at the door, keeping an eye on the service. Some people were coming in for a drink, or for lunch. With the consummate tact of a born maître d'hôtel, she took the plate of chicken from Alberto and brought it herself, and poured some more wine into the glasses.

"A wonderful woman," remarked Laos when she had left.

"In what sense?"

"In the sense of a woman, interesting, alive. I see, especially highlighted in her, the very stuff of philosophy — human emotions, human desires. The virility of that woman, her faith in herself. She knows what she wants in life. A philosopher is liable to lose himself in his own world of ideas, to fall in love with his imaginary laws and cycles of history, his inner necessities and inescapable conclusions. He juggles with them, arranges them in his own imaginary order. He forgets human beings, the men and women. I aim my bead at her when I deal with philosophic questions. I'd rather aim too low, than too high. . . . Eat the chicken with your fingers. That is the best way, and wipe your fingers on the bib."

The bib was tucked below Eurydice's neck. It proved most useful when it came to the green noodles with the splashing red tomato and meat sauce.

The chicken, spiced with garlicky flavor, was certainly heavenly.

"Philosophy is made for man, not man for philosophy. The twentieth-century philosophers were like dress designers making dresses, but feeling no obligation for any woman to wear them."

"You are pragmatic," said Eurydice wiping her fingers on her napkin.

"It is a good word. In Greek, *pragma* means a business, a job to be done. We have to take the phenomenal world as it is. Life is a job to be done, not to be argued about."

"May I ask you a question?"

"Certainly."

"I was impressed by the Ireniki prayer inscribed on the porch of the Athenaeum. I like its open-eyed quality, its simplicity."

"I am glad you like it."

"Tell me something about it."

"Well, I spent a good deal of thought on that. In the first place, you will notice that I do not say: *We believe*, but rather, let us try to believe. I am so afraid of incrustations of the mind. I want it only to be a statement of present, common beliefs, of a common attitude, in words simple and flexible, so that it will remain a prayer, a mental attitude, and not a code of articles. I don't want it to become a creed. You agree that creeds are a series of definitions, intellectual in character; a prayer is a matter of the heart. The Bible states, but does not define. Creeds were formed when the Christian fathers began to argue. What does the great Chuangtse say? 'It is said that one who argues does so because he does not see certain points.' People who like to argue have an inveterate belief in words, in speech, not knowing how tricky words always are. You agree that the creeds are not found in the Bible, do you not?"

"True," replied Eurydice.

"Of course. Why do you think creeds were formed at all?"

"I suppose the early Christians wanted to agree on what to believe."

"Is it not true that they wanted others to believe exactly the same things as they did?"

"That must be the reason."

"Do you not think that men who wanted others to believe exactly as they did must have been sure that they were right?"

"I am sure they were."

"Is that a good sign or a bad sign?"

"I do not quite follow what you mean."

"I mean that such men must be one hundred per cent sure that they are absolutely right, and others who differ from them absolutely wrong. In other words, they must be dogmatic, to wish to lay down for others, and for all posterity, what they themselves believe, and to permit no discussion of it hereafter."

"That must be their intent. Those who disagreed would be heretics."

"In other words, creeds were formed when men's minds began to harden instead of remaining soft and pliable. Is that a good or bad sign?"

"Bad, I say."

"Could you quarrel with certain articles of the creed, if the subject were open for discussion? I am asking a hypothetical question; I know it is not. I mean if your mind were free, could you have differences of opinion regarding some of the beliefs of your religion?"

"Conceivably yes."

"And after these thousands of years, do you find that you can quarrel with the Lord's Prayer?"

"Certainly not."

"There you are. You see what I mean."

"I follow you."

Laos had torn the meat from the drumstick; for some time he had been nibbling at the tendons around the joints. "I hope I am not interfering with your chicken dinner. Go ahead and eat. It is a bad habit of mine, asking questions."

"I don't mind at all."

Holding the bare drumstick, Laos leaned back in his chair, now and then brandishing it at her as he talked. He poured himself another glass.

"As you have a perspicacious mind," he went on, "you must have perceived a sequence in the thoughts of the Ireniki prayer. The arrangement is not casual. Since the Enlightenment of the eighteenth century, a great change has come over the spiritual content of modern civilization. More and more attention was paid to matter, less and less to man. For the eighteenth-century rationalists the whole of the prayer was common knowledge. And the eighteenth-century men were the most optimistic of all. The opportunity to live the good life was the concern of the philosophers. It was in fact old-fashioned in Voltaire's and Leibnitz' days. Up to Kant, the last part about wonder of the universe was still good. But Kant was already desperately retrieving what was slipping; in the search by critical reason, what he called Pure Thought, the reasons for working fruitfully, enduring nobly, and living happily found no basis, and the optimism of the rationalists was thrown into academic contempt. The eternal beauty of the stars above and the small voice of the conscience within were classified by Kant as categorical imperatives. That means he could not define them, reduce them or prove them, except that he was immediately aware of their existence. But the men of the mid-nineteenth century were still able to believe in it, to affirm it — witness the stentorian voice of Carlyle. Can you imagine a twentieth-century Carlyle?

"The generation of Carlyle and Darwin and Spencer saw a critical change; optimism and pessimism hung in balance. The voice of social reformers could still be heard from Comte to Spencer — society is ours as we create and improve it. Matthew Arnold still spoke of seeing life steadily and seeing it whole, as the ancient Greeks did. Now our scholars of the Old World are concerned only in seeing life in highly specialized aspects of highly specialized departments, each scholar content with an exact but somewhat tortuous view of some inconsequential fragment. The whole of the prayer except the first sentence had been scrapped out of the realm of philosophy. All that remained of philosophy was history of philosophy.

"As for the men of the first half of the twentieth century, only the first line remained valid. Certainly, neither in science, nor in the so-called social sciences, was the central problem of war and society marked by simplicity; rather confusion and artifices of the mind, by which I mean the academic quasi-scientific terminology like 'behavior pattern' and 'anti-social tendencies,' and 'integrated individual'— a kind of diluted English, dehydrated, effeminate and robbed of virility. Can you imagine anyone growing enthusiastic about 'behavior patterns,' any more than about blood counts and cardiographs in a laboratory? Thought had been systematically purged of its moral content. Their social philosophers were scared of the words, right and wrong. Science is concerned with the true, not the good; hence their social philosophers, who insisted on being 'scientists,' were afraid to touch the good, and thought their function was merely to give an accurate historical description of man's social behavior. Environment and heredity absolved man from all sins. If the social scientists could account for Satan's strange behavior by reference to his father, or to an episode in his childhood, their work was done; it was considered a gain in knowledge.

"Then toward 1950, only half of the first line, 'Let us take time to think,' had any semblance of validity. Man was still trying to think, and think hard. After 1970 thinking became impossible. Men were too busy escaping bombs and ruination. And after the psychic exhaustion of the wars of 1989 to 1998, I imagine man's prayer was further shortened to 'Let us take time' only — to do what, they did not know. Nowhere else in the history of philosophy and of human civilization, East or West, ancient or modern, was philosophy so completely divorced from the conduct of life. Most extraordinary. Thus ended a complete cycle of man's psychic exhaustion, until we come around, with a certain naïveté, to man's moral problems where the eighteenth-century man had left off. Thus during the past two hundred years man has been thinking furiously and very successfully about matter, but very little about man, and the opportunity to live the good life has been lost."

As Eurydice sat listening, she imagined she was experiencing the airplane crash she had so many times feared on her trips, when everything around her went up in a burst of flame.

"And so," Laos concluded, "the logical development of civilization was thwarted; the opportunity to live the good life was lost. Nature abhors vacuums; man's moral philosophy had become a vacuum. Of course there had to be wars. Between the four wars, unprofitable learning filled the rest, great wonderful learning, heaps of it, more than we could comfortably digest. But there was no clearing house. Man was smothered by the sheer weight of knowledge he had piled up around himself. That was how the dinosaurus became extinct, because of the enormous disparity between bodily weight and brain. There was nevertheless sufficient advance in knowledge of matter to maintain the illusion that human progress was being made."

Laos had spoken easily, fluently, but with conviction, a heretical fire shining in his eyes. How he could talk, summarizing the thought of two centuries in a couple of paragraphs. Of course, it wasn't that simple; he made it look simple. Eurydice, forgetting all about the chicken, had listened, inspired. That was Laos all right; she had a glimpse of his world of thought. The sharp knife of his mind had fallen on a huge Gordian knot of entangled ideas.

Ah, the caffè diavolo! The French would call it café diable. Coffee with a sting in it.

"Few things, Eurydice," said Laos, his eyes gleaming, "few things can so reconcile us to this earthly existence as a good meal. Don't you agree?"

"Why does everybody call me Eurydice?"

"Since we have made you a life captive, a permanent member of our community, we thought we should give you a pretty Greek name, the prettiest we could think of. Eurydice, the beloved of Orpheus. Don't you like it?"

"I like it. Are you trying to make me lose my sense of identity?"

"Not at all. Certainly I wouldn't call you Miss Maverick. And Barbara — that suggests *barbarikos*. No!"

Chapter XXI

BETWEEN SIPS of the Devil's coffee, time hung heavy. The other guests, having finished their dinner, took out their pipes and sat, engaged in slow, good-natured prattle, or in throwing dice; others, more nobly inclined, stretched out their legs and did nothing at all. Time always hung heavy on this island. Everybody got up at ten on this island, it seemed. Oh, the sensuous delight, the pleasurable laziness of sleeping late, with nothing on one's mind, and the enjoyment of a perfect sleep!

"Have you decided to move over and live with Iolanthe?" asked the philosopher.

The green noodles with the rich Bolognese sauce had not quite agreed with Eurydice. But the coffee had helped. She lowered her lashes.

"I haven't even met her. Is she a heretic — like yourself?"

"You mean is she sane like myself? She is, very sane — and captivating. I really think you should. I think you will really be more comfortable. And Emma-Emma is like a hermit; research is her life. She loves your company, I am sure, as a fellow American. But a scholar is usually sufficient unto himself. You can still always come and see her of course. Perhaps it might be more convenient for her. She has Bowena. . . ."

The mention of Bowena recalled to her last night's episode. "Bowena," she said and abruptly broke off.

"What about her?"

"Bowena is a good girl," she said rather flatly, not wishing to

173

purvey gossip and cause her trouble. "Tell me about Iolanthe. Isn't Prince Andreyev her father?"

"Yes. Her mother, a Greek woman of Smyra, is dead. She came here with her father when she was a child of ten or eleven. Andreyev saw to it that Athanopoulos fell in love with her. And she was extremely attractive — a mixture of Russian and Greek, you know — dark hair and all that, and accomplished; good brains, not like her father. We used to call her Princess. She dropped it when she grew up. They used to have liveried servants. She dropped that, too. She always had a mind of her own, even as a child. I don't blame Athanopoulos for falling in love with her. Perfection of body, brilliance of mind, yet gay and sensible and feminine. One of Nature's successful experiments — rather rare, I must admit. Frankly idolatrous — you will frequently find her speaking without inhibitions. But you will like her."

"Does she get along with the Countess?"

"Yes, they are friends. She usually includes her in her parties. She is now the widow. It was all so long ago."

"You say she is idolatrous?"

"Yes. She says it makes her happy to believe in the stars, to people the heavens with gods and goddesses, Orion and Daphne, and all that. All nature is alive for her. She feels it, believes in it, and there's no use arguing with her."

A man strode up to the table whom she recognized as Groucho. Tall with an athletic figure, he was easily distinguishable from the other guests, if only by the lilt of his walk, the walk of a shambling peacock. Suave, friendly, easy, he looked the picture of a man happy with himself, confident of himself, lord of his destiny and captain of his soul. He exuded male virility; broad shoulders, hairy chest and a short-clipped, stubby beard, and that peculiar amble, a sign of superabundance of energy, which marked either the human male or the peacock displaying his feathers before the weaker sex.

Eurydice had not seen Groucho come in, so absorbed was she in Laos' conversation. While having his lunch, Groucho repeatedly tried to catch her eye, but without success. This was a mortifying experience. He thought of walking right over to say "Hullo," perhaps even giving a friendly pat on her shoulder. He had not seen her since the day of the funeral. And here was Barbara Maverick, from his own country, the U.S.A.; an Ohio girl if he remembered correctly, young, lonely, marriageable, exciting. All girls were exciting, but Barbara — he mentally called her Barbara — in a special sense. She was the only American young woman on this island, and he the only American man, and she was a lady in distress; in his own language and way of thinking, a dame in a hot spot. She was behind the eight ball, all right. He remembered Paul. Not much of a man, was he? Paul with his spectacles, his hand shaking with the gun. And Barbara looked and talked like a college-bred girl, a little too high-class for him. But wasn't she a woman?

The point was, he had not seen an American girl for a long, long time.

He decided it was better not to disturb their conversation now. He would wait until after dinner, and then he would have a better chance for a real talk. Perhaps he would be able to take her out. Yes, that hairdo, that unmistakable gait and pace and that look of independence and hearty gaiety, of one able to take care of one-self, was distinctly and to him familiarly American. He felt so homesick; he had not felt so for years now. The old dream came back to him, a dream long forgotten, the fulfillment of his life ambition. He had, while a boy, pictured himself, tall and hand-some in his white overall, owner of a filling station, friendly, inde-pendent, a smile for everybody, looking over broad spaces along some highway, and able to detect and locate engine troubles and give advice to women drivers, hearing the pleasant ding of the bell when a car drew up, bringing in money to his business. He had taken lessons at a night school in automotive repairs and service. Then the war came and he was drafted. He was still handling instruments as a navigator pilot. Then the crash-landing and all that followed. A long, long forgotten dream!

"Hello there," said Groucho.

Eurydice answered with a mild "Hello," with less fervor than

Groucho had expected, as being due to a fellow American. She disliked him. She remembered he was the first man to demand that Paul put down his gun, with that swaggering tone she knew so well; he had been part of the plan to betray her and Paul, to act as decoy while they destroyed their plane. Of course, Laos was responsible, had ordered it, yet she did not hold it against Laos. It was rather the young man's coarseness, his unthinking masculine pride and facile assumption that every girl must admire a husky male like himself and his cheap reference to girls, which aroused her resentment, particularly because he was a fellow American. There was no difficulty in understanding him. But she would rather not have America represented by that type of female-conquering he-man. Emma-Emma was a scholar. Emma-Emma thought; he didn't, she was sure. She wondered what he was doing here. Had he gone to seed, lost himself in drinks and women, perhaps?

"Glad to see you about. I hear they are calling you Eurydice." He had straddled a chair, eyes gazing at her, simple, direct and a trifle familiar.

"So they do."

"That's a swell name for a gal. Your real name isn't that."

"Barbara Maverick."

"Well, Barbara!"

"Call me Eurydice, or call me Miss Maverick."

"Why, what's the idea? You are not sore, or anything."

"No. Why should I be?"

"All right, Eurydice. Me thinking that here's a long time I haven't seen an American gal, and we should be good pals, shouldn't we? Ain't yer happy to see a fellow American out here?"

"Sure."

"Me thinking that perhaps you will be glad to find one who can talk good English with you."

"Cut out your thinking," said Eurydice pertly. "All right, Groucho. I call you Groucho, and you call me Eurydice. Is that all right?"

"Sure, sure. That's fine. I can show you around. I know everybody here. Laos, don't I?"

"Where are you from?"

"Oklahoma City, Oklahoma. A great town. Have you ever been there?"

"No."

"A great town. A fellow has a hell of a good time there. A lot of fellows moved up from Texas, as the climate changed. Rivers all dried up."

"Do you miss America?"

"I did. What could I do? Buried in this island; no news, no radio. . . . Well, I adapted myself. Now I like it. The only thing I miss is the baseball season."

Light came into Eurydice's eyes. "Oh, yes. Do you know what? The day before I left San Felipe I heard on the radio the Milwaukee Braves were three games ahead. Angelo Reese had had the flu. . . ."

"Who is Reese?"

"Say, where have you been? No, I suppose you wouldn't know. The best pitcher in the world. He yielded two walks to fill the bases in the ninth inning and they had to take him out of the game."

"That's sad."

"He may be back pitching again, and here we are talking twaddle. It's criminal."

The mention of baseball suddenly obliterated Eurydice's antipathy toward the man, made her feel friendly.

"What are you doing here?"

"What do you think?"

"I can't guess. Not coaching baseball by any chance?"

"No. I work at the electric plant here."

Laos had been listening amused. He said, "Quite a mechanic. He is doing fine."

Groucho visibly sat up, waiting for him to go on. Laos didn't. "Sure, I am doing fine."

Laos smiled. "He wanted to fight everybody when he first came. All of us were honored with the name bastard. Then we discovered he was quite a genius at tinkering with machines. He fixed up the movie projector for us."

"Why don't you get yourself a Greek name?" asked Eurydice.

"Groucho is quite Greek, I am told."

"How is the solar motor?" Laos suddenly asked.

"It's producing three and one-half h.p. I figure that if we could get the temperature up to 1,200 degrees, through black body radiation, we might really have something. Dr. Artemos is working on it. Then we'll have to build a more powerful compressor, with safety cut-out switch."

Eurydice felt good to hear all this, proud that this American did not disgrace her nation after all. Groucho turned to her:

"It's working all right. Not as cheap as hydroelectric power. But it works. I think we have the right approach. We've made a start. One can always improve when the right approach is found. I'll be glad to show it to you."

"Where is it?"

"On the dam. Right in the electric plant. We are experimenting with a small model of course. Say, will you have dinner with me?"

"Perhaps. In a few days. I am moving."

"Where to?"

"Iolanthe has invited me to stay with her."

"Say, you are getting class."

"Why?"

"She has never invited me. So you are moving to the top. Of course, a pretty young girl like you. But don't try to put on that highbrow stuff with me."

Eurydice said to Laos, "I thought — Emma-Emma told me you wanted to put a moratorium on scientific progress, and here you go inventing a solar motor."

"I don't know what she told you. I am not against scientific progress, I am for making more intelligent use of it than man has done. Electric power, for instance. Why should any sane man be against it? We imported the whole machinery here for the hydroelectric plant. And this solar motor is different. It is a new, fundamental source of power. I am very enthusiastic about it in fact.

And I believe we are succeeding in harnessing the power from the sun's heat. Once that is done, we'll usher in a new world. Do you notice one thing? Electric power is an unqualified boon to humanity. It hasn't augmented in any appreciable degree the explosive power of war. And with the solar motor, we'll actually only be producing electric power, store it up as a source of energy."

"That will be something, won't it?" said Eurydice, getting interested. "When we can harness the vast atomic energy of the sun. The scientists in the Old World — as you call it — have been working on it for decades. And it will be a cheap, almost costless and inexhaustible source of power."

Groucho said, "Cheap and inexhaustible. That's it. The enemy of utilization of sun's heat is radiation. I think we've licked the problem. We've found the right high-temperature alloy."

"I think you ought to go back and take a nap," said Laos. "You should take good care of yourself in this climate."

"I don't take afternoon naps," replied Eurydice. "I am not used to it."

"Everybody does on this island. A siesta is good for you. Go and live with Iolanthe. It is much cooler higher up. There's a continual breeze from the sea at the crest."

"I think I shall. When shall I go?"

"Any day you like."

Groucho said, "I shall be glad to be of service. I shall come and get your things for you."

"There's really nothing. I haven't even a suitcase."

They rose. Laos insisted on paying, but Joanna would not think of it. She sent them to the door and asked particularly Eurydice to come again.

"Do you come here often?" Eurydice asked Laos. "I hear you have a very good cook at home."

"Oh, Eugénie is getting old. She bosses me," said Laos pleasantly. "And I sometimes want a change."

Outside the door, Sister Teresa had been waiting quietly. She said sweetly to Laos when they came out:

"Can you come to the convent when you are free? Clymene

wants to speak to you. Hello, Eurydice, when are you coming to see us?" She was a picture of innocence and sweet piety. Her few English words, clearly pronounced, were charming. She understood the language better than she spoke it.

"I shall come. This is only my third day out."

Laos said he would go to see Clymene. He said good-by to Eurydice, who thanked him heartily for the dinner.

"Drop in any time at my house," he said.

Eurydice felt very grateful to the generous old philosopher for giving her so much of his time, as she saw him leaving the square, a masculine figure in his white long tunic and his thought-packed head covered with a mass of white hair. The excitement she had felt in talking to him person-to-person hadn't entirely left her; the novelty of his ideas still caused a minor stir in her breast.

Groucho said he would accompany her home, but she told him there was no need; it was such a short distance. Besides, Sister Teresa seemed to claim her attention.

Slightly rebuffed, Groucho said good-by. "Be sure to call on me if there's anything I can do for you." This meeting had not been entirely satisfactory, but it also had left him not entirely without hope. Eurydice saw his long, ambling strides disappear across the square and thought him extremely funny.

She turned with Sister Teresa toward home. They entered the narrow, shaded alley.

"You are well, I hope?" said the young nun.

"Completely. Thank you."

"God bless you! Please do come to the convent. It's very *pittoresco* on the other side of the *collina*."

"I shall be going to live with Iolanthe."

"Oh, Iolanthe!" Her young voice chirped. Her breast heaved a little. A perceptible color mounted her face, and then she compressed her lips and her face assumed a limpid purity again.

"I hear she is a very attractive woman," said Eurydice. "Everybody on this island is so kind."

"Yes, very beautiful and very unreligious. Are you going to stay there long?"

"I don't know. She has invited me to."

"I envy you. You have met the Prince, her father?"

"Yes. Prince Andreyev Somovarvitch." Eurydice giggled. She loved to pronounce that name.

"Why do you smile?"

"Something very funny in that name. You won't understand. Something not very proper for you to hear."

Teresa's lips formed a surprised circle. The innocent girl said involuntarily, "Such a tall prince, like what you see in storybooks. A real great-grandson of Czar Alexander III. He stands a full head above the others in the church. He sings, too, out of key, but he sings. He will never follow the organist; he leads. We have a little organ; sometimes I play during the service, sometimes Margherita. Margherita, she follows him, catches up with him. I don't; I play louder and resist him, try to keep him in line. But it is no use. He must lead; the Prince must always lead. Such a manly voice! Once he spoke to me after the service; he asked why I was not following him. He said we must praise God with vigor, in stately, martial measures. Do I express myself correctly?"

"Very correctly."

"Yes, stately, martial, like himself. And before Father Donatello concludes his prayer, while he is invoking the name of the Holy Father and the Son, he says Amen. He does not allow Father Donatello to say the Holy Ghost. So Father Donatello says Amen after he says Amen."

"What did you say to him when he spoke to you?"

"Why, I could not say a word. I blushed. He is so tall! He says we must be more hearty, more spirited, when worshiping God, whether singing or praying to Him — with more — how do you pronounce that word? — entusiasmo. A very difficult word for me to pronounce."

"We say punch in America. It is easier to say."

"Punch, you say? Like in boxing?"

"Yes, pray to God with more punch. . . . Doesn't Father Donatello dare to speak to him, ask him not to interrupt his prayer?"

"He told him. The Prince said he was sorry; he could not help it. He was always bursting to say Amen, it poured out of his heart. The next Sunday, he did the same. He says God does not like lazy people."

"What do you sisters think of him?"

"We adore him. Margherita says she loves him, in the spiritual sense of course. I love him, too, in the spiritual sense. You'll be seeing a lot of him, then."

"I believe so."

They had come to Emma-Emma's cottage. Sister Teresa said she should not tarry. She had come to bring Laos a message from Clymene, Oaxus' wife. She had tarried too long already. Mother Superior would not like it.

Chapter XXII

"BUT, LAOS, BE REASONABLE," said Thrasymachus in Iolanthe's house a week later. Iolanthe was giving a party for Eurydice. There were the people she had met at the Countess', and a few new faces, too, including Thrasymachus and the Orthodox priest Aristotimus. The two latter gentlemen were equally tall and made a pretty picture with Prince Andreyev. "Be reasonable. You and Athanopoulos promised us when we came that the tax would be only 10 per cent. Why should I pay 12½?"

"Is it not fair?" replied Laos. "The Council of the Republic have decided. The music and song tax, 3 per cent; education tax, 3 per cent; welfare tax, 3 per cent, and public administration 1 per cent. The total is still 10 per cent. In your case, why did you choose to go ahead and produce a fourth child? What if everybody did the same? The island will be overpopulated in a generation or two, and there will not be enough food for everybody. Where are we going to emigrate? We will be shut up on this island and try to eat one another. Those are the regulations, officially adopted by the Council. I don't see why you should be made an exception. And if you insist on going ahead with multiplying Thrasymachus babies, it will be raised to 15, 17½, and 20 per cent, progressively. That's the decision of the Council."

"The Council!" said Thrasymachus. "You are the Council. I, for one, find it hard to prevail against you at the deliberations. Your music and song tax! Wasting the public's money on amusements for the people. Why should public administration get only 1 per

183

cent while what you call music and song tax take away 3 per cent."

"You forget that the 3 per cent includes the religion tax — up-keep of the church festivals. It costs money to support the Institute of Comforters of Men's Souls, to train singers, dancers, musicians. Unfortunately, these things are expensive; unlike restaurants which cater to our physical needs, they cannot bring sufficient income and support themselves. Left alone, the arts die out. I wish you well, Thrasymachus, but the Institute has received more applicants than it can take care of. Your own daughter benefits from it. A little contribution from you will help take care of a few more applicants."

Thrasymachus was unhappy. It appeared he was one of the original founders of the colony. A good Christian of peasant stock, he had joined the S. S. *Arcadia* on a mistaken private theory that the friendship of a multimillionaire like Athanopoulos was worth cultivating: the opportunity for forming an intimate friendship was bound to be present when they were on board the same ship and on the island. He had not believed in the nonsense that the S. S. *Arcadia* was never going to return, that a man of Athanopoulos' wealth was going to quit his millions and settle on some primitive island. He was sure that the millionaire had something up his sleeve, that there was a treasure island, or at least some incredibly lucrative venture afoot, for which he needed the assistance and labor of a large colony. So he told his wife. No, Athanopoulos was not mad; he was just imaginative. Perhaps he would return after five years a co-partner of Athanopoulos, Incorporated, a millionaire himself. He had given up a well-established chandler's business, selling ship supplies at the port of Piraeus. When he found that S. S. *Arcadia* was going to sail back, never to return, he was distraught, puzzled. Not in his forty-five years had he seen such madness. Disillusioned and profoundly shocked, he changed his mind. His sharp business acumen enabled him to see the many business opportunities present. There was not much prospect in ropes, wool, furniture. But wine and tobacco, above all, wine! Everybody was going to smoke and drink. Thrasymachus' brew would be the universal liquid to quench the tropical thirsts of the islanders, Irenikis and Thainians alike. He was absolutely right. His brewery prospered, practically the only big industry on the island. He had at first, with rare perceptiveness, supported the music and song tax since Attic festivals as he knew them were conducive to the bacchanalian spirit — gallons and gallons would be consumed. Wine and music and song were related; consequently the promotion of music and song would be a favorable factor in the long run for the consumption of spirits. To that extent he was justified. He had grown rich; was in fact one of the richest men in the colony, a parvenu, as compared with Iolanthe, but respectable and respected. Of course he had fought tooth and nail at the Council meetings against a wine and tobacco surtax — and had succeeded. He had consistently opposed money on the "idle arts." They had been wrangling at the Council meetings ever since.

When Athanopoulos died, Thrasymachus' seniority, his businesslike ability, and his long beard and his wealth, gave him a position of great importance in the community. He had long given up the idea of returning to Piraeus and made up his mind to found a dynasty of Thrasymachuses, chiefly by thrift and denying himself the good things of life. His daughter Eretrea and his two sons Andreas and Laertes hated him for the pusillanimous meals they had at home. But he had risen to become a pillar of the Ireniki community, was made treasurer of many public funds and was one of the ten elders of the island. He fought Laos at the committee meetings. The two minds just never met. Art was an extravagant waste, a frivolity, an amusement, like schoolchildren chalking figures on walls, having no place in the serious world of adult responsibilities. He had disapproved of the project of the Museion when it was first brought up, and of course saw no point in the Institute of Comforters of Men's Souls. Good Christians, he avowed, should not permit the pagan custom of having hetaeras. He had some mistaken notions of the Institute himself. He found himself standing alone, even in his own family. Against his wish, his daughter Eretrea had entered the Institute to receive its training. He found he was fighting with the support of only a few women, against a floodtide of pagan instincts and beliefs, long suppressed at home, now overrunning the island under the leadership and encouragement of Laos.

The daughter Eretrea was the youngest. It had almost been a catastrophe for him; he had counted upon three sons. He had named the child before it was born, and Eretrea it remained. That was why he was caught. He would try a fourth child. He was big enough; the law was for the small fry — Anacharsis had said. The cobweb was for catching the small insects; he was a big insect. He had not expected Laos to be so doctrinaire about it. The fourth child was born a month ago; it had turned out to be another girl. And now a 12½ per cent tax! It was an injustice, an outrage, an imposition on his good nature and a lack of appreciation for his contributions to the Ireniki society. What was worse, if he did not fight it now, and if he had a fifth child, the tax on his income would be revised to 15 per cent. Of course the Council could vote an exemption in his favor, in recognition of his lifelong devotion to the advancement of public welfare, etc.

That was why he had taken this opportunity to draw Laos to a corner and try to influence him. He knew Iolanthe of course. In fact, he was quite friendly to Stephan. He was thinking of Eretrea, of the day when the House of Athanopoulos and the House of Thrasymachus might be joined together in a happy union. He protested against the general characterization of the young son of Athanopoulos as a witless, useless young man. Witless, but certainly not useless, he maintained. Stephan would come into the vast inheritance of Athanopoulos. Let Stephan provide the property. He himself and his son Andreas could provide the brains, apparently so lacking in Stephan.

In short, he was both friendly and fatherly to Stephan. Now the young people were playing cards in one of the side rooms.

It was yet early for supper. Iolanthe, subtly dressed in a long muslin veil and a swathing silk wrapped around her body, was standing, grace itself, by the parapet of the white terrace overlooking the southern shore. She had promised Athanopoulos on his deathbed never to let down her long beautiful hair for another man's eyes to look upon, and she had kept her promise. Her hair was partly done up in an upswept coil, pinned to the veil by a glittering brooch. She was talking with Eunice who came in her frightful high-collared, white-laced frock. The Countess was inside occupied with young Wriggs.

Eurydice, who had moved in three days ago, was delighted with the place, situated on the breezy heights, and its superb view. She was standing on the terrace with the hostess and Eunice, looking out on the southern shore. To their right spread the lagoon and the falling slopes of the country, with patches of green and yellowing corn in the shade, and straggling cottages with pale pink walls blushing in the setting sun. To their left, Mount Ida stood in the full glory of the evenglow, its brazen-tinted craggy summit now perfectly outlined against the eastern sky. The ridge upon which the Residence was built extended on their left in the southerly direction following the irregular bulging shoreline, covered with pines, baring its western edge in sharp, perpendicular, reddish-brown cliffs, pitted with sea birds' nests, some three hundred feet above the sea. Further south, the land rose once again to form a hillock upon which stood a white convent, named after St. Catherine, and then swept by graceful slopes slowly toward the valley beyond.

Eurydice rather envied the striking dress worn by Iolanthe, designed to bring out the beauty of a woman's head and shoulders. The dress hung upon her shoulder on one side in a long continuous flowing line to her ankles, leaving her arms completely bare, arms of compact flesh, *sarkopagos*, as the Greeks called it, delighting in its supple comeliness. In spite of her forty years, she still retained her model's figure, the figure in imported marble Athanopolous had commissioned Melitus, teacher of Philemon, now deceased, to commit to immortality, standing modestly in Athanopoulos' bedroom, which Eurydice was now occupying. Eurydice herself was dressed in a light fluffy, gathered blouse, low-necked, worn over her tight-fitting black matador breeches, ribboned below her knees, now called "sleeks" in contrast to the sloppy slacks, and that pair of dyed and refurbished high heels. It had become the general fashion for young American women to prefer the pajama effect. For evening, trousers of soft silken materials, cut very broad toward the ankles, like bloomers, in pink, peach and pastels, had taken the place of long, trailing skirts. The women called these "swaddles"; sleeks for daytime wear, and swaddles for the evening; it is difficult to account for the origin of words. Fashion critics spoke of this vogue in the 1990's as the "Persian period." Iolanthe had urged her to keep her sleeks; it was novel, unique and exciting at Thainos; and she had a pair of swaddles cut and made for her according to her instructions.

"I think I'd better go in to change," said Eurydice.

"I am sure it will be stunning," replied Iolanthe.

"She is very pretty, isn't she?" said Iolanthe after Eurydice left them.

"And quite intelligent," replied Eunice, "it must be difficult for her to get adjusted to our ways."

"I had a long talk with her, as between women, you know. A girl of twenty-five . . ."

"How do you know?"

"She told me herself."

"I thought American girls never told their age."

"Probably she is different. A girl of twenty-five can judge men pretty well; she won't find it so easy to find a man to satisfy her. I mentioned Groucho, not seriously, and she laughed. Naturally, she is confused, somewhat bewildered. She used to work hard. Now suddenly she has nothing to do. We have to find something for her to do, or she will be bored."

"I have caught her listless looks from time to time."

"Of course. The sudden loss of her fiancé upset her, left her adrift. She is lost and alone. That's why I have invited her to come and stay with me." She added with a knowing blink, "But don't worry. She will find a man, and then everything will be all right. That's what I told her. We had a long talk, and she was quite frank about it."

"I like her keen, open eyes."

"Too keen, perhaps. Looks as if she always readies herself to tackle something. Too undeceived, too open-minded, too American. Actually, I think she is more charming when she is a little listless. When she lets her eyes be veiled in thought. Helplessness in women always fascinates men. It never fails. She will learn."

Eurydice now appeared in her "swaddles," banded in deep Oriental brocade. The deep lavender agreed with the soft tan of her skin. "How do I look?" she said, eyes beaming.

"How flattering!" said Eunice.

"Divine!" exclaimed Iolanthe. "A woman is never quite happy when her dress does not do full justice to her figure, don't you think?"

"Or her undress," remarked Eunice dryly. "The public always likes a well-undressed woman."

"You are funny, very funny."

"But it's true. Praxiteles' draped Venus did not survive the ages; his undraped one did, don't you see?"

"Joking apart," said Iolanthe, "I must say that those swaddles are very becoming. . . . Here comes Chloe. She is walking in a dream."

Chloe and Philemon had come out to join them. Philemon's eyes surveyed Eurydice's costume critically and appreciatively.

"Where are they, I mean the men?" Iolanthe asked Philemon.

"Thrasymachus is talking with Laos, and the Countess is talking with Wriggs, sipping apéritifs."

Philemon made good company for the ladies, serious without being stiff, and gay without being frivolous. He started to ask if Eurydice had been to the library again. She said she had and was greatly impressed. It made her very happy to find so many books to read, and she had taken a few home to while away the hours.

"Have you seen the solar motor yet?"

"Not yet. I am just trying to get settled."

"Of course." Philemon was the soul of courtesy. "I shall be glad to take you there."

"Thank you. I have already promised Groucho to go with him."

"Have you invited Dr. Artemos to join us?" Philemon asked the hostess.

"I am sorry I haven't. I thought the old professor didn't come out to parties any more, and in any case he wouldn't enjoy it. He is so occupied with his experiments."

"What are you doing at the Institute?" asked Eunice of Chloe.

"I got so interested in Lucretius that I am learning it. In the third chapter now. Otherwise we are studying Plutarch."

"How is Berenice?"

"She is reading Xenophon. But everything is upset. We are rehearsing a play for the Irenicia. It's barely four weeks from now. Everything else is put aside. Everybody is busy, practicing song and dance besides the play, and making the new dress for Athena."

"What is the Irenicia?" asked Eurydice.

Iolanthe explained that this was the big festival of the island, corresponding somewhat to the Panathenaea of ancient Greece. Laos had this revived, and it has become very popular with the people. There would be songs and poetry recitals and gymnastic contests and water sports, besides the play given at the amphitheater. The whole island went mad for three days.

Over the apéritifs at tea tables on the terrace they sat and chatted. Philemon was jaunty, carefree and easy, knowing that he was always admired and welcome in ladies' company. He commented favorably on Eurydice's dress.

"I am surprised," observed Eurydice, "that you people really dress for dinner."

"Dress is civilization, isn't it?" said Iolanthe. "I cannot imagine a civilization where women do not wish to beautify themselves."

"When I arrived, I saw so much nakedness around that I thought you people had gone native. Now I admire the innocence of the young girls in the streets, and I sincerely believe that it is much simpler and healthier, especially in this climate. I have seen enough naked tribesmen of course. But the dress of Ireniki girls must be considered unusual for Europeans. Is it due to the influence of the natives, or the climate?"

Iolanthe replied, "I remember it started as a joke. I was a child when the colony was started. The men, newly arrived, wished to express their sense of freedom, and they did it by growing beards. The women protested, said that it was a matter of personal appearance, and that everybody shouldn't just start to do whatever he pleased. 'If women dressed as they pleased, would the men like it?' one of them said. 'Sure, go ahead,' said the men. 'Dress as you please. We've put the Old World behind us.' 'And are you sure you would not mind?' said one woman — I remember her name was Hypatia; she was very pretty. 'What, for instance?' asked the men. Hypatia replied, 'If you men insist on growing beards, then we would like to strip to the waist in this hot weather. Wouldn't you mind?' 'Sure, go ahead, we don't care a bit,' replied one of the men. She started then and there to divest herself of her upper clothing in a spirit of derring-do, winning the applause of the men. With much encouragement from the men, all the girls did it. It is of course simpler. But don't you worry." She was addressing Eurydice. "The girls love to dress. They are dying for a brassiere, or something or other to decorate themselves with."

"I have noticed how they play with their shawls."

"The instinct to dress is perfectly natural with women," commented Eunice.

"The point is," said Philemon rather professionally in his suave, even tone, "the point is, all men and women love to dress. Savages tattoo their faces, believing it makes them beautiful or impressive; or put a ring in their nose or a stack of metal rings around their neck. It is perfectly natural. For the women, a black wart may be considered a point of beauty; hence the beauty spot. Or a pair of earrings, an artfully set curl, a belt, or ankle bells. Why not? Some American women have put real peanuts and cabbages in their hats in the belief that they were thus enhancing their attractiveness. Back thirty years ago, I was told, fashionable ladies of New York put blinkers in their hair, blinking off and on by means of a concealed battery. Anything to attract the male. Essentially, there is no difference between peanuts in

American women's hats and the scraping of legs by crickets to attract the opposite sex." He playfully stuck a Brazil nut in Chloe's hair; she at once took it down. "Look at what women have done with their hair; they sweep it up, let it down, coil it, plait it, bunch it together, spread it over their shoulders like a mangy lion, or again clip it short, then curl it, straighten it, dye it black, white, purple, livid or mottled — in an endless variety. And the men like it."

"Dress is the fine art of deception, of creating an illusion of beauty. An appeal to the opposite sex," said Eunice. "In the human race this function of the peacock, of making an artful display of feathers, has fallen to the female sex. They do this by withholding, by concealing, and yet by not altogether concealing. All women's dresses follow the basic technique of revealing-by-concealing, alternating between the avowed desire to dress and the unavowed desire to undress. Women have found by experience that it works; it is part of the courtship technique among animals to attract by running away. Actually, this makes for neuroticism. If women never permitted their earlobes to be seen in public, these organs would become at once a powerful, provocative, erotic symbol. It is all custom, of course. For myself, I like the simplicity of the natives. It is healthier, more open, less neurotic, and more beautiful."

"The point is," said Philemon, "I was going to say the point is, dress should not in any way interfere with the noble form of the human body, but should only accentuate and enhance its natural grace and beauty. That should be the principle. A wrap is often more beautiful than a tailored suit. Most women overdress, as most men overeat. While dressed, they should not permit themselves to be ashamed of any part of their body. The whole line of the female form should be simple, flowing and harmonious. Like Iolanthe's dress, for example. Too much emphasis, I think, is placed upon external make-up, too little upon the female form itself, its natural grace, its movements, carriage, postures. After all, dress is only drapery; it must have a good body to hang on. That is where I believe our Ireniki girls are ahead. Our girls are invariably graceful, with very few exceptions."

"The whole art of women's dress," said Eunice, pursuing her own thoughts, "the whole art lies in women dressing themselves to suggest how they would look if they were undressed, in bed."

Eurydice laughed with the others. She said, "Why do you drape yourself then, right up to the neck? Why don't you follow your own ideal?"

"I wish I could. I would love to. There's an Ireniki law — actually it is the influence of Laos."

Laos, entering the terrace along with Thrasymachus, heard this part of the sentence.

"What Ireniki law are you ascribing to my influence?" he asked. "I don't make the laws, do I?"

"Does the philosopher also practice the art of deception on himself?"

"Tell me then what you are talking about."

"We are discussing the subject of dress and undress, and the law which forbids older women to strip themselves in public. Eurydice was asking. You had better explain it to your American friend."

Laos' fine face creased into a smile in the dusk. "My American friend? Yes, she is my American friend."

He sat down at the tea table. Slowly he said, "Eurydice dear, this subject, I assure you, has been very painful to me. It is true that there's such an Ireniki law, and I confess I had a hand in it. Nudity is not very beautiful; most of the time it isn't, with the exception of young men and young girls. God has made animals and covered them with furs, and thick hides, and armor, but has left man as defenseless as a worm so far as his body is concerned. The biped is a noble form, a beautiful form, not necessarily more graceful than a young deer — but it is noble and beautiful. In the course of life, however, most of us lose that perfection of form which we see in a child in all his movements. The law reflects our Hellenic sense of form and good taste only. Mothers who have given birth to three children and

breast-fed them are entitled to some concealment of their imperfections. And so with many old women — you will grant
that women who have a coarse or wrinkled skin should not be
permitted to offend the public's good taste by exposing what
is less than truly beautiful. All the elders agreed. Public bathing
is a different matter. I am speaking of dress in general. Don't
you think it is sensible?"

Eurydice recalled the few times she had been to the opera,
and what she had seen in the golden horseshoe and during the
intermission, where the obscenity of jewels had replaced the
natural simple beauty of a young human form.

"Very sensible," she said.

Thus they sat and talked and sipped their apéritifs until the
moon had come up over Mount Ida and they went in for dinner.

Chapter XXIII

A HUGE GLITTERING Venetian chandelier and a row of candles on the dining table lit up the gaily dressed company of laughing women and smiling, white-bearded men. Five or six Thainian maids, in their native costume and bare feet, lined up on both sides of the long table, with Roxana, the chief maid, standing behind Iolanthe. The hostess, sitting at one end of the table in the glowing, subdued light reflected from the white tablecloth and the silver, emanated by her beauty of flesh and glistening necklace, style, elegance and nobility of atmosphere. This was the illusion they had spoken of on the terrace. Iolanthe, a woman in her early forties, looked thirty; she could have graced the court of Louis XIV with her elegance, her courtly, knowing glances under her dark lashes, and her gay, infectious, silvery laughter. One would have liked to capture that illusion, to impress it in painting, or celebrate it in song and ballad, to evoke like music a memory of what was essentially a fleeting, evanescent mood and tone and color. Dutifully she had kept her muslin veil over her foaming black tresses, faithful to her promise to Athanopoulos that this billowy torrent of loveliness should not lie exposed to the gaze of other men. It was only a formality, expressing a sentiment; she let her locks escape gracefully over her clad shoulder, her orange robe swung diagonally across her bosom to her waist, leaving her other shoulder bare. This note of eccentric charm, of enticing feminine forethought, might be appropriately called scandalous in the old-

195

fashioned twentieth century, but it made her look like an exotic Macedonian princess.

The older people — Iolanthe herself, the Countess, Laos, Eunice, Aristotimus, Prince Andreyev — were gayer, more relaxed, more attuned to the atmosphere of friendly joviality. The younger set, spread around the middle of the table, looked by comparison tense and serious. That was as it should be. They lacked the serenity of age, the ability to take life at its face value and accept it. Also they were somewhat awed by the superior wisdom, the inexplicable ease of knowledge of the older generation and the flowing brilliance of their conversation. And, too, on this island, the young were supposed to be respectful to the old; they were to sit quietly, to listen, to learn what the older generation was saying. Of the older men only Thrasymachus looked occupied and unnecessarily serious. His daughter, Eretrea, tall and thin and in a dress of outrageous transparency, was sitting next to Stephan halfway down the table, dividing her attention between halfheartedly carrying on a conversation with the young man and listening to what was going on between Prince Andreyev and Countess Cordelia della Castiglioni at one end, and between the more brilliant group of Laos and Iolanthe and Eunice at the other. Emma-Emma had planned to come, but was unable to at the last moment because she had had to rush to the Thainian village to attend the celebration of the first moon of a baby born of a Thainian mother and an unknown Ireniki father.

The hostess, as has been noted before, was a thorough pagan. Her banquet was usually a function of great joviality, always preceded by the Ireniki prayer.

"Let's say the prayer," she said happily.

Everybody stood up. "O friends, let us take time to think," ending in "grateful for having enjoyed this short but precious gift of life. Amen."

"That prayer is an appetizer," she said as she sat down.

Eurydice said, "I like your prayer. It has a true religious feeling, it makes one feel grateful for the gift of life instead of apologizing for being alive."

The lights from the chandelier were clicked out. Only the glowing row of candles lit up the table of well-dressed women and happy men, standing out against the encircling dome of darkness. It was very flattering to the ladies. Iolanthe knew this well, that lights from above accentuated shadows on their faces, while lights from below were flattering to their cheeks and necks and made them look fuller and younger, obliterating all blemishes and the inroads of time on their physiognomies.

The chatter began. Laos on the hostess' right was next to Eunice, while Eurydice on the other side was placed next to Alcibiades Wriggs.

"What are you doing?" Iolanthe asked to put the young man at his ease.

Alcibiades, alone of all the men faithful to the English tradition in his uncompromising tuxedo and bow-tie, was at that stage of youth when he had learned to cover up his lack of ease not too successfully with the usual courteous phrases. His hair was in beautiful order, parted on the right; his manners rather deliberately quiet.

"Oh, nothing, nothing worth talking about."

"Don't be modest," said Iolanthe.

"I've been reading up some authors." A cloud passed over his puckered brow. He had seen so many pictures of Edward-to-be-VIII when he was Prince of Wales.

"Who are your favorite authors?" Iolanthe was determined to egg him on, to thaw him out of his reticence, his punctilious stiffness.

Alcibiades was a little surprised. He had never expected to be the center of attention. And he had not of course expected to be placed next to Eurydice.

"Oh, Balzac. And Dickens. They open up to me a world of characters. I am beginning to think I almost know Paris and London. And I hope," he added modestly, "to learn something from these great masters."

"I hear you are trying to write a novel," said Laos.

"Don't be misled by the Countess," Alcibiades said deprecatingly. "I don't think I shall ever be more than a scribbler."

"Every young man is entitled to try, to find out where his talent lies and develop it."

"I realize that I am laboring under a handicap; that I do not know the world sufficiently. I have never even seen artillery, or a double-deck bus, or a crowded tenement house. I try to learn as much as I can from reading, from studying photographs, and from my mother. But it is distressingly inadequate."

"Why should you try to write about a world you have never seen? Why don't you write about people you know, about this island?"

"It is too quiet and peaceful, isn't it?"

"Quiet!" blurted Eunice, directly opposite. "There is drama where there are human beings. Even among the Thainian tribesmen, there is a world of desires and emotions once we come close to them. I wish Emma-Emma wouldn't spend so much time collecting sociological data . . ."

Iolanthe said, "What Laos suggests is right. I think it is perfectly useless to write about what one has never seen; it will never be authentic." She went merrily on; the service was so smooth that she never had to worry. "Read Balzac and Dickens for the characters, but not for the details of milieu. I'm afraid you are under their influence. It is natural for a young writer. On the other hand, I think one comes to maturity by breaking away from mere imitativeness. We are discussing the general principles of art, of course. What do you think?" She turned to Laos.

Laos said, "Why don't you write a play, where the element of milieu is less important than in a novel? Aeschylus wrote, and Sophocles wrote, on conflicts of concentrated human emotions. That is the quality of all true drama, human emotions elevated to a higher level. All novels and plays deal in the last analysis with human emotions, but the element of milieu is suggested rather than portrayed in a drama. Of course Shakespeare wrote *Julius Caesar* without even seeing Rome, out of the

flow of his genius, but if he were to write a novel of ancient
Rome, he would have to do an enormous amount of research.
And research kills the immediate inspiration. Perhaps one day
you can write a play, a play about kings and nobles, or of the
common people of Thainos, for the Comforters of Men's Souls
to put on during an Irenicia. Look at Prince Andreyev. He is
good material for a drama, isn't he?"

From the other end of the table bellowed the Prince. "I protest. Your remarks are ambiguous. You seem to include me
among the common people of Thainos."

Laos smiled. "I didn't mean it. I mean he could write about
the common people of Thainos, *and* about our uncommon Royal
Highness."

Roxana, the first maid, pushed forward at this moment a service cart containing an enormous clay pot. She lifted the pot
cover for the hostess' inspection. Iolanthe smiled approvingly.
It was a famous, sensational dish — whiting en casserole, cooked
in a deep brown sauce with truffles, capers, mushrooms, a
smidgen of thyme, a sprinkle of white wine, pre-fried chopped
garlic and slices of bacon.

"Oh, the whiting!" exclaimed Eunice.

"I never tire of the whiting, do you?" said the hostess. "It's
a Roman dish, I believe, handed down from the culinary tradition of the Roman Empire, with modern improvements. My cook
learned it from a chef of Abruzzo. It reminds me of something
I tasted once in Casablanca. Probably it has Arabic elements
in it."

"The human palate is international," remarked Eunice, "en-
dowed with the same sensibilities. All cooks talk a language
which the different nations can understand. I once read something about the American pumpkin pie," she said to Eurydice,
"golden-brown and peppered, with a steaming heavenly flavor.
It greatly increased my respect for your American civilization.
All of a sudden, it made America beautiful to me."

"You are not joking, I hope."

"No. I had never eaten a pumpkin pie before. You see, American pumpkin pie would be a contribution to world civilization, to better living. I think international understanding could be reached through the stomach. And I believe we usually falsify our ideas of civilization, associate it with philosophy and science, and advances in knowledge. Civilization, as I see it, is merely what adds to a better and more gracious living."

"So you mean by the perfection of the pumpkin pie my country has made a positive contribution to world civilization?"

"Exactly, it means she has by the peculiar genius of her people made a positive contribution, however small; has brought civilization a step forward. It means that behind the façade of scientific progress she has not forgotten how to live. Culture and the arts are something else again. What do you think?" She addressed the question to Laos.

"The distinction between civilization and culture is not easy. These words, like all words, grew in their meaning through usage. I would say that civilization refers more to our material advances, culture to the spiritual gains. I would say that a nation which does not know how to cook whiting en casserole is less civilized than one which does. I have tasted once fried abalone steaks: in that respect, Americans are still savages, mere children in the morning of civilization. They don't know the ABC of cooking abalone. The accent on good living will grow as a nation grows to maturity. I do not think anybody can deny that all the scientific advances should have no other aim and goal than as a means to a better living; only the goal is so often lost sight of. On the other hand, I think a man can be civilized without being cultured. The advances and gains of civilization are physical, they are something added extraneously to the man; culture's influence is chemical, it enters into the man's inner being and changes him."

"And progress?" asked Iolanthe.

"Progress is neutral. It simply means going forward. It does not say going where. A man going in a circle in a wood may quite well believe that he is going forward by the mere act of taking steps and strides. Isn't it curious that in the Old World everybody took it for granted that mere movement — no matter in what direction — was a good thing in itself? Nobody attempted even to define the goal or had any inkling of a notion what the goal was to be. It means simply we are today somewhere else than where we were yesterday. That is all that progress means. That is why I say the word 'progress' is neutral. It is like the words 'progressive' and 'reactionary' as used by the Communists. It assumes too much. Once the goal is fixed, then we can talk of progressive and reactionary, or forward and backward, in reference to that goal. It would seem to me that a man who in belief and in practice is moving back toward slave labor in the times of the Pharaohs, or toward a rule of absolute autocracy and naked fear in the times of the Czars, or toward denial of all the gains of the human spirit in the last two or three thousand years, is reaching backward, a true reactionary. They assume too much — for instance, that voting on a single ticket, with no opposition allowed, is a more progressive form of democracy, while allowing the people to make a choice between two parties is not only reactionary, but downright decadent. So why argue?"

Iolanthe said, "Isn't there something in what Eunice just said? That civilization has a goal, the goal of good living?"

"Quite frankly yes. And further than that, I believe world civilization can be built only upon the common basis of international living, a combination of all that is best and finest in each civilization. The ideal life would be, I think, to live in an English cottage, with American heating, and have a Japanese wife, a French mistress and a Chinese cook. That is about the clearest way I can put it."

A sunny smile played about Laos' face as he went on. "I remember once I attended a dinner in New York, back in the 1960's. A grand annual dinner given by the Sigma Phi Kappa, American Society of Dietitians. Absolutely matchless, unforgettable! A dietitian is by definition an expert on food, a man who concerns himself with the gastronomic, as well as nutritive values of food. Or so I thought. I was stunned. We had ox tongue with cherry sauce! I could not believe my eyes. On a side dish was broccoli with a sweet lemon sauce. One taste of it almost made me throw up. No, I am not exaggerating. There was mayonnaise with maraschino cherries! No doubt, the spirit of experimentation was alive, reminding me of those modernist paintings. To crown everything, we had for dessert apricot with peanut butter, appearing under the title 'apricot surprise.' Apricot, mind you, with peanut butter! No doubt it swarmed with calory content. For an alternative choice, we were invited to sample a dessert with a fancy name, South Seas Delight — coconut with slices of apple."

"Mr. Laos," said Eurydice, "I believe you are making up a tale to blackmail the United States of America."

"Why should I? I kept that menu for years, to show to my friends."

There was a murmur of amusement and of dissent.

"Laos loves fooling," said Iolanthe to Eurydice. "Broccoli with sweet lemon sauce would be a horror, to my way of thinking."

"Anyway, scientific eating is a piece of idiocy," said Eunice.

"Believe it or not," Laos continued, "I tasted that apricot with peanut butter myself. To make you feel better, Eurydice, I must make it clear that this menu was given at the dinner of the dietetic scientists, not of the New York Gourmet Society. It was just a limited company of unlimited fools. But this is only typical of all modern knowledge. A dietitian, according to the practices of those days, was a man who knew all about the calory values of food, and nothing about its flavor. He was a *scientist*, concerned only with one special aspect of food; a Hottentot, so far as culinary flavors are concerned. Man learned to know more and more about less and less. Society became dupes to a host of scientific experts — psychologists, child-care specialists, efficiency engineers — each knowing a great deal about his own subject and nothing whatsoever about human life. It was so easy to impress, to talk of calories and proteins and carbohydrates, to say science knows. Educational psychologists told you that you must never say 'don't' to your child, forgetting the common-sense value of discipline, the wholesome moral value of spanking. The child was to grow up with no elder ever saying 'no' to him until he met his business boss, until life itself said 'don't' to him. And there were enough half-educated fools to believe them. Babies' feeding hours were to be strictly regulated; it took a long time for the experts to find out — I think it was in the 1950's — that the best time to feed the baby was when he was hungry. A baby duckling would die of eating too much or too little if left to itself, according to these experts. Those dietitians forgot that the baby turns his mouth away from the bottle when he has eaten enough. That late recognition of a simple fact, observable by any mother with a modicum of common sense, was made in 1972 after an exhaustive series of experiments. And those dietetic hoodoos forgot the simple fact that you digest better when you enjoy what you eat. No official recognition was made of this fact up to the time we left. No, everything went preferably by percentages and measurements. What the dietitians failed to tell you was that the body manufactures its carbohydrates out of proteins, and vice versa according to its bodily needs."

He paused and added, "What am I leading up to? Simply that there was a failure to recognize the individual in the mass, to appreciate fully the wisdom of the body, the subtle, flexible mechanism in the human body and the capacity of the human mind to adjust itself. The individual tended to be judged by mass standards, arrived at by group statistics. Those coarse specialists, masquerading under the name of science, became a positive menace to society. And so, in a broad sense, was modern knowledge, expert knowledge, where a whole view of the capabilities and needs of man — physical needs and psychic needs — was lost sight of."

"That reminds me," said Eurydice. "In times of yore, there was quite a fashion for educational psychology, and especially for psychiatry. Back in the 1940's, I believe, there was a professor of psychology of Bennington College who said you could evaluate a man's character by observing the way he crushed his cigarette butt. If he crushes it violently, he has a hidden sadistic complex, destructive, repressive tendencies; if he crushes it deliberately, he is a methodical, calculating colleague; on the other hand, if he simply leaves it burning, he is liable to be careless with his savings, a shiftless person who besides is likely to be insensitive to his fellow men's feelings. You got to a point where you dared not crush a cigarette in a psychologist's presence. It became a little mystical. He sounded oracular, reading meaning in a few shadows and forms like a crystal gazer. It is difficult to tell where science ends and charlatanry begins. Don't you think that is exactly what the scientific method tries to avoid — reading meaning into things, drawing dogmatic conclusions from a few, inadequate facts?"

"I think," said Eunice, "it was this oracular character which made psychology popular. People love oracles. They do. Palmistry, handwriting analysis, astrology and psychology, anything that tells you what you don't know."

"In those times," said Eurydice, "a psychologist was a man who rushed about examining baby's diapers. If the baby's bowels were loose, he was likely to grow up into a generous character; if he was inclined to constipation, he was likely to be a little tight with his money when he grew up."

Even Thrasymachus roared.

"I've never heard that one," said Iolanthe, tittering sweetly.

"But it was true," said Eurydice.

"I believe it," said Laos, "considering the fact that Freud was looking for the human soul somewhere very near the seat of the pants."

Eunice protested. "That is unfair. For one Freud, there were a thousand frauds."

Laos said, "I don't mean to disparage Freud. At least he was trying to look for the human soul. He brought knowledge of the human mind a vast step forward. He had an almost Oriental, uncanny intuition; practically discovered a vast continent for the Western world. Had to develop his own method, too. The word *soul* had become so inextricably bound up with theology that the natural scientists respectfully left it alone. Freud had to go back to ancient Greek and reintroduce the word *psyche*. I think it is clearer. We had no words to describe those mysterious forces, racial forces, controlling our mind and body. So he had to invent the *id*, and the *libido* and *eros* and predicate them almost as mythic entities."

"I wish he had chosen the word *sarks*," said Iolanthe in a languid tone. "It means the flesh — and psychology must deal with the forces of the flesh, mustn't it? At the same time, it also means human nature, human kind. Wouldn't it be a sounder basis to go upon — let us say, a more fleshly understanding of psychology?"

"There is really no need. The term *human nature* is perfectly good and adequate. Psychology should be a study of human nature. It comprises everything, from our carnal longings to our spiritual aspirations and lofty ideals. Freud has to be given the credit for returning to the problem of the soul. The natural scientists had fought shy about that word; they did not know what to do with it."

Eurydice said, "I think I heard you say once that science is concerned with the true, not the good. Of course they had to leave it alone."

"It is all a question of method — and of the proper goal of human knowledge. We have agreed that the goal should be the art of better living, of living well. Why should any inquirer after truth shut out the realm of the good, and willfully say to himself: The realm of the good is no concern of mine? That, I think, was the most destructive feature of twentieth-century thinking. All thinking was trying to be quasi-scientific. The fault was not that of the natural scientists who deal with rocks and metals; the fault was that of the social scientists who tried to ape their technique. It was a fiasco, a disaster; it created an intellectual vacuum. Only true and untrue, no good and bad, no right and wrong. Science wants to measure; it has to. Once you introduce the method of natural science into the humanities, however, you discard one by one that which you cannot measure — God, good and evil, sin and repentance, artistic creations, noble impulses. But that was where it led until the behaviorists came along and hit upon the notion of creating a psychology as the study of the human mind without a mind. Everything was reduced to sensory stimuli and animal response. That, the behaviorist was sure he could measure. The psychologist then became a man who rushed about among cages of rats and chickens. Of course Watson started as an animal psychologist and ended where he began. Everything of the human mind — imagination, memory, love, impulses (outside the animal impulses for food and sex) — was scrapped or thrown out the window. Mother-love as the reaction of endocrine glands was a proper subject for study; mother-love as a result of a human relationship and growing understanding and pride in one's boy's achievements wasn't, simply because there was no way of measuring the latter. He believed in that way and only in that way could psychology become a true science. In that very limited sense, he was right."

"All fools are not dead yet," said Iolanthe.

"No, definitely not."

Chapter XXIV

THE CHATTER OF VOICES was now broken by the
clanking of spoons against glasses, when the dessert of banana
sherbet topped with whipped cream was served. The encircling
dome of playful thought was broken. Everybody had reached
that state of happy satisfaction toward the end of a meal; the
wine had been good and the whiting superb. Laos' face glowed
a little, as did Iolanthe's. From the window behind Iolanthe's
back, Eurydice could see the moon over Mount Ida. Iolanthe
was especially pretty when she had drunk a little, when a distant
look came into her eyes. The night was delightfully cool at the
ridge.

"What do you do for sports?" Eurydice asked Alcibiades.

"Swimming, and fishing. Some days I go with the fishermen.
There is good swimming in the lake and in the lagoon. Do you
fish?"

"Oh, I have played at it sometimes. Only as an amateur."

"We are all amateurs. And there's good clamming, too, way
out near the sandbars. I'd like to take you out some day. I sometimes spend a whole day on the sandbars, alone."

"Alone? You are a strange person."

"I take my notes along, or perhaps a book. I have a rowboat.
My mother packs me a couple of sandwiches, and I have everything I need in the boat, including a kettle for making hot coffee."

"How delightful!"

"There's not much else one can do on this island. A little hiking
perhaps. I try to keep myself fit."

"How about Groucho?"

"What about him?"

"I mean what does he do for sports? I ask because I wondered what an American would do for sports out here."

"He lives on the dam. Frankly I don't know. Swimming in the brook below perhaps. A lot of us go swimming in the morning in the lagoon; some in the late afternoon, and some gather at Chiron's or Giovanni's for a drink."

"I think we'd better have the coffee outside, don't you think?" said the hostess.

The company rose. As the Countess had sat at the other end of the table, Eurydice had not been able to see her or talk with her at all. Now she came over, charming in her low-cut beige dress, beaming an open smile straight toward them.

"Well, did you have a good chat at dinner?" she asked young Wriggs, casting a sidelong glance at Eurydice standing close by. "I overheard some of the things they were discussing at your end of the table."

"Oh, I was listening most of the time. About food and psychology. Every time Laos said something, it upset some scheme of mine. I was just taking a bite at behaviorist psychology. It is so upsetting, isn't it? He was advising me to write a play, to try at least."

"I heard that part of the conversation. Not a bad idea. I think you could profit from his advice."

"But I would have to change all my reading again. Take up Euripides perhaps."

"Nothing that has been read is lost. . . . How are you, Eurydice? Did you enjoy the dinner?"

"Thoroughly."

"I am so glad to see you looking happy."

"I was suggesting to Eurydice," said the young man, "that one day I might take her to the sandbars."

"Spendid — splendid!" said the Countess.

They had been swept along to the terrace, and now caught up with Chloe and Philemon.

"How are you, darling?" the Countess said to Chloe. "How are you coming out with the play? Aristotimus was telling us that you are rehearsing for the Irenicia."

"We are just starting. It takes a lot of practice, with the song and chorus and all that."

Aristotimus walked toward them. Eurydice remembered seeing him at the head of the funeral procession. His tall figure, his skullcap, his inscrutable eyes and his exceptionally long beard gave him the very dignified air of the spiritual head of the community. He was enthusiastic about the Irenicia, and always got very busy in the month of preparations preceding it. There was nothing incongruous in his taking an active interest in the pagan festival in honor of Pallas Athena; he was a Greek himself. He was a practical, adroit man. Athanopoulos, with his anti-clerical leanings, had tolerated him, but soon came to respect his counsel and his wisdom, and later to like him. Father Sebastian Donatello, the Italian priest, called him Aristotimus the Apostate — Father Donatello who had joined the community on the pure strength of the Countess' friendship.

"Has any one of you ever read all the epistles of St. Paul straight through in one sitting?" he used to say. "You get an impression of a man of extraordinary ability, of true greatness, molding the first amorphous ideas of the Christian fathers into an order, giving sharp definition to certain fundamental doctrines of the Church. A Jew of the Dispersion, imbued with Greek learning, conversant with the religious rites and mysteries of his times, and beset with the divergent quarrels and domestic problems of the churches, the doubts and relapses of Christian converts, their licentiousness, their unchaste widows and the false prophets among them, and their tendency toward holy-rolling and speaking of tongues, he was able to hold together all those international elements, in Rome and in Thessaly, in Corinth and in Ephesus, and forge them into an international church by the sheer power of his intellect and his selfless, fanatical devotion, rising to the height of St. Peter, without being one of the Twelve Apostles. He stood above local customs, above baptism and circumcision. At one stroke, by refusing to place prime value upon a Jewish custom, he made it possible for Christianity to rise from a Jewish sect to a cosmopolitan religion."

Aristotimus held forth that local customs should be permitted to exist side by side with Christ's teachings. He of course refused to baptize. He did not believe in, and did not enforce, the veiling of women's heads during worship. He said that St. Paul insisted on the veiling of the head, not because it was a local custom of Asia Minor or Magna Graecia, but because he shared in the belief of the inferiority of the female sex. "Wives, submit yourselves unto your own husbands." "For man is not of the woman; but the woman is of the man. Neither was the man created for the woman; but the woman for the man. For this cause the woman ought to have power over her head because of the angels." The modern Christians pretended still to believe in those words, but no preacher he had known had so far dared to preach a sermon on that text.

As for the religious rites and local customs of the different peoples amongst whom the Christians lived, St. Paul was quite explicit. His remarkable first letter to the Corinthians made everything sunlight clear. His great principle was expediency. "All things are lawful for me, but all things are not expedient; all things are lawful for me, but all things edify not." Specifically about eating idolatrous meat, he prescribed, "If any of them that believe not bid you to a feast, and ye be disposed to go; whatsoever is set before you, eat, asking no question for conscience's sake. . . . Conscience, I say, not thine own, but of the other: for why is my liberty judged of another man's conscience? . . . Give none offense, neither to the Jews, nor to the Gentiles, nor to the church of God." The earth was of the Lord's, and the fulness thereof. Why abstain?

It took the greatness of St. Paul to ride over national barriers, and it took the genius of Aristotimus to lead in the jovialities, gaieties, idolatry and drunkenness of the Irenicia festivals.

For all this, Father Aristotimus still presided over Christian as well as pagan rites, believed in the sacraments along with the worship of Athena, holding that both were symbolical rites, himself a symbol of shining liberalism which enraged and inflamed the sterling orthodoxy of Father Donatello. The Irenicia festivals had come about naturally. Soon after their arrival at this island, the founders of the colony wished to celebrate the anniversary of their landing. The men and women, mostly from Attica, wished to signal their gratitude to a deity who should be worshiped as the patron god of the colony, and naturally believed that their loyalty was to Pallas Athena; the Delian shepherds and fishermen were inveterately loyal to Apollo, but being in the minority were overruled. It began with the setting up of an inscription on stone. "To the Goddess Pallas Athena Coryphagenes All Honor and Veneration from the Colony of Irenikis for Her Divine Protection." Later, a statue of the goddess was voted by the public and duly erected.

When the question of the patron god was brought up, Aristotimus had insisted that St. Nicholas, patron saint of sailors far away from home, should be given the honor. The inhabitants, being Christians in theory but pagans at heart, did not openly object, and Christmas, which was originally a festival in honor of St. Nicholas, was duly celebrated. But a patron saint could not be arbitrarily designated; it had to come from the people's belief and the strength of their votive offerings. Once in this mid-Pacific island, the tenuous thread which had bound these Hellenic peasants to Christianity was broken. The paganism in their blood which had never died out during the centuries now burst forth in their uninhibited fervor and childlike exuberance, which could not be suppressed and was insuppressible as far as Father Aristotimus was concerned. Christmas was a small, unglamorous affair compared with the festival in honor of Athena. Somehow it failed to arouse the enthusiasm of the populace shown in the celebration of the landing anniversary, which, under the adroit leadership of Laos and Athanopoulos, was modeled after the Panathenaea of ancient Greece. The song and dance, the feasting and drunkenness and gymnastic contests and poetry recitals struck a responsive chord in their Athenian hearts. Laos had intended that in the worship of Athena, religion and song and poetry should be joined into one; it was to be a revival of the religion and the sunny spirit of Athens, a joining hands of art and religion, of beauty and piety unmarred by the Christian sense of sin. Why, Laos had asked, in the division of piety and impiety, should Satan be given all the pleasures, and God all the pains? It did not make sense to him, or to the Mediterranean souls. Aristotimus saw that it would be senseless to fight it, or wise to stay out of it. A folk festival was a folk festival. It would be as senseless to stop it as to try to stop the celebration of Mardi Gras among French Catholics. The thing to do was, rather, to make Athena a Christian deity, as the English had done with St. George who slew the dragon.

It must not be inferred that Aristotimus was a man without principles. He followed the great principle of compromise. Laos had read Morley's essay on "Compromise" to him and said that compromise was "half of statesmanship."

"Chloe," the priest said now to the young girl, "be sure you girls make a good new dress for Athena, as lavishly beautiful as possible. Secure the best materials from Iolanthe. It is the Great Irenicia this year, which comes once every five years. What play are you girls going to put on?"

"The story of Ariadne."

"Well, make it good, especially the last part. I suggested to Laos that we should put on *Lysistrata*, but he thought there wouldn't be enough men who could act to make it a great success."

The lights had been lighted, a series of colored lanterns which fringed the edge of the terrace. Groups of men and women were standing or strolling in clusters. The subdued glow of the lanterns was not such as to obliterate the view of the sea now lying far below, scintillating with streaks of reflected moonlight. Many young men and girls who had been invited to come after dinner for the dance were now streaming in.

Iolanthe and the Countess were approaching them, talking together. Iolanthe, without being tall, was easily noticeable in any company; her warm silvery voice, her ready laughter, her dark

lashes radiated a tone of elegant gaiety, a guarantee against
dullness and insipid vulgarity, which men so often feared might
befall an evening party. Her white flesh and dark tresses, and
her perfect carriage, trained in the Institute, still retained a stat-
uesque effect, which was helped by her veil and tunic. She was
confoundedly beautiful. What was most outstanding was her
eyes; from those orbits played a light changing with her moods,
of incredible virginal innocence, or of placid languor, or again
of a flaming, Oriental passion of unknown depths. No wonder
Athanopoulos had fallen in love with this woman. The Countess,
on the other hand, was of a conservatively simple and happy disposition, of a naturally warm and affectionate nature. Ten years
older than Iolanthe, with streaks of white hair at her temples,
she was the kind of person in whose company a young man could
relax. That was why young Wriggs had been able to feel close
to her, as he could not with Iolanthe.

"Will there be a water-trial this year?" Iolanthe asked the
Greek priest.

"I do not know. There have been a few people shut up for
minor offenses, but none charged with felony."

"It's disappointing, isn't it? An Irenicia without a water-trial
won't be quite perfect. It will lack a sort of climax."

"Don't say that, my daughter. You should be proud that we
have not killed a man for crime these last five years."

"It just does not seem right," said Iolanthe coldly, almost
mystically.

"Don't be so horrible," said Countess della Castiglioni. "I think
there's a streak of Romanoff blood still surviving in you."

"Perhaps. Just Russian blood. I don't think it is right that
there should be no killing at all, no punishment for wickedness
of the human soul. It is not in the scheme of things. Don't misunderstand me. I don't mean we should gratuitously slaughter
human beings. But somewhere in the universe there are surely
dark forces, forces of evil. I always feel better when I see a
water-trial. I don't gloat over the killing of a condemned criminal. I don't relit it. I suffer, and it profoundly moves me.

But it has, I think, a cathartic effect on me. While I suffer with the condemned, I cannot keep my eyes away from him."

"I never could look at it," said the Countess. "You don't like it, do you?" She addressed the question to young Wriggs.

"Of course not. But I see what she means. I can quite see that life even on this island isn't all perfect, and it might be just as well to have it out and dealt with rather than hidden. Of course I don't stand for the inhumanity of the water-trial."

"Isn't he a sweet boy?" said the Countess quite inconsequentially. "Where's Thrasymachus?"

Aristotimus replied, "He is still locked in argument with Laos in the Prince's room. I left them just a while ago, fighting about the twelve-and-half per cent tax on account of his fourth child."

Music had started, a few violins, soft and agreeably clear in the open tropical night, adding liveliness to the chatter of men's and women's voices. The musicians were the girls themselves, from the Institute of Comforters of Men's Souls. A few couples had started dancing.

"Why don't you join in?" the Countess said to young Wriggs.

"May I?" Alcibiades said to Eurydice.

Eurydice beamed and followed.

Chapter XXV

We CAN BE REASONABLY SURE," said Laos, "that we shall never go beyond the tithe. Ancient Chinese law, Hebrew law, Mohammedan law all speak of it. Without wars, and without a complex government trying to interfere with everybody's business, a ten per cent tax should be sufficient for any public administration. And we can also be reasonably sure that laws must be held sacred and inviolable, and that once exceptions are made for individual persons, they will soon become unenforceable for the public."

Prince Andreyev had listened patiently to the wrangling between Laos and Thrasymachus over their coffee. His room, if not exactly breathing royal opulence, was luxuriously carpeted and furnished with a sumptuous divan and long wooden chairs, heavily carved. The walls were a blur of oil portraits, miniatures on ivory, and faded photographs. The room, forty by thirty, was spacious, the ceiling high, originally built for Athanopoulos as he had wanted it. On a piano, in one corner of the room, stood an iron goat, a foot high. The frieze of the walls itself was filled with designs of an odd variety of curving and straight goat's horns. In a special glass case, placed on a niche built into the wall was a copy of white marble of the Hermes of Praxiteles in Olympia. This jumble of antiques and old photographs of the Prince's ancestors and royal relatives, while not artistic, did give the room a special atmosphere of fallen nobility.

The Prince was ensconced in his chair, especially adapted to his size, smoking a long pipe. His head was enormous by comparison with the others. The combination of size, superstition and a certain amount of idiocy made him every inch a Romanoff. He certainly would not disgrace the throne, as King of Thainos, if Laos would let him occupy it. Laos constantly pointed to Stephan, his grandson, as an example of the danger of a hereditary government; Stephan, too, in spite of his brilliant mother, was an atavistic reversion to type, with the royal vacancy of mind and futility of purpose. The point is, you cannot train a royal house, from generation to generation, to mannered movements and accepted routines, to pose as figureheads, without having some of that mannequin quality impressed on the physiognomy of the royal descendants. After the first president, Athanopoulos, died, the Prince had been elected President of the Republic. Nevertheless, with or without a throne, he stood for God, the Church, and law and order. Strictly speaking, on the island of Thainos, he was an incongruity. How did such a consummate humbug produce a jewel of intelligence and beauty like Iolanthe?

"I don't see why we should ever have to go above ten per cent, seeing that we do not have to maintain an army," said Laos.

"And I don't see why the public officers, the administrators of law and order, should be paid only ten per cent out of the total revenue. I would not be able to live if I had to depend upon it."

"I know you don't have to. I do not see how the support for educational and religious institutions, or for public welfare and poor relief, can be cut down. Our tax system reflects accurately the emphasis we place upon certain values."

"Music and song tax!" spluttered Thrasymachus. "Never heard of such a thing! If people want to hear music, let them pay for it each time. And sculpture! Have you ever seen me once in the last five years go into the Museion, to look at those stone figures? Have you?"

"No. I am afraid I have not had that pleasure. Nor am I likely to accuse you of ever being seen going into the Athenaeum except for the committee meetings, or of being found with a volume in your hands. You forget, however, that musicians and dancers have to be trained. We pay for what we love. Artists don't spring up all of a sudden overnight. Let's not argue about it. As for increasing the pay of the public administrators, it is contradictory to our very purpose of discouraging people from entering government service. This evil, the rush for government jobs, is a social disease which has grown up in many countries. It has happened in the United States, in France, in Communist Russia. In the first case, the federal employees swelled to millions. In the second, the system of families feeding upon the ministries as a hereditary privilege practically strangled the government, ate up the revenue, bankrupted the fiscal system, destroyed young men's initiative, crippled reforms, and made everybody poorly paid. There would be a sudden spurt of energy if the government employees and parasites were cut in half and their pay doubled. They would not impede each other. It is an evil spiral, creating work for an excess of employees so that everything can be done with as much paper and as little efficiency as possible, to keep the parasites busy. Government by paper — it has happened in Washington. There is a point of diminishing returns, a limit to the size of an organization beyond which efficiency cannot be expected. How papers and documents have a way of getting lost! If a business firm were to do that, it would go out of business in no time. No, government work and government pensions, subsidies, breed lethargy and indolence and attract those who wish to be idle. . . . As for Communist Russia, every hospital nurse and every veterinary surgeon who ought to be working out in the field prefers to sit behind a desk in Moscow or in some provincial office, issuing directives, directives, and more directives. It is our desire to avoid paper bureaucracy — the most unproductive work ever created by the mind of man.

"Now in this Republic of ours," continued Laos, "we have been at particular pains to discourage any possible swelling of the ranks of public employees. We have tried to penalize our rulers, as it were. But they have their reward. It is in a way a gratifying form of self-expression for those who sit in offices; some people have an inborn aptitude for signing papers and making others work for them. There are two classes of men as far as I am concerned; not economic classes, but classes of human beings: those that mind their own business, and those who are not happy unless they mind that of others. This latter class have to express themselves. It is also a form of talent, which calls for self-expression. As a class, they have a talent for oratory, for rounded periods and choice phrases and the deliberate manner. While pleased with their authority over others below them, they have a power of self-control, of exquisite patience, of self-abnegation before those above them. It is a type. They thrive in such an atmosphere. And they have a special nose for a soft job with high emolument. I do not say that these ruling talents do not serve their purpose. I wish to say, however, that we should do nothing deliberately to offer ointment to the flies. They *are* the flies in our ointment. There will always be men willing to work for the honor of the office and the service for humanity with little pay, or with no pay at all. Your Royal Highness, for example."

What Laos said was true. It had always been the practice of the elders of the Republic to select young men, handsome of mien and tall of stature, with a promising baritone voice, and train them for public office. Among a group of apprentices in a carpenter's shop, there was always one whose hand was inclined to be idle, but who talked with a natural facility for words. Such a boy might take ten days to finish a bench while others took five. He pursued his trade without distinction, without enthusiasm, but let any trouble arise, and he could be trusted to stand up on the bench and harangue the other apprentices. Clearly he was a misfit in a carpenter's shop; it would be a pity to waste his gift of eloquence, so much prized and so well cultivated among the Hellenes. Or among a group of shepherd boys, there might be one who, being idle and absent-minded, had the tendency to lose his sheep, but who had no difficulty in blaming the loss on others. Other boys, in whatever group, were noticed to have the special ability of contriving to make others do things for them. Coincidentally, none of them was a good craftsman himself. Such boys were carefully picked from their individual professions, and sent to the School of Public Administration, where oratory, elementary and advanced, was a compulsory subject, given a place of central importance in the program of studies.

But the course of oratory, or public eloquence, as they called it, must not be supposed to cover rhetoric only. It included the art of silence. They studied, of course, Demosthenes and such translations of Cicero and Cato as were available; the beauty of language, the rounded periods, and the artful choice of words to influence popular feeling were carefully pointed out and studied. For those who had the gift of languages, even Burke and Daniel Webster were included. But, "Fine speech is like silver, silence is gold," ran one of the maxims for the school. The beginners were put through a rigorous training in keeping secrets — more simply, in keeping their mouths shut. A fierce sense of loyalty and esprit de corps was developed among them; nothing they did in the school was to be divulged to the public, even if it was the most harmless kind of information. If a boy told his mother that they had had cold lamb for lunch, he was severely reprimanded. To such questions, the older students usually replied in dignified tones, "No comment."

Laos had himself, with his own painstaking labors, translated a Chinese essay. "Pointing Out the Ferry Across the Official Sea," or more simply, "Keys to Success and Political Advancement." In this famous ancient handbook, the successive stages of the art of equivocation were clearly outlined, beginning with not saying what was on one own's mind, proceeding by stages to saying what was on the other's mind, then saying what was not on one's mind, and finally to the most accomplished and difficult stage, of saying half of what was on one's mind. This last stage presupposed a thorough preparation, a fine mastering of vocabulary, a flair for double-entendre and innocent ambiguities, to the end that the accomplished servant of the state should always be able to affirm what he had denied, and deny what he had affirmed. If future events made desirable a shift of course of action, the public servant should always be able to deny that he had said what he had said, that what he had said did not mean what he had said, but in fact exactly the opposite. It was categorically stated, according to this Chinese handbook, that officials who had risen to governorships and cabinet ranks had practiced the art of saying half of what was on one's mind to perfection. Inasmuch as this last accomplishment required great polish and refinement of language, it was the most difficult of all. Compared to the sonorous beauty of these state memoranda, a curt reply of "no comment" by the officials of the Old World sounded crude and very much like fear of battle.

But, says·the Chinese manual, even the dullest, provided he had the will to learn, could overcome, by assiduous practice, the first stage, namely, not saying what was on one's mind. This consisted in keeping one's mouth shut. Students of this stage could qualify for copyists, operators and third-class secretaries. Those who had mastered the second stage, of saying what was on the other's mind, were considered promising. This consisted mainly in saying "You are right, sir," no matter what was the subject under discussion. Young men who showed such promise were given the rank of second-class secretaries, in which position they were permitted to interview the less important emissaries, guests and representatives of public bodies. Some of these were given the position of departmental chiefs, a rank equivalent to serving as *taotai* magistrates in the provinces. In this position they had the opportunity to learn from the older, tried-and-true mainstays of the department the art of saying what was not on one's mind, with the employment of charming ambiguities and fine nuances. Ten years of such governmental experience were usually required. This went on of course with an excellent training in self-discipline, in never losing one's temper. Many of the officials, the run of the mill, never got beyond this step, or practiced it only with indifferent success. As for the cream, the fine flower of mandarinate, the handbook avowed, only a few could aspire to reach such austere heights of culture. Diplomats and cabinet ministers and great governors were born, not made.

But then the nation could do without everybody aspiring to governorships and cabinet posts.

In practice, Laos explained to the students of the School of Public Administration, which was housed in a small building, he had found this true of the Western world, that Chinese wisdom was universal in application. From his own experience, Laos told them, he had always found third-class secretaries able to talk only in scared tones of whisper. Not so the truly born diplomats! Why, he had sat a whole evening with such diplomats. Suave and graceful, and apparently frank, full of anecdotes for either evading an embarrassing question or leading away from it to some trivialities, some amazing experience in Alaska or Iceland, or an innocent encounter with an Australian peasant girl, the diplomat could rattle off all evening. "Isn't he amazingly frank and agreeable, not at all tight-mouthed?" the hostess would say. And at the end of the evening the hostess discovered, or you discovered, he had not let out one scrap of vital information as to where his government or he himself stood with regard to a burning question. Such men were the despair of the lesser artists.

Following this principle, Laos had assisted in forming the program of instruction in rhetoric, or eloquence, as they called it. The students were given ample opportunity for practice. Debates on public issues were frequently held; the state would perish if there were no orators. A subject was chosen for debate. The merits were strictly given on the basis of who could talk longer and say less. The graduation ceremony was always a brilliant affair on the island, greatly enjoyed by the parents and the public. Two students were selected to give the valedictory, carefully chosen from those who had distinguished themselves in their class. The fireworks of rhetoric started, the parade of phrases began; the delivery was always flawless, the inflections perfect, the flow of euphonious sounds charming. Nobody understood, or hoped to understand, what they were saying. The speakers always received a deafening applause. But all of them who graduated at all were conferred the degree of M.E., which spelled out in English conveniently as Master of Equivocation. But the better speaker of the two received the *magna cum laude*.

Such a bright young man, the audience usually commented, will one day become the President of the Republic.

Of course, rhetoric was not the only subject taught in the School. The training in political science was different in character from that given in the colleges of the Old World. Some jurisprudence was taught, but it was thought impractical to teach the students the varied and complex laws and institutions which belonged to the past. Above all, Laos, following Confucian ideals, had always insisted on simplicity of administration and law court proceedings. Government was at best a necessary evil. The School of Public Administration was conceived primarily to fit a person for public office. As it was the habit of a democracy to fix responsibility for actions and hold its public men to promises they had made, the basic principle of this training was defense against responsibility.

It must not be supposed that Laos had deliberately set out to wreck the political machinery of the Republic; rather it was his desire to inculcate, by the most indirect means possible, a healthy public distrust of government, which was the bedrock of democracy. A strong government always spelled the destruction of a democratic form of government. By contrast, an insidious distrust of their rulers was the best guarantee for keeping the spirit of liberty alive. The chief ruler, such as the President of the Republic, must be popular of course, but not too popular. God forbid! Let the rulers be bright, but not overbright! A great general is made by the exposure of tens of thousands of skeletons on the battlefield, so runs a Chinese proverb; and Laos inferred, a strong government was established over the ruins and wreckage of the people's liberties. Hence the weaker the government and the more it was held in public contempt, the brighter burned the lamp of liberty, fraternity and equality for all.

That the public servants of the state might not appear too impressive, that efficiency of government might be appropriately lowered, these students were carefully instructed in the various

arts and subterfuges for defense against responsibility and against
any precipitate promptness of action. (Such at least was Laos'
unavowed intention.) As the people demanded responsibility, the
government must learn to evade it, without being actually rushed
into action. Anyone who expected to survive in a public career
had to familiarize himself with the working of this principle, how
to appear to be always planning to do good things for the
public without doing them, and without arousing any suspicion
of his integrity of character.

Basically, this was taught in three cardinal tenets: the principle of collective responsibility, the principle of reference, and
the principle of gradual progress, the last requiring no special
explanation. The principle of collective responsibility was em-
bodied in the forming of various committees for the purpose of
avoiding individual responsibility, since no one need be held
responsible for a committee decison. That was why there were
so many committees for so little work done, and why the time of
the public employees was spent in all-day committee meetings.
To avoid duplication of labor, committees to co-ordinate committees were established. Secondly, there was the principle of
reference. There grew up in time quite a formidable system of
interdepartmental memos, digests, résumés, various squares for
ticking off, and certain formulas like "in re's" and "forward to
your attention" which kept everybody happily busy — limited
only by the supply of paper. Even so, a disproportionately large
amount of paper was consumed; in one instance, seventeen committee meetings, evidenced by 248 pages of reports, and an exchange of some thirty-odd letters between the departments, invariably marked "In re Resolution 211.07, the transplanting of
two trees," preceded the actual transplanting of the two trees
aforementioned from the back of the amphitheater to the square
of the Athenaeum. But such delay was not only desirable in
itself, but rather helped to pass a screen over the activities of
individual officers. When the public wanted something done on
which it was difficult to foresee the consequences, the principle
of reference was put to work. A foolish, raw recruit in govern-

ment service would come out in the open for or against it, but
the mature man would refer it to somebody else, preferably in
some department other than his own. And when the smooth
politician wanted to say no to someone's request, he had another
department write a memo to himself, which was appropriately
forwarded, without giving offense to anybody. When a question
had been the subject of interdepartmental correspondence from
three to six months, the likelihood was that the public had already
forgotten about it; and if it had not and inquiries were made,
the situation had become so cloudy by the volume of correspondence that it was hard to pin the responsibility for action
or lack of action on any one individual. This technique, plus the
technique of guarded expression already taught in the course
of advanced rhetoric, guaranteed anyone a comfortable, unevent-
ful, but successful lifelong career in the service of the nation.

The net result of all this was that committees were identified
with the democratic government. When anything was to be
done, let a committee be formed. Let no one take individual
responsibility for decision. A generous moral tone for faring
and sharing alike was thus generated. The people were convinced that they governed themselves, or felt they did.

All in all, the system of government put into operation on the
island had been suitably conceived to discourage the rise of a
strong and efficient government. That made the people very
happy.

Simple laws, a weak government and low taxes, said Laos,
were the three cornerstones of a happy republic. That was
why Laos held out, against the Prince's entreaties, for a dis-
gracefully low pay for their public employees. Service to the
Republic and the honors of the office were their own rewards.

Chapter XXVI

FATHER ARISTOTIMUS had come in to join them.

"Why, Thrasymachus, are you still at it?"

"Laos is stubborn, stubborn as a mule."

Prince Andreyev had stood up to give his chair to the priest. In all his simplicity of heart, he always held the venerable priest in great esteem, as representative of the spiritual power, as he was of the secular power. Athanopoulos was dead, but Thrasymachus had filled in the place of the fourth Apostle — a reference to El Greco's painting of the Twelve Apostles. The four of them looked in fact remarkably like them — by reason of their height, especially the Prince.

"Have a glass of water, or do you prefer some liquor?" The Prince was being very cordial.

"No, no water, please," answered the priest affably. "What does St. Paul say?"

"You are full of St. Paul."

"I am. 'Drink no longer water, but use a little wine for thy stomach's sake and thine often infirmities.' I Timothy 5:23."

"You seem to have a special aptitude for quoting St. Paul. You certainly know your Bible."

"I confess I do."

"Jesus drank of course," said Laos.

"Why, you amaze me," said the Prince.

"He drank with the publicans. That is what the Bible says, in fact what the priests of those days accused him of. Small virtues for small men. Jesus turned water into wine at the wedding in Cana. Did he ever turn wine into water?"

The Prince roared, and the priest roared with him. "Capital! Capital!" exclaimed Prince Andreyev, as he stepped forward to pour another glass from the decanter for Laos. Aristotimus rolled his hand over his stomach, a sign of comfort and contentment.

"Where's Philemon?" asked Laos.

"He is dancing outside, with Chloe and the other young people."

The sound of the music wafted across the terrace, mingled with the sound of young laughter. Prince Andreyev stood up, laid his long pipe down, and slapped his arms about his body.

"I think I will join them."

Thrasymachus, having Eretrea and Stephan in mind, also went out to join the guests on the terrace.

It was not long before Chloe came in, eyes glittering, followed by Philemon.

"Do you want to speak to me?" asked Philemon.

"No. I was just asking. Go ahead with your dancing."

"No. How about you?" he asked the girl.

"It does not matter. I enjoy listening to your conversation if you prefer to sit inside and talk."

"I heard Eurydice talking with the Countess in the card room."

"Why, I just saw her dancing with Alcibiades. Do you think . . .?" She blinked playfully.

"Who knows? I think they were saying that they were coming over."

The Countess was already standing in the door, Eurydice and young Wriggs behind her.

"Oh, here you are! Isn't it a little hot in here? It's very cool on the terrace."

"Come in and sit down," said Laos.

"I thought you were coming out. It is so beautiful on the terrace. But if we are going to talk, probably it is quieter here."

"What is Eunice doing?" Laos asked.

"Playing chess with Lysippus."

Eurydice and the others came in and took seats on the divan.

"Talking about Dr. Lysippus," said Eurydice, "I feel sort of ashamed to meet him. I can't pay of course, have nothing to pay for his services. Emma-Emma says it is taken care of already. I don't know whom to thank."

"Thank nobody," said the Countess. "Nobody pays the doctor. He is paid by the state."

"Oh, I see. That is why the doctor seems to have no use for his patients."

"He is not tempted," said Laos, "to encourage patients to imagine they are ill. You might almost say he is a doctor who is a Christian Scientist."

Eurydice somehow thought this extremely funny. It was like saying someone was an agnostic priest. She was ready to smile at anything tonight. She had ceased to be surprised. She smiled a soft, indulgent smile.

"But he is an expert ornithologist and an astute, extraordinary chess player," said the Countess. "He always pooh-poohs the idea when I tell him I am unwell. A marvelous doctor for dismissing pains and restoring the patient's confidence in himself. When I complain of a headache, he says 'Let's play a game of chess.' It is true: after a game of chess, my headache is gone. I don't know about other people. I am perhaps more impressionable. It works in my case."

"Don't disturb him if he is playing chess with Eunice," said Laos. "I thought Eunice would enliven the talk a bit with her dry, salty remarks. . . . Are there many people outside?"

"Oh yes, a lot of people have come. Naturally a lot of girls from the Institute are there. Berenice and Doris and Phyllis and Dorothea are all there. Iolanthe loves it. She wants lots of young people and noise and gay laughter. And they of course love to come to the Residence when they are invited."

"Well, it's good for the young people to be able to enjoy themselves."

"It makes me feel young, too. Ah!" said the Countess, her eyes slightly brimming. She wasn't crying; she was just happy. "Youth, life, love, dance, movement! It's all so spontaneous. I love to look at them."

"Dancing is good for them," said Laos. "I think we can be proud of our Ireniki girls. Dancing is only the natural expression of harmony and grace of movement, as it should be. They have so much in them to express, so much innate sense of rhythm. No unruly excitement of the spirit. Old Confucius was so right. By a nation's dance, you can judge its character. He was quite a student of music, too."

"I thought he was only a moral philosopher who spoke in proverbs," said Eurydice. "I have the impression that he was a rather dull and austere schoolmaster."

"Nothing of the kind. One of his most important works was a book of songs, all set to music, edited and checked by himself. Music and rituals. Music and rituals as the alpha and omega of government, from the beginning to the end. He had, as a matter of fact, no faith in laws and administration of justice. He went for the subtler influences on human character. Rites and music, childhood habits and influence of home and social customs and sense of honor. His famous doctrine of filial piety was only to say that good habits are formed at home, in childhood. If a boy did not begin with right mental attitudes toward his parents at home as a child, he would never have rectitude of character later. He would be blaming everybody: society, neighbors, his boss — everybody but himself. Quite a psychologist, Confucius. Moral righteousness begins at home. He went rather to the extreme, of course, in his emphasis on education and the arts, but he was the philosophic type. Never could keep a job in government — out and in all the time — but mostly out — traveling in the wilds — running into bandits and rebels — insulted, detained — but never left his guitar, or what was the equivalent of a guitar. Singing in the rain, comparing himself to a homeless, wandering dog and making a joke of it! True philosophers are like that. Like Plato, he gave up all thoughts of putting his ideas into practice late in life and went back to teaching. A great man. It took a great man to say simple things. When asked what was his dream for a peaceful society, he said that his dream was that the young should be able to enjoy themselves and the old live in affection and public esteem. That's what I call simple. Yet after thinking and reading up all social philosophies, you don't find better things than that. The greatest good of the greatest number seems cold in comparison."

"You love simplicity," said Eurydice.

"I do."

"It's quite a gift. It's not easy, is it?"

"No, it's not easy. But I say to myself, if a man cannot think clearly, how can he make it clear to others? Any thinking which has been digested becomes clear, and any which has not remains unclear, beclouded with a lot of pompous words. The man himself is befogged, treading in a cloud of dimly perceived shapes and forms. They are a danger to mankind, because the habit of unclear thinking is a danger to mankind. There ought to be a law requiring a professor of philosophy to explain his thoughts to his maidservant. If he cannot do that, he ought to be disqualified, disfranchised, summarily dismissed. He will be passing on his dimly perceived shapes and forms to the youth. I suspect, very often, if you strip him of his academic jargon he really has very little to say to the common man. The diplomats have a right to be unclear, the professors don't. Look at the clarity of Hellenic thought, their mode of expression! The clarity of the Ionian sun. That was how the human spirit achieved sweetness and light. Now academic thought, professorial thought, hangs like a wet limp kitchen rag. It's not neat and it's not pretty."

"But life isn't simple. Modern life isn't simple," said Eurydice. "Society has grown complex, and thinking with it, don't you think?"

"Of course it isn't simple. The question is what will you have? Life can be looked at simply; no? If you face the sun at dawn, stand erect upon the earth, canopied by the open sky, your thinking becomes clear, too. Only in the cloistered shadows of universities, or in the cavernous shades of cathedrals where men brood on their sins, do thoughts become unclear."

Philemon said, "Eurydice has a point there. Philosophy is the study of man, of human nature. But man is a highly complex creature . . ."

Eurydice interrupted to say, "I heard you talking at the table about Freud. Now isn't the human mind extremely complicated?"

"Of course it is. It is philosophy's business to make it simple, or at least make it clear — clear as to what man most wants in life, and get a tight grip on it, refusing to let go. You have seen the fishermen drawing in their nets; it's so important to keep a tight grip on the main lines and let the entangling net take care of itself. Everything falls into place if the master lines are held firmly in hand."

"And what are those master lines?"

"All men want different things, and want them differently. But you do not get away from the four things: food, rest, work and love. Is that simple enough?"

"Does that cover all?"

"It should. These are the four things which we need, which influence our fleshly nature, and which make us happy or unhappy, according as we have them the way we want or not. We don't get away from food of course — our primary need. Rest covers the comforts of a house and shelter, a bed, a good mattress, a nice armchair, clothing, a good bath, soap — everything that contributes to the comforts of material living. To enjoy these things, man has to work. The farmer plants his corn, the artisan beats out a kettle, the weaver makes a basket, etc. — to make his living. It justifies all his multifarious activites. Here between making a living and the attainment of those comforts you want, slips in the entire complex structure of economic facts, of trade and industry and international commerce — all the way to shipping and insurance. That's where the modern man is caught, and effectively stopped. He never goes beyond that, or thinks much about it. The mere act of making a living weighs him down, puts him in harness, cramps his style, warps his spirit and corrupts his mind. All right, modern man is progressive, civilized, enjoys all the luxuries and conveniences denied to kings and queens two centuries ago. The question is: what price these modern conveniences? No man but can put his pipe in his mouth and count on his fingers the few things he really wants. Different men want different things. For me, a good mattress is very desirable. But when I have that, I am the equal of anybody: the world's richest millionaire does not sleep on a bigger mattress because he is a millionaire. His bed cannot be longer than mine, save a matter of inches. Nature makes us equal. The short span of life makes us equal. Old age and death make us equal. Death is democratic. Because Nature is democratic. An ulcer-free stomach may be all a millionaire will pray for. Nature compensates. Man imagines there are numberless things he wants. It is not true. He wants them only because he does not have them; when he has them, he does not want them. Pleasures grow stale. So as far as material well-being and happiness are concerned, there are only a few things. Epicurus reduces all to one thing, the absence from pain — all the rest are temporary, subject to loss. Am I ascetic? No, I wallow in the material comforts of life. I have what Santayana calls animal faith."

Philemon said, "I suppose you mean the old-fashioned saying that the best things of life cost nothing."

"Old-fashioned, yes. But it is true. The trouble is in modern life they don't cost nothing any more. An open river view from your window in an apartment house costs about ten dollars a month; one segment of sky, five; half a sky, ten; three-quarters, nearly twenty-five; as for a whole rounded sky such as is enjoyable from a penthouse — it's for the millionaires or near-millionaires. There used to be a paper in New York called the *Herald Tribune* which had a project that was named 'Fresh Air Fund.' Literally, you had to have a fund to enable city children to enjoy fresh air. It, the fresh air, had stopped costing nothing."

"You haven't spoken about love, and love is much more complex, I suspect," said Eurydice.

"Yes, I believe I was carried away on the subject of making a living. So much of his time is taken up with making a living that man forgets to face up to the whole of himself. He makes of his spirit a slave to his body, as the Chinese expression goes. He loses his freedom. He forgets what he loves, the poor fool. Man is a curious animal; he has psychic, as well as physical needs. As I said, we must face up to the whole truth about man. And his psychic department is much more complex than his physical department. Man's psyche is a box that contains many wares, sometimes very curious wares. Philosophy, or love of wisdom, of knowledge and learning, is only a rare flower — wanted as a matter of fact by the very few. Man's life is dominated by other loves. It is these loves that dominate human life. Consequently we cannot even begin to philosophize about human life unless we know what these loves are."

"I have noticed that philosophy means in Greek the love of wisdom. Was it Pythagoras who invented that word? He refused to be called wise, but just a lover of wisdom. It was so charming of him. You seem to have a lot of words with *phil* — from philter to philosophy. The Greeks must have loved that word."

"Yes, they loved love. They *phil* everything. They *philip.*"

"Philip?"

"Yes, *philip* is to love a horse, or be a lover of horses (*philohippos*); *philadelphia* is the love of friends, brotherly love (*philoadelphi*). There was a Philadelphia in Asia Minor, west of Antioch."

"They really love so much."

"They do. It is a Hellenism. You make a category of words expressing the various loves in a language, and you have a pretty complete picture of its national psyche. The Greek language happens to be extraordinarily rich in this category of ideas. There is the love of chatter, of meddling in other people's business, love of violence, of food and sleep, love of riches and gold and sensuous living, of wine and noise, of the chase and war. They have special words for all of these. On the fair side, there is the love of the bride and groom, love of beauty, love of wisdom, of learning, of a good joke, of labor, and of the arts, of the lyre, of the Muses. Pathologically, there are quite a few

words for love of groaning, of lamentation. Homer speaks even
of loving the woman's breast. Quite extraordinary, don't you,
think? These are, as it were, the ingredients of human life, and
we have to make of it as good a dish as we can."

"How would you make a good dish? Certainly some loves are
more important than others."

"I have thought a great deal about these forms of love — these
desires that keep men and women so busy. Certainly love of
the family, of one's natural kin, of friendship and of one's own
country are some of the strongest and most noble forms of human
love. There is no use trying to classify them. However, all
human life seems to be dominated by four *philos* — two of the
ennobling kind, *philosophia* and *philomusia,* and two of the more
material and often degrading kind, *philosomatia* and *philodoxia.*
According as we give expression to these loves, placing higher
value on the one or the other, we change the tenor of our social
and spiritual life. They are the motivating forces of human life
and human society."

Laos went on: "*Philosophia,* the love of wisdom, the steady,
free pursuit of knowledge, is certainly the noblest and fairest
form of love. It includes science as we understand it today, the
free and fearless inquiry into the nature and cause of things.
Of course you know the Greeks understood by philosophy something quite different from the modern connotation of that word.
The Greeks meant by that word love of wisdom, inquiry into the
good and beautiful life. Socratic philosophy was ethical philosophy, concerned with the conduct of life. Modern philosophers
would be horrified if you told them that was their function: they
don't want to be turned into schoolma'ams. That is to say, for a
whole century philosophy had nothing to do with human life.
It was emaciated, castrated, sterilized of all moral purpose, and
truly monastic. It coiled itself like a conch shell further and
further back from sunlight until it reached its own tail. There the
shellfish meditates about the theory of knowledge, about the
possibility of knowledge and its relation to reality. How do I
know? That is the great question of shellfish philosophy. How

can I possibly be sure that I know what I know? Whitehead caused quite a stir, an academic *éclat*, when he announced, after due meditation, that knowledge is a *function* of reality, not an extraneous factor added to it. He had given a clear answer to a formidable problem! A revolutionary thought! Quite an animated flutter of feathers in the academic fowlyard! That was where philosophy had come to.

"Next comes *philomusia,* the love of the arts, the muses — music, poetry, song, dance, sculpture — those things that satisfy the spirit of man, as philosophy satisfies his yearning for knowledge. It is for this reason that here in Thainos we are trying to create an atmosphere favorable for the development of the arts. In the practice of the arts, man is nearest to the gods, for he is a creator, a maker of things. In this sense, the maker of a bronze kettle or a cane chair is not to be despised. There are applied arts — *philotechnia* — just as creative as the pure arts if they are the product of human skill. Folk art is an expression of the people's creative fancies at play. The trouble with the industrial age is that men have stopped making things. They do not make shoes; each man makes one part of many shoes. They do not make wheels; each man makes one part of many wheels. He is not called upon to exercise his skill and ingenuity so far as the product of his hand is concerned. He does not make or follow his own design; the design is made for him. He turns a wheel — no, not a wheel, a switch for a wheel. It is not only a dead loss of human intelligence, of the man's necessary expression of his artistic genius; it is a wrench, a violence to a very essential part of his nature, the creative part."

"You exaggerate a little, if I may say so," said Philemon. "The skilled mechanic is as proud at the lathe of the fineness and precision of his work."

"I do. Everybody exaggerates when he scores a point. Then we turn a half-truth into a whole truth; therein the danger lies. But in the main, the essential truth of what I say cannot be denied."

Chapter XXVII

At THIS MOMENT Eunice appeared at the door, wearing a happy smile, her eyes glinting more brightly than usual. The limping figure of Dr. Lysippus was behind her. She must have won the game of chess.

"You people have been apparently having a nice chat together," she said placidly.

"Who won?" asked the Countess.

"She did," said the doctor.

"Brains, my friend, brains," Eunice croaked.

"A woman with brains is the abomination of the Lord," said the doctor with his usual Biblical rhythm. "Pshaw! Brains! Whichsoever step she took, I stopped her. And we sat, and we sat. She knoweth not what I think and I know not what she thinketh. She availeth not against me, and I avail not against her. And so we sat. Then I spake unto her, It is thy move, lady. And she saith, Is it? I thought it was thine. Then she taketh away one of my chessmen, and I take away her knight. And it cometh to pass that she saith not a word and cometh like Amalek and smiteth into my camp from behind. . . . Yea, a woman with brains is the abomination of the Lord. We shall have another game tomorrow — agree? — when I come to minister to Her Highness' headache."

"How do you know I shall have a headache?" protested the Countess.

"Thou shalt have one, and I shall cure thee."

Young Wriggs was finding it impossible to stifle his laughter.

"By the way, Doctor, why do you speak like the Puritan fathers?"

"Puritan fathers? I know them not. I speak the best English, the English of the Bible. Doth not Her Highness say so? She is my teacher. And I love it. Such beauty of rhythm, such elegance. My God, I love it."

"Far be it from me to say anything to the contrary," said young Wriggs. "Go on. I love it, too." He threw a glance at Eurydice. Eurydice was very near hysterics. Eunice was standing silently, a study in black.

"My God, I love it. English is a great language," repeated the doctor, his enthusiasm having not yet worked itself out. "I cannot stop speaking the language. Only King James, only King James for me. Many pleasant hours have we together, Her Highness and I, reading the Deuteronomy, don't we?"

"You really do!" said Eurydice.

"What else can I do?" said Countess della Castiglioni. "It is good reading. Eurydice, why don't you start to learn Greek now that you are with us? Alcibiades will be glad to help you, I am sure."

Young Wriggs turned to Eurydice. "Will you? I shall consider it a pleasure."

"I would love to," said the American woman. "It struck me I might start with the Ireniki prayer. 'O philoi . . .'"

"I am glad to hear you say that," said Laos, laughing. "I am sure you cannot do better than that. 'O philoi.' You've got it exactly right. You do like us, I hope?"

"I do, immensely. If I am to be shut up here for the rest of my life, I might just as well make a good beginning. It will be useful."

Laos, observing everything, saw that Eurydice was more at ease, more her natural self. Her absent-minded looks, her moments of tense silence, when she would prop up her chin in her hand, were gone.

"Is your new pair of sandals ready?" he asked.

"They will be ready in a day or two, I think." It amused her that Laos should remember about her shoes. It amused her also because she remembered that little episode in his home, how childishly they had argued about the question, how seriously she had taken it at the time.

"The time may not be far off when I can be thy succor and thy strength," said Dr. Lysippus cryptically.

Young Wriggs threw up a glance of despair.

"No doubt he means he can be of service to you," he whispered to Eurydice.

What did he mean? thought Eurydice. This doctor seemed to go round wishing people headaches and other illnesses.

But the doctor was pursuing his own thoughts. "As a student of English, I think the English language very funny. You have a phrase, child psychologist — the psychologist is not a child; and you have sick room — the room is not sick. I look up the medical terms. And husbandman — he is not a husband. And middle wife may not be a woman, it may be me."

"You don't mean midwife perhaps?" said Wriggs.

"Yes, I do. Middle wife, of course. Me, a man, a middle wife for you, Eurydice. Ha! Ha!"

The idea gradually dawned upon Eurydice. She was not so much amused as embarrassed. What was he insinuating?

"In America," said Eurydice, a little piqued, "one does not expect a girl to have babies unless she is married."

"Here we do," replied the doctor. "In America you don't talk about it. The difference is, you give them to orphanages. Here we let the mothers keep them."

While the Countess laughed broadly, Alcibiades Wriggs bit his lip. It was so nice of him. Such refinement of manners.

"By Jove, you are funny, Lysippus." That was all he said.

Eunice thought the doctor had gone far enough. There was no telling what he might say next, things perhaps that might offend the young woman's sensibilities. Tactfully she said: "What were you discussing?"

"Laos was telling us about the four *philos* when you came in," said Philemon.

"Oh, I am so sorry," said Eunice as she took the seat vacated for her by young Wriggs. Where he had learned that chivalry, those fine manners, nobody knew, but of course he had read Sir Walter Scott and Thackeray and others. It was perhaps his instinct; he was more English than the English.

While Philemon explained what Laos had been saying, Iolanthe came in.

"Oh, everybody is here! I was looking for the Countess."

"Won't you sit down?" said Wriggs.

"No, thank you. I prefer standing and listening to your talk. I have to look after the people outside. Our girls are becoming quite accomplished musicians. Each has brought a boy friend, and they take turns playing music and dancing. Please go on."

Laos said, "I was talking about *philomusia*, wasn't I? As for the other motives dominating men's lives, money and power, we cannot laugh them off. They are more powerful than the fair desires to pursue wisdom and beauty. A moment ago I was speaking about man's material needs, needs for the comfort of the body, man's fleshly inheritance. *Philosomatia* covers these pretty well. Man has a body, *soma*, as well as a soul, *psyche*. Frankly I would rather that he look after his body well; a good beautiful soul flows from a healthy body. A recognition of the body, of our fleshly inheritance, is the beginning of wisdom. Why do our philosophers sound so high-flown, as if we had only a soul, a mind, a spirit existing in itself, to look after? Such a point of view is evidently lacking in common sense. We must eat well, sleep well, before we can think, can feel the strength of purpose, the love of fellow men and the beauty of the spirit."

"Thou art right," interrupted Dr. Lysippus. "The body is the house of God; it must be clean . . ."

"Please," said Eunice.

Laos continued. "We should be on much sounder ground if we paid more attention to our material comforts." (This from Laos, thought Eurydice in surprise.) "More material comforts so that the soul may be released from the yoke of the flesh to attend to its own functions and the exercise of its powers. And to a certain extent, the twentieth-century man was right — all labor-saving devices are good; they release men and women from the toil of labor. By 1970, no woman in the United States knew what washing laundry meant. The washing machine did everything, from washing to rinsing and drying. The millennium could have come already, if philosophy had caught up with progress, and if they had been able to solve the problem of world peace. Men and women could have leisure, could think, could feel — without the pressure of work. Of course under the circumstances, they couldn't. The economic pressure was greater than ever before. This push-button culture was advanced pretty far. Press a button and *presto* — everything. As far back as 1953, there were radio-clocks. You didn't even press a button to turn on a radio; the clock turned it on for you and turned it off at the hour set. Electric ovens roasted a chicken, automatically, cutting off the current when the chicken was properly browned."

"May I say something?" said Eunice.

"Please do. You are always refreshing."

Eunice was not ugly, in spite of her peeping mustache. Thin, but not ugly. You forgot her manly octave when you listened to what she was saying, "It seems to me that laziness, not necessity, is the mother of all inventions. Why does the electric light drive out the kerosene lamp? Cleaner of course, no labor to keep it bright. But essentially because it is lazier and more comfortable to click a light on than to strike a match and light a kerosene lamp. To lie on a couch and turn on the radio is distinctly more comfortable than to go out on a wet night and attend the opera. Laziness is the prime motivating force of industrial progress. It may or may not be good. How did the Greek genius blossom into such a fine flower in the age of Pericles? There were about 20,000 citizens to about 10,000 foreigners and 40,000 slaves. Approximately two slaves to a man. It meant ease and comfort and luxury which made the flowering of their intellectual and artistic genius possible. But it seems this ease and luxury were their own undoing — as in Rome. It sapped their moral fiber. The flowering of the Greek genius was a flash in the pan. Plato and Aristotle lived to see its downfall. Today we have machines for our slaves. Even so . . ."

"There you are off, I am afraid," said Laos. "I wish the modern man would surrender himself to ease and comfort, would live up to its much preached gospel of rising standard of living. He hasn't. Having invented machines to save labor, he went ahead and worked harder than before. He got lost somewhere in the maze because of the fast pace of progress and never got out. When I say ease and comfort, I mean literally ease and comfort. Strange thing, though, laziness was frowned upon, enjoying leisure was dishonorable, and doing nothing was a sin. What can you do with the Anglo-Saxon conscience, the Nordic doctrine of the strenuous life? No danger, as far as I can see, from letting their moral fiber grow flabby in the lap of luxury. Man was cruel to himself. He stopped driving the donkey and the horse, and started driving himself. I heard it rumored that American offices and firms did not close for lunch. Half an hour for a snatch of a sandwich, perched on a high stool before the soda fountain, and off again to work. Work! Work was divine! When I was in New York, the lunch counter high stool greatly puzzled me. A dog, when he got a piece of meat, would take it to a corner and eat it in a more comfortable position. You cannot tell me that those high precarious stools were invented for the convenience of the waiters behind the counter. Why not the convenience of the customer? Why not? Where did one get the idea that the convenience of the waiter came before that of the customers? I puzzled and puzzled and could find no satisfactory answer except that the average American despised the comfort of a chair at lunch. A quick lunch. Ah, that's it. A slow lunch would mean that you were unemployed or unwanted and unneeded at the office, that your time didn't count much. So there you are. No, rest and repose had no part in the American *philosomatia*.

"Come to think of it," continued Laos, "all these inventions, you will note, belonged strictly in the category of conveniences, none of them necessities, and therefore touch only on the peripheries of living. Man was ashamed to be seen loafing, to be doing nothing, to be happily unemployed. A demon pace rushed them on. Onward, Christian soldiers! Marching as to war — to invent a machine to save time to have time to work harder than before! The magazine editorials fairly bristled with pep-up talks. Success, hope, success! Onward march! The clergy joined in. More confidence in yourself. Overcome fears. Stop worries. Have faith. Satan was hesitation, lack of confidence in yourself. Onward march! God is behind you. A great change had come over Christianity. The people wanted the religion of success, and the clergy knew it. It was a great cheering, rousing kind of religion to fight the Devil — failure. Why, religion was a spiritual force, a terrific force, tapping a divine source of energy by putting you in contact with the Divine, a help to success! Like the radio, yes, like the radio antennae, receiving invisible power from above, catching messages from on high. Religion, in other words, will help you to success, raise your position in the company and in the eyes of your colleagues, increase the value of your services to the company and of your pay check. If a religion did not help one to fight on, with faith in God and confidence in oneself, to become a vice-president, why, it was no religion at all."

After this long-winded peregrination, Laos came to a halt.

There was the noise of laughter from outside, a swarm of merry voices.

Eurydice asked, "Isn't this love of good living, of improved material well-being, perfectly natural?"

"Of course it is. Of course comfort and ease are noble aims of life. Then hold fast to that aim. Be comfortable. In all these inventions, the peripheries were touched; man's center remained the same. The human body is uncommonly flexible. Over-emphasis may be placed on mechanical inventions. It is so easy to forget that life wasn't bad, wasn't bad at all in Vienna when Johann Strauss wrote his waltzes, or in Stratford-on-Avon when Shakespeare wrote his tragedies. Shakespeare's bed, the school bench the boy sat on, were not quite as comfortable as in modern days. It gives us the illusion that we have progressed."

Iolanthe had preferred to stand listening all this while, one white arm resting gracefully on her hip.

"Have you finished?"

"Why?"

"If you have, I am disappointed."

"Have I said something you disagree with?"

"Oh, no. I am fascinated. You were talking about *philosomatia*, but forgot the most important part of the pleasures of the body."

"And what is that?"

"You just mentioned Shakespeare's bed. And his school bench. The pleasures of the bed are more important than the pleasures of the bench — no?"

A ripple of laughter started somewhere and traveled across the room. Eurydice was bemused, but Alcibiades Wriggs blushed almost scarlet.

"You are horrible, Iolanthe darling," chided the Countess.

"I am trying to be philosophical. We are discussing the pleasures of the mind and pleasures of the body. It does not become us to omit to say something in praise of Cupid and Venus."

Dr. Lysippus had sufficiently caught the meaning to say "Sanctify love . . ."

"You've provided the word," said Iolanthe. "Yes. And sanctify love. The love of all loves. The world will be much happier if men and women have a clearer view of love, if they are not so ashamed of it, if they will invoke Venus more frequently and give her the honor and veneration and gratitude that is her due. It is she who gives beauty to the world, the song of the birds, the fragrance of the flowers, and the vernal glory and power of women over men. What would we women do if men were eunuchs? We would have no power over them; our beauty and our magic would not avail. For it is magic, the gift and boon of Venus. Christianity is certainly the religion of love. Yet they have assigned this love of bride and bridegroom to a place in the attic. When will the Christians ever grow up?"

"Now, now," said Laos. "You have inserted a useful reminder. I knew you would say something I was going to say. But you say it much better as a woman. But we must go on."

"And *philodoxia*," asked Eurydice. "Love of praise, I presume? The doxology business."

"Oh, yes. That is the desire to excel, to be exalted among men. A form of vanity, starting from self-admiration. We all have a grain of it. Only the very ugly and deformed and the stupid are exempt from it. But this love of praise, love of flattery found in all leaders, this belief in themselves and sheer love of power to rule others, can become a mania. Bismarck believed absolutely in Bismarck, Hitler adored Adolf, and Roosevelt was simply charmed by Franklin Delano. When a man begins to believe himself a demigod, he becomes a danger to mankind. Our Prince Andreyev Somovarvitch has shown vague symptoms of a delusion of grandeur. I have done my best to humiliate him, to sow in him a healthy doubt of himself. All of us will be doing a fine service to him by helping him in that direction. Let's try to keep him sane. For like *philosomatia,* this love of praise and flattery and rank and honors can become a disease, and then it becomes a terrible force. Love of money often makes a man a coward, but love of power always makes a man a brute. It is the most degrading love of all. Love of material well-being seldom hurts others, but love of power and glory always does. The former makes slaves of the common people; the latter makes slaves of the great. Napoleon. Hitler. We all have a bit of this, the love of the good opinion of others, a legitimate pride in our own work, a harmless vanity. But when it becomes pathological, it does not stop at slaughtering millions. In a milder form, it is not so rare as you think. Our Prince Andreyev Somovarvitch is not too bad a case. He is perfectly satisfied with a few ribbons. . . . The case of Adolph Hitler was pretty bad. Hitler saying 'Heil Hitler!' If I said to myself, 'Good morning, Laodamus,' in public, you would send me to the insane asylum, wouldn't you? And this doxology business was carried further by comrade Joseph Stalin than any man in the memory of history. Tens of thousands of almost identical telegrams flooded his birthday. 'O Thou Shining Sun, Savior of Mankind, Our Father who art in Moscow . . .' That sort of strain was music to his ears. I wonder if he believed it himself . . . I wonder . . ."

Chapter XXVIII

THE PRESIDENT OF THE REPUBLIC OF THAINOS
was snoring. It was perfectly all right. Everybody snored in his
own bedroom. His bedroom was full of full-length mirrors, besides
portraits of his mother, Princess Ilyana, his great uncle, Prince
Kharkovsky Alexandrovitch, and many other such valuable relics
of history. A royal scabbard, which Princess Ilyana had smuggled
out of Soviet Russia along with their baggage, hung diagonally
across the wall, its gilt handle scuffed and black with age — an
heirloom of the Czars. Those kindly, yet dignified eyes of his
mother, looked down on him from a faded photograph, taken
in Smyrna. His eyes always brimmed over with tears when he
looked at that portrait. A sweet, saintly soul. How he loved and
adored his mother! His fierce loyalty to the Orthodox Church
was part of his loyalty to his mother, and of his belief in God's
scheme in the universe. An honest, sterling soul, he had not been
ashamed to say to the councilors on assuming the office of
President, with tears in his eyes, "How my saintly mother would
rejoice at this moment!" And the councilors were greatly touched.
They loved him for being so devoted to his mother.

His inauguration speech was a great success, if merely by reason
of his kingly voice — marred only by a slight detail. The speech
had been written for him by Laos. But he was carried away.
He spoke honestly from his heart. At a dramatic moment, he
swung his arms wide open and then embraced in a closing gesture
the imaginary people of the Republic: "My people, the people of

this blessed island empire." It was most distressing to have someone tug at your toga at such a moment. He coughed and went on
"— this island Republic. It is our pleasure —" Another hideous,
annoying tug "— my pleasure — it is my pleasure — and honor
to pledge at this moment to give our entire devotion to the welfare
of the — ah — Republic."

He really, at moments, had murderous thoughts about Laos, but
being of a peace-loving nature, he did not entertain such thoughts
for long. Laos had handled him like a child. The Prince had protested at the original draft containing the phrase, "to give my
service to the welfare, etc." He had been firm about it. Why all
the hypocrisy about being a "public servant"? He would rather
forgo the presidency than say he was to "serve" the people. And
Laos had obligingly changed the text and replaced the word
"service" with "devotion."

One habit, however, remained. He referred to the Irenikis as
"my people." He simply had to. And they left him alone.

Just now, he was sleeping in his red plush chair, placed opposite
a mirror. He opened his eyelid ever so slightly to see how he looked
in his sleep when his eyes were closed. His fingers searched his
beard and gave it one or two gentle flattering fluffs. He snored
again. He had the special ability to snore before he was asleep,
having come to the conclusion that the very act of a well-regu-
lated snore induced a happy disposition for sleep. He often took
a little snooze after supper in view of his nocturnal habits. The
island not only looked prettier in the starlight. It looked bigger,
and more majestic, more pregnant with a dark power. It *was* an
empire, with his loving subjects so peacefully asleep, so loyal, so
devoted to him. That was why he enjoyed the nightly strolls.
But then why was he often so sad, so contrite, so humble, so
religious when he came home in the early hours of the morning?

He had thus dozed for half an hour, while the guests were discussing philosophy downstairs. The sound of violins had stopped,
replaced by the strain of an accordion and castanets. He stood up,
took a fleeting side glance at himself in the mirror — one never
really got, ever, a satisfactory image of his own profile — tilted

his chin and walked toward the window. The moon was at its zenith, the sea dappled with golden ripples. The heavy timber on the ridge leading from the left was coated with a glow of luminous silver. Below on the terrace, the young people were dancing, while others sat in chairs along the edge. Eretrea, the daughter of Thrasymachus, thin and tall but not bad-looking, was sitting next to his grandson, Stephan. The climbing parvenu. Imagine marrying a Romanoff to a brewer's daughter, and such despicable brew, too! Well, that was life. There was no nobility in sight outside the Countess, and she was without an heir. Stephan was all right. A little gangling in shape, he had grown too fast; no doubt he would fill out after twenty. The youth breathed that odor of boredom and vacuity of mind, that deceptive aloofness and silence, that peculiar quality of having nothing to say so akin to profundity — every inch a Romanoff. The Prince himself had nothing to say, either, in the presence of Laos and Eunice. Ah, there was Countess della Castiglioni, coming out with the rest. She was different, warm, easy to understand. Divine Cordelia! Such a full bosom, and always friendly. There was a woman, a true woman, all woman. Eunice was scrawny as a donkey — no doubt that was why she was so intellectual. Why had the Countess refused his courtship? She had offered him friendship and everything but said it was much better that they remain this way. Divine Cordelia! How he and she together would grace the Republic! A Cioni and a Romanoff joined in the service of the nation. He snorted suddenly. "Service! Bah! Service!"

His hand in his pocket, his fingers fumbled and touched a piece of paper. It was a note from Margherita. He at once felt a glow of warmth and tenderness. How he wished that Margherita were here, gay and happy under the colored lanterns! Iolanthe had made a point of not inviting the sisters from the convent to the dance, and of course the Mother Superior had been strict about it.

Down at the terrace, dancing was still going on. Only a few couples were on the floor. The music was desultory, informal, a little haphazard. The girl accordionist kept pace with the dancers, rather than the reverse; she played snappily when a couple rose to dance, and let it gradually die out when there was no one on the floor. Doris and the other girls from the Institute were sitting together, thinking of going home.

Berenice came over to Chloe. "How is everything, Chloe?"

"Fine!" Chloe purred; she was so happy.

"You must come tomorrow. We are getting really busy. Why didn't you come yesterday and today?"

"I was so busy, helping with the preparations at home, and running a few errands for Philemon. He needs my help."

Philemon was within hearing. He smiled. "Chloe is indeed a great help."

"I want him to be left completely free to do his work. And Eurydice has been telling me marvelous things about the Old World. How they build buildings underground thirty floors below, all electrically lighted, and completely ventilated."

"Thirty floors below?"

"Yes. To escape atom bombs. A complete underground city, with elevators and streets and all that. And they found the temperature was much more constant, warm in winter and cool in summer, and free from storms. It must be a dream! No one builds skyscrapers any more. And of course they have sun lamps to give all the tan you need . . . oh, I must introduce Eurydice to you."

After the introduction, Berenice said, "Chloe has been telling me about your underground buildings. They must be wonderful. Do you grow gardens underground, too?"

"We tried to, but not very successfully, with artificial sunlight and chemical fertilizer fluids. But it's never quite the same. We have electric fans to simulate the breeze for the flowers and showers from perforated ceilings to simulate rain. Somehow the flowers don't like it. Then we turn the lights on for twelve hours, and off for twelve hours. The flowers want to sleep, too. They like the cycle of dawn and sunset and day and night. A few hothouse plants survive, but most die out. We tried everything. We thought we had forgotten about the bees; perhaps flowers like to be sucked by bees, even if they do not depend upon their transfer of pollen. They just love to be sucked; it is in their nature. We let out the bees regularly from nine to twelve, then another turn between three and five. It never quite worked. The flowers just died."

"What about the cows?"

"Oh, we leave them on the ground surface. There is much more pasture land available since most buildings are built underground. A few people refuse stubbornly to go under. But everything is so much more convenient with modern inventions and facilities. Some advantages are undeniable. You can understand that it is easier to deliver milk in quantities underground than up a sky-scraper. Less pressure, too, is required for water in the mains."

"Don't you come up to the ground surface at all?"

"We do, for a stroll, or a whiff of fresh air. Things are apt to be a little seedy-looking on the surface, with long stretches of country, and not a house in sight; only funnels sticking out of the ground blowing smoke. Where dozens stand in a row, with a blue haze over the area, you know there is probably a street underneath — the way you detect crabs in the sand. We don't call these chimneys, but ventducts; they rise two or three feet above the ground to prevent snow and water from seeping in. There is just as much business going on — people selling and buying, though we are a quieter race as a whole. We get the subterranean outlook — the groundhog point of view. Some show a tendency to hibernate, and become quieter, more philosophical. But people work and are happy all the same. If you have not been there, you cannot imagine what it is like. Science can do everything; light perfect; ventilation perfect; you forget you are underground at all. We call these structures unsinkable skyscrapers. Those skyscrapers they used to have in New York and Chicago belonged to a past era. We do not have too much respect for the twentieth century — so old-fashioned and marked by four big world wars, from 1914 to 1998. We are hoping to do better in the twenty-first."

"Come on, we must go," said one of Berenice's friends.

After the girls left, the others remained chatting for some time. Eugénie, Laos' fat French cook who had come over to help with the dinner, now appeared. She said to the old philosopher: "Come on. It is late. You must come home."

Laos rose obediently. It looked from the sharp intonation of her voice that she would have laid her hand on his arm if he had not.

"If she tells me I must, I must," he said good-humoredly.

Eugénie, in black, wobbled away with Laos, swinging her broad shoulders a little on account of her weight. "She is a woman of peasant stock, from Bourgogne — you know what I mean. Never sick a day," said the Countess to Eurydice. Laos' tall erect figure needed no support. But the old French cook believed that he did, and Laos let her usher him out. True, her steps were fairly steady, and she was shorter of stature. It was open to question, however, as to who would have to support whom in case they both stumbled at the same time in the dark. Anyway, the old philosopher went home like a good schoolchild.

Even a philosopher met his match in a woman.

Prince Andreyev was already off for his nightly stroll.

Chapter XXIX

EURYDICE was lying in bed, having been waked up by the profuse bird calls, though she had retired late. After the guests had gone, Iolanthe had come into her room and sat and talked for a while. She had been given Athanopoulos' own bedroom, on the southeast corner, commanding a view of the mountain and the sea. It was perfectly delightful. The bird cries came from the forest on the ridge, where a beautiful shaded walk led straight to the white convent.

She was vaguely conscious of a happy feeling. Not from what Laos had said. It was all a blur; she could not remember a word of it. She remembered only one remark of Iolanthe's, "When will the Christians ever grow up?" That was a funny way of putting it. Did she have such a low opinion of Christendom? Ah, yes, she was an Athenian anyway. She had an idea that the two points of view would never meet. Iolanthe was such a thorough pagan: she literally believed in Athena and Diana and Apollo and all those broods of Zeus, legitimate and illegitimate. Athena born out of the brain of Zeus! (Eurydice still thought of Zeus as Jupiter — it was a habit she acquired at college.) That was why she was surnamed Coryphagenes. There was a wide gulf between Iolanthe and herself. Iolanthe said, what did it matter? She could not say, what did it matter? It was either true, or not true. She envied Iolanthe for being able to say so, and thought that her own scientific training was perhaps a handicap.

What was she happy about? Young Wriggs, of course. That

young English youth intrigued her. (Though Alcibiades was twenty-four, he had blushed like a boy at a little harmless pleasantry.) He looked like a young man sure to get into trouble. And where had he picked up such perfect manners, such delicacy, such a poetic attitude toward women? On the other hand, Groucho was easier to understand. Charming, frank, easy to talk to. The very fact that Groucho could take care of himself made him less interesting; he lacked the element of novelty for her. A young man who had dreamed of owning a filling station — she had known so many of them. But Alcibiades was clearly a young man who filled his head with ideas, inexperienced, likely to be hurt, a rare botanical species that required special handling. Why, she had to take care of him! How could his mother understand him? Alcibiades, with Eurydice all evening, had not by one word or gesture ventured to suggest that he thought of her as a woman. Yet the strangest thing was that he made her feel like a woman. All woman.

Except for the bird songs and the distant swish of the seashore, a stillness hung about the house. Iolanthe slept late of course. And Prince Andreyev, whose room was at the other end of the enormous house, was never seen before twelve, though this morning, if Eurydice had known, he was wide awake, more troubled than usual. She sat up in bed, propped against her pillow, and gazed at the nude statue of Iolanthe in white marble, standing in the corner, about which the original had asked her most casually if she liked it. Of course the form was divine. Done when she was thirty, it was surprising that Iolanthe had managed to preserve her form so well. In the soft light, the marble seemed to come alive, so subtle was its witchery of line. The light rippled over a crooked arm lost in long tresses and the sloping, velvety surface of a body thrown forward from the waist down, head tilted to one side wearing a mysterious alluring smile. It was a triumph of the sculptor's art, an expression, through a material medium, of what was no more than a spirit, a wordless thought, a feeling, seized and captured for all eternity. It said something to her, had a message. It was as if the sculptor were saying, "There is a vision of human perfection in spirit and in form." With all her derring-do, Iolanthe did not have this replica of her nude self placed in the reception hall. Perhaps it was Athanopoulos' wish that this sight be kept from common eyes, to be shown only to his best friends.

Eurydice enjoyed a feeling of being settled — it was her fourth or fifth day in the Residence. She experienced characteristically a sudden spurt of energy. She was feeling fine, young, completely recuperated from the recent tragedy. Blood flowed through her veins. She knew it by the unmistakable sign that she wanted to tackle something, was ready for anything. Even though it might be only a breakfast. Gone forever her survey trips, her geodetic instruments, her papers, reports, population figures. She must re-establish her regular habits of living. What more can I want of God, she thought to herself? This beautiful house, Athanopoulos' room with a golden ceiling, this view of the sea, and this hospitality all around me. From now on, she was going to get up regularly at eight and do things. No more five or six cups of black Chilean coffee, working at documents at night with Paul. She must get up early, have regular habits, do something. Primed for action, that she was. There were so many things to do, so many places to go, so many people to see. A trip out with the fishermen, perhaps; or clamming near the sandbars out in the lagoon, as Wriggs had suggested. There was Emma-Emma, and Bowena. Dear Bowena. What was happening to Oaxus? There was Joanna, and on the other side of the fountain, Theodota and her husband Chiron. She had not talked much with Theodota and would like to know that quiet Greek mother better, when she had learned enough Greek to speak without too many hand gestures. And of course Groucho and his solar motor. And Sister Teresa. She had promised Teresa she would visit the convent. She must pay a return visit to the Countess, too.

But of course she must go and get the new pair of shoes. They would be ready. Something to do for today; a sense of immediacy and definiteness among all the other floating schemes for the future. She was going to show Laos that her toes were not deformed, that she could walk as well in sandals as any Ireniki girl. Barefoot perhaps in three months. She was going to show Laos. Education for her toes — that old philosopher had insulted her by the very suggestion of it.

She heard Chloe telling the cook that she was going to the Institute, and would not be home till evening.

After tackling her breakfast, she wanted to tackle something else. She looked at the grandfather clock on the wall. Five minutes past eight. She was happy. But where could she go? A visit to the Athenaeum to borrow some books, perhaps. But not at this unearthly hour. Everyone in the house was asleep. She thought of taking a walk through the forest.

She put on her "sleeks." Everybody had told her that she was charming in them.

The forest ran along the ridge overlooking the sea below. The path, named after the first president of the island, was called "Athanopoulos Walk." A few palms stretched their long necks like giraffes above the lower cedars and widespreading banyans. It was beautifully cool in the morning. Walking alone, she was able to think. Solitude was good for the soul. She thought of the cunning purpose of Iolanthe in placing Alcibiades next to her, and of Countess della Castiglioni in suggesting Greek lessons. At least, it meant one thing clearly: that the two older women had a good opinion of the young man. It was quite obvious; she didn't have to be told. Why was she thinking of Alcibiades? Because he was practically saying that he had failed in trying to write a novel. If he had boasted about being a novelist, she would not be able to stand him.

After coming in sight of the white convent, she turned back, fully satisfied with her walk.

Roxana came out to tell her that her mistress had heard her footsteps on the path and would like to see her. She went in and found Iolanthe sitting up in bed having her breakfast. Eurydice wondered if she should try this continental custom, but she didn't think she would enjoy it. She liked to be all dressed when she had her breakfast. The hostess asked her pleasantly if she had enjoyed a good sleep, and if there was anything she would like to do. She even complimented her on looking so young and fresh this morning. That was right, she said; Eurydice should give some thought to being a woman. She had heard that Eurydice had been rushing about between Brazil, Peru and Chile for the service of humanity.

"Don't be a fool," Iolanthe said. "Be a woman, find a nice young man and marry him."

Eurydice admired the way she said it, with that knowing laughter in her eyes. "You have pretty good assets. Nice hair, bright eyes, small lips, and a good figure. You don't mind my telling you as an older woman. . . ."

"Not at all."

"I guess you were the studious type at college. You should have outgrown it by now. There are more important things than books. I can see from the way you stand. You are the studious type all right. Why does a young girl like you bend her head while standing or walking? Cultivate grace. Grace and mystery. A woman must always have some mystery about her. Never mind what. Something that men can't understand. Men adore it. For instance, don't be too logical with them, and don't argue. Frankly, I don't know if Athena was born out of Zeus' brain or not. But say you do. It will puzzle them, and they love it. It flatters them a little maybe; makes them think they are superior intellects. Don't meet them on their own ground, but on yours. It will be dangerous to try to compete with them. And foolish. Because it isn't pretty for a woman to have the broad shoulders of a man, any more than for a man to have the broad hips of a woman. Nature makes it so, and don't fight Nature. Be whimsical, have a few convenient superstitions and abnormal fears, and above all be mysterious and a little helpless. Do you get what I mean?"

"I do. You don't believe for instance in nudity for women."

"Of course not. It destroys all the mystery. Half undress is better than total undress. Leave some mystery concealed. A good merchant conceals his best wares. And above all don't believe in all the nonsense about sexual equality: there is no more equality between the sexes than there is among men or among women. Equality is not the word; why compare banana with orange? Each has its individual flavor. Men have got what we haven't got, and we have got what men haven't got. That's all there is to it. I don't think another word need be said about sex."

"You mean the sexes attract each other by their differences and not by their common characteristics."

"There. Your college education has spoiled you. Be a little more graphic. Say: man attracts by being manly, and woman by being womanly. That goes for everything, from toenails to cerebral functions."

It was just a few casual words between the older and the younger woman. Coming from Iolanthe, they impressed Eurydice more than if another woman had said them. Iolanthe understood her sex.

Eurydice told her that she was going down to get her shoes and take a look at the town.

The Residence was situated on about the same level as the Athenaeum, some two hundred yards away, connected by a country path. She could have taken another route to town, more gradual and easier walking. Somehow, without any reason clear to herself, she found her feet going straight to the Athenaeum. She remembered she wanted to borrow a few books of course.

The square was lying in the clear sun, with the bronze Athanopoulos and his goat in the center.

She went through the massive portal into the darkened interior, and saw the dim row of bookshelves. When her eyes got fully adjusted, she spotted Alcibiades there, bending over a volume. He had not seen her coming in. She approached lightly, in slow leisurely steps. He looked up.

"Why, this is a surprise!" he said with an obviously glad smile.

"A surprise?" Remembering Iolanthe's advice, she tilted her chin up a little. "I came here to browse around a bit, perhaps find

a few volumes to take home. What are you reading?" she asked
in a warm interested tone.

"Euripides." He showed her the volume. "I like him. He is
jolly good. Enjoyable and deep at the same time. What are you
doing for lunch?"

"I am going down to get a pair of shoes ordered over a week
ago. Then I thought I might drop in to see Emma-Emma."

"We are going to have Greek lessons, remember? Please have
lunch with me. I have to get through this. Then I'll be free all
afternoon. At Chiron's — all right?'

"Whatever you say. Do you think this light is perfectly all
right for your eyes?"

"I like it. It is a little dim, but so quiet. As you see, not a soul
is studying but me. Once in a while, some people come. That's
all. The girls of the Institute are getting busy. They've come
in to borrow quite a few volumes. Homer and that sort of thing.
If there's any book you want, just tell me. I know my way
about here."

"Well, see you at Chiron's about lunchtime then," Eurydice
said as she turned to go away.

"No. Hang it all. I'll come with you. I will show you a short
cut, straight down. It's much nearer."

"Don't you want to work a little longer?"

"No. It is not so important."

He collected his notebook and pencil, put the book on the
shelf, then followed her out, in his open shirt and shorts, the notebook under his arm, walking briskly.

"Not half bad, that old fellow," he said as they came to the door.

"Who? Laos?"

"No. Euripides. In fact I found him jolly good. Here and
there a few bright, interesting lines. So polished. His name sounds
a little like yours. Eurydice. What a beautiful name."

"You like it?"

"I do."

It was the first time Alcibiades Wriggs had said anything
personal about her.

The short cut consisted of a flight of sharp steps going down. Alcibiades lent her his arm, gently, without any suggestion of intimacy. A soul of honor. Eurydice was pleased.

They went into the shoemaker's. It was difficult to say who was more pleased when she put the shoes on, the shoemaker or herself. Pride shone in the cobbler's eyes.

"I knew they would fit perfectly. If there's anything wrong, I'll fix it for you. All hand-stitched. Strong and comfortable," he said with many hand gestures. "You can't get a better pair made by the hands of man anywhere in the world."

They came out of the narrow pebbled alley into the square where Chiron's tavern was.

They had *fritures,* heaped in a wooden bowl. Fish was cheap here, cheap and good. There was an Ireniki law against selling stale fish, or vegetables that were not picked on the same day, fresh from the garden. With the *fritures* were pickled cucumber and large, ripe black olives; and then Laodicean sausages, which went well with red wine, and some unknown fabulous Greek pastry.

"How are you going to start the Greek lessons?"

"Oh, I can go over the grammar with you. Get the inflections straight of course. Then a few words a day. You will pick up the vocabulary as you go along, after you know the grammatical pattern for the words to fall into."

"I learned a lot of Greek grammar at college. It was of no earthly use to me. Else I wouldn't have to begin all over again."

"You know of course that they speak modern Greek here. Quite different from the classical tongue."

"Do you mind," said Eurydice, "if I suggest an easier way? I am learning a living language. There is as much difference between a spoken language heard through the ear and the written words, as there is between hearing an orchestra and reading the music score. The music score never makes you hear all the nuances, all the variations of heard music. The same is true of the written sentence. It just isn't the same thing as the spoken sentence — a living thing, with accented, emphatic words and slurred indistinct syllables strung together, and modulations of tone and all that."

In his notebook she drew a picture of the sentence as it was actually spoken.

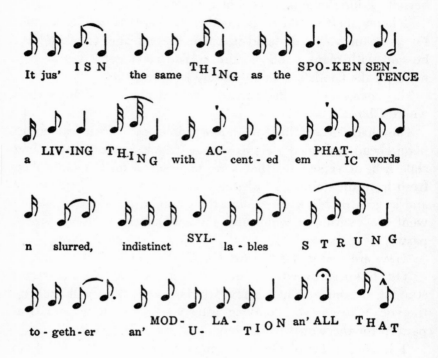

"Now," she continued, "how can a student ever get a correct picture of the varying speeds and intonation from a printed line? Why don't we forget about grammar and just learn it all by mouth and ear, as the child does?"

"That's fine with me."

"Then when there are questions of grammar, of the laws of the language, I will ask you."

"Maybe you are right. No laid-down laws, until you have tried it out first. By Jove, you are right."

"But where? Where shall we learn?"

"That makes it easy, doesn't it? Your way. Perhaps lying on pine needles, or on the sand. Just talk. By the way, have you ever gone swimming in the lake?"

"I have. Just once."

"We can go after lunch to the woods near the lake. A few people usually go up there for a swim. We won't be entirely alone. Then when you feel like it, we can go in for a dip."

"A delightful idea. Are you sure we won't be alone?"

"It won't be right, will it?"

"I was just asking."

"Oh, sometimes a few persons come for a dip. They often do. I just want you to feel that we are doing the correct thing. We shan't be alone."

Eurydice felt inwardly amused, but she did not say anything. Alcibiades the incorruptible, who wished the world well. Bless his heart!

Chapter XXX

EURYDICE was as playful as a kitten, lying on the pine needles on the lake shore. She wriggled her toes, consciously. She was barefoot. She had been barefooted before — on return from a swim, obligingly, as a concession to the sand, not to get it into her shoes. This time it was different. The very fact of her bare feet, the movement of her toes, was pregnant with a philosophic significance. Re-education, readjustment of something cramped and deformed, restoration of lost ancient liberties, emancipation and recovery of the Ionian spirit. That was the way, almost the way, Laos had put it.

"*Keimai, keisai, keitai,*" she chirped. "At least that's a good beginning. It is amazing how everything one learns slips back to the teacher after leaving college, the student retaining very little, if anything."

"Yes, it's a good beginning," said Alcibiades, looking at her. They had just come back from a short swim. Eurydice was quite properly dressed — beach style. No false immodesty, she had said to herself, following Iolanthe's advice this morning. The wise woman leaves herself a little mystery. It does seem true that a private garden open to the gaze of the public is less of a private garden. It is always more enjoyable, more peaceful, with a screening hedge.

And not alone her toes. She was beginning a new chapter in her life. A metamorphosis was passing through her whole being, a slow, concealed process similar to what happens to a chrysalis in the cocoon. She was going to lie still, to vegetate, to absorb

everything there was about the island. There was magic in the
insolent beauty of the island sky, the tip of Mount Ida visible
from where she lay, the proud cedars raising their noble heads
in the pure, blue sky, the alluring blue of the lake water. The
magic of the island — and the confusion over the violent assaults
upon her conventions and beliefs, upon all that she had held
sacred and inviolable, including the gospel of the rising standard
of living. The dissolving of the past, shred by shred, particle by
particle, and the emergence of something so new and yet so old,
like Florentine Italy or ancient Hellas. The delirious fever of her
spirit had left her. A moment ago, lying on her back on the lake,
she had let the cool caress of the water obliterate from her all
memories of the Geodetic Survey, her feverish desire to serve
humanity. Eunice had once told her, sarcastically, that the desire
to serve humanity was gone after one had discovered oneself.
Curiously, while she was working for the Geodetic Survey, her
earthly labors had seemed lofty and noble; now her most lofty
thoughts seemed earthly. It was like a Copernican revolution in
her mind. The first impact had been painful; it was as if all her
thought processes had been inhibited, blocked at every turn, for
ideas did not follow through to the usual conclusions. Yet,
strangely enough, she now felt happy and contented and at peace.
She felt vitally alive, happy down on earth.

Now looking at the sky above through the leafy canopy of
the pine forest, memories of her past floated back. What was happening to her? She thought with a nostalgic pain and pleasure
of work shared with Paul, struggles with problems of food and
population pressures, adventures down dangerous trails, the multifarious activities which had kept her so happily busy that she
never had time to think of herself.

"What are you thinking about?" Alcibiades asked.

"Just thinking."

"Of what?"

"Of my work with the Geodetic Survey. Things past and gone.
It seems so remote, so unreal. People working for peace and
preparing for war. The people of the Old World seem like a
dream."

"Dreams are protests against reality, aren't they?"

"Maybe."

"Eurydice, you are very beautiful."

"Am I?"

He had already looked away. Eurydice's lips curled, bemused to think that she always fell for the scholarly type. Paul was like that, too.

"Come on," he said. "Do you want another swim?"

"I do. But I thought we were going to study Greek."

"Come on. The water is good."

Eurydice had as a matter of habit set up bars against her instincts, due to her Episcopalian upbringing, had always passed for a conventional woman, but had always thought sin delightful. Alcibiades probably didn't even think that.

Out in the middle of the lake, they took it easy. Alcibiades outdid Paul. He was carrying on a conversation in water about Iphigenia in Tauris he had just read about in Euripides.

Then other boys and girls came along through the forest and joined in the swim.

"Would you like to visit my empire?" he asked when they were about ready to depart.

"What is that?"

"The sandbars on the lagoon. We can spend a day there, learning Greek if you like. I will ask my mother to pack us some sandwiches."

"Sounds wonderful."

"Meet me at the beach, then. Preferably early."

"How early?"

"Seven o'clock. Is that too early?"

"No. I love morning swims."

The morning was misty. A stillness hung upon the shore. Eurydice was there early, alone. The sky was laden with dark gray masses, a vast thick screen of vapory shapes hanging over the horizon. A coating of whitish mist lay spread like a gauze over the surface of the lagoon, keeping it warm. Horseshoe crabs and other small fish came at this hour to feed in the shallow waters. But some of the rays of the morning sun broke through some rifts in the clouds with shafts of quivering gold, stirring to life the sea of misty vapor around, drawing it upward in lazy veil-like movements to join the upper layers. In long, slow, satisfied strokes, she swam out about fifty yards. Lying on her back, she heard a voice breaking through the stillness of the morning.

"Hey! Eurydice! Hey!"

Young Wriggs was there, holloaing, in open shirt and shorts, a basket in his hand.

Quickly Eurydice swam back. She saw him going to unfasten a rowboat from the rocks, and having deposited the basket, tugging it down into the water.

"Get in. I will row you out."

Shaking her wet tresses, she adjusted herself in a seat in the small rowboat. For just a flickering second, the thought flitted across her mind that she was placing her trust in this young man. Half Greek and half English — was that not a dangerous combination, with explosive possibilities? The thought was instantly dismissed from her mind. She ought to feel as safe with Alcibiades on a desert island as if she were with Sir Walter Raleigh himself. This particular young Sir Walter was perhaps just looking for a lady in distress. He would go to the ends of the earth, dare death itself, to defend the honor of a lady, to judge from his past behavior.

His voice was vibrant and enthusiastic, as he threw her a towel. "There! Wrap it around you. Do you want a coat?"

"No, thank you. It's not as cold as all that."

"My mother will blame me if you catch cold."

Eurydice's heart tickled. He was too sweet for words.

"You told your mother you were taking me out?"

"Of course. There's good water in the pot. Will you help light the fire? By the time we reach there, we shall have the pot boiling."

"I don't see a percolator around."

"No. Just throw the coffee in when it boils, and take it off the fire. Pour through that strainer. Isn't it simple?"

"Look," he said again. "The fog is lifting."

Eurydice looked. While a gray heaviness still hung about the water where they were, the sea, farther out, was bathed in the morning sun, limpid and smooth like a sheet of silk. The little sandbars stood clear as thin black lines on the surface. At her back, the sun coming over Mount Ida cast long shafts of bluish shadows, printing a zigzag outline of the peak on the sea. The boat cut its way through a smooth watery surface, wrinkling it behind them.

Wriggs told her about his mother. He was born on this island, the only child of his parents. His young, blue eyes, his dashing smile, his fine athletic figure, the fine proportions of bone and flesh, made him handsome to look at. He had read all he could about England and the rest of the Old World, about the Spanish Armada, the Charge of the Light Brigade, and the Dardanelles, and Chinese Gordon — a hodgepodge of English generals and admirals. All this and what he had read about soccer made him inordinately curious about the world lying beyond. He regretted profoundly that he was born on this island, and not in the time of Sir Francis Drake. He would follow that old buccaneer to the end of the earth.

"I wish I could get out of here and see the Old World," he said.

Eurydice looked at him in surprise.

"What are you talking about?"

"I know I am talking nonsense. But it is not impossible that the Geodetic Survey people will come in search of you. I had half hoped they would, and then I might beg them to let me fly out with them."

"I had a dim hope, too. I have given that up."

"Look," he said. "You have seen the Old World, I haven't. It's not fair. I am like a baby tortoise born in a well. Maybe I have Viking blood in me. And I want to see Madame Tussaud's wax museum, and the Eiffel Tower . . . don't you understand?"

"Don't be silly. They have all been destroyed, evaporated, some thirty years ago," said Eurydice.

"All the same, I keep reading about those things and staring at those photographs until I want to go mad. And I want to see my own people — hundreds of them, thousands of them. I am the lone sample of the species out here. My mother is of a different mind. I can't talk to her. She has had enough of the East End, never wants to go back."

When they had reached the sandbar, they hoisted the boat up. The coffee, camp-style, tasted good in the cool morning. Eurydice felt as she had during her expedition days in the Andes. Not a bush or a sprig of green could be seen on the long, narrow islet. There were four or five of them, connected by shallow waters. Only stretches of muddy sand and a few boulders, covered with seaweed and a few sun-bleached logs.

"This is my empire," said Alcibiades. "I often come out here and write, all by myself. In case I run out of provisions, I go around and dig up a dozen clams. Ridiculously simple, isn't it? Sometimes in the afternoon, I beg one of the returning fishermen for a mackerel or a sea bass and broil it. All I need is salt."

"I don't see why you should even want to leave the island."

Ignoring her remark, he said, "Do you want me to show you?"

"Show me what?"

"Clamming. I know a good colony. Practically inexhaustible."

"It must be fun," said Eurydice enthusiastically, keenly observing the young man.

Having finished their breakfast, they strolled into the water again, Alcibiades with a large pail in his hand. He showed her how to feel for a clam and grip it out of the water between her toes. Eurydice tried, but couldn't do it. Luckily the sea bed was sandy smooth, not difficult to walk on. She was interested in the clams, quite excited when she bent down and caught one with her hands. But she was more interested in clamming with him, in being in his company. Alcibiades had wandered on. They were about thirty yards apart. Once in a while she heard a sharp thump and knew he had thrown another into the pail. In no time at all, they had picked up several dozen.

"We have enough," said Alcibiades, turning back.

Swishing through the shallow waters, they returned to the sandbar. Young Wriggs opened the clams with his jackknife like an expert. They were small, but tasted delicious.

"I wish there was a way to get out of here," said Alcibiades. "Don't you wish you could go back?"

"I do and I don't. I don't know."

"Don't you want to see your home folks?"

"I have been away from home all these years. I have only an aunt living and some college friends. And what's the use thinking of the impossible? I think the island is magically beautiful." Remembering what Iolanthe had said this morning, she added, "Don't you think that it is really protected by some genius, a patron saint, Pallas Athena herself?"

"Do you believe that?"

"Why not?" Eurydice gave him an ingenuous look.

"Now, of course, Athena and Diana and Poseidon are all charming in mythology. You don't believe that these deities are really alive today."

"I don't see why not, if they are spirits."

"How charming!"

"And I really believe that she could have been born, without a mother, out of Jupiter's brain."

Alcibiades laughed. "I am surprised at you. You have traveled a great deal. You have gone through college. You don't mean you actually believe all that charming nonsense. Athena Coryphagenes, and Orion born out of Jupiter's urine!"

"The way I look at it is, if Jupiter was a god, he could do anything, couldn't he? There are forces controlling our lives that we have no means of knowing anything about." She was determined to appear feminine.

"That's only superstition."

"You may be right. I can't explain. I just feel."

Alcibiades felt relaxed. A softness came into his eyes. Eurydice cast him a direct open gaze.

"You don't believe?"

"I can't. I like myths as myths, and truths as truths. I hate getting them mixed up together."

"What about Father Aristotimus and Laos? They all seem to believe."

"I never can understand Laos, I must say. It must be the Anglo-Saxon blood in me. A lot of charming nonsense. Jupiter turning Io into a cow, and so forth."

"They all believe. I tell you what I think. I think the island is under a magic spell. Look at its extraordinary colors! Why, we could believe ourselves in the garden of Hesperides. Some patron god certainly must be protecting this place. The colony has not been discovered all these years."

"This from you!" said Alcibiades. "An American college-bred woman. I think you are as superstitious as the ancient Greeks."

Eurydice kept quiet. At this moment, she looked even demure, believing, artless, ingénue, and of course very feminine. She could see that a color had crept into his blue eyes. He looked at her as he had never done before.

"Eurydice!"

"What?"

"The gods are casting a spell over me now."

Alcibiades had visibly reddened.

"A spell?"

He looked straight into her eyes. "It's so sweet to hear you say these things. It makes me want to believe them. I guess I can never understand women."

"You had better, if you are going to be a novelist, don't you think?" Eurydice was unusually gay.

To her great surprise, his hand sought hers, and he bent over and kissed it. Eurydice chuckled. Very continental, she thought.

"You are not offended?" he asked.

"No. Why should I be?" she answered. "Tell me, what are these water-trials they put on during the festivals!"

Alcibiades' eyes sobered. "The water-trial? Oh, yes. They try a criminal who has committed murder or some other big offense on the beach, the accused standing in the water."

"How is that?"

"Have you heard of the story of Phryne, the famous ancient courtesan?"

"No."

"She started the water-trial. Some say it was she, the model of Praxiteles, some say it was another Phryne. It does not matter. She was the toast of Athens. She was so beautiful and so much sought after that she ruined many Athenian homes, including those of prominent citizens. The wives hated her and demanded that she be put on trial and condemned to death. She agreed, her only condition being that she be tried in water. She gladly admitted that many husbands had fallen in love with her, but what could she do about it? When the trial started, she stood naked with the water coming up to her neck, while she listened patiently to the successive accusations and complaints against her. To all this she said nothing in her own defense. When the testimonies were concluded, she walked slowly and majestically up from the water, like Venus born out of a shell, her long flowing hair dripping wet. After every few steps, she stopped, to let the men judges drink in the perfection of her shoulders, then her bust, then her eloquent hips—she invented the water strip-tease as you might say. She was certain of changing the mind of the judges. With a serene smile, she came up higher and higher, confident of herself, while she observed how the men's opinion of her criminality began to waver. A strong suspicion entered their minds that she was not to blame, was in fact adorable, as they inclined their heads in whispers. By the time her shapely legs and ankles were revealed, she stopped. Casually wringing her tresses upon her shoulder, in the manner of the famous Cnidian Venus, she asked leisurely, 'Well? Am I guilty or not?' To a man, the white-bearded judges and all the elders of the city shouted, 'No, thou art not.'

"Odd, isn't it?" concluded Wriggs. "The classical Greeks just could not associate beauty with evil. They thought or believed that such perfection of body, such harmony of proportions, must be an embodiment of divinity — Venus herself, worthy of the sac-rifices of men's honor and women's happiness."

"She was acquitted of course."

"Triumphantly. Odd, isn't it?"

"Do you think it odd?" asked Eurydice.

"I do, don't you? I don't see the point of it. They never would have behaved like that in England. Phryne could never have got away with it."

"With the French she would."

"Tell me, what are the French like? I have never seen a Frenchman in my life. I read Maupassant and Balzac. Do all the senators have a mistress?"

"Practically all. Alcibiades . . ."

"Call me Alie, will you? Sweet of you."

"You call me Eudy. Sounds like Judy, doesn't it?"

"With your permission, you shall always be Eurydice to me. It's one of the prettiest names. Not cheap and common. A wonderful name for a young lady. No Bessie and Maggie and Dolly for me."

Eurydice was terribly amused. Iolanthe's medicine was already working. What did the young man see in her? A goddess on a pedestal — sweetheart of Orpheus?

"Alie," she said. "There is one thing about you."

"What?"

"You are very English."

Young Wriggs was visibly relieved; at the same time a perceptible smile crept to his lips. "Oh, thank you. I am trying to be."

"I thought you were going to stand up and make a bow or something. Alie, come close. Relax."

Any threat of a romance was dispelled when Alcibiades next spoke. "I want to tell you something."

"Yes, Alie?" Eurydice was tense.

"I do believe there's a radio somewhere on this island."

"Oh!" A tone, not of enthusiasm, but of visible disappointment.

"I do believe that Laos has access to news about the outside world."

"Why do you think so?"

"Because after you came he was seen going into the locked

room in the Museion. I believe there's a radio set in there. Nobody but Laos himself has the key to the place."

"What of it?"

"I don't know. I thought if there was a way of sending out news about you, the Geodetic Survey would surely come for you. This sounds like treason, I know; betraying the secret colony. But I couldn't help wondering."

"Forget about it. At most he would have a receiver."

"You seem perfectly contented to remain here."

"Perhaps I am."

As Eurydice looked at his dreamy gaze upon the ocean beyond, she felt a sense of pity for this young man, restless in this isolated island, adventurous, longing for action. She realized how such a young man with an imaginative turn of mind must feel. There was something fine about his young enthusiasm, his English integrity. Quite clearly, the island was too small, too confined, the peace was too static, for such a dreamer-idealist as he. A little quixotic, too. He would live up to the code of the gentleman on a deserted isle, or on the Sahara Desert. A moral hide difficult to prick through. Alcibiades idly tapped his lips with a clenched fist, intense, buried in thought. She laid a gentle hand on his shoulder.

"Don't fret. All young people are restless, I know."

"I am not fretting." He looked up at her and dropped his glance again to the sand. His face seemed to relax. Then he looked up at her again, tenderly, as a woman.

There they sat and talked on that deserted islet, and Eurydice learned some Greek. As they came away in late afternoon, she was happy that he had been so decent, honor bright. She was aware that she had not been so sure of herself.

Chapter XXXI

A WEEK OF SUCH HAPPINESS passed. And then, to her complete puzzlement, a cloud came over their romance. Eurydice searched her own record, if there was anything she had said or done which made her seem cheap and common, like "Bessie and Maggie and Dolly" as Alcibiades had expressed it. She could not understand. She had seen him at the Athenaeum and had had a few more swims with him on the lake. Nothing had changed. But he had. The previous day she had come to see him, and he had said, "Eurydice, leave me alone. I beg you."

"What is this?"

"Just leave me alone."

"I won't. Perhaps you study too much. Come on. Get some fresh air. I will walk with you."

"No, Eurydice, believe me. I mustn't. For your good, I mustn't."

"Are you in trouble? Tell me, tell your Eurydice."

"No, it's nobody's business but my own. I must bear this alone."

"Don't be quixotic. Bear what alone?"

"I am sorry," he said in very firm tones. "I can't talk about it."

"You don't want to see me any more?"

"No. I am awfully sorry, but I shall appreciate it if we stop seeing each other for a while."

"But, Alie, what have I done?"

"You are all right. You have not done anything. I have. I just don't want to talk about it. This is not something I can discuss with you or anybody, including my mother."

"Not about the radio?"

"No. Please!"

"Anything I am to blame for?"

"No. Not you, Eurydice. But please!"

His tone was emphatic, manly, even a little heroic.

Dejectedly, Eurydice walked out of the library. She didn't know what to do. She wouldn't talk to anybody about it. That was that. A romance busted before it was half begun.

She went back by the narrow path toward the Residence. It was about ten in the morning. Where could she go? Hugging her own thoughts, she headed for the forest as she was approaching the Residence. She wanted to be alone, to have time to think. Aimlessly she jogged on. Then she remembered Sister Teresa. She had wanted to see the convent, but had not been able to during the past weeks. Sweet Teresa. Such a face of virginal beauty and purity.

Quickening her steps, she went to the end of the forest, where the road rose slightly. There stood the convent with its white walls, on a beautiful isolated spot facing the sea, enclosed by a deep wood on the south and east.

She rang the bell and a nun in black came to open the gate. She said she wanted to see Sister Teresa.

"Oh, Eurydice," said Teresa very sweetly when she came out. "I am glad you have not forgotten me. Why did you wait till now to come to see us?"

"I have been so occupied."

"I am so glad you have come. You are staying with Iolanthe, I hear." Her English was quite tolerable.

Sister Teresa took her around, and showed her the buildings, mostly grouped around a yard in cloister style. Because of the moist climate and the shaded light, the cut stones, partially covered with vine, looked already aged, almost ancient. A gurgling fountain in the center of the yard was spewing up several thin streams, dripping with a pleasant sound into the basin below. Owing to the proximity of the forest, the atmosphere was unusually cool. In a separate court, on the more sunny south, were a group of lay women who had come here to take their rest from their husbands.

Eurydice was introduced to the Mother Superior and the sisters. They were all very much interested in this young woman from the Old World. Mother Superior Luella wore her thin lips tight; she was naturally a good disciplinarian, or looked so. She said not a word too much.

"Why don't I see you about the town at all?" Eurydice asked Teresa.

"We don't go out unless we have something to do."

"Are you happy here?"

"Very happy. There is so much to do all day. Services and the garden and study hours. A day is gone before we know it."

"Where's Margherita you once mentioned to me?"

"Margherita — oh!" Her face was suddenly drawn. She tried to smile again. "She can't see people today."

"Why?"

"She is not permitted to . . . I am so sorry for her. I have prayed and prayed for her."

A cloud seemed to pass over her face. She seemed not quite willing to talk.

"Why is she not permitted to see people?"

"She has been locked up. Crying all day. It tears my heart out. Poor Margherita, she was so happy before, so full of fun."

"Wasn't she the organist you mentioned?"

"Yes. Margherita was peculiar. She used to walk in her sleep. And she saw visions."

"Saw visions?"

"Yes. Visions. She was so religious. She would pray for hours, and fast. And then she saw visions."

"What visions?"

"She said St. Francis of Assisi spoke to her. Tall and half naked. He had given his last shirt to the poor."

"Did you people believe her?"

"We don't know what to think. She was apparently very honest. She told me; she would not lie to me. I am her best friend. Then she walked in her sleep again. We caught her several times walking in the dark corridor. We waked her up. She didn't know a thing. She said St. Francis was calling her. She must go. It got so crazy that it quite upset us."

"You mean in the middle of the night?"

"Yes. Sometimes early; sometimes late. And we were all excited about it, when she said she was going to meet St. Francis, for if we didn't let her, she said St. Francis would be angry. She must not keep St. Francis waiting. What could we do? We wanted to follow her, but she said 'No'; St. Francis wanted to speak to her alone. Nobody must be about, or he would not appear."

"What did Mother Luella say?"

"She let her go the first two times. Then she refused. She said it was all her imagination — a sacrilegious thing for a mother superior to say. She forbade it. Sister Margherita started sleep-walking again."

"Is that why she is shut up?"

The young nun's face colored a little, and she paused.

"Not exactly. Oh, I am so sorry for her. I am."

"Because she is not allowed to see St. Francis?"

"Not exactly. She is expecting," said the young nun as she lowered her lashes. "This time, she changed her story. She said during one of her night meetings, waiting for St. Francis to appear, suddenly a black giant covered her mouth from behind, dragged her to the ground, and overpowered her. She didn't tell us. She was so scared. And now she is expecting, poor Margherita, weeping all by herself."

"Does Mother Superior believe her story?"

"She did not say anything."

"What will happen to her?"

"She will be expelled, I'm afraid, taken back to her mother."

"Poor Margherita," said Eurydice sympathetically. "What do you think?"

"She was so good, so pure. Somebody may have violated her. It is quite possible. A girl seen frequently alone in the wood at night."

The next day, about the same hour, Eurydice was wrestling with the problem in her solitary walk through the forest. The story of the black giant was too comical. Laos had once told her that Confucius' own mother, a young woman married to an old man, was thus overpowered by a black giant, while walking alone on the shores of a big lake. Such things had happened before. So Confucius was born "out of wedlock." Okay, she thought. What difference does it make? Confucius' mother must have been a very pretty young woman, to be married before her elder sisters were. What difference does it make? Confucius was a great teacher, wasn't he?

Occupied with her own thoughts, she suddenly raised her head and saw the wobbling figure of Father Donatello accompanied by Alcibiades Wriggs coming in her direction. Wriggs, of all persons!

"Alie!" she cried. "What are you doing here? Where are you going?"

Alcibiades' face was grimly serious, the furrows on his brow particularly noticeable.

"Oh, just walking." He was evidently excited to see her, and appeared awkward, uneasy.

Father Donatello lightly touched his hat.

"Hello, Eurydice. Haven't seen you for a few days."

Eurydice said to Wriggs, "Not studying now?"

"No."

"Alie, chin up! Don't look so restless."

Wriggs suddenly relaxed, and said with a laugh, "There's really nothing. I've got some business to attend to. That's all."

He seemed impatient to go on.

"Cheerio!" he said, with that good old smile she loved to see.

"Cheerio!"

Father Donatello waved a hand, too. "*Churo, churo.* You must come to church. Come with the Countess. God bless you!"

The party of two proceeded, to the great mystification of Eurydice. Why should Alie be going with the father to the convent? Could it be that he was involved with Margherita?

All day, and after she had retired that night, this kept returning to her thoughts. She refused to believe it. It must be somebody else. Not Alie. The soul of honor. She knew him well enough. Then her mind turned to Margherita, and her sleepwalking stunts. The whole thing was so indescribably funny that she chuckled aloud in bed. The more she pondered over the highly improbable meeting with St. Francis, the louder she chuckled. Imperceptibly, it became a roar, and then a scream until her tears came. It was so fantastically funny. Margherita must be a nympholeptic. What was Margherita like?

Chapter XXXII

IT WASN'T SO FUNNY the next day. Gossip buzzed. The whole town knew it. Alcibiades Wriggs had seduced a nun, and made her pregnant. He had confessed it, and had gone with Father Donatello to take her home. Iolanthe heard the story. Chloe heard it. Prince Andreyev Somovarvitch had heard it before them. Iolanthe believed it. Chloe believed it. And Prince Somovarvitch swore by it.

It made Eurydice very, very angry.

Stunned by the scandal, she went down to town. Everybody knew. So that was why Wriggs had avoided her, had cut her off. Was he going to marry Margherita? If he did, he would indeed be a poor fool. He would be sure to find a sleepwalking wife hanging on his upright neck all the rest of his life. She was not going to allow it.

But of course, there was not much hope. Wriggs had confessed his guilt openly, and had taken the expelled nun home to her mother.

She must find out what was going to happen. Emma-Emma would know. What did Ireniki anthropology say?

She found Emma-Emma at home. The old woman was working very hard at her desk.

"I heard about it," said Emma-Emma quietly.

"Do you believe it — that a perfect gentleman like Alcibiades is capable of doing such a thing?"

"A young man is capable of doing anything when a pretty girl is around."

"Is she very pretty?"

"Very pretty. The typical Madonna oval type, you know, the type you see very frequently in modern Italy — dark hair, straight nose, a tapering oval contour."

The old anthropologist was exasperatingly scientific. Wait till her Bowena was involved. She bet Emma-Emma would not be so coolly objective then.

"What's going to happen to Wriggs?"

"Marry her, I suppose. Of course they can settle it out of court. His mother will have to be prepared to give gifts to the girl, if she will change the story from rape to fornication. It is a little hard for a nun to say so, you know."

"Will he be punished if he is convicted of rape?"

"Ten years of imprisonment, including three years' hard labor."

Eurydice was visibly shaken.

"But I was told it won't come to that. Fornication, by mutual consent, it will be," said Emma-Emma.

"Who told you?"

"I heard it from Bowena. Bowena heard it from Dr. Lysippus, and Dr. Lysippus heard it from Joanna. Joanna knows."

"What happened?"

"I was told that Margherita confessed that she loved Wriggs, that it was not rape."

"Then he will marry her."

"Not necessarily, not if the girl doesn't want to. She can be a perfectly respectable unwedded mother. That is the Ireniki custom. If she weren't a nun, everybody would forget about it. All children are natural on this island, including the legitimate ones. It is up to the two of them."

The news was a little better than she had at first feared.

"All children are either natural, or supernatural, as you know. There are no 'unnatural' children, a term which we curiously apply, by implication at least, to all children of happily married parents. Practically all great men of ancient history had supernatural births credited to them. But those supernatural births

have stopped in the last thousand years or so. I don't seem to be
able to recall a single instance . . ."

The garrulous anthropologist was waxing eloquent. It threatened to become an hour-long lecture. She certainly had the
material for it.

"What exactly did Joanna say?"

"She never said anything *exactly*. I think the impression is
that the girl hasn't yet made up her mind whether to marry him
or not. She must love him a great deal to acquit him of rape,
or she may have been bought. Joanna said she saw somebody
going into Margherita's home, and bringing her lots of presents.
Joanna avowed the presents were from Wriggs's mother."

"So it is entirely in Margherita's hands whether they will be
married or not!"

"That's the Ireniki custom."

It was confusion worse confounded, for Eurydice. She was
furious about everybody, about Wriggs, about Father Donatello,
about Emma-Emma, about all the Irenikis and their confounded
customs, their cursed perversity. She hated even Laos. She felt
a little vicious.

It suddenly dawned upon her that Margherita was Margaret
in English, and therefore "Maggie." No, it was utterly impossible. Her pure, noble idealist Alcibiades was innocent. She knew.
He wouldn't fall for a "Maggie." He couldn't.

She must speak to Iolanthe.

Dejectedly, her head bent, she left Emma-Emma's house and
entered the narrow alley. Reaching the fountain, she heard the
noise of roaring laughter in Giovanni's restaurant, Joanna's high
piping voice coming clear above the rest. At this morning hour, the
restaurant was packed with an idle, gossipy, seething humanity,
very much alive. Seldom had there been such a delicious scandal.
In the absence of railway disasters and airplane crashes and gun
battles between police and gangsters, this topic of a fallen angel
was bound to occupy their talks and their thoughts for another
month. Opinions were divided, about the character of Margherita
and of Alcibiades respectively. These two personalities were suddenly invested with great importance: every detail of their re-

spective childhood was passed in review. The sleepwalking habits of the nun were discussed at length, for this feature of the story, too, had become known. Above all, the story of a fallen angel was inherently interesting; it proved that nobody was saintlier than themselves.

Eurydice vaguely sensed what they were talking about. She hated the noise and laughter and quickened her steps. She knew that she had attracted the attention of some people in the square. Lots of heads were peeping out the restaurant door at her, and the air fairly rang with ribald laughter. She did not know what they were saying, but she did know that some people were enjoying themselves tremendously. Without reason, she felt as if she herself had been part of this dismal affair.

Reaching the outskirts, her pace slowed down. She was terribly mad at something, at this hateful, wicked Ireniki humanity. Almost by instinct, she avoided taking the short cut up to the Athenaeum; of course Alcibiades would not be there. She took the long, winding path leading to the crest.

What was Alcibiades going to do? she asked herself. This thought suddenly dissolved her anger. She sympathized with him, as a person like herself, alien to the community, incompletely absorbed. And this affair did not sound like Alcibiades Wriggs at all. She could not bring herself to believe it. Was there a crowd, such a jeering crowd as she had just seen at the square, when he brought the nun home to her mother? She thought of the day they had spent out at the sandbar. Sir Walter Raleigh could not have behaved better. Of course! She had it. Sir Walter Raleigh spreading his cloak in the puddle of mud for Queen Elizabeth to walk over. Ah, that's it. Covering himself with mud to shield someone. Who? But he had told her himself that he had done something wrong. What did that mean? The whole thing was most extraordinary. Above all, what was he going to do? Would Maggie (she could not think of Margherita otherwise than as Maggie) — would Maggie have a claim on him? Shouldn't she seek him out and talk to him, warn him against that somnambulist charmer? She had better not; he would resent it as intruding upon his affair. Now it was clear. "I must bear this alone." And if he was not guilty, but doing this for some inscrutable idealistic reason, what a cross it was for a soul of shining honor to bear! It was so English; he wanted to bear it alone, to suffer in silence.

The net conclusion of such reflections was that she should leave Alcibiades alone, until time healed his wounds.

Iolanthe saw the excitement on her face when she entered her room. Iolanthe was exasperatingly calm. She must have already heard the story from her daughter.

Eurydice told her about what Joanna had said, and about what Sister Teresa had told her herself — the story of the black giant, and Margherita's sleepwalking habits.

As Iolanthe listened, she looked far away, an Olympian aloofness coming into her eyes. Then they focused again.

"Why are you so excited about it?" she said.

"Because — because I believe Wriggs is innocent, as innocent as you and I."

Iolanthe laughed a languid laugh, the kind that was partly nasal.

"You don't get away with the basic fact that he confessed."

"But it is impossible."

"Why impossible? The power of Venus is like wine. Both of them are young, normal, not above the temptations of young flesh. I know Margherita. The tense, nervous, emotional type. She sleepwalks all right. And Alcibiades is so handsome. Forget about him, Eurydice. There are plenty of fish in the sea."

"So you believe he is guilty."

"What else can I think, when they both have confessed to a mutual attraction for each other?"

"He was such a gentleman with me."

Iolanthe opened up one of her diabolical laughs, a sensuous, cynical, thoroughly wicked laugh. It sounded so convincing. Yet it was not. Eurydice was sensitized to all the emanations in the room. There was something wrong about that laughter — too well modulated, the laughter of a practiced, deceiving courtesan.

Why should she be like that? It raised a further mystery in

her mind. Why did Iolanthe believe, so emphatically, in his guilt, like Emma-Emma, like everybody at the square?

That night Chloe came back for dinner. They talked of inconsequential topics. Prince Andreyev was his grave, dignified self, not having much to say.

After dinner, Eurydice sought Chloe out on the terrace. Chloe talked freely, gaily, as usual; nothing on her mind. Everybody was like that, except herself.

"What have you heard?" she asked the young girl.

"I hear that they are hushing up the whole affair. That nothing further will happen. No punishment for Wriggs. But it is such a disgrace for the convent. She was just about ready to enter the Holy Order, having been there for three years."

"Has Philemon said anything to you?"

"No. He just says they are going to hush up the matter. Margherita will have her baby in her mother's home unless she chooses to marry him. But of course Wriggs will have a long time to live it down. It is such a despicable thing to do."

"Don't you think that he could be innocent, that he could be taking somebody else's blame?"

"Why should he? One does not do a thing of this kind to oblige one's best friend. There's just no reason to do so. And he is an aloof sort of person."

"What will happen to him?"

"Nothing. Except that very few girls will want to marry him."

Eurydice felt very uncomfortable and tried to talk of other things.

There were lights in the Prince's room upstairs.

"I thought His Royal Highness usually went out for a stroll about this time of the night. Hasn't he been going out these nights?"

"No — I really don't know. Why?"

"Nothing."

Eurydice retired to her room, not because everybody's opinion was against hers, but because she could not do anything about it.

Chapter XXXIII

ALCIBIADES just disappeared from her sight. Many times she felt tempted to go into the Athenaeum, in the hope of finding him there, perhaps seeking solace in Euripides. She decided she should not. She knew him well enough now; he would persist in bearing his silence alone. He must have taken this step after due deliberation. She had, time and again, come to her own conclusions. She put two and two together. She suspected who the black giant was. And yet not one person whispered the same thought as her own. And what compelling reason was there for Alcibiades to make the confession if he was not guilty? It did not make sense at all. She hid herself for a day, fathoming the mystery, and discovering for herself that she cared very much for Alcibiades. There was no use talking with Iolanthe; it would make her look foolish. She couldn't stand the silence, the easy, wicked acceptance of Alcibiades' culpability by the Ireniki people. She wanted to talk with someone.

She found her steps leading toward the Athenaeum, where she loitered at the colonnade, gazing upon the bright blue sea, looking around in the hope of catching a sight of young Wriggs. There were very few people at the square. She followed the colonnade and entered the porch of the Athenaeum, reading lazily the Ireniki prayer, timidly peeping through the portal into the dim interior, in case Alcibiades was there. There was not a sign of anyone inside. She made bold to enter. Wriggs was not there; the table where he had worked and pored over his volumes was vacant. She fell into his seat, and felt as if she wanted to cry. Where was Alie? No, she wouldn't mind if he entered this minute and found her there, her eyes slightly moist. She leaned back, crossed her arms behind her head and looked up vacantly at the high dome of the library. Her eyes traveled to the Euripidean inscription overhead, "Happy is he who has learned the value of research." Wasn't that a motto for Alie, who found his best company among books, aloof and silent in society? What tore this young man from his books, his writings and made him go out like a fool and take an expelled nun home? It occurred to her that there was something melodramatic in this contrast, in this sudden spurt of action, and that it was this melodramatic character which appealed to him. Whom was he trying to help? Margherita's honor was not by any means saved. It made less sense than ever.

She came out, went by the back of the library, past a wooded patch, and reached the lake. Sitting in the shade, quite alone and restless and furious, she imagined things. Paul was here a month ago, Alie was here with her chatting happily about Greek grammar only a week ago — both gone. The pine needles under her breeches pricked; she was all nerves. She took off her clothes and plunged into the lake. The sun was shining upon it. Deliberately she sought the shaded side and swam along it. She fancied she could almost hear Alcibiades' voice in the water, his head all wet, discoursing on Iphigenia before she was sent to Tauris.

The brief dip in the lake did her good. As she came out, going in the direction of Emma-Emma's cottage by the sharply inclined paved walk, she saw Dr. Lysippus limping ahead of her.

"Hello . . . Dr. Lysippus?"

The doctor looked back and waited for her.

"Where are you going?"

"Nowhere whatsoever. I watch birds. I will go whither thou goest."

At the sound of Dr. Lysippus' Biblical English, Eurydice forgot all her troubles.

"You watch birds?"

"I watch birds, even as thou sayest. What is ailing thee, Eurydice?"

"Do I show it?"

"Have I not eyes? He that hath eyes can see. Art thou in tribulation?"

Eurydice pursed her lips. "No."

"Thine heart is filled with trouble. Ah, Dr. Lysippus can see. It is my duty. I keep everybody well, everybody happy. Everybody happy on this island except Clymene."

"Clymene?"

"Yes, Oaxus' wife. Father Donatello spake unto her, to maketh her come home. Oaxus went to the convent to maketh her come home. It availeth nothing. She wilt not, and Oaxus is mightily angry. There is big wrath in him, very big wrath. Come home, he saith, for the day of the Irenicia is drawing near. But she willeth not."

"You see Alcibiades?"

"Yes, I see him. I see everybody. He the young fool."

Eurydice sharply drew up. "Where is he?"

"Where is he? Hearken to me. He is young fool."

"Where is he?" Eurydice repeated.

"He? He goeth out to the ocean."

Eurydice's heart leaped. She gasped involuntarily.

"He goeth to the ocean, all by himself. You see the sandbar. That's where he goeth. I stand on the shore and see his tiny boat and him, a small black shape. He liveth unto himself."

"Is he there now?"

"I see him this morning. He must be there."

"Why do you say he is young fool?"

Dr. Lysippus' sharp eyes narrowed into slits, as he threw a glance at her.

"He taketh a young nun and maketh her lie with him. Ha! ha!" Dr. Lysippus broke out into a loud laugh.

Blood throbbed in Eurydice's young face.

"What is so funny about that?"

The old doctor was still laughing.

"He, Alcibiades Wriggs, taketh Margherita to bed. Ha, ha! you believe that?"

"I don't know what to think."

"No. Why not say Father Donatello did it?"

"No!"

"Of course not. Not Father Donatello. I like not his religion. But Father Donatello good man."

"Do you know?"

"No, I do not know anything. I watch birds. I have eyes. He that hath eyes can see."

"I am sure you know."

"I know. But I do not tell. Alcibiades, he the young fool."

"Then why? Why did he confess?"

"Do not ask me. I do not tell."

It dawned upon Eurydice.

"You say you watch birds. You must get up pretty early."

"Yes, very early. The birds wake up about half past four in the morning. He that watcheth birds seeth many things. Beautiful birds in that forest near the convent. He that watcheth birds picketh up things. But I do not tell."

"Thank you, Doctor," said Eurydice, as a mysterious happiness surged through her veins.

They had reached the cluster of houses at the end of the slope. Eurydice said good-by to him cheerfully and turned impatiently in the direction of the seashore.

There beneath the glittering sun, she saw in the far distance a tiny black speck on the sandbar. She focused her eyes on that black shape, to see if it moved. He was standing up. He was walking about. It was Alcibiades all right. It could be nobody else. Thank God, he was safe, and above all alone, not in Margherita's company.

One afternoon, after visiting Emma-Emma out of sheer boredom, she was coming back past the square when she chanced upon Groucho at Giovanni's. He rushed out and invited her in for a drink. She hated his joviality, his carefree manner, his complete self-sufficiency. Of course, she had been less than fair to him as a fellow American. They should have gotten together, perhaps talking baseball, or exchanging news about their mother country.

"Oh, Judy! . . ."

Where did he get that? Nobody had called her Judy. She bit her lip in disapproval.

"All right, all right. Miss Maverick, if you insist. I am not trying to be fresh, am I? I thought a gal like you wouldn't try to be stuck up with a fellow American."

"Okay, fellow American, how is that?" She was surprised that her cocky, pert tone, that light tone of playful raillery, came back so readily when she talked with Groucho. "What is all this about Alcibiades Wriggs?"

"I don't know a thing. It's not in my line to seduce a nun, is it?"

"Cut it out. You don't know a thing? You haven't heard?"

"Naw. I heard it from Joanna only two days ago. It's none of our business. What do you care what that English guy does?"

From his tone, she gathered that he really didn't know, not even about herself and Wriggs.

"What have you been doing? Hibernating?"

"I've got so much to do. I seldom come out. Haven't the time, Miss Maverick." His tone was facetious.

"What do you do?"

"That solar motor I told you about. I work in the lab even at night, then hit the mattress, and sleep like a top, Miss Maverick." He said it with a grimace.

"All right! All right! Call me Judy, and don't try to break your jaw calling me Miss Maverick."

"Judy, sure. It's easier. What does a gal want to be stuck up on this desert island for? Now, honestly, you must come and see my solar motor. Dr. Artemos and I work together. He is sick most of the time but I get his instructions. Come tomorrow. What do you say?"

"Okay," said Eurydice cheerfully.
"That's more like it."

The rolling hum of the electric generator filled the power plant near the dam. A rambling shed, some fifty feet wide, situated at the back of the plant and filled with a number of lathes and drills, constituted Groucho's workshop. It was connected with a platform outside where a small model of the solar motor had been installed. Only about seven feet high, it consisted of two big cylinders, tubes, wheels, crankshafts, various gauges and valves, and long pipes, condensers, etc., ending in a piston engine, the whole not so different from a steam engine minus the boiler.

"Inside these cylinders," Groucho explained, "are specially constructed high-temperature metal alloys, completely insulated against radiation. When the sun shines on them, they are capable of producing eight-hundred-degree heat through steady accumulation and by black body radiation. That heat is transferred immediately to surrounding tubes of water which, transformed into steam, is carried through those long pipes to turn the generator. That's about all. The secret lies in the search for the alloy. The heat is thus transformed into electric energy and is stored up for use. I think we've got it. It produces three and a half h.p. Theoretically it is possible to increase it indefinitely."

Eurydice was enthusiastic. Without being a mechanic, she appreciated what it was supposed to do. She felt proud of Groucho.

"How long have you been working at this?"

"For about three years. I think we can still improve it. It is all a matter of controlling accumulation and radiation. We've tried everything, vacuum, asbestos — we couldn't get fiberglass of course. But it is already working."

"Wouldn't it be very expensive to build a big model?"

"Yes. On the other hand, once it is built, the source of power is practically costless — and inexhaustible. They could have discovered it long ago, if the people of the Old World had set their minds to it, with the same kind of co-operation and concentration with which they built the atom bombs. But of course they didn't."

Eurydice glanced at him as he talked. She saw the genuine joy in mechanics and machines that she knew so well. She said approvingly, "It may be one of the most important discoveries of the century. The harnessing of the sun's energy direct."

They came down from the platform, and went back to the main building, where Groucho led her into what might be called an office, furnished with a table and chairs. He closed the door to shut out the noise of the generator. He was wearing overalls, unbuttoned, free, easy.

"What do you think of it?" he asked.

"I think it is marvelous."

"Don't you think that once the invention is perfected one might sail across the Pacific without other energy than what is supplied by the sun?"

"It won't run in a storm."

"That's true if the battery runs out. Crude perhaps. But theoretically it is possible. There may be days waiting for the battery to be recharged. But in the case of a small yacht, say, twenty or thirty feet long, it can be done. The solar motor will keep working, creating energy whenever the sun comes out. It won't work wonders, but it will push the little toy boat back home, right through the Golden Gate."

"What are you talking about?"

"Nothing. I was saying — going right through the Golden Gate, wasn't I?"

Eurydice was silent as Groucho paused. Then she said, "Are you dreaming, too?"

"Dreaming? What do you think I devote my time and energy day and night for? It may take years yet. I don't care. Then off goes Groucho Marx, oh, boy!"

"Aren't you a little unguarded in your speech?"

"Not to you, Judy. Next week you'll see my electric boat popping across the water. I've told Laos about making an electric boat. He approves. I think I can get it ready for exhibition during the water sports of the Irenicia festival."

"You haven't told him you are planning to escape."

"What if I do? It's like saying that you want to kill a man, as a joke. One can joke about murder and not be punished. By the time I can develop sufficient power, they are not going to catch me. Not with rowboats."

Groucho swaggered a little. That was his way. Eurydice didn't know whether to believe him or not.

"Look," he said. "Believe me. During the Irenicia, I will have a small speedboat careening around the lagoon for your amusement."

"I wish you luck."

"Thanks, Judy."

After this talk, Groucho grew perceptibly in her opinion.

Chapter XXXIV

THE CHURCH ORGAN pealed through the small Italian chapel. Eurydice was sitting with the Countess, who wore a black broad-brimmed hat very becoming to her, but very inconsiderate of others sitting behind her. Sister Teresa in her white surplice facing the organ at the side presented an exquisite profile. Margherita was not there. And Prince Andreyev's voice did not ring out as it had before; he did not set the pace for the organist to follow.

Even inside that chapel, you could feel the spirit of the Irenicia festival coming. There was a gladness about the place; the vault and the walls were ornate with red and blue flags and pennants, fringed with yellow tassels. Sparkling candles lighted up the image of St. Thomas in a niche, the saint being in the eyes of the Christian followers the patron deity, chosen because he had sailed across the seas to faraway lands like themselves, and died in India. A new robe had already been prepared; on the day the Greeks celebrated the festival of Pallas Athena, the Faithful Flock was going to celebrate theirs.

The indefatigable Father Donatello was a practical man who rose to the exigencies of the situation faced by his church. He did not forbid the believers, mostly Italians, but including some faithful Greek women, from joining in the sports, the festivities and revelries and the poetry contests, which were all part of the three-day celebration of the Irenicia. Why shouldn't they participate in the civil, joyous customs of the community? But

291

he cautioned his flock against joining the procession of the robe
of Athena. They were to have their own procession — no doubt,
shorter, smaller but no less impressive. Statesmanship required
that he should work out a policy of peaceful coexistence and
mutual respect between followers of different religions; that
mutual recognition did not imply approval of the other's doctrines
and beliefs, but that each should be free to follow the dictates
of his conscience and worship God in his own way.

The competition faced by the Italian Christians was formidable;
pagan gods and goddesses were so vivid and appealed to the
popular imagination. Father Donatello was not so foolish as to
imagine that his church stood a chance if he taught belief only
in one invisible, abstract, formless, non-corporeal deity, recalcitrant
to reduction into human forms. The believers would not know
what it was all about. St. Thomas, for instance, was a person,
with an image they could see, a symbol of course only, but a
real visible help to devotion. Worshiping God in the spirit
only was a difficult assignment; mortals being what they are must
worship God with the flesh, with the eye, for example, and all
sensuous aids at their command. Fortunately, there was a complete hierarchy of angels and saints; Christianity had never lacked
subjects for pictorial representation throughout the medieval ages.

Father Donatello had searched the Bible for such subjects for
graphic representation. He was not going to let the pagans get
away with all the vividness and appeal to imagery. He wanted
to be careful, however, lest anything unorthodox crept in. In
the Book of Revelation he found what he wanted. On one of the
silk banners, for instance, there was a hand-painted image of
the fall of Babylon on the Day of Judgment, the foreheads of the
Babylonians printed with marks of the beast they worshiped,
the smoke of their torment ascending up forever and ever, while
fire and brimstone filled the sky with orange flames. In the foreground were, very realistically painted, all manners of merchandise, of gold, and silver, and precious stones, and fine linen, and
all manners of vessels of ivory, and wine and oil and fine flour
and horses, and chariots, and slaves and souls of men. The merchants were weeping and mourning, for alas, for the mighty

city, "no one buyeth their merchandise any more." Even more striking were some other flags portraying the Last Day, of the seven angels blowing trumpets, the four angels standing upon the corners of the earth, and the four and twenty elders, and the pale horse, etc. Above all, most artistically done, was a picture of the red dragon, with seven heads and ten horns, and seven crowns upon his head, his feet as the feet of a bear, and his mouth as the mouth of a lion, standing before a woman about to deliver her child, for to devour her child as soon as it was born. No, there was no lack of subjects for graphic representation. More questionable in good taste was the picture of the woman of Babylon, arrayed in purple and scarlet, holding in her hand a golden cup supposed to be "full of abominations and filthiness of her fornication." Even more questionable was the representation of the Son of Man as a figure clothed with a garment, his head and hairs white as snow, his eyes as a flame of fire, his feet like fine brass, holding in his right hand seven stars, and strangest of all, a sharp two-edged sword projecting from his mouth. It was just questionable how far one should go in permitting an over-richness in such graphic representation of a spiritual subject, even though he had this image copied strictly from the Bible. Father Donatello, left all on his own, had to make his decision. Certainly, these banners added color to the procession of St. Thomas. He even took the liberty of changing the date of the festival of St. Thomas, so as to make it easy for the Faithful Flock to have an excuse for some gaiety, during the Irenicia, even as the early Christians adapted and incorporated a Roman spring festival into Easter.

In conformity with the spirit of the coming Irenicia, Father Donatello had made it a practice to read several chapters at a stretch from the Book of Revelation. It never failed to move his congregation. He chose it also because it contained warnings against corruption by the surrounding sea of heathendom, faced by the seven churches of Asia Minor, a situation analogous to their own. Just now he was reading the chapter about the woman of Babylon. His voice rose and fell in stately cadence.

"And the angel said unto me, Wherefore didst thou marvel?

I will tell thee the mystery of the woman, and of the beast that carrieth her, which hath the seven heads and ten horns. The beast that thou sawest was, and is not; and shall ascend out of the bottomless pit, and go into perdition: and they that dwell on the earth shall wonder, whose names were not written in the book of life from the foundation of the world, when they behold the beast that was, and is not, and yet is."

Father Donatello paused and shot a glance in the direction of Prince Andreyev, who was sitting in front of Eurydice.

Eurydice was not listening at all. Vaguely she heard "that was, and is not, and yet is." She sat up. She looked at the back of the Prince's head, and imagined ten horns growing out of it.

She was thinking of other things, too. She was thinking of Father Donatello — the man with the secret. She had met Alcibiades going to the convent in the father's company. Undoubtedly he was the man who knew. He must have persuaded young Wriggs to confess, by some mysterious appeal to his idealistic impulses. Why did the priest choose to blacken a young man's honor, and why did young Wriggs consent? It must have been for some compelling reason.

Father Donatello had been very busy these days. He had come up to the Residence — a very unusual thing — and sought to have a word with the Prince the morning after the people had heard the news. Eurydice was having her breakfast when Chloe told her that Father Donatello had come and asked for His Royal Highness to go out and have a word with him.

She wished she had the courage to go up to him after the service and ask him what it was all about.

Luckily, there was no need.

Eurydice felt good. She had not attended church for so long. The music, the candlelights, the banners, the group of persons — Father Donatello, Teresa, the Countess, Joanna and Giovanni and their son Alberto — joined together in a common devotion to things spiritual. She was in a religious mood. She had felt lost and alone; it was good to be in a community, to have the knowledge that there were other people with their problems besides her own.

Father Donatello was standing at the chapel door, shaking hands with the departing congregation. Teresa and the other sisters were slowly coming out, following Mother Luella.

"How is Margherita?" asked the mother superior of the priest, her face unnecessarily stern and tragic.

"She is all right. She'll get over it," said the priest.

The Countess and Eurydice were already standing outside in the sun. So was the Prince.

"Won't you come and join us for dinner, darling?" asked the Countess.

"No, thank you. Not today," answered Prince Andreyev. "There is good attendance today, don't you think? Unusually good."

"People get a little more religious when the Feast of St. Thomas is drawing near," said the Countess. She buried a thought that perhaps many had come in the hope of hearing more news from their neighbors about the expelled nun, perhaps even catching sight of Margherita herself. Unfortunately, Margherita had not appeared.

Sister Teresa was coming out with the others. Passing the Prince, she gave him a sweet look.

"How are you, Your Royal Highness?"

"Fine, fine. Your organ was a bit slow, spiritless."

"Why didn't you lead?"

"Well, I thought for once I ought to let you do it without my help. Don't forget, God will be displeased if you do not praise Him with joy and strength and conviction in your heart."

The other sisters all looked up at His Royal Highness with admiration and awe.

Father Donatello was watching from inside the door. He saw the sisters pass and leave, and Prince Andreyev was turning to go away. "Thank God!" he muttered, placing his stubby fingers on his chest. A crisis had passed. A near-scandal had been astutely and firmly avoided. He had been so worried, so afraid. If the Prince, the pillar of the church, had fallen, the church, already fighting to avoid being engulfed by the tide of paganism, would fall with him, dragging down the convent with it.

Back in her home, the Countess removed her hat, and taking

up a fan, sat down in a chair for breath. The walk of a mile under the hot sun had always been a trial, but she had never missed a service.

"Sit down, darling," she said to Eurydice. "Did you enjoy it? I think it was a fine service."

"I did. Sister Teresa looked so delicate, so pretty."

Timalpo the "Moor" was standing with a glass of water.

"Where is Eunice?" Eurydice asked.

"She is in her room. She never goes to church."

The Countess turned to Timalpo.

"Is she up yet?"

"I think she is still in bed. She says you may go ahead with dinner. She has a headache."

"Oh, well," said the Countess, a little sadly, "she always has a headache on Sundays. I always feel a little uneasy leaving her. She may have a heart attack or something."

"I've taken in some sandwiches to her. She does not want anything else," said the Moor.

"Oh, well . . ."

The Countess and Eurydice sat down to dinner. Fried chicken and the usual things. Eurydice thought it a splendid opportunity to be alone with her.

"I hate all this," said the Countess. "I would have asked Alcibiades to come. I always do, on Sundays. Such a fine young man. But of course you know what has happened."

Eurydice looked straight in the Countess' face.

"Look here. You know Alcibiades. He is not that kind of man . . . the whole thing is false."

The Countess' voice was soft and warm when she said, "You don't believe he did it?"

"No. I can't believe it."

The Countess took a piece of celery, idly bit it, looked down, then glanced up at Eurydice swiftly.

"I am awfully sorry. I had thought that you . . . that Alcibiades was such a fine young man with such perfect manners, and so right-minded. There are not many like him in this place. That was why I suggested you take Greek lessons with him."

Eurydice colored perceptibly. "And now this thing has happened!"

"What do you think?" asked the younger woman. "Do you think he is capable of a thing like that?"

"I don't know."

"Why is everybody so easily convinced? I am sure he deserves the benefit of the doubt from his friends. There must be friends who believe in him, in his innocence, and are willing to come out and say so."

"But what's the use? He has confessed himself." There was a note of exasperation, even of sympathy, in the Countess' voice. "He has chosen to confess. He didn't come to me when he decided to do so."

"You don't believe that he did it, then."

The Countess was a sunny, open character. She could not lie successfully.

"No, I don't."

"I met Dr. Lysippus. He told me something."

"He did?"

"Didn't he tell you? He implied that he had picked up something."

The Countess' eyes opened wide. So Eurydice knew.

"Yes, he said something. Dr. Lysippus talks too much. I don't think people will believe him. He knows I am his friend, so he told me," said the Countess.

"Whose friend do you mean? Alcibiades'?"

"No. He knows I am Prince Andreyev's friend. He knows of my loyalty to the church. The father, the Prince and myself — we are deeply concerned in keeping the church going. He knows I would not talk."

"So you know."

"Yes, I know. Eurydice, darling, you mustn't get excited, and you must not breathe a word of it. I am telling you because you already know something, and because I am glad that you stand for Alcibiades, believe in his innocence as I do. Nobody knows about it except Father Donatello, the mother superior and of course Andreyev himself. You promise not to tell?"

"I promise."

"You will swear?"

"I will swear by anything you say."

"After dinner when we can talk privately I'll tell you all about it. The poor boy. It breaks my heart. It makes me want to cry for him. I am so glad that you have not lost faith in him. That's the important thing."

It appeared that the Countess had suspected the truth. She had wrung it out of the Prince, had confronted him with point-blank questions. His night strolls and Margherita's somnambulistic habits! The Prince need not lie to her. Then she had had a talk with Father Donatello. Why had not the father told her? They might have thought of some other way out.

Father Donatello had been very frank about it. Here was a pretty situation, involving the reputation of the convent and the most prominent member of the church. Even from a civil point of view, the honor of the President of the Republic must be saved at all costs. Who was going to believe the story of the black giant when Margherita's sleepwalking habits were known? The story was bound to come out. Mother Luella was deeply worried; she had been derelict in her duty in the first place, by countenancing the young sister's meetings with an imaginary St. Francis in the beginning. Of course, she could expel her and not say a word about it, but what would the town gossips say when her child was delivered? It simply would not do. Father Donatello knew young Wriggs. He was a student of human character. A restless, noble young man, full of honor and high ideals, capable of sacrifice, with the madness of an idealist, untamed by experience. A perfect gentleman, too, who could be counted upon to keep his mouth shut. It would be difficult to find another person so well cut out for the job.

Father Donatello said that he had no difficulty in persuading young Wriggs to put on the knight's armor and save both the church and the state, rushing open-eyed to his own perdition, in the manner of the famous doomed Light Brigade. It was such an inspiring, heroic thing to do. The most wonderful part of it was that no one was going to give him a cheap, brass medal for it, but that he would carry within his breast the satisfying knowledge of having done a secret good deed, of character beating situation and overcoming it and being master of it. Why, to give one's life, one's body, for the Queen was nothing; to give one's own honor, to smear one's coat of arms with the mud of gossip, then to go away and suffer alone, like a wounded beast, to bear the stings of insult and ignominy in silence — that was a greater, more soul-stirring, demand upon the noblest qualities of manhood. Would he, Alcibiades Wriggs, sacrifice his life if the foundation of the church and state were at stake? He would gladly, without a second's thought. Would he, Alcibiades Wriggs, not sacrifice his all, if he could do something to save the community? He would. Would he not risk his life to save a few virgins if the convent caught fire, perhaps even risking an arm, or an eye? No question of that. Would he do even a greater thing, ascend to a still greater spiritual height, blacken his own name, distress his mother, dishonor his family and compromise his whole career, if the sanctity of social and religious institutions could be preserved by such an unusual call upon his sacrifice? What was it all about? asked young Wriggs. Father Donatello slowly unfolded the situation and its implications. Father Donatello had pondered deeply. God had spoken to him in the middle of the night. He had heard a voice distinctly in the dark. It said: Wriggs — Wriggs — Wriggs. He had no doubt about it. Father Donatello would speak to Margherita and bind her by oath not to take advantage of the situation, not to bind him to her in marriage, but would charge her to bring up the child as an honorable unwedded mother. He, Father Donatello, would be the witness; he would with his own hands tear the young nun to pieces if she went back on her word. All that he demanded was that young Wriggs suffer a temporary social disgrace. All would be forgotten in God's good time.

Cheerily, Alcibiades Wriggs had gone to battle with a shining armor and literally held up the walls of the convent with his bare hands. A Samson Agonistes, with this difference, not to destroy the temple, but to push back the toppling cornices and keep the temple intact.

Of course, Eurydice saw in her mind's eye, there was the young lion now, curling up on the sandbar, licking its wounds — alone.

"The whole thing is so unfair, such an imposition upon his good nature," concluded the Countess. "On the other hand, I can see the father's point of view. If Margherita talked, Prince Andreyev would be held up to ridicule and would drag down the church with him."

"But still it is unfair. Nobody gives him the benefit of the doubt," said Eurydice.

"Do you think Iolanthe knows?"

"I have a feeling that she has guessed as much. But everybody who knows keeps his mouth shut and lets him bear all this humiliation. It is so unfair to Alie!"

"Alie?"

Eurydice colored. "Yes, that's what I call him."

"Eurydice, darling, this shouldn't make any difference to you. I should love him the more for it. . . . What are you thinking?"

Eurydice glanced up. "I want to go and tell him that I believe in him, that nothing has changed. I must."

Countess della Castiglioni paused, "I wonder. I wonder if you should."

"Why not?"

"Because he wouldn't like it. Let it come naturally. You have plenty of time. Let him sit it out for a few days. He must have preferred it that way; nobody forced him to do it. And now let him have the pleasure of thinking that he is taking the full consequences of his sacrifice. Don't rob him of that pleasure and don't disturb him. Then of course, at the first opportunity you come across him naturally, let him know clearly that you alone believe in his innocence."

"But I can't stand it. I might help him at this moment by showing my faith in him."

"No, you'd better wait. It will do him no harm. He must be feeling pretty strongly about what he has done. Don't break his encircling doom. I do believe that after this adventure —

the only adventure he has had in his life — he may feel less restless, happier and surer of himself."

At this moment, Eunice appeared in her house frock, and they stopped talking. She said:

"Oh, dear, how I love Sunday mornings when you are not in the house."

They went on to talk about the coming Irenicia, and Eurydice soon left.

Chapter XXXV

IT WAS UNREASONABLE to ask Eurydice to wait to see Alcibiades. While she waited and kept away, she was thinking every moment of him alone. She could not stand it any longer.

The day of the Irenicia festival was already approaching. Excitement was in the air. Chloe came home for supper and went out in the evening again. She and her fellow students had been rehearsing feverishly the play *Ariadne*. The Institute of Comforters of Men's Souls had been closed for a month, so that the girls could give their whole attention to the dramatic recitals, the songs, the dances.

Eurydice went over one afternoon to talk with Emma-Emma, to get her advice, and to have a better idea of the consequences of Alcibiades' action.

"Do you think," she asked the woman anthropologist, "that Wriggs will be a social outcast for life, and nobody will marry him?"

Emma-Emma took off her spectacles. She seemed to have been working at her papers in her study-bedroom all day. She brushed a few locks of white hair up from her temple and smiled softly.

"It is not so tragic as that. There have been a lot of irregularities — unwedded motherhood — on this island. This is a more serious case, looked upon with more disapproval only because a sister of the convent is involved."

"What will happen?"

"After a while it will be forgotten. Wriggs is not a bad boy. I suppose some girl will marry him. Of course every young man makes mistakes. We don't take it quite so seriously as in the Old World."

Insensibly, Emma-Emma drifted into a discussion of Ireniki customs with regard to courtship and motherhood in general. Eurydice was glad to listen, having nothing to do, and Emma-Emma's tone was quiet, scholarly and imperturbable.

"You will find that some of our customs are very sensible, and some not entirely so, at least not to you. They clash sharply with your established notions and beliefs: some are delightfully novel, some bordering on the comical, possible only among a population gifted with a very lively imagination. Others seem possible only to a people given to the spirit of inquiry and free and fearless discussion of ideas. To philosophize — *philosopheon* — to pursue a subject scientifically is a common practice among them, not limited to academic students as in the twentieth century. You remember I told you about the sex cycles among men and women I have been trying to verify."

"I do. Seven for women and eight for men?"

"Correct. Girls celebrate their puberty at fourteen and boys at sixteen, but they are not to marry, in principle, until they are fully mature, girls at twenty-one, and men at twenty-four. The interval between beginning of puberty and full maturity is called *adoleschia*, a word which suggests artless frivolity or guileless innocence."

Thus, Emma-Emma went on to say, there was a period of enforced courtship before taking on the responsibilities of parenthood. Marriage and parenthood should neither antedate full maturity, nor lag too much behind it. During the period of puberty, as it was called, there was considerable courtship between boys and girls, or innocent frivolity, as they called it. This is to be expected in a race whose gods set such examples of amorous conduct (the domestic affairs of Zeus and the scandals on Mount Olympus were notorious). The gods' amorous exploits tended to condone some laxity among the young. Also it must be remembered that Nordic frigidity was unknown in Mediterranean peoples. The whole atmosphere of this island was against false prudery of any sort. Thus extramarital parenthood was frowned upon, not so much on account of illicitness, as on account of its taking place before the period of full maturity. Motherhood, wedded or unwedded, was held in public honor.

This was the point most difficult for Eurydice to grasp. The Ireniki people were somewhat surprised when they learned that Eurydice had reached the age of twenty-five without yet being married. She was neither crippled nor deformed. This was considered in Ireniki society as unnatural, and what was unnatural was a sin against nature. Not that the islanders placed so much emphasis on fruitfulness, for they were concerned about overpopulation in a strictly limited island area; but they held motherhood to be the sacred, innate and inalienable right of every woman. Enforced sterility in a woman was like enforced barrenness in a fruit tree. The Irenikis believed rightly that it was the nature of fruit trees to bear fruit as it was the nature of women to become mothers, and that only by becoming mothers, could women fullfil the laws of their being. Barrenness in women, unless due to physical causes, was a perversity, a crime committed by them upon society, a moral wrong. It was difficult for outsiders to grasp this attitude, just as difficult as it was for the islanders to be told that in the Old World motherhood often had to bow its head in shame. *Expectant mothers are a part of divinity*, ran one of the Ireniki proverbs. This was a case of self-adulation of the islanders, based on a sound instinct for race survival. To them, motherhood was something sacred, to be treated with reverence. Hence, much as they tried to discountenance unwedded motherhood, before the age of twenty-one, the unwedded mother was as much protected by law and custom as if she had been legally married. No social opprobrium was attached to natural children, first because, they reasoned, the children were not responsible for their own birth and, secondly, because there was only one way in which children could come into this world, and theirs was no different. "But," said Emma-Emma, "the islanders are not reckless about it.

"Strange as it may seem, when I left the Old World, public birth-control clinics were legal in all non-Christian countries and illegal in a good many Christian communities. Epidemics were no longer regarded as the 'will of God,' but a succession of unwanted children born to unwilling parents still was. Floods were brought under control, but the arrival of children was not. Beards were shaven, and hair was cut, but childbirth must take its natural course, even though the mothers were thereby subjected to daily drudgery and aged prematurely. It is difficult to reason when religion steps into the matter; for a Sikh to have a haircut is an offense against God.

"As a number of the Ireniki were good Christians, the problem precipitated a heated controversy. Laos knew that the welfare and future happines of the islanders depended upon a sane solution of the population problem. He thought the stubbornness of the priests was primarily due to the fact that the priests were not women. The priests sincerely thought that they knew the will of God in this matter; if they were women, they would think differently. Anyway, bachelors should leave the matter alone, having no experience of this subject. Let them talk warily about conception and 'natural' control and women's 'labors.' In matters principally concerning women, Laos reminded the islanders, women should have some say in it. Let no one presume to know what was pleasing in the eyes of God. The women had to bear the burden of childbirth; therefore let them speak out what they felt was the wise thing to do.

"An overwhelming vote was registered by the women in favor of birth-control clinics. It was then the decision of the Council of Elders that women should have access to birth-control clinics established for the public benefit; that to deprive them of proper knowledge of the mysteries of childbirth was a piece of male prejudice and antiquated savagery; that in principle, women after thirty-five should be relieved of the pressing fear of childbirth, but those between twenty-one and thirty-five were urged to produce children not in excess of three; that women who had given birth already to three children, regardless of age, were urged to consult the clinics, and finally that no restraint should be placed upon parents of whatever age who had not yet produced an excess of three children.

"This," concluded Emma-Emma, "is merely one of the examples of how the thought of the colonists is directed more to man than to matter. It sounds incredible that in the Old World, the invention of jet engines and discovery of galaxies in the heavens occupied the thoughts of men, but little thought was given to this homely topic. Their thinking on this subject had remained almost stationary since 1 A.D. Never had it once entered their heads that mortality should be related to maternity. The world's population was to 'take its natural course.' Such abysmal ignorance in the twentieth century was unbelievable. And they called themselves scientific people living in a scientific age."

Chapter XXXVI

TELL ME ABOUT these Comforters of Men's Souls. What sort of a set-up is the Institute?" asked Eurydice. "I mean what kind of program Chloe and Berenice and the others study. They seem such wonderful girls, and such accomplished musicians."

Emma-Emma smiled. "Program? They study man — man, the male sex. They are a privileged class of girls, chosen from the prettiest and most gifted of the daughters of the island, corresponding somewhat to the group who attend finishing schools in some countries. Such girls are much sought after as wives. The character of the training program of these public entertainers is somewhat difficult to describe. Paradoxically, it is a very exacting kind of training. In the first place, they have to distinguish themselves physically and mentally to qualify. The general education of the daughters of the island is thought lacking in the final touches for marital happiness."

"So they are a select group."

"Yes, the best. They have to be good, physically and mentally above the average."

"What kind of general education do the average girls get?"

"Ah, there's quite a story about the girls' school we had at first. When we first came, we naturally kept up the girls' education. We had some quite good teachers with us, men and women, and a girls' school was established. Incidentally there were some precious educational experts — I don't know where Laos had found

307

them. It soon proved impracticable, first because the girls' services were needed on the farms and at home, to assist their parents and take care of their younger brothers, but principally because, after a number of years, the girls who had been shut up in school and separated from their homes were found to be more ignorant of life than those who had not been at school. They had no chance to learn cooking by experience; a class in culinary science was therefore introduced at school, and still the girls made lamentable cooks. They had no chance to act as older sisters at home and help take care of babies; a class on baby care was therefore instituted, with a real baby contributed by some parents, for them to take care of at school. Then it was said they did not morally develop an all-around character because they were deprived of proper parental influence. My friend Pausias, a great educational expert, after years of intensive study, came to the conclusion that children learned as much from observation as from books on group behavior, and that girls should not be denied the natural influence of parents. A Parents and Teachers Association was formed, in order to discuss, with much learning, the problem of group behavior and social attitudes and any antisocial tendencies among the growing daughters. It all sounded very modern. The problems appeared very complicated; how was it possible to take girls out of their natural life, shut them apart for years away from adult society, and then reintroduce the various natural elements of life and provide them with a vicarious experience of life? The educational experts used to delight in such speculations, for it required as much technical knowledge as for a good chemist to devise ways and means of extracting the various vitamins from milk and then putting them back in desired proportions and quantities into the milk again. In the Old World they labeled it Revitaminized Milk, prepared by a patented process. The girls resented this treatment as much as the milk would if the milk had anything to say about it. They did not want to be revitaminized, they preferred to be natural whole milk. Because of their natural feminine instincts, they resented this more than the boys did.

"Then a little incident occurred which, small as it was, caused a revolution in the educational system on the island. One day Phoebe, the daughter of Hephaistos the flutemaker, complained that she did not understand how a hen sat on eggs to produce chickens. The principal of the girls' school called a conference of an educational psychologist and an educational sociologist to determine what was wrong with Phoebe. Was she mentally subnormal? The factors of environment in Phoebe's case were properly gone into — it was found that Hephaistos, a widower, never kept poultry. The experts agreed that it would be very desirable to have some chickens in school, so that not only Phoebe, but also her schoolmates, would have a chance of "duplicating life experience" and observing how a hen actually sat on eggs. A mother hen was properly installed in a glass case in the biology room and became an object of great curiosity among the girl students. For twenty-one days the mother hen occupied her throne with regal dignity and aristocratic indifference to all around her, and when the time of hatching of the chicks came, the biology teacher gave a solemn lecture on how the young chicks pecked their way out into the glorious new life. Such 'progressive' tendencies in this school were greatly frowned upon by the directors, in particular by Thrasymachus, whose daughter Eretrea was then in school.

" 'What is the modern school coming to?' he asked. 'Our school is understaffed, our classrooms are overcrowded, and our educational equipment is daily growing in variety. First you introduced frying pans; then you introduced cradles and diapers, and as if that were not enough, you have now introduced mother hens and let them take up valuable school space. Is it not more economical and sensible to send the girls home for half the day and let my daughter learn all about frying pans and diapers and chickens at home?' "

Emma-Emma went on to tell the story. Thrasymachus was an important supporter of the school. The matter was passed on to the Parents and Teachers Association and diligently gone into. A resolution was subsequently passed, which stated: "Inasmuch as it is recognized that the purpose of education is to prepare the young for life and the consequent shaping of the school program should, as far as possible, simulate life, it is the considered opinion of the majority here foregathered that it would be infinitely simpler not to simulate, at school, life in all its four-dimensional complexity, but to send the schoolgirls back to life for half a day each working day, with the hope that they will, without relaxation of effort, continue to study the use and handling of frying pans and cradles and diapers in Real Life (*capitals original*) and pursue, with unabated diligence, observations of such biological phenomena as the hatching of chickens." This unnecessary wordiness of the declaration was a heritage of the educational claptrap of the Old World with which the older generation had grown up.

The Ireniki girls therefore grew up without too much schooling. Music, gymnastics, the recitation of commemorative songs and the telling of legends (in place of history), and some simple arithmetic were about all that was required. What they lacked in quantity, they made up for in quality. It was thought that they should work toward the ideal of doing a few things superlatively well, rather than a lot of things not well at all. Grace and strength, in body and mind, were the objects of their culture; this combination was their ideal, according to Laosian esthetics. Naturally the boys majored in strength and minored in grace, while the girls majored in grace and minored in strength. Their ideal had always been a healthy mind in a healthy body. The school punished a girl more severely for a sloppish gait than for bad memory of history dates; and signs of tuberculosis or pallor in the face were considered backwardness in educational developments — these girls were liable to be called up by the Dean of Studies. Gymnastics, swimming, archery and dancing occupied a great deal of the school program. To learn correct posture and a graceful carriage, girls were made to carry pitchers full of water on the head and gyrate their bodies, or put themselves through various reclining motions by first bending one knee forward and then the other. The graduating ceremony always included such a pitcher parade by the graduating class which usually elicited great applause from the admiring parents. Monthly tests were held, and a senior who had not yet learned to walk properly or was awkward with her pitcher gave the principal more concern than if she had failed in mathematics or history, for the school was anxious that the pitcher parade be a vision of female beauty and perfection.

"What about the Comforters of Men's Souls?" asked Eurydice.

"The especially bright ones are given, after graduation, special training free in the Institute, which is supported by the community. We regard the training of a class of perfect females as a means of keeping alive the highest ideal of feminine beauty and accomplishment. Such a class of desirable femininity is almost religious in its concept, in upholding the tone and value of the moral content of our society. For it is recognized that the ideal of beauty is to be found in women of a certain age, and our young girls have the duty of keeping the esthetic tradition alive, from generation to generation, as living symbols of the eternal feminine. When the feminine ideal crumbles, civilization starts on its way to decay. They are to be perfect in grace, cultured, and psychologically trained in dealing with men. It is such an honored privilege that, exacting as the training is, many more girls apply than are admitted. All of them are required to have shown some talent in one of the musical arts, and some readiness of wit.

"No intelligence tests are employed, because these have fallen into disrepute along with other forms of mnemonics — the faith in figures as such and the belief that everything can be measured or reduced to statistical figures, which was the rage in the first half of the twentieth century. It had already been shown that the twentieth century mind, influenced by a strange quasi-scientific aberration, had become stupidly mechanical. About 1960, it was thought that there was a correlation between a person's intelligence and the sparkle in his eyes, and a Columbia professor of educational psychology had invented an electronic colorameter for measuring this sparkle, able to detect and record all the subtle changes on the spectrograph. As the professor was one day peering over the instrument, a rival professor who had invented a method for recording and measuring spasms of laughter clubbed him from the back. There was a scuffle and both dunderheads perished. As late as 1993, a professor of the Theological School in Texas, trying to put theology on a scientific basis, developed a complete Chart of Conscience, and by putting sinners to a list of questions, was able to measure accurately a man's moral degradation in centimeters.

"However, for us a sparkle is something too indefinable to measure. After their qualifications have been ascertained and approved, the applicants have to undergo a public test, somewhat similar to the beauty contests of the Old World. The judges rely on their personal reactions instead of using tape measurements as was done in the twentieth century — the announcement that a girl had a waistline of so many inches was considered the lowest prostitution of the statistical method. We think the allure of a young woman's eyes and the length of her eyelashes and the suppleness of her flesh much more important. So many other factors enter into what constitute a good figure and feminine beauty.

"After the judges have made their choice of the successful candidates, each of the graduates is given a dummy clay book which she is later to throw into the sea, for real books are much too valuable on the island to throw away. This ceremony is symbolic of the thought that these girls have sufficiently dealt with books and are now ready to deal with men. The chosen girls continue to read poetry and history, etc., of course. But Laos insists that the proper study of woman is man. Stars, flowers, clouds and minerals can come later."

"What about the proper study of men? Shouldn't the men study women also?"

"They can't. There's no use teaching them. They can never understand women. All of them choose their women blindfolded, somewhat as a male walrus chooses a female walrus. By instinct. It must not be thought that this Institute serves the selfish interests of the male sex. Rather it is based upon the assumption that men are difficult to handle, that they are essentially babies and have to be wheedled and cajoled, and patted on the back. To do so, however, requires maximum skill, and for a woman to do it without losing patience outwardly or offending a man openly requires years of training. That is what the Institute is for. This seems to be the major object of their training. Many girls have plunged into the matrimonial sea without knowing the first rudiments of navigation. Our Comforters are permitted, and even encouraged, to lie to the men, if it flatters them or humors them. They are given daily examples of tired men, drunken men, vain men, mentally sick men, short-tempered men, to deal with, and these are supposed to come away from their company feeling better than before. All wiles and tricks and jokes are permissible so long as the men are stopped from whining about themselves. And it is true that tired, nervous men and unhappy husbands regain control of themselves when one of these girls merely lays a gentle hand on their foreheads."

"Why are they called Comforters of Men's Souls?"

"Because experience has taught the Ireniki wives to send their nervous, irritable husbands to them for treatment. No fees are charged because the institution is supported by the public, but upon admission a man must make a statement that he is approaching a nervous breakdown, or is guilty of beating his wife — such persons are regarded as emergency cases. Normally men are admitted merely upon stating that they have been boorish, or short-tempered, or fatigued and depressed. Choice wine is served them, but they must drink in moderation or they will be expelled from the place. Most men value the privilege of admission too much to take this risk. Also the girls are allowed to slap their faces if they do not behave, exactly as they would slap their babies. Consequently, an etiquette has developed and the Institute has become a synonym for polite intercourse and civilized manners. Our girls are usually gifted in some musical instrument such as the lyre, the flute, the guitar, or the violin. They are taught philosophy — a world apart from that of Bertrand Russell or Alfred

North Whitehead. They have the witticisms of great writers at their command, and are well acquainted with the sayings of Confucius, Epictetus and Epicurus. Doris, one of the girls, is quite an expert on Democritus and his theory of the atom. Part of their training consists in memorizing the lyrics of Sappho and reciting famous passages of epic verse. Pork is served with poetry and philosophy with filet. The men tell them jokes and anecdotes at table in exchange for what the girls tell them. Consequently, the latter are placed in an atmosphere peculiarly fitted for developing witty and polite intercourse. Many of the more learned men prefer to come here for their company, rather than talk to their semi-illiterate wives."

"I guess they would."

"It is thought that this constant association with men, in their best and their more seamy aspects, fits the girls to become better wives, by furnishing them with many object lessons in human nature. Husbands who have just beaten their wives rush to them and tell them their domestic woes. The girls sit listening, all understanding and sympathy, or mildly exclaiming 'How horrible of her!' A wild-eyed husband will tell his story and conclude by asking, 'Now is that reasonable?' And the listener's eyes will darken and she will reply sweetly and sympathetically, 'I am *so* sorry.' By the time they have been at the Institute one or two years, the girls know a lot about the complexities of husband-wife relationships. With the frankness about sex that exists among the islanders, the girls sometimes have to listen to intimate details which the married men confide in them. This is slightly embarrassing, for the girls themselves are unmarried. But unmarried clergy often are forced to listen to lurid details and perversions in sex relationships, or even question their believers on these points. At the Institute, no such confession of intimate relationships is obligatory, as is the case of the Old World."

"What about their love affairs?"

"Naturally, young men come to court them. There is a sharp separation of their professional duty as public entertainers and their private love affairs. What they do outside is their own concern. Many of them fall in love, for they have no lack of suitors. Many marry in their second or their third year. The term of their training is three years, but if they marry while at the Institute they have to resign. The community deplores these early marriages inasmuch as it is desirable to keep a good class of entertainers at the place, and also because according to the custom of the country, it is not considered desirable for girls to marry before twenty-one. However, their places are readily filled by waiting applicants. Younger sisters have been known to beg their older sisters to get married so that there would be room for them at the Institute. . . . You are going to see their play during the Irenicia. It's usually quite good, because the acting and the chorus and dance are always excellent."

"I imagine it will be very gay."

"Very gay. The girls at their best. There is the procession of the robe, and before that a pitcher parade by the girls of the high school. Their graduation ceremony is part of the Irenicia festival. It will be a vision of beauty and health and gaiety you have never seen before."

Eurydice had something on her mind. She said, "I am going to persuade Alcibiades to come out of his hiding. He will need friends to assure him that they accept him in spite of what he has done. Can I bring him to you?"

"Certainly. He made a mistake, a young man's mistake. Bring him to me. We want him to feel comfortable, and help him over this difficult period."

Much edified, Eurydice left. It would be ridiculous for Alcibiades to hide away in self-immolation while the festivals were going on. She would not allow it. She decided to go to him, tell him everything and persuade him to forget his troubles and join the festivities with a glad heart. She could not enjoy them if Alie stayed away. She didn't care if people gossiped.

Chapter XXXVII

THE MORNING FOG was heavy, visibility bad. Eurydice was splashing about near the shore, waiting for Wriggs. She knew he would come. She waited half an hour and he still did not appear. Not a soul was in sight; there was not a sound except the occasional squawking of sea gulls calling to their mates announcing the happy discovery of clams or soft-shell crabs.

At last, growing impatient, she swam out a little. The water was quite warm in the shallower part of the lagoon. She could see only fifteen yards ahead of her. All around was a vapory whiteness which shut out the sun. Turning on her back, she paddled leisurely and thought. A sound of splashing penetrated the fog. She stopped and listened. She recognized the familiar creak and swish of oar strokes, and headed for that direction.

"Alie!" she cried as she saw the bow of his boat and his figure loomed into view.

"Hullo, Eurydice! What are you doing here?"

"Waiting for you." She swam toward him.

"What do you want?" He did not seem particularly pleased to see her.

"I want to speak to you, Alie . . . Alie, I must speak to you . . . do you hear?"

Alie had already swung his boat away. For a time, she maintained a speaking distance. "Alie! . . . I am coming with you . . . don't row away! . . . Alie!" She swam as fast as she could after him. Alie's oars stopped long enough for him to turn back and

say, "Don't be foolish. Go back, Eurydice. Leave me alone."
Then he quickened his strokes, and disappeared slowly behind
the vapory screen.

She was mortified. Wriggs had never been so rude. Wasn't
it foolish of him — to sulk alone, speak to nobody, and retreat
to his lonely empire of thoughts? Slowly she swam back to the
shore.

Of course he did not mean to snub her, passing a lady in water
and refusing to take her in. It wasn't that at all. She understood.
But wasn't he unnecessarily heroic?

Once her mind was made up, Eurydice determined that she
was going to speak to him whether he wanted it or not. She
got in one of the Thainian fishing boats and when the fishermen
came down to the beach with their gear she asked them to take
her out to the sandbar.

Young Wriggs was surprised when he saw Eurydice jump off
the boat and swim toward him. Of course it was a compliment
to him, but why had she gone to such trouble? Didn't she know
of his disgrace? Of course she knew. And Eurydice was really
charming when she waded lazily through the shallow water.
He forgot all his resolutions.

"Why, Eurydice," he shouted, wearing his normal smile, as
he splashed toward her.

Eurydice put her arm around him as they walked back toward
the sandbar.

"It's so foolish of you. Why do you keep alone — away from
others, yes, but why from me? Alie, you know, I never believed
a word of that sorry business."

"You didn't?"

"Not a word of it, even though you confessed."

"Why?"

"My heart tells me. You are not that kind."

Alcibiades relaxed, and turned his head toward her.

"It is so wonderful of you to believe in me, against my own
evidence. Why not? I could have committed a folly. How do
you know?"

"Intuition. Even if you insist on it now, I refuse to believe you."

"How about the others? What do they think?"

"What do you care?"

"I don't."

"Then let them think what they like."

They had come up on the patch of bare sand. Reaching his blanket, they sat down.

"Don't hide yourself. The Irenicia begins day after tomorrow. I am looking forward to it, curious to know what it is like. You mustn't make yourself conspicuous by your absence."

"It will be a bit awkward. I didn't quite realize what I had done. It is hard, very hard."

"Of course it is hard on you. But you can't hide yourself forever like this. I'll be with you — in public. No nonsense. We'll pretend nothing has happened. And the Countess knows. She stands by you."

"How does she know?"

Eurydice had to tell him.

"We won't talk," she continued, "but the Countess and I and some others will stand by you. You will be in good company."

"Really you will appear with me in public?"

"Gladly. Alie, you know how I love you." She turned her face up, and he bent over and kissed her long and passionately.

"Are you free?" she asked as she drew her breath.

"Yes, I am free."

"How about Margherita?"

"It was all understood from the beginning. And she is pledged under oath never to divulge the secret. I brought her home to her mother. That is supposed to be the end of the matter."

"Is it? Are you quite sure?"

"I'm quite sure. She has no claim on me. How Father Donatello swore he would deal with her if she ever talked of the matter again. Poor Margherita! I never saw such misery."

"And the Prince?"

Wriggs's face was suddenly tense. "That humbug. He got so scared. He continued to deny it, and he got Father Donatello to find a way to get him out of the difficulty."

"Why didn't he confess and marry her?"

"Not a sister of the convent! He was in a blue funk."

"Margherita really loved him, I suppose."

"How do I know? I hardly ever put my foot inside the convent. And I never go to church."

"You know what?"

"What?"

"Do you know what I call His Royal Highness? From the first time I heard his name mentioned, it struck me as indescribably funny. I call him Prince Sonuvabitch."

Wriggs exploded in loud laughter. "It's jolly good. Sonuva-bitch. Jolly good. I never thought of it."

For the first time, Wriggs completely forgot his troubles . . . "Sonuvabitch" . . . he started to laugh again.

Chapter XXXVIII

REHEARSALS FOR THE FESTIVAL had been going on for weeks; sometimes, walking in late afternoons past the Institute, Eurydice had heard the girls practicing their chorus. There was also the work of training the twelve virgins between twelve and seventeen for their part in the procession. As for dancing, the young damsels of the island required very little instruction. The great festival was peculiarly a young people's affair, because of the contest in gymnastics and water sports, but it was also an affair of the entire community. Laertes, the gymnasiarch, had his hands full, making ready the amphitheater and organizing the groups of contestants. The inhabitants from Macedonia, Thessaly, Delos and Lesbos organized their procession groups and vied with one another in the offerings of oxen and lamb for the big feast. The Delian farmers who lived up on the middle slopes of Mount Ida brought with them the best wines. Some older men had been invited to join in the recital of poetry. For this was the great holiday of the year, consecrated to the worship of the goddess Athena, the patron saint, and the happiness of the colony.

On the eve of the Irenicia, a prayer service was held at the temple of Athena, situated half a mile above the dam, facing the great fertile valley below Mount Ida. Eurydice had gone up with Alcibiades to watch the ceremony, before going to Emma-Emma's for supper. Ill at ease, Alcibiades had preferred not to go. However, Eurydice persuaded him to make the best of it. A beginning had to be made, and he might just as well do it now, be seen in public with her, rather than wait till the morrow. He had to pull himself together. The invitation to supper with Emma-Emma was the first assurance that he had not lost status with respectable society. Besides, Eunice had informed him that he was invited to lunch with Laos after the procession the next day.

"Countess della Castiglioni has invited you, too, but I don't think you would like to attend."

"Why?"

"The Countess said she was giving a party for Father Donatello and others. She usually does that; she says. It is also St. Thomas' Day. She is inviting the sisters of the convent. It would be a little embarrassing. But Laos has invited you."

"Was it at your suggestion?"

"No, no," Eurydice denied quickly. "I'll be going to Laos' party. You'd better come along."

Many candles were lighted before the altar inside the grotto sacred to the goddess. Father Aristotimus had carried his compromise with paganism a little too far, in Eurydices' eyes. He still wore his Greek Catholic robes, a long white beard covering his chest. He had not joined in the prayer to the pagan god, but owing to his age, was the official leader of the community. What was more, a statue of St. Nicholas which had been erected on his insistence, stood on the side wall of the grotto, and kept company with Athena in front. The curly-bearded face and bare shoulders of the Christian saint were illuminated by many prayer candles. Yet no one felt the incongruity of this juxtaposition. St. Nicholas, Eurydice thought, had been admitted among the deities on Mount Olympus, or so it seemed.

Chloe came up to Eurydice after the ceremony was over. Excitement was upon the young girl's face as they left the grotto. She showed Eurydice the new dress Berenice had made for her.

"What am I supposed to do tomorrow?" asked Eurydice.

"Wear white, worship God and enjoy yourself," replied Chloe.

It sounded so remarkably simple to her. Worship God and enjoy yourself!

Chloe looked at Alcibiades intently. So did some of the other girls. They treated him with the same awe as somebody who had been to the North Pole and killed three polar bears with his bare hands — mysterious, wicked and great. A few strolled up and said "Hello!" Alcibiades did not like it at all. Had he suddenly become a popular hero with girls?

"I don't think I should attend Laos' luncheon. I know — he gives it every year on the day of the procession. The whole crowd will be there. Including Prince Sonuvabitch."

"Alie, you mustn't hide away from society. Once it's over, it's over; and this luncheon is important. You will meet the people you always meet. You'll be a guest of Laos; Laos has accepted you. That is enough. As for the Prince, what do you care? Chin up, Alie."

The last two words possessed an intrinsic magic for young Wriggs. Yes, chin up. He must remember that.

At Emma-Emma's table, they talked of what they had seen at Athena's grotto.

"How many patron saints have you really got on the island?" Eurydice asked.

"Three, I believe," replied Emma-Emma. "It is a little confusing, isn't it? The Catholics have decided in favor of St. Thomas. Father Aristotimus had at first insisted on St. Nicholas, the famed protector of the sailors. It was just bad luck, they had a poor crop the following spring. St. Nicholas was thought to have been derelict in his duty. He couldn't be much of a patron saint, could he? The Greeks deserted him and went for good old Athena. That is why you find St. Nicholas' statue back in the grotto, while that of Athena stands in front."

"Doesn't it strike you as incongruous?" asked Eurydice. "A Christian saint and a Grecian goddess sharing the same grotto."

"I think it's a little messy myself," said Alcibiades.

"What is Father Aristotimus thinking of?" asked Eurydice.

"Perhaps you don't understand," said Emma-Emma. "He sincerely believes that he is still a Christian priest. Tomorrow you will see him heading the procession of the robe of Athena, but he continues to officiate at Christian rites. During the first years after our arrival, he saw the paganism in the hearts of men. He decided, like a practical person, if pagans would not come to the church, he would bring the church to the pagans.

"He settled this matter with his conscience, by the help of historical and ecclesiastical learning. Laos, who had done his research on the influence of Oriental ideas upon Pythagoras, helped him to equate his conscience with his conduct. Laos was familiar with the Greek and the non-Greek elements in the religion of the early Christian fathers. The conflict of popular beliefs and pure Christianity was known to the early fathers, and the Christianity which was born was a resolution of this conflict, of Hebraic and Hellenistic elements. Jesus said nothing about the mortification of the flesh, but Pythagorean and Orphic rules of abstinence and continence clearly became a part of the Christian doctrine. It was the Greek ascetic Antisthenes who expressed the wish to 'shoot Aphrodite, who has ruined so many virtuous women.' Christ never said anything about shooting beautiful young women. Remember Mary of Magdalene? And of course, neither the Gospel of St. John nor St. Paul's first Epistle to the Corinthians, Chapter Thirteen, can be understood without reference to the Greek Logos philosophy. Though he was a Jew of the Dispersion, St. Paul had absorbed the knowledge of Plato's doctrine of the soul and the mysteries of the Egyptian gods.

"The upshot of it all was that in addition to the basic Christian teachings of hope, faith and charity, Christianity borrowed its effective forms of worship, its sacramentalism, its mysteries, its eschatology and even its icons from prevailing Mediterranean polytheism. Why should not Father Aristotimus make a similar concession to poor human nature? When the first festival of Athena was celebrated on the island and he saw the zeal and enthusiasm of the virgins in embroidering the goddess' white robe and their joy and pride in carrying it, he did not have the heart to say to them, 'Go back, you idolaters.' He was a good shepherd; he knew his flock too well.

"This attitude of Father Aristotimus in adjusting, directly under the influence of Laos, the differences between his own orthodoxy and the rather lively polytheistic imagination of the Ireniki, was of great consequence in the life of the people," Emma-Emma, the student of comparative religion, went on to say. "It enabled the people to take sin less tragically than the Christians did. Sin is an element of error in human conduct, to be corrected and be ashamed of, but it is not an all-inclusive, all-dominating, basic key structure of their religion. Laos pointed out that an American president, Calvin Coolidge, once summed up the Christian religion very well and pithily, in the one word *Sin*. On the other hand, if Dr. Artemos, former Dean of the College of Science of Athens University and a great mathematician, had been the leader of the Ireniki society, he would not have tolerated such dramatic fancies of the people, but would have condemned them as ignorance and superstition. He would have carried into this island the Aristotelian tradition, which in the modern world has forced a final divorce between science and religion with such tragic results, and the philosophy of the good life would have perished, as it perished around the year 1900 in the Old World. As Laos put it, science, like a monster, had eaten up religion and transformed it into one of its internal organs.

"If Dr. Artemos had won, such a joyous festival, making the myth the language of both science and philosophy, would have become impossible. He would have made the universe completely rational, human society included. Not that Laos feared the Irenikis would ever come to such a humdrum existence: Laos has defined a completely rational human society as one in which nobody ever goes crazy at some time of his life. It would be positively shocking, if it was not unthinkable. Luckily, it is unthinkable, because the shepherds and peasants could never change, whatever Dr. Artemos says. So while Dr. Artemos kept on explaining to them that the sun was a prosaic piece of intensely hot ball, deriving its power from exploded atoms, the peasants ignored him completely, and continued to wonder and see in their imagination Apollo's chariot being drawn by white steeds across the skies."

Because of this combination of circumstances, the Irenikis were still able to celebrate their pagan festival.

Chapter XXXIX

EARLY THE NEXT MORNING, the bells of St. Thomas' rang merrily to announce the Saint's Day. The tropical sun was shining upon those who lived in the verdure-covered island that morning. Eurydice wanted to believe that the sun god Apollo was particularly glorious that morning. Except for a few dark strips in the distant horizon, the sea was an opalescent band of white, shooting golden sparkles as the rays struck it. The morning air, cool to the skin, was noisy with the twittering of birds in the nearby groves. At this time, the eastern peaks cast long shafts of blue over the island, while the town and valley still lay in the cool shade. The vineyards in the uplands usually glowed a reddish purple, for the moisture of the night winds had deepened the tint of the red soil. At the heights, a stiff ocean wind had broken up the clouds into strips and ribbons and turned up the whitish backs of the olive leaves in waves as they swept down the valley. Eurydice was all dressed up and happy.

Chloe had gotten up early and gone to the Institute by herself. Iolanthe was up, too, at the unearthly hour of seven. Eurydice heard the tolling of the bells of St. Thomas' Chapel. Father Donatello was at his job. The joyous clarion notes rent the silent air of the morning. Probably he was pulling the ropes himself. Athena or no Athena, it was St. Thomas' Day for him. The bells at St. Catherine's Convent answered with clear, if softer, notes.

Hastily finishing her breakfast, she prepared to go down. From

325

the terrace she had a glimpse of the open gate of the convent, through which some nuns were coming.

"You'd better hurry if you want to see the graduation ceremony. You'll be at lunch with Laos?" said Iolanthe.

"Yes."

"With Alcibiades?"

"I hope."

Iolanthe smiled. "Meet you at lunch, then."

Eurydice strode down the easy slope, toward the town. She saw flags on the amphitheater. Otherwise, the streets were yet quiet. The graduation ceremony was not to begin till nine. Alcibiades had said he would be at the procession, but did not care to see the pitcher parade.

She thought she would see Emma-Emma. She was in town and there was nothing to do.

Emma-Emma was up early and very much alive for a woman in her seventies, possibly eighties.

"You are dressed in white, too?" Eurydice asked. "Are you going to join the procession of the robe?"

"You bet I am. I have lived here for thirty years, and have never missed one." There was a glimmer in the old woman's eyes. "It has done something to me, I don't know what. But it tones you up. Makes you want to live forever."

"What is it, do you think?"

"It is difficult to describe what it is. One feels a hundred per cent happy. In the Old World . . . Come on. I will go with you."

She told Bowena to lock up the house and take the whole day off. She would not be home for lunch. As they left the house, going through the narrow alleys, Emma-Emma pursued her thoughts as if the conversation had never been interrupted. "This was not possible in the Old World," she said, "except in states of intoxication — intoxication of alcohol or of love, which has the power of obliterating for a moment the sense of our social guilts and imperfections, makes one feel divine while its effect lasts. As soon as a man sobers up, he feels all his weaknesses, his confusion, his insufficiencies, his guilt. Subconsciously, we all felt guilty, a psychic residue of our contemplation of sin on Sundays. Hence no one was ever one hundred per cent happy; the guilt complex was always there, suppressed and hidden, and was, socially speaking, responsible for many of our sadistic, destructive tendencies to see ourselves and others punished. We were subconsciously demanding that somebody should die for our sins. This straining for divinity as an ideal of perfection was ruining us, and produced the curious twists and turns in our behavior. We sang hymns one day and went forth to kill our enemy the next. We were indeed a very funny people. Emotional instability is what I call it. Divinity is necessarily an impossible ideal for man . . ."

"I am afraid I don't quite follow," said Eurydice hesitantly.

"I mean attempting the impossible only creates a psychic tension in us; this straining after perfection does no good to anybody."

"You mean we should not try to be perfect as God is perfect?"

"I mean we shouldn't try to imitate our betters, to keep up with the Joneses. The effort makes one unhappy, and usually causes a mental breakdown. No, there's no use trying to be like our betters. The gods would think us contemptible asses for trying, a bunch of despicable social climbers."

They had come to the fountain. Looking up at the statue of Hermes, she said, "The Greeks did an infinitely wiser thing. They made the gods imperfect like ourselves and relieved us of the striving. The ethics of Mount Olympus are rather low, you are no doubt aware. The gods and goddesses, practically speaking, are a gay, drunken, amorous, polygamous lot. Zeus himself makes a bad-tempered, irascible and far from exemplary father, difficult to live with — not to mention the unspeakable scandals inside his household. He probably holds the world's record for the number of illegitimate children. That is why the genealogy of the gods is so confusing. And think how many girls Apollo tried to rape — Issa, Daphne, Cyparissus, Leucothoë, Bolina, Coronis, Clymene, Cyrene, Chione. . . . Quite a Don Juan. Can you imagine a Greek feeling guilty when he worships Apollo? Juno tried to destroy another woman's child by her husband, just like the daughters of the earth. The Greeks made the gods like men, instead of trying to make the men like gods. So everybody is relieved. As you can see, no woman can say a prayer of repentance to Juno, 'O Goddess, forgive me for I have killed the child of my husband's mistress.' No man can pray to Apollo, 'O Apollo, forgive me, for I have harbored thoughts of fornication with many virgins, strangers and friends.'"

"And you think that easing of tension is good?"

"Anyway, it makes me feel a better woman, for the gods are just about like me. I used to study comparative religion. I stopped comparing when I found the Greeks. And it did another thing. We can worship God and enjoy ourselves. It is a gay, sunny religion, a religion of cheerfulness and beauty and joy. I think that is what religion ought to be. And this worship of Athena is but the symbol and the climax of that joy of spirit which made the development of Athenian art and philosophy possible."

Men and women, clad in white tunics, were already passing through the grove, congregating near the gymnastic ground.

"Come on, let's join them," said Emma-Emma, a lilt in her voice and a spring in her step as if this old woman had suddenly come alive.

Eurydice felt happy, in spite of her critical reason which told her that she and all the rest of them were crazy. She felt emotionally stirred when she heard the sound of flutes across the grove. She gladly surrendered herself to the senses, to the smells and sights of this day, and thought it a wonderful, simple idea to worship God in the open. The Nordic custom of building cathedrals to shut out the sun and worship God in the cavernous gloom of an eternal twilight was all a mistake, she thought. It was understandable in view of the bleak winters and the blustering storms of the Brittany coast. The Christians just had to keep warm.

"What are they going to do this morning?"

"First, the pitcher parade and graduating exercises, ending with the throwing of books into the sea. The procession of the *peplos*, or robe, of Athena begins about ten. Then the procession of St.

Thomas. Father Donatello is an extraordinary genius. Of course, it is a shorter procession. With the sisters and some school students and the Faithful Flock, it can't be more than seventy or eighty people. The procession in honor of Athena numbers in the hundreds. But he also manages to make it seem a mile long by making the whole crowd follow it."

"How?"

"You see when the Greeks go up to Athena's grotto, the Christians stay behind. Some thirty minutes later, they start. They go as far as the top of the ridge and wait. The Athena worshipers have to return, don't they? When the ceremony at the grotto is over, and the pilgrims are coming up the ridge, the procession of St. Thomas starts again and leads them back to town. St. Thomas, I imagine, must be quite pleased to see such a big crowd. At least, Father Donatello is. Once he said to me, with inimitable self-delusion, 'They shall go as pagans, and return Christians.'"

"Like those religious revivalists who make themselves believe they have converted hundreds, sometimes even thousands, on a single day," remarked Eurydice.

"And just as happy about it," added Emma-Emma. "The father is a fanatic. He is driven by a tremendous force inside him; never stops, never wavers, never allows his purpose to be obscured."

On the gymnastic ground, gaily decorated with pennants and bunting, a platform had been set up. A throng was already gathering, waiting for the appearance of the schoolgirls. Men and women and children, principally families of the schoolgirls, had begun to arrive, wearing the customary white. Another crowd had gathered around the chapel nearby. Now the schoolgirls filed into the ground, led by the teachers.

The graduation ceremony began. Thrasymachus, Laos and the directors of the school were seated on the platform. Prince Andreyev, as the civil head of the community, was there, too; he took a deep interest in the education of the boys and girls. Busy as Father Donatello was this morning, he rushed in at the last minute to be present at the ceremony. The man, as usual, was working himself to death in his zeal to be a fine example of devotion to the general welfare of the community. He believed that in this sea of heathendom, it was no time to think of his own pleasure, that he should redouble his efforts against the false prophets and the engulfing sands of their doctrines, and that those young growing minds could be shaped so that some of them might grow up to be true Christians.

The Ireniki prayer was said; the principal made a speech; the girls sang, and prizes were given. The names of those who had been selected to enter the Institute, for advanced education, were announced to the great applause of the public. Then began the breathtaking pitcher parade, given by the graduating class, numbering some twenty girls between sixteen and eighteen. Each one picked up a pitcher, half filled with water, weighing about twenty to thirty pounds, and put it over her head, holding it with one hand, the other arm akimbo. They went up the platform on one side and came down on the other and then, both hands down and spread open, they began to circle the grounds. The eyes of their teachers, no less than those of the parents, looked on with pride at the ease and seal-like grace with which the girls carried themselves. The weight on their heads seemed to enforce a perfect sense of balance, and they countered any unevenness of the ground with a slight movement of their hips. The ease with which they did it was a joy to see.

After completing a full circle, they threaded their way, with the pitchers still on their heads, toward the beach. The audience rose and followed them. This part was more informal, and they were permitted to hold their pitchers with one hand. It was at the beach that the real graduation began, so far as the girls themselves were concerned. There the line broke up, and each girl picked up a clay book and with great glee threw it into the sea as if to say, "Good-by, books, good-by!"

When they returned, the whole town had already come out to join in the procession of the *peplos*. Aristotimus, with his long white beard, Laos and others were consulting with Laertes about the arrangements. It was a gay holiday crowd. All the men and women, in honor of the occasion, wore wide, flowing cloaks of white. Most were standing along the maple lane. Laertes rushed back and forth seeing about the order of the procession. Eurydice saw Alcibiades, Groucho and Philemon among the group of young men. She walked up and greeted them.

"You must come and look at my speedboat tomorrow morning," said Groucho.

"I certainly shall. Where will it be?"

"Right in the lagoon."

Eurydice had to find her place among the young women, for the men and women were separated. "Worship God and enjoy yourself," she said to herself, quite amused.

She met Laos.

"How are your toes?" he asked, glancing at her sandals.

"They are doing well."

"Becoming more normal, straightening out a bit?"

Eurydice remembered their argument over shoes.

"Not so bad," she replied.

"Well, see you at lunch. And bring young Wriggs as you promised."

"I shall."

She fell into place, always keeping an eye on Alie to see if he was happy or was suffering. She saw his fine head and shoulders, his gentlemanly carriage. It was hard to tell; he never spoke much anyway. His emotions, if he had any, were deeply hidden under a smooth, dignified exterior.

The bells of St. Thomas' were clanging merrily at this moment, their tones throbbing through the olive grove where the procession was to be formed. From the distance came the sweet strain of organ music and the singing of hymns. A service was going on at this moment. It was really very thoughtful of Father Donatello to change, without permission from the Vatican, the date of St. Thomas' Day. The Christian flock was having a great celebration, too. The church had not been caught asleep. Father Donatello was reading some more chapters from the Book of Revelation. It was no time to be lazy. . . . "So then because thou art lukewarm, and neither cold nor hot, I will spew thee out of

my mouth" . . . Incredible as it might seem, the father's rich
metallic voice, setting the whole dome of the small chapel to
reverberation, could be heard as a clanging whir at the grove some
hundred yards away. The metallic whir rose and fell. He was
preaching with special vigor this day. Then, suddenly, silence.
After a while, to the strain of a sacred anthem, the statue of St.
Thomas was carried out of the church.

But of course, the Christian procession was not to begin yet.
There now began again the tolling of bells, gay, joyous, lingering.
The red banners were carried out. Meanwhile, the Italian followers waited. The Prince and a few others were coming toward
the grove, watching the procession of Athena's robe being formed
— detached, but friendly.

The new robe for the goddess had now been placed in position,
hoisted up like a ship's sail on a contrivance. Not every year
did the Greek goddess get a new robe, but this was the Great
Irenicia, falling once every five years. It had to be embroidered
by the hand of selected virgins. Now it was being held by two
of them, who were clothed in long white robes banded with gold.

The arrangement of the procession followed the pattern of the
Panathenaea of ancient Greece, the older people in front, the
younger behind. First came the older men or women carrying
green boughs of olives, called *moreiae,* sacred to Athena. After
these came women, all in white cloaks, carrying water pots, the
hydraphori, and then the younger men, and select virgins, the
canephori, or basket-carriers, who held baskets on their heads,
containing things needed for the sacrifice. Father Aristotimus,
still in his Christian priestly garb, walked in front of the *peplos,*
which was followed by the girls of the Institute, specially trained
in dance and song, who in turn were followed by the men musicians. With the beginning of the music and singing, joined in by
the men and women, the procession started.

Emerging from the grove, they came upon the country path,
now bathed in the bright sunlight. The procession wended its
way up toward the ridge, a short distance from Athanopoulos'
Residence. They stopped for a while near the right, where the

road lay in the shade of tall palms. All the colors of the island on that bright morning exercised a hypnotic effect. The sea on the south lay under the dazzling rays of the sun, a pale lucid green near the shore, deepening into aquamarine and then a fiery, rich turquoise. Below lay the red sands, washed by moving bands of frolicsome waves. Up above, jutting out on a headland, was the white St. Catherine's Convent, partly hidden in the thick forest. All along the road, straggling bougainvilleas flamed in lavish profusion.

Surmounting the ridge, the procession went eastward by a few gentle ups and downs to the Grotto of Athena. A pleasant sea breeze was blowing in their faces. Worship God and enjoy yourself, thought Eurydice.

When the procession reached the Grotto, the ceremony of putting the new robe on the goddess was performed in the midst of more music and singing. Athena wore a helmet with an engraved cock at the top and winged shoes on her feet, and held a distaff in her right hand, rather than a spear and shield, for the goddess was deprived of her warlike qualities on this island. Over the grotto was an inscription: *To Pallas Athena Coryphagenes Musica.*

The procession had broken up. The believers went up individually and kissed the big toe of Athena, some going in to kiss the feet of St. Nicholas standing on the side, believing that it was safer to kiss both. However, the big toe of the Greek goddess was more shining and smooth.

As was to be expected, the Greeks met the procession of St. Thomas at the ridge on their return. Prince Andreyev and the Countess were with the Italian Christians. This Italian procession started to return to town when the Greeks were straggling back. They were not in formation, but they could not but become a part of the procession of St. Thomas, so cleverly had Father Donatello contrived to capture them for the glory of what he regarded as the only true and proper patron saint of the island.

Now Emma-Emma had joined Eurydice. Youths and girls mingled freely on their return. Alcibiades lost no time in coming up to

them. Once back to town, the holiday spirit broke loose. Many
of the young people had prepared baskets of lunch, and they
dispersed in groups, spreading out in the grove and around the
chapel and near the gymnastic ground, wherever there was a
shade. Some headed for the shore. Some girls had divested themselves of their cloaks and were chasing and gamboling in the
woods like sylvan nymphs.

Laos joined them.

"How did you like it?" he asked Eurydice.

"I think it was beautiful. The young faces look so cheerful and
healthy and gay. It reminds me of America."

"I am glad to hear you say that. Comeliness is next to godli-
ness. We try to develop in them a harmonious character. And
the basis of a harmonious character is quite plainly a correct
figure."

Involuntarily Eurydice threw her shoulders back a little. She
had been too studious.

"We must find ourselves before we can serve the world, mustn't
we?"

Eurydice stammered a "Yes."

Any encounter with that old man always upset her a little.
He was too kind. He was of the peripatetic school, going about
handing out advice. He turned to young Alcibiades, and checked
his steps with him. Alcibiades nodded in appreciation.

Eurydice asked: "Is the Prince coming to lunch?"

"I think not. I have asked him of course. But I believe he is
going to the Countess' party. He is more at home with the Countess and with Father Donatello than with me. . . . the humbug,"
he added with a smile.

Did he know?

Chapter XL

WHILE THE PRINCE was having a roaring good time at the Countess' villa, to which a select group of Father Donatello's followers had been invited, Alcibiades Wriggs and Eurydice went with Emma-Emma to Laos' house for lunch. There were Father Aristotimus, Iolanthe and her daughter Chloe, Philemon and others. Eunice had joined them; she always preferred Laos' company.

"What are we going to have for lunch?" asked Eunice.

Laos replied: "How do I know? Ask Eugénie."

Eugénie had already laid a fine table for the guests. Eunice went over and asked her something.

"Lobsters sautéed," whispered the fat French cook.

"In butter and garlic?"

"Yes."

"Put some capers in. Try," suggested Eunice.

Small talk filled the table as they sat down to lunch. Eugénie announced to the guests that she was not serving anything "heavy" because of the big feast to come that night. Everybody laughed.

Emma-Emma was sitting on Laos' right, Iolanthe on his left. Emma-Emma said: "Eurydice and I were talking last night. She was asking about the girls' education, and about the Institute. I quoted the Institute's motto — 'The proper study of woman is man.' She asked me what was the proper study of man, would it be woman? I couldn't reply; I said there was no use teaching man about woman. Am I right?"

"You are right," replied Laos. "God, I think, intended woman to be elusive, mysterious. That is her role in courtship anyway. Man is the pursuer, she the pursued. Consequently the more elusive she is, the more she attracts. What do you say, Iolanthe? What is the proper study of man?"

"Man, isn't it?" replied Iolanthe. "I should say the proper study of man is man, and the proper sport of man is woman."

"You incorrigible heathen," said Emma-Emma in sweetly chiding tones.

Laughter rippled over the table. Alcibiades colored. Eurydice saw it and liked it.

"What's wrong with that?" replied Iolanthe. "The eternal, unending sport, the oldest sport in history, man chasing after woman, isn't it?"

Eurydice was trying to remember the story of Ariadne, which was the subject of the play the girls were giving that afternoon — how Ariadne, a sweet princess, helped her lover Theseus to find his way out of the labyrinth and kill the monster Minotaur, how they eloped and he married her and then deserted her after their arrival on an island, how finally she turned to Bacchus.

Eurydice said, "The ancient Greeks were fabulous tellers of myths. No other people tell such charming stories about their gods and goddesses. How is it that modern man cannot create myths any more?" The question was addressed to Philemon sitting opposite her.

"I think the Greeks had a playful fancy and there lurks in them always a Rabelaisian humor. It lies in a realm beyond true and false. Modern man demands that a thing must be true or false. That kills all myths, of course. For me I prefer this marriage of poetry and religion. It makes them laugh while they worship the gods. I think the decay of religion began with the separation of poetry and religion. It is a pity. The earth is the poorer for it. Aphrodite no longer rises from the waves and Poseidon no longer rules the sea. You see how impossible it is in this scientific era to be religious, to exalt in the earth, in the gift of life. Bales of cotton and loads of jute sacks make ugly gods. The modern man has quite a problem to recapture that poetic spirit, the spirit of gay laughter which hovered over ancient Greece. Religion should be a matter of the heart, of feeling and spirit, as philosophy is a matter of the head. Modern religion is a little leaden-hued and moldy-smelling, don't you think?"

"I hardly know what to say," replied Eurydice. "What do you think, Laos? I know this worship of Athena is sunny and gay. But somehow I find it impossible to take it seriously."

"You shouldn't," said Laos. "That would be a mistake — a mistake in approach. As Philemon says, it lies beyond the realm of true and false. Why should we try to place God exactly where he is? We wish to codify God and never ask whether God wishes to be codified by us. When you feel inspired by a very beautiful object, or are moved by a great experience, you know ordinary language fails. True lovers always stammer when they come to the declaration of love; they don't know what to say, or how to say it. You express that great glorious feeling of love, or of experience of God, by poetry, or music, or you revert to the language of myths and symbols. It is a different thing altogether. You cannot demonstrate, explain, prove or define. You adumbrate, suggest, and leave the feeling there. Santayana was the only philosopher who understood the connection between poetry, symbolism and religion. Mythology is that language peculiar to the union of poetry and religion. It is the translation of an immediate mood into imagery, the identification of a playful fancy with a sudden glimpse of truth. As for the inability of the modern man to create myths, I think the simple reason is that our poetic fancies, owing to a more scientific education, have run dry. One important part of our psyche is atrophied."

"But isn't there a distinction between a true and a false religion?" asked Eurydice.

Eunice said dryly: "I think you have used a wrong word. I think you mean by true religion the right religion, religion of the right kind, worshiped by the right people. On the right side of the track, as one might say. The kind you belong to respectably, bearing the unmistakable stamp of social approval. It is a great social institution. You are never in doubt about the people you rub shoulders with. Church bazaars, charities and parochial schools and that sort of thing. All confirm your opinion that your religion is indubitably the right one. You cannot imagine a Catholic president of the United States, or a Protestant one in Ireland. The people won't stand for it. It just isn't right. That's about all we mean by the true religion. Don't imagine for a moment that the churchgoers bother much about its dogmas and articles of belief. They are points settled long ago and put out of the way. As for real thinking about the truth about God, nobody has ever reached a knowledge of God by the staircase of logic. Even the prophets didn't. They didn't argue God out of heaven. They simply saw God, or heard voices. And we have to take their word for it."

"All that you say is very enlightening. But Philemon was talking about the union of poetry and myth and religion. Isn't there a danger of approving even a false religion? Surely there is one true God, and plenty of false gods," protested Eurydice. She had a feeling that she had found herself in a nest of polytheists, idolaters.

Laos had something to say. "True religion is an ugly phrase. It smells of orthodoxy and arrogance and willingness to fight somebody for it. That was how the Mohammedans went to battle with the Koran in one hand and a scimitar in the other. The Crusaders and the Saracens all had a good time defending the true religion and cutting down the enemy. The Russian Catholics had a grand time staging pogroms against the Jews. As Eunice has just said, no one has learned to know God by the staircase of logic. As a matter of fact, all the world's great religions are monotheistic. Hinduism, Judaism, Mohammedanism, Christianity and Taoism — all affirm the oneness of God. But if there is only one God, what is the fight about? The quarrels center about the prophets only. Savage or civilized, never a thinking man breaks the petals of a tulip but is driven to postulate a god, a creator. That feeling of religious wonder is universal. There is nothing to quarrel about. Then logic begins to play havoc with that feeling. Wise old men began to discuss, and to *decide*, whether God was outside, or inside that tulip; whether God was transcendental or imminent. If outside, he was a monotheist; if inside, a pantheist. You see how silly it all is. The Brahmin leaders thought God was in everything. Yet you cannot deny that the Brahmin is a monotheist, believing in the one Brahma. Polytheism, the belief in many gods, is merely fragmentized monotheism, arising out of the human need to visualize God. Divine order. How are they going to worship divine order? They want divine disorder, a god popping up here and there at the beck of your finger to interfere and alter the course of things in your favor — if not God himself, then a pettigod, a saint perhaps. Make the wind blow north when you are sailing north, and blow south when you are sailing south and damn the bastards who are sailing in the opposite direction. That is the kind of god they want — a sort of personal attendant with supernatural powers. Who says we want a universal God who treats everybody exactly alike? If He prefers to run His affairs in His own way, indifferent to our prayers, all right, let Him run them."

"But surely, you can prove the true God," protested Eurydice.

"Proving God? The prophets never tried to prove God by reason, but rather by unreason, the antithesis of reason."

"By unreason?"

"Yes, the populace wanted to know how do we know that what the prophet said was true. Now God proves his truth by the order and beauty and reason of the universe; the prophet had to prove his truth by some element of disorder, some inexplicable insanity of the universe that could not be explained by reason. The burning bush. A temporary suspension of law and order, defiant of all logical explanation. It is a tragedy that legally, an earthquake is considered an act of God, but the tinting of tulips isn't. Miracles, of course. If Aaron's snake ate up the Egyptian magician's snake, Aaron's god was true, and if the Egyptian's snake ate up Aaron's snake, the Egyptian's god was the true one. The psychology is practically universal. There is no greater conception of the order of the universe than that of Buddha, yet his followers try to prove their gods and goddesses by miraculous answers to prayers, by those inexplicable upsets of the normal course of the universe. You see, the beauty and delicacy of pansies and tulips can only prove the existence of one universal god, which is unsatisfying to the popular mind; the disturbance of that beauty and order — such as an instantaneous, inexplicable withering of the tulip, or blossoming out of season of the flowers — some such local disturbance, however minor, is necessary to prove the truth of some particular god or goddess. In ancient times, the proof of a 'true' god was usually more violent. You want hails and brimstones from heaven to demolish an enemy, desolate a whole town; or floods, ravaging plagues, wars and conquests on the battlefield. Any good mass slaughter will do. The gods of those days were unusually violent. Like Ezekiel's god, for instance. He promised that the Israelites should be seven months burying the corpses of Gog of Magog's men, and should 'eat the flesh of the mighty, and drink the blood of the princes of the earth.' The demonstration was effective, the conclusion inevitable. 'And I will rain upon him, and upon his bands . . . an overflowing rain, and great hailstones, fire and brimstone. Thus will I magnify myself, and sanctify myself; and I will be known in the eyes of many nations, and they shall know I am the Lord.' A rather dramatic way of proving the true god, don't you think? That was what was meant by 'true' in those days."

"That is not fair," said Eurydice. "The Israelites grew out of that notion of a tribal god long ago. There are no traces of that tribal god in the New Testament."

"What I was saying was that once that was the way of judging or proving whether a god was true or not, by the power to smite its enemies and deserters. And even today the believers insist God must be proved, not by reason, but by upsets of reason, by the universe going mad for a while."

"It is true," remarked Aristotimus, feeling extremely Greek and patriotic. "It is true the Hebrew god was temperamental. He was angry most of the time. He certainly was not particularly kind to other tribes. He loved smashing into the Hittites and Moabites."

"Do you doubt the Bible?" asked Eurydice.

"I doubt the Bible? Impossible! Ezekiel — Jeremiah — I could recognize all their voices. Ezekiel said all those things which Laos said he did. Each nation conceived God in its own image and made God talk its own language."

"Exactly," joined in Eunice. "The French say in their Bible that Jehovah was *irrité*, irritated, where the English Bible says he was filled with wrath and fury. Imagine Jehovah being irritated! If Ezekiel had been an Englishman, he would have said that God was terribly annoyed, but not ruffled. His God would keep a stiff upper lip and walk away, muttering some inaudible curses under his breath without losing a whit of his composure. He would not waste his breath on the hoi-polloi, a bunch of silly idolatrous blighters."

There was a general laughter over Eunice's sally and her clever imitation of an English accent.

"There would be no Ezekiels and Jeremiahs at all," said Philemon. "Jeremiahs and all sorts of sentimental rantings would be considered bad taste, don't you agree?"

Alcibiades, finding the question coming home to him replied, "I suppose it would not be good taste, would it?"

Eurydice said, "I think some of the words used by Ezekiel and Jeremiah would not be permitted on TV in the United States."

"What, for instance?" asked Iolanthe.

"Jerusalem the whore, for example. And quite a few other expressions."

"I think the English have a wonderful gift of gritting their teeth and bearing their troubles in silence," said Iolanthe, as she threw an admiring glance at young Wriggs.

This came closest to Iolanthe's hinting that perhaps she knew about Wriggs's heroic sacrifice. It was strange. The company seemed to think so well of him. Perhaps Iolanthe knew. Eunice too, being so close to the Countess. So might Laos. Eurydice thought it was nice of them not to mention the affair of Margherita. One reason perhaps was that the subject involving the Prince was strictly taboo.

Chapter XLI

LUNCH OVER, they spread out onto the terrace at the back, enclosed by a low embankment of cut stone. It was now shaded from the westering sun whose beams throbbed against the opposite valley, lighting up the pinnacles of Mount Ida in shades of phosphorescent red and purple. To the north, the outer ocean spread out in a white, almost colorless film, marked by large grayish patches of cloud shadows which revealed its substantiality. Below the peak, the vineyards and red roofs of the Delian colony dotted the uplands.

It was yet early. The dramatic recitals in the afternoon at the amphitheater would not begin until about five, when the actors and the audience would be in the shade and the air had cooled off. Eunice, Philemon and Chloe had gone into Laos' library; the others strolled about on the terrace.

Alcibiades and Eurydice stood hand in hand before the embankment, enjoying the view of the valley. Laos himself had always favored this view from the back of the house; it was his private universe, with Mount Ida and the green valley cut by a stream below. Clouds were racing in the upper regions of the sky. A playful group of stray misty bands hung about the lower shoulders of the peak, like the low-cut dress of a lady, whimsical, irresponsible, changing their fancies and shapes, driven by the winds at the heights, now resting quietly like children tired of play, and now starting to chase one another around the crevices and gaps of the rocky rampart.

Laos was enjoying the view with them. "Clouds are to mountain peaks," he said, "as hair is to a woman's head. They make the peaks alive, forever new, like a woman changing her hair style every day. You never get tired of looking at them. Peaks without clouds are like bald-headed women, and clouds without peaks are like children without a barnyard to play around in."

He seemed to merge into the background. It was his habit while talking to tilt his head slightly and dart a swift, appreciative glance at the mountain top.

"It is beautiful," said Eurydice in an inspired tone. She was so happy that Alie had come back, that nothing had changed. "Almost like a Utopia."

"Utopia be damned," said Laos. "It is like writing a check which is not expected to be cashed. When you are writing such a check, you think nothing of adding a few zeros. All Utopias are uncashed and uncashable checks, uncashable in any foreseeable future. Millenniums are so easy to construct. You just spin them out of your heads. And the people like it. Karl Marx knew that he did not have to deliver the goods — the classless society. No, it is the millenniums that lead the millions astray. Millenniums and messiahs. Most of those too well ordered millenniums sound like a well-run salmon-canning factory to me."

Alcibiades' gaze was fixed upon the craggy top of the mountain.

"I've been up there, at the very top," he said to Eurydice.

"Don't be a fool," said Laos to Eurydice. "He may want to take you up there. Mountain tops are to be looked up to, smiled at if you like, but not spat at."

"Nobody is spitting at it," protested Alcibiades.

"You are now — mentally. You want to conquer it, get even with it. It is an old European malady, this habit of taking Nature by the throat and trying to strangle it. Like Jacob. Jacob wanted to grapple with God on the ladder to heaven and got one of his joints smitten. Jacob never tired of telling about the dream, each time embellishing it a little. At one time he said he was grappling with one of God's angels, then he changed his mind and said he grappled with God Himself. It made a nicer story, sounded better."

Iolanthe, Chloe and Philemon now came out.

"Where is Aristotimus?" Laos asked.

"He has left. He has things to attend to."

"And where is Eunice?"

Iolanthe smiled. "She is snoring in your library. What are you people talking about?"

Wriggs said, "Laos was accusing me of spitting at Mount Ida, or grappling with it. I only scaled it once."

"But you are the only one on the island who ever did it," said Laos. "I was only making fun of the psychology of climbing Mount Everest. But this is merely symptomatic of our attitude toward Nature, our relation with Nature. If man cannot learn to be humble before Nature, he will never learn humility any other way."

"Just what do you mean?" asked Eurydice.

"I mean there is a pre-established harmony between man and Nature. When that harmony is upset, man is destroyed. When man is deep-rooted in Nature, he becomes healthy and normal again. Nature is man's element, as water is fish's element. Deprived of his element, man's nature changes also; his feelings, his emotions, his ambitions all change. He gets a mild form of megalomania, thinks of himself as too clever. He loses his scale of values. . . . Are you a mystic?"

Now this, just after a lobster lunch, Eurydice thought. She didn't want to be dragged into probings of mysticism. She answered quickly and stupidly. "No. Why?"

"Because what I am going to say may sound mystical to you. It isn't really. It is difficult to explain. Man, through hundreds of thousands of years, has developed a mechanism of response to wind and sun and rain, to mountain and wood and stream, and to the changes and the rotation of the seasons, to all the sights and sounds and smells of nature. There is nothing mystical about that. One may say that organically we are adapted to this earth, which is our element. The thing is far subtler than we think. I suppose it is permissible to speak of the subtle radiations of all these forces of Nature; there is an established harmony between our nerves and muscles, our sight and smell and touch and the heat and cold, and the smell of the soil and all that. Take man away from Nature and he perishes like a fish out of water. The harmony is destroyed. Do you believe that?"

"I can see there's something in it."

"Well, sometimes people make it sound mystical — unnecessarily so. Like speaking about radiations of occult forces. What I mean is simply that man is physiologically attuned to Nature's harmony. Put a red Indian in an air-conditioned apartment and he physically suffocates; his lungs are used to larger quantities of oxygen. Put shoes on him and make him walk on concrete pavements, and he dies like a sparrow in a cage — you've seen those scrawny lions in cages at the zoo. These are very subtle things, like changes in the blood when we move to high altitudes, or cold regions. Physiology is a world of subtle responses and processes in itself. The wild mountain sheep grows a thicker wool in anticipation of a severe winter. Trees start shedding leaves at the first touch of autumn, and, mind you, without nerves that we know of. Potatoes in the cellar put out sprouts in spring — equally without nerves of any sort. How do you account for that? We are as much part of that Nature's harmony as the potatoes. You may not believe me, but when a gardener, his hand caked with damp soil, watches that soil whiten in the warm breeze, he gathers new strength. When the cool wind passes over the plowman's brow and clears the sweat on it, he, too, gathers a new strength."

"You mean we should get back to Nature."

"It is an over-used phrase since Rousseau's days. Trite, perhaps, but we may not disobey the laws of Nature with impunity. I mean simply that we belong to this earth, are physiologically attuned to it. The worship of Demeter is not pagan or Christian; it merely celebrates an eternal truth. I would rather say that we should imitate the earth."

"Imitate the earth?"

"Yes, imitate its serenity and its patience. You see that gulley and those uplands there. The spring freshet washes the earth down; it is exposed to the frost and the snow and the wind and sun. It is gray, yet contains in its bosom the pastel of the violets and the tulips and the orchids. It is acrid, yet it is sweet with the apples, and vanilla and mint. It is dumb, yet is alive with the orange and the grapes, and it gives fragrance to the lilac, the profuse song of the sparrows and the meadow lark. You get mystical when you think of these things. See how silent, how quiet and peaceful the valley looks now!"

As if to make mockery of this last remark, the bells of St. Thomas' suddenly pealed an alarm, to the surprise of everybody.

Chapter XLII

THERE WAS NO REASON for the bells of St. Thomas'
to be sounded now.

"Whatever for?" said Philemon.

"It's mysterious," remarked Laos.

They listened. The notes were unusually fast, energetic, a little
bit frantic, more like a fire alarm than like the joyous, serene
call to devotion. Then, as abruptly, they stopped.

"It's probably some children, or some young people playing
pranks on the holiday. Some fellow may have got drunk."

After a while, the frantic tolling began again, this time apparently in earnest. It lasted about two or three minutes.

Philemon and Alcibiades rushed out to see what it was about.
Eurydice and Chloe followed. By the time they had reached
the colonnade at the Athenaeum, the bells had stopped again.
Evidently, Father Donatello or the man at the bell had not made
up his mind. Coming to the edge of the square overlooking the
town, they could see people rushing here and there.

"Oh, look! There's a ship!" exclaimed Chloe pointing in the
direction of the south shore.

Far out at sea, surely enough, a medium-sized tanker was
slowly plowing across the water, perhaps four or five miles
away yet.

Seeing the commotion at the colonnade, Laos and Aristotimus
and Eugénie now ran up. Everybody was excited. They had
not seen a ship since Telemachus had made his farewell trip eight

347

or nine years ago. Young Wriggs was beside himself. So was Eurydice along with everybody. They could not believe their eyes.

Laos' face darkened, wrapped in puzzlement. Slowly he said, "Perhaps it is Telemachus."

Iolanthe said to her daughter, "Chloe, go and get the field glasses. I left them at Laos' house."

Chloe was starting to go, when Philemon said he would go in her place. Meanwhile the ship was looming nearer, cutting its way through the wrinkled surface of the ocean.

When Philemon came back with the field glasses, Iolanthe looked and then gave them to Laos.

"It is Telemachus all right. I can see its name: *Athanopoulos*."

Alcibiades was all impatience, waiting to take a good look. His hands were trembling, and perspiration poured down his forehead as he stared into the glass.

"Are you sure it is Telemachus?" Iolanthe asked.

"I am sure," replied Laos, considerably relieved. "I thought he was never coming back."

Now many people had come up to the square, among them Prince Andreyev. He had been the first to spot the ship from the Countess' villa, as he was strolling on the shore of the promontory. Everybody rushed out to see. Then Father Donatello left immediately to ring the alarm, so that the "corpses" stored in a back room of the rectory could be taken out and laid along the shore. Then later the Prince had sent word to stop the alarm. The priest, however, had decided that whatever the ship was or her business, he should ring out the alarm so that the colony would be warned. Father Donatello himself was now, with the help of many people, spreading the corpses about the shore. Many of the people had now come up to the Athenaeum to get a better view of the approaching ship.

Prince Andreyev was greatly relieved when Laos assured him that it was the old skipper, probably returning for a visit to the island.

"Are you sure?"

"I am quite sure. This will upset the ceremonies this afternoon. But we have two hours yet."

"Let the poetry contests and the play go on," said the Prince. "At most, we may be held up for a while."

"That's it," said Laos suddenly. "It can be nobody else, to arrive on the thirtieth anniversary of our landing. Telemachus must have timed his arrival for the Irenicia. He was so enthusiastic about it the last time he was here."

This unexpected event broke up the party. Laos was going down to the shore. Hundreds of people had already gathered there. The ship, approaching from the southeast, was already looming up beyond the lagoon.

There was one man who was not there, and that was Groucho. His electric boat had been readied for launching in the lagoon for an exhibition the next morning, when the water sports would be held. Among all the Ireniki colonists, there was no one more excited than Groucho. He had been invited to lunch by the Countess. The moment he saw the ship coming, he knew his chance had come. "Boy, oh, boy!" he shouted when he sighted it. Without further ado, he dashed out of the Countess' villa and returned to the dam. He ran as fast as he could to the small speedboat lying at the mouth of the river.

The appearance of the speedboat in the lagoon even before the ship arrived surprised everybody. Now he was making a dash across the water toward the ship, and encircling it. Human figures could be seen on deck. The colonists and the Thainians were watching. Some even thought that the speedboat belonged to the big tanker. In the general excitement, the corpses were trampled over, Laos having assured everyone that it was not necessary to take the usual safety measures. A few rowboats put out to sea, and the big fishing boats were weighing up anchor. The excited voices of men and women shrilled along the beach. It was the most exciting event in years.

The old skipper came ashore in a small lifeboat. Groucho had at first appeared to be following along, but it turned out that he was towing the lifeboat ashore. For a moment the popping electric boat overshadowed the excitement created by Telemachus' arrival.

Laos, Iolanthe, Prince Andreyev and Father Donatello were standing on the sand to welcome the old captain. The latter was wearing a sun helmet and an open shirt. A short-clipped white beard edged his well-tanned face. With a ringing shout, he hugged Laos. Then he greeted the others.

"Where is Athanopoulos?" he asked.

Iolanthe was silent, and the old skipper understood.

"I thought I could make it. You must be celebrating the thirtieth anniversary of the founding of the colony. But a stiff headwind slowed us up a bit."

"You remember the date of the Irenicia," said Laos pleasantly.

"Certainly I do." The captain's voice was young and buoyant. "I've brought you a lot of things, medicines and other supplies."

"Let's go up to the Residence."

The party went up. Groucho tied up his speedboat and accompanied them.

"How long can you stop?" Laos asked the captain on the way.

"Two or three days."

"Why don't you drop everything, and come and stay for good?"

"I would love to. But I have to go on. If I do, I'll have to bring my family here. I have two grown-up grandchildren. I've come to pay a special visit to my old friend and see how you people are getting along."

Telemachus was not surprised to hear about the death of Athanopoulos. But he was greatly moved when he reached his friend's house. In the parlor, they talked of various things, reminisced on the old days. How Stephan and Chloe had grown up! They were kids when he saw them on his last trip. Telemachus was doing well; his ships plied between the West Indies, North Africa and South America; his firm now owned six of them. Athanopoulos' first wife had died, but his two sons were carrying on. Prince Andreyev, Laos, Eurydice, Alcibiades, Groucho and Emma-Emma were all in the room. No, he had not forgotten Emma-Emma. She was keeping so well. He always remembered their first trip to the island. His mind constantly reverted to his old friend, the founder of the colony:

"A great man. A very great man," he meditated. "But I miss the goat smell. This place used to stink all over."

Iolanthe laughed. "We have taken down the goatshed at the back. You must see the statue we have erected in his honor."

At last the Countess appeared with Eunice. She was breathing heavily when she walked into the room.

"Oh, Cordelia!" The old skipper stood up, opened his arms in a great gesture and hugged her.

"You haven't changed a bit!" he exclaimed.

"Thank you. But you don't fool me. I must have, haven't I?"

"Not in my eyes. You haven't."

Telemachus, full of vigor, said he would like to see the house once more, for the pleasure of refreshing his memories. Iolanthe guided him. He stopped for a moment on the terrace, admiring the view, then went through the house. It was almost like seeing his old friend. He also saw Athanopoulos' room, now occupied by Eurydice. He had to be told who Eurydice was, and how she had come. It was arranged that he was to be put up in the house for the night, and that the next morning, he would have his men bring up the supplies he had thoughtfully brought for them — wines, cigars, newspapers, magazines, medicines, clothes, silks, etc. He said he owed everything to Athanopoulos. The poetry recitals and dramatic performance were to begin at five o'clock. No, he would not miss it for anything. He had come specially to attend the Irenicia. He would be able to see Athanopoulos' statue on the way there.

"Does nobody know about the colony?" Laos asked.

"No. I gave Athanopoulos my word. I never told anybody."

"How about your crew this time?' '

"They don't know anything. They only know they are somewhere in the eastern South Pacific."

Alcibiades asked, "Can I go out to the ship to take a look? I have never been aboard one."

"Surely, you can. Provided you don't tell the crew what this place is. They are mighty curious."

What was going on in Alcibiades' mind and in Groucho's mind, particularly Groucho's, was something weightier and more important, far more important than the exhibition of the speedboat. It opened up a ray of hope for Groucho to return to the Old World, and for Alcibiades to visit vast new continents which he had only read about and which he longed to visit. Groucho would not have to wait for years till the solar motor was perfected, if he could only get Laos' permission. He had already learned that the ship would not be leaving for three days. Now he did his best to cultivate the skipper's friendship. He had not come here voluntarily; he had virtually been held captive with no means of escape. He would ask Laos, and if Laos had objections to his going back with the ship, he would know what to do.

"Why, here's our chance," said Groucho to Eurydice. "Don't you want to return to the U.S.?"

"This is so sudden, so unexpected. Why don't you ask Laos?"

He went to speak to Laos, while the skipper was on a tour of the house. He presented his case as strongly as he could.

"Look, Laos," he said. "Here's a chance for me to return to my country. I am not one of your original colonists. I crash-landed here. You destroyed my plane. I am virtually a captive held here against my will. Now there's a chance . . ."

"Isn't that putting it rather strongly? I don't like to hear you regard yourself as a captive. Haven't you enjoyed your life here?"

"I have."

"And the Republic pleases you, I hope."

"It isn't that. Every man feels differently. This is not my country. The U. S. is my country. Naturally I want to go back."

Laos thought a moment, and said, "What about Eurydice? She is in the same situation as you."

"I don't know about her. It is her business whether she chooses to stay or return."

"This question has never come up before," said Laos enigmatically. "You are the first person ever to express a wish to leave the island. Naturally, I am a little disappointed. We do want you to stay. Then there's the matter of not wanting anybody outside to know. Our colony is a closely guarded secret."

"I can swear I shall never tell anybody."

Laos glanced at him with an appraising look. "Perhaps. I don't know. Perhaps I can trust you. You see, nobody knows our secret except Telemachus. His loyalty to Athanopoulos cannot be questioned. Frankly, I don't know. Then if I let you go back, I'll have to let Eurydice go, too. We love you too much to wish you to leave us. We shall certainly miss you, and I don't think we have quite as fine a mechanic to take your place."

"How about me?" said young Wriggs, standing on the side. "Why can't I go with Telemachus and see the Old World?"

Laos smiled indulgently at the young man. "You are restless, Alcibiades, I see. How about your mother? And how are you going to come back?"

"What's all this?" said the Countess, who had been listening. "Oh, dear, Telemachus' coming is already causing trouble. Alie, darling, how can you even think of such a thing? You belong here. And Eurydice is here, and we are growing so fond of her just now."

"You see," said Laos to Groucho, "you are setting a bad example. Eurydice hasn't said a thing. Probably she is not even thinking of leaving at all. I don't want to hold anybody here against his or her will if I can help it. Let me think it over."

It did seem that everything hinged upon Eurydice. If Eurydice insisted on going back, too, it would make Groucho's case stronger. And Laos would probably stretch a point for her. Laos did not like it at all. Keeping the whereabouts of the colony secret was his paramount consideration — the only defense for the island against outside interference. Once someone leaked out the secret, troubles would begin. Not whether the Ireniki Republic would let the Old World alone, but whether the DWC would let them alone. Even if there were no political interference, the invasion of tourists alone would be enough to vitiate the peace of the island and spoil its characteristic ethos and mores, as had been done in Tahiti and Bali.

Eurydice had not thought about it at all; it had been so sudden.

She had gone along with Chloe and Stephan and Iolanthe, showing the house to the skipper, almost like a member of the family. When she came back to the parlor, both Alcibiades and Groucho spoke to her about the opportunity of leaving the island. She didn't know what to think. She was just beginning to like the island and the people, fascinated by their original philosophy and way of life. Certainly she had not yet had enough of the island. If the ship had come a year later, she might readily seize the chance to go back. But she had been here only a little over a month!

Chapter XLIII

IT WAS IN THIS CONFUSED STATE of mind that Eurydice went in young Wriggs's company to watch the dramatic recitals at the amphitheater. The ceremony opened late, waiting for the appearance of Laos and Prince Andreyev and the newly arrived guest. The amphitheater was partly in the shade, the weak afternoon sun shining upon a section of the tiers, which were cut into the hill, looking down upon the stage in the west. The orchestra, boasting four violins, a cello and flutes, started to play when the distinguished leaders came in to take seats in the front row. Also ranged in the front were the girls from the Institute, all dressed in white.

All eyes were turned to the new guest. His arrival overshadowed the performance itself in public interest. Laos went to the stage. After an invocation to Athena, he gave an opening speech, then introduced the skipper, with many genial sallies at his old friend, which the audience seemed to enjoy greatly. Telemachus strode up to the stage amidst much applause. He said briefly that he had come all the way to attend their Ireniki festival, and recalled vividly the adventures during the founding of the colony. He spoke in Greek. It was his happiest day; he had never forgotten about the colony in all his voyages; he had dreamed about returning for a visit to see how they were all faring. Then he recalled, with much evident emotion, the founder of the colony, and asked the audience to stand up in silence in honor of his memory.

All this while, Eurydice's thoughts were turning about the unexpected chance to return to her old country. At this moment, she felt a nostalgic pain about the Old World she had left so far away.

The recitals began. Two old men, Sardanopoulus the Phrygian and Demagoras of Epirus, who claimed to be a direct descendant of Neoptolemus, son of Achilles, gave moving dramatic recitals, partly sung to the lyre. They regaled the audience with selections from Homer, long passages about ancient wars and warriors, of which the audience never tired.

It was the custom for Laos to recite one of his own compositions at the annual festival. He mounted the stage amidst a thunderous applause. It was evident that as the father of the colony, he was held in great esteem. His well-tanned face, his white hair brushed back from his brow, and the gentle but bright glow in his eyes spoke of a man having reached a happy old age. The audience's murmur subsided as he cleared his throat to read the short poem he had written for this occasion.

He announced the subject of the poem, "The Atom," and explained in a few words the structure of the atom by analogy. He pictured a magician whirling a number of tiny balls at the end of a number of strings; as he whirled faster and faster, the orbits of the balls grew bigger and bigger and the magician grew smaller and smaller until finally he became a shadow without mass and weight, and what remained was a blurring whirl representing a field of force, practically empty except for the tremendous force keeping the balls in motion. Any object hitting its orbit would feel it like solid metallic wall. The magician was the nucleus, and the balls were the electrons.

> The fairy tales of science can now be told,
> Surpassing the brave dreams of manhood's youth,
> When faith was a creative guess at truth,
> Investing Nature with elves and sprites of old;
> Or our own childhood fancies, free and bold,
> When kinship love made all the universe move,
> When twinkling starlets whispered from above,

And the beetle's back was prettier than gold;
Till adolescence shed a cold, gray tinge,
And bat-eyed reason paled the magic lure,
And all is matter dead, exact and sure,
All mysteries gone, and nothing wondrous strange.
But the earth is alive! Once more we can
Recapture the joy and wonder of ancient man.

Ah, eerie is Nature, magic in the flesh!
The atom is a prison of fairy ions —
The insubstantial fabric which our science
Is weaving into a cosmic, ethereal mesh;
While she forges the cipher key to crash
The phantom fortress by a million volts
And pry loose the infinitesimal bolts,
So freeing ions to serve mankind afresh.
This was the vision which the sages saw
That matter wore a spiritual hue.
And somewhat chastened now, we stand anew
Before a speck of dust, staggered with awe.
Such the new faith: the stars of heaven pour
A golden liquid same as a blade of straw.

What if the atoms be smashed! and out there came
A thousand trotting angels trooping the earth,
Swift-footed Mercuries, with high-powered mirth,
To run our errands, quick as lightning flame!
What if the merry throng, without a frame,
But with Herculean powers, cross the shores,
Wing over seas and oceans to do the chores
For man, without a thought of praise or blame!
Yet shall we not ourselves escape the Tao,
Nor have the wit to shake this mortal coil,
But fears and worries and unceasing toil
Shall fill our human lot, until somehow
With larger comprehension, strife shall cease,
And war and turmoil shall give way to peace.

Now the dramatic presentation of the story of Ariadne was
to begin. For the audience, it was the great event of the day's

program, making vivid by song and chorus and action an ancient legend very close to their hearts. The girls had been practicing for weeks. For them it was the culmination of their training in grace and beauty and music and eloquence. For Laos, it was the justification of all the expenditures and labors incurred in the promotion of the arts, so that once a year the high level of culture and artistic expression should be manifest.

The stage was simplicity itself, having for its backdrop the sky in redolent sunset, glistening above the tree tops. At this time of the day, a stillness hung over the island and sea. The very clouds seemed to have congealed into patterns of citadels and columns and a desert of fleece, piling up miles high in the distant sky, motionless. In that upper region, those white forms were coalescing and dispersing, regrouping and reforming, so gradually that at the great distance the changes were imperceptible. By watching steadily, one might notice after a few minutes that a castle tower was dissolving at one corner, or cracking in two, embankments had widened and thickened, shapes of beasts and dragons had altered or vanished. The air had sufficiently cooled for the audience to relax and give themselves wholeheartedly to the enjoyment of the drama, the chorus and the dance being enacted in the arena.

It was a superbly beautiful presentation. The girls carried the audience with them, by their song, their dance, their zest, and the beauty of their voices and gestures. The audience knew the story anyway. It didn't matter. They loved the songs and they loved the story — first the love scenes of Ariadne and Theseus, the fight with the monster Minotaur, the escape and marriage, and then the desertion of the girl by Theseus, and finally the entrance of Bacchus. The simple devoted girl became a knowing, laughing, licentious woman who mocked at man's infidelity. Toward the end, in the bacchanalian scene, the audience grew a little rowdy and joined in the chorus.

Phoebe, who played the part of Ariadne, stepped down from the stage to a deafening applause. The play apparently had no moral. It was just a commentary on human nature. Ariadne ended up as a star in heaven. Nevertheless, Eurydice rather liked it.

Now the people retired to the feast which had been prepared. The day's festivities were nothing compared to the celebrations of the night, by feasting and dancing and song. Oxen and lamb contributed by the wealthier families had been turning on the spit over open fires. The people gathered around the fountain, to amuse themselves with food and wine and a night's revelry. For on this night the law against drunkenness was suspended. The square around the fountain was brilliantly illuminated. Housewives offered stewed hare and the most delicate pastry and enormous raspberry pies. To this feast, the native servants, field workers, and some of the Thainian neighbors of the different families were invited. The square was packed solid with a milling throng, overflowing to the connecting alleys and outer spaces. It was noticed, however, that many young lovers preferred to carry their food to the surrounding grounds, where the long day permitted a soft twilight to linger around the clearings. A long stretch of lights led along the path from the square to the gymnastic ground.

Some fireflies appeared, weaving patterns of light through the branches overhead and among the grass. The air was noisy with the cries of insects. The warm wind from the sea made their limbs relax. Over at the square, the air was even suffocating and moist from the congestion. The crowd, after helping themselves to the food, flowed out in all directions, while some fiddlers perched on a high stand continued to play lively tunes and add to the noise and gaiety of the night.

With the wining and feasting, a few people were quite prepared to get happily intoxicated. The Ireniki holiday was gay, noisy and a bit rowdy. All bars were down. Oaxus was seen toddling about in a happy inebriated state. The Thainians, too, had come out in great numbers, joining the throng of revelers and waiting to see the torch race at ten o'clock. The laughter of men and women rang in the woods.

Eurydice was excited, as she should be, enjoying the feast

with Alcibiades, Philemon and others. Now Philemon and Chloe
were gone. Emma-Emma, who was with Eurydice, saw Bowena,
plate in hand, going into the woods with Tihualco.

"Are you enjoying yourselves?" she asked the Thainian girl.
Bowena smiled beatifically.

"I think I should go back now," said Eurydice. "Telemachus
and Laos have left."

"Nonsense," said Emma-Emma. "I am going home. I have
seen the torch race so many times. But you young people. This
is a young people's night. Unthinkable!"

Left alone, Eurydice said to Wriggs. "Where shall we go?"

"I would hate to go into the woods. Let's go off where it is
quiet. We'll go to the beach. We'll row out and see the torch
race from the sea. It will be held on the beach."

Alcibiades' mind was occupied. Hand in hand, they strolled
toward the beach. The night was moist and warm. Lots of boys
and girls were already there. Wriggs loosened the boat, pushed it
into the water, and they got in. The air, vapory, smelled of the
sea. Lights were visible through the forest; there were bonfires
here and there, and the sky above the square glowed. As they
rowed out, the noise of revelry became subdued and distant;
they had gotten out of the overhanging mist, and the tropical
sky glittered with starlight.

Wriggs rested on his oars, and let the boat drift.

"I hope you are not going to leave," he said sadly. "Unless
we go together. It will be like a dream fulfilled for me. Groucho
has spoken to Laos."

"I have an idea that Groucho will go anyway, whether Laos
consents or not. He can manage to slip aboard ship. He is getting
on with the skipper. Or he can go in his speedboat and meet
the ship at sea."

"I am going aboard tomorrow. I have talked with the skipper.
I've never seen the inside of a ship in my life. How I dreamed
of this! A chance to see the Old World. There will never be another."

"How would you get back? You'll be leaving the island for
good."

"I don't care. I just must see the world. I don't mind working as a sailor, scrubbing the deck to earn my passage. The skipper seems like a decent fellow. How about you? Here's your chance. We can go together. I'll be like an ignoramus. Everything will be new to me. Cars, railways, subways, your underground palaces — everything will be new."

Eurydice said nothing. Such a difficult decision had been forced upon her just when she was getting used to the island, and beginning to like it. She loved all these people who had been so kind — Iolanthe and the Countess, the young, vivacious Chloe, and the contented, scholarly Emma-Emma. Emma-Emma seemed so perfectly happy here. Yes, she loved all these colorful characters, even Prince Andreyev Somovarvitch and Father Donatello and the limping doctor-ornithologist Lysippus, and the loud-voiced, vital Joanna. She had not forgotten Bowena. And Philemon. Philemon and Chloe, what a happy young couple! What did they care whether they saw the outside world? Philemon was so talented; and remarkably well-read for an artist. No, he was not just a sculptor. She had always enjoyed the conversation of Philemon and Eunice and Laos; she hadn't heard half enough of what she wanted to hear. A world of new ideas had just opened; she could learn so much more. It had all been very bewildering, perplexing, upsetting. Boys majoring in strength, and girls majoring in grace. She had not had a chance to hear Laos talk of his esthetics yet.

Above all, there was Alie. Laos had said something very enigmatic to her, just before he left with Telemachus after the feast. It was very curious because he suddenly asked her, "Where did you go to college?" She answered, "Colorado." Laos paused. "What about it?" she asked. "Well, never mind," he said. "I was thinking if you will stay with us, we will make you our Librarian at the Athenaeum. You'll get enough Greek in another few months. You said Colorado?" "Yes." And he had said, "It's not so important what college you went to, is it? It's more important what kind of man you marry." And he just turned and left.

Laos confused her, as he always did. Was he trying to suggest something? Or was he perhaps trying to keep both her and Wriggs from going away?

The torch race had begun. Against the bright lights on the shore, she could see dark, jumping, leaping figures. Apparently, there was quite a swarm of people on the shore. Some other couples, too, had paddled out to get a view of the race from the sea.

"Let's get out of here," said Wriggs.

"Alie! Whatever for?"

"I know the beach on the other side, beyond the Thainian village, on the other side of the river. Let's get away from all this noise."

Eurydice was terribly amused. The man, with his books and his thoughts, perpetually seeking solitude.

Wriggs started to row out past the sandbars and turned east. There was no noise except that of their boat swishing through the water and the creaking oars. Only the sea and stars remained.

"Isn't it strangely warm tonight?" he said.

"Yes, it is."

The current was strong where the river from the dam joined the sea. After some hard rowing, they pulled the boat ashore. Wriggs took a blanket and spread it on the sand. He was not himself that night. Tumultuous thoughts and passions thronged his heart and brain. A fateful decision had to be made.

Eurydice, too, was purring in happiness. She knew she loved Wriggs, the young, impressionable, restless soul of honor. "It's not so important what college you went to; it's more important what kind of man you marry." Laos' tricky words echoed in her ears. She could not forget them.

"Will you go if I stay?" she asked.

He was looking down closely at her face in the dim starlight.

"Eurydice, I beg you. Why don't you make up your mind to leave? I am sure Laos will let you. Then there's no question at all. Eurydice, you know how I feel about you, from that day you came to see me on the sandbar."

"Alie, don't talk."

Her arms closed around him, and their lips touched in a passionate, young embrace.

They had lain thus on the sand for an hour, thinking their own thoughts, Eurydice of her future, and Alie of his.

"You've never been up Mount Ida, have you?"

"No."

"We can go up now if you want to."

"Alie, you are crazy. What you want is sleep. Tomorrow you'll be seeing the ship."

"I can't sleep. It's really an inspiring view from the mountain top, especially at night. It's not so high as it looks. I love walking in the starlight."

Chapter XLIV

$\mathbb{I}$T WAS ALMOST DAWN when they came down from the peak. The sky was already faintly tinged with white. They had had a rest on top. But it was a good half-hour's walk coming down to the shore. Eurydice was tired, and sleepy. Finding their boat, they got in, and Wriggs rowed over to the lagoon side while she fell asleep.

The island was asleep, too. It should be. That night many lovers had fallen asleep in the woods. What surprised them was that when they approached the town, they saw lights burning in Chiron's tavern. The noise of some people talking could be heard in the dead of the night. They were angry voices, too. Eurydice heard the rich voice of Bowena. What was she doing out at this time of the night?

"Let's go and look," said Eurydice.

There had been an appalling murder. Bowena was in tears, having received several cuts on the arms. She had not informed her own people yet, or Emma-Emma. A group of young people, both white and brown, were at the square, some standing around the fountain, others inside the restaurant. Tihualco, Bowena's lover, had been murdered, his throat cut with a knife. The girl had screamed and waked up many people passing the night in the woods. These people had seen Oaxus, brother of Theodota, Chiron's wife, running through the trees. Some had seen him throw away a knife. An officer of the law had been informed, and had gone to the spot to inspect Tihualco's body. There was going to be trouble when the Thainian chiefs heard of this. Greatly upset, they came away, Wriggs taking Eurydice home as the dawn was breaking.

The news of the murder did not take long to spread as soon as the villagers were up. Laos and the Prince were informed. Oaxus was caught snoring in his bed, and arrested by the officers of the law. Emma-Emma herself came to the square to find out all the details. The Thainian chiefs had been informed and were coming. The town was buzzing with gossip.

So while the water sports were going on as planned and Groucho and Wriggs were helping with others to bring the presents of supplies from the ship, the story of the murder was very much on people's minds. The case was pretty clear. Oaxus had been arrested snoring in bed, his clothing stained with blood; the knife thrown among the underbrush had been found near the place of the murder. His wife, Clymene, was crying her eyes out. What was going to happen to her two children if their father was condemned to death? There were marks of a fight, and Oaxus could have pleaded self-defense, but he was so dead drunk that he really didn't know what had happened.

They were sure there was going to be a water-trial the next day. Athena had been made their goddess of justice, and it was their custom to try a serious crime on the last day of the Irenicia. Cases like murder, patricide and other forms of felony would be reviewed in court and the offender shut up in prison until the last day of the Irenicia when the grand trial would take place on the shore. The whole town was excited. There had not been such a water-trial for years.

The fact that a Thainian was the victim heightened the tension. The tribesmen's faces were grim that morning as they came to watch the sports. There was no telling what they might do if Oaxus was not found guilty and punished.

Eurydice was catching up on some sleep in her bedroom. Late in the morning Laos came up to the Residence with the skipper. Men were bringing ashore boatloads of supplies of all sorts, including hams and canned goods. The wines alone cost hundreds of dollars. Most interesting, however, were the newspapers and magazines. The house was astir with the clumping of men's boots.

Hearing that there were newspapers and magazines, Eurydice came out of her room. She looked at the newspapers. They were of no use to her; they were a month old. There was nothing about the baseball series that she did not already know.

She met Laos.

"Did you sleep well?" Laos asked.

"Marvelously. What time is it?"

"You can see for yourself."

The morning sun was shining full upon the terrace. She was yawning.

"I can't believe it."

"Believe what?"

"That I am here. I had a strange dream, nonsensical in fact."

"Tell me. Perhaps it is not entirely nonsensical. You were so excited yesterday. We all were."

"I dreamed that I was back in Minneapolis, visiting my aunt. There I met a college friend of mine, Iris. It seemed I had been far away and had just returned. Yes, I told them about this island and some of the things you people do here. They wouldn't believe me and called me a liar. I swore it was true. Then we went out to do some shopping. The people in the streets saw me walking on my bare feet and thought me insane. I attracted so much attention that the policeman came around and hailed me to court for disturbing public order.

"To my great mortification, my aunt and Iris told the court that I had been talking stuff and nonsense. I told the judge the same things, that I had been to Thainos, that there was an island free from the threat of war, that people actually built homes on the surface of the earth instead of in subterranean tunnels. There was great laughter in court. The judge said I was very ironic, and said if I persisted in my story, he would sentence me for contempt of court. I said, Your Honor, I am irenic, not ironic. He said I was talking Greek to him. I said that I wasn't; I was talking good

English, and as a college-educated person he should know. I asked if he knew what irenicon means. He said he didn't. I told him to look up Webster. The police looked up at the judge. There was a moment of silence. I wanted to be kind. I explained to help him out. I said, I am irenic, peaceful. I said he must have heard of girls called Irene; that was Greek for peaceful.

"I looked up at the ceiling and twiddled my thumbs, and the judge twiddled his. After this thumb-twiddling had gone on for some seconds, the judge recovered himself. He said that if I was irenic, I was ironic, that he would call in a psychiatrist to determine whether I was qualified for an insane asylum. I said, If you people don't believe my story, that there is a corner upon this God's earth where people are not threatened with war, you people are insane, not me. Not I, corrected the judge. Not me, said I. I was in a spiteful mood. Your Honor, I said, you seem to have learned English from grammar books. You don't know good English when you hear it. That's not the King's English, said His Honor. Where's your king? said I; I talk the people's English. The court was set in an uproar.

"This diversion created an atmosphere in my favor. Lots of people in the audience were sympathetic toward me. Somebody with a mousy-colored beard stepped up and whispered in the judge's ear. It is clearly established, said the judge, that the defendant has broken the law of the United States by creating public disturbance through her most unusual attire. It is most disturbing and indecent for a young, grown-up woman to appear barefooted in the streets. He was permitted by the law to sentence me for indecent exposure. However, it was possible, even probable, that I was suffering under some psychic disturbance and had dreamed all this up about the Ireniki settlement.

"He called for a copy of Rand McNally, to verify if there was an island in mid-Pacific by such a name. It's not on the map because nobody knows about it, I protested. Not even Mr. Rand, or Mr. McNally. This only confused them more. I was sure they would not find it on the map, which would be unfavorable to me. So I said, Bring the Webster, too, if you want to bring Rand

MacNally. You bring the Rand McNally, said the judge to a court officer. Yes, bring the Webster, I said after him. The audience was mystified.

"At this moment, you appeared, just as you are now. You glanced at me with a quick smile, and I cast you an imploring look. Tell them, I said, tell them that it is true. Serenely, you walked through the aisle right up to the judge and said, We are making such fuss over nothing. This is all a dream. This policeman is dreaming that he arrested Eurydice. Turning to the policeman you said to him very sharply, You are a dream. The policeman gaped in surprise. Before he could close his mouth, he vanished, just dissolved like a ghost. Then you took care of the judge, who was dumbfounded at what had happened. And you said, Your Honor, you are dreaming, too, that you are sitting here judging between a dream policeman and a dream defendant. His face seemed to dissolve, become transparent, and he just disappeared. Just like that."

Laos was greatly amused by the story. His lips curled up in a smile, and he said, "Perhaps you and I are such stuff as dreams are made of also. You, Eurydice, you are a dream, too, dreaming that you are telling a dream to a man called Laos about a dream judge and a dream policeman in a dream court, who believe they are real and take themselves very seriously."

"Perhaps."

"Did you hear about the murder last night?"

"Yes, I did."

"Where were you last night? Did you hear Bowena's screams?"

Eurydice's face colored a little.

"No. I was at Mount Ida."

"At Mount Ida?"

"Yes. Alcibiades wanted to get away from all the noise. We rowed out to the other side."

Laos' eyes gleamed for a brief second.

"What is going to happen?" she asked.

"Oaxus is foredoomed, I am afraid, although I personally believe he is guilty. There might be mitigating circumstances; he was drunk. But it is a dangerous, explosive situation. The tribesmen want to see blood. I have invited their chiefs to sit in judgment with us. And then, if and when he is found guilty, they will deal with him in their own way."

"What do you mean? Eat him up?"

"No, they are not cannibals, though there is a good argument for cannibalism when a man is killed."

"You are shocking."

"Not at all. We don't kill a man with a knife; we drown him in the sea. But when the tribesmen take it over, the drowning is much more subtle, refined. It is turned into a kind of sport — like a bullfight, or a gladiatorial combat. A curious point of human psychology — the Ireniki people love it, too."

Laos paused and added, "Are you going to leave us?"

Eurydice's eyes opened wide. "Are you suggesting I should?"

"Groucho was asking me yesterday, and this morning again. He said he was held here against his will. I feel a little hurt, of course. I don't want to hold people here against their will. I've thought about it. Your case and his are identical. If I let him go, I will have to let you go, too. The choice is yours. The only thing is, I have to trust your honor. Groucho and you have to give me your word of honor that you will under no circumstances divulge the whereabouts of the colony. Just as in your dream, people might think you insane and subject you to a psychiatric examination when you tell them about it. Of course, you can add a few melodramatic details, say you are spat out of the belly of a fish, like Jonah, for example. They will surely confine you to a hospital for mental cases."

"What about Alcibiades?"

"What about him?"

"Will you let him go?"

Laos' laughter was brittle. "How can I? I have made quite an exception for you and Groucho. His case is different. I don't think Telemachus will take him. Depend on it. Even if I agree to his going, the skipper won't; he is stubbornly loyal to us. Then perhaps there will be many more young men who want to see the

Old World as a matter of curiosity. I cannot allow that. And it won't be fair to let him go. I am sorry."

Eurydice tried to puzzle it out. Perhaps it was Laos' plan to keep her on the island without appearing to compel her to do so.

"When will Telemachus leave?" she asked.

"We want him to stay as long as he likes. He seems decided to go tomorrow afternoon." He glanced at her kindly, and added, "We shall be sorry to see you go, if you do insist. Take your time, and think about it. Remember you have been offered a job as the public librarian on the island. The offer still stands."

Leaving the house, she met Groucho coming up. He was a new man. He had come alive.

"Eurydice," he said, "Laos is letting me and you go back with Telemachus. Boy, oh, boy!"

"Have you considered whether it is possible for Alcibiades to come along?"

"I don't know. Why should he go?"

"Because he wants to very much, to see the world. Do you think you could arrange it, as a stowaway perhaps?"

"That may be difficult."

"Certainly you can, with your speedboat. He can go out in the dark. He need not be discovered until the boat is on the way. After that, I will take the whole responsibility; I believe I can handle the skipper."

"I am sure you can."

"Have you seen Alie around?"

"He has just gone out with the skipper to look at the ship."

Eurydice strolled by herself toward the beach. The water sports were over, and people had gone back for lunch. The gymnastic contests would be held in the afternoon. She stood alone looking at the ship lying just outside the lagoon. There it was, the connection between her and the Old World. A few weeks ago, it would have been the answer to her prayer, a means of delivery from her confinement on this island. Her days had been so happy, so full of surprises that she would be sorry to leave now. She did not know what to think.

There, she thought, was Alie on that ship at this moment, all excited, praying for a chance to go with her and set sail to the world beyond. For all his self-taught manners, he was still very inexperienced, immature, hardly prepared to knock about in the wide world without landing himself in some noble, but foolish, adventures. Like that episode with Margherita. Impressionable, excitable beneath his reserved exterior, living very much to himself, would he not be as easily disappointed as he was now enthusiastic about a world he had glamorized in his imagination? Might he not change once he set his foot on the continents of the Old World?

She wanted very much to talk to somebody. Her steps led her unconsciously back to town, past the square, into Emma-Emma's cottage, the cottage where just over a month ago, she had received the first hospitality of the old American woman.

Bowena had gone back to her village. Emma-Emma was alone, her face grim. She was very much worked up over what had happened to Bowena. She was worried, too. She knew there might be a communal riot if Oaxus were acquitted at the trial. This interracial relationship was a ticklish business, stirring up one of the deepest instincts in the human soul, the instinct of the herd.

Emma-Emma was glad to see her. She saw the expression on the younger woman's face, weighted with thought.

"Laos told me that I can go back if I want to. Groucho is going. I hate to leave this island and all you people. What do you think?"

"I am surprised at Laos' decision. He has never permitted anybody to leave the island. We don't want the integrity of this island to be compromised just as we are happily established."

"What should I do?"

"It's up to you. But Eurydice, I thought you liked us here. I tell you what. I know Laos will feel hurt if you choose to leave. He has told me; he thinks you are a very intelligent girl, and this choice he is giving you is not so much a test of you as of himself; on the success of his social experiment. You've come as an outsider to look at our way of life, and I imagine he likes to know how it strikes a visitor from the outside. . . . I don't suppose young Wriggs will be permitted to go with you."

"No," Eurydice said sadly.

"Don't be a fool," said the anthropologist.

"What do you mean?"

"I say don't be a fool. I believe you are mature enough to know what you want, instead of chasing around the globe to save humanity."

"You don't think I should go?"

"It's up to yourself entirely."

Eurydice asked about the trial of Oaxus, which was to take place the next morning.

"It is going to be a sensational trial for everybody on this island," Emma-Emma said. "They had better convict Oaxus, or there will be trouble. Oaxus is guilty. Of course he is. I have advised Bowena to testify about the rape, now that the affair has gone so far. And Bowena will, without my telling her. Poor girl, she loved Tihualco so. He was a fine young man, and they would have been married soon. How she hates the murderer!"

"I hear they are going to punish him by some sort of slow torture. What is it like?"

"It's a kind of gladiatorial combat in water. The poor fellow hasn't got a chance. I have seen it once, how the Thainians punished one of their own men. They put the condemned man in water and chase him all over the sea with good swimmers and boats. The man fights for his life. He hasn't got a chance. If they would put a spear through his body and throw him into the sea, he would be dead in a few seconds. But they turn it into a sport. The man ducks in the water to avoid his captors of course. He bobs up here and there to get his breath. But soon he will be exhausted, and they finally get hold of him, like the tired bull. He fights back, and gets away again. They catch him again, haul him overboard, and put a black sack over his head and tie his hands behind his back, and throw him back into the sea. They are all good swimmers. By the primary law of instinct for survival, he cannot let himself drown; certain animal reflexes work against his self-destruction. There he floats in the water, able to kick about, but unable to see, exposed to the sun and the water, completely blind-folded, sometimes for a day and a night, until he gives up his ghost."

"How can you people tolerate such a thing?"

"We've discussed it. It's difficult to stop an old tribal custom, when it is one of their own men. I'm afraid Oaxus is getting it, this time. It's one of the rawest instincts, this love of revenge. The question is whether they will be satisfied with a quick drowning."

"It's terrible, even to think of it," said Eurydice, as she visibly paled.

"I don't like this cruelty any more than you do. There's a point about it, though. I've discussed it with Laos, the whole subject of killing a man."

"What does Laos think?"

"Killing is never noble. Apart from this unnecessary cruelty of the Thainians, capital punishment is unavoidable, I believe. Men have killed men for less justifiable reasons. In war, for in-stance, taking the life of a stranger you have never met before, stabbing him in the belly with a bayonet, or even shooting him from the back, is considered both honorable and heroic. There are lots of silly things men do."

"Of course, war is war. Your enemy ambushes you. So you have every right to kill him from the back."

Emma-Emma said, "The point is, we are not so far from savagery so long as war is not abolished, however civilized we may think ourselves to be. I mean the physical part of it, crawling in the slime to avoid being detected by enemy sharpshooters. A most humiliating position, I should think. Or crawling in the jungle like a hunted criminal, trying to avoid being seen by another hunted criminal. We laugh at the Roman gladiatorial combats. Are we any better? What difference is there between throwing a Christian to the lions in the arena and sending a son freshly graduated from college to be stabbed or blown to bits on the battlefield? What difference? A professional gladiator had a better chance against a lion than a grocer's son against the crackle and spitting fire of a machine gun. We believe that we are civilized and superior to the Romans only because we are not that grocer's son. Once you identify yourself with that grocer's boy, you don't think so. I tell you we are all savages. It is possible only by the grossest lack of imagination on the part of the stay-at-homes to maintain the illusion of human civilization. Blood is blood, says Laos, and it smells exactly the same whether one is torn limb from limb by a hungry lion or by an exploding shell. Progress? Huh!"

"You are speaking of killing in general."

"Of course I am. Man kills for religious sacrifice, for food, or for sport; rarely for a good social purpose, such as capital punishment. The whole nation's wires buzz when a criminal is about to be sent to an electric chair, but of course the slaughter of a few hundred soldiers is reported as a quiet day on a quiet front. The Thainians are supposed to be cruel, insensitive; we pride ourselves on a finer sensitivity to human suffering, even suffering of animals. Mistreating a horse is horrible, but bombing, shooting or clubbing a young boy to death is simply refined, noble, patriotic and civilized. It is a matter of racial conditioning. The most non-sensical killing is of course unplanned killing. Between 1954 and 1964, a little under half a million people comfortably killed themselves and others on the highways in the United States alone, averaging a little better than 38,000 per year, or well over a hundred a day. More citizens of the United States were killed in one year by this folly than in the entire Korean War. That's about the most foolish form of killing. Then there's killing for food and killing for sport. There is, however, one essential difference between animals and men. As a rule, animals do not kill their own kind. They have more wisdom. Two lions may fight each other to death for love, but it rarely comes to that; the lion who loses is usually permitted to slink away in defeat. Wolves do not slaughter another pack of wolves of a different color. But the human species does — usually in the name of God and righteousness."

Eurydice's mind was preoccupied when she left Emma-Emma's house. She thought she should go and see the Countess. She could not make up her mind. The Countess was so warm, so understanding.

"What's the matter?" Countess della Castiglioni said when she entered her house. "I hear you are leaving us."

"Who told you?"

"Alie was just here."

"I never said exactly that I was going."

"Oh, darling, you musn't, unless you are crazy. We all love you. Don't you like us?"

"I do. Who told you I was leaving?"

"Alie. He said he heard it from Groucho."

"Where is he?"

"I don't know."

A sudden, unreasonable fear seized Eurydice. She explained to the Countess that she was hoping there might be some way of arranging for Wriggs to go with her in case she was going. "But I really have not made up my mind."

"Don't you know he would never consent?"

"What do you mean?"

"He came to me. He told me all about it. Groucho told him if he wanted to go, he might be able to smuggle him into the ship, as a stowaway."

"He told you?"

"Yes. And, darling, you ought to know. He is such a sweet boy. He said, 'How can they expect me to do such a thing, sneak away like a thief?' He would not even consider it for a second."

Eurydice was stupidly silent. She did not know what to say.

"Darling, listen to me," said the Countess. "I don't know what you are thinking. I don't blame you if you want to get back to your country and your work — what do you call it? — the Geodetic Survey. But I think you would be acting foolish to go away. It's a choice between the Geodetic Survey and Alie. I know you care for him. Even if you speak to Laos and are able to persuade him to let Alie go with you, I don't think it is wise — from a woman's point of view. Here on this island, he is yours. Once he goes out to the wide world, I don't know what may happen. He may want to do one of those foolish things, save a young girl in distress, perhaps. He may meet other girls. They will all be new, exciting, exotic to him. I would consider carefully if I were you."

At last, Eurydice said, "So he thinks I am leaving the island anyway?"

"That's the impression I got."

Eurydice left the house exasperated. She was almost sure, by a kind of feminine intuition, that he had gone into hiding again. He was that sort, seeking retreat into himself when he was in trouble. There was no use looking for him on the gymnastic ground where the contests were going on. She went to the beach and peered toward the sandbar. His boat was safely tied on shore. Where was he? She walked up to the Athenaeum, found the door closed for the holidays, and went around the lake in vain.

She decided to go home and wait. Surely he would come to say good-by, if he thought this was her last evening on the island. All night, she tossed in bed. She thought of the words of the Countess. A choice between Alie and the Geodetic Survey. What would she do when she got back? Report to the Democratic World Commonwealth. . . . Statistical data, beautiful charts on graph paper, committee meetings, memorandums, a nice feeling, never quite too sure, that she had a place, doing her bit, in a huge, unthinking machine trying to bring peace to the world. She wished she could be sure that that was what they were actually doing, that there were thinking brains actually coming to close grips with the fundamentals of world peace, that it was not a pious hope placed in a gigantic organization of delegates working at cross purposes, sent there to represent their own respective countries and not the common good of mankind, each struggling with his own individual problems. And what about herself? Committees, papers, committees, papers. She felt a little tired.

What if she chose to stay? she thought. Suddenly everything became clear, simple, a job as librarian at the Athenaeum, and Alie. No perplexities, no ambiguities, no doubts. She decided not to leave at all.

Chapter XLV

SHE DIDN'T FEEL SO GOOD when she got up the next morning. Her first thought was to find Alie and tell him. Her mind was made up, but she was nervous from a sleepless night.

Iolanthe was up early that morning. She still maintained her mystic Russian philosophy that punishment for sin was good for the soul. Not just Tolstoy, or Dostoevski; it was in her Muscovite blood. There was something inherently noble, soulful, in perceiving and experiencing atonement for sin. She was not like the Countess who could not stand looking at the chasing of a doomed man in the water; she was going to see it. It performed, as she said, a cathartic function on her soul.

At breakfast Eurydice announced to Iolanthe in firm and pointed tones: "I am not leaving Thainos."

Iolanthe was delighted. "Laos told me you were not leaving."

"How did he know?"

"I don't know. He just thought so perhaps. I am so happy that you will remain with us. Laos will be proud."

Chloe had come in, too. Eurydice rose nervously, and said, "I am going to look for Alcibiades."

"Are you coming to see the water-trial?" asked Iolanthe.

"Yes, of course."

Eurydice left. She did not know what she was nervous about, but she was. She wanted to tell Laos, Groucho, Telemachus, everybody, that she had made up her mind to stay on Thainos. But

377

above all, her heart was not at rest till she had seen and spoken to Alcibiades.

Alcibiades was not around. No one had seen him.

Oaxus was a powerful man. Not a particularly gracious creature of God. God was nodding perhaps when Oaxus was conceived. Philemon had characterized him rightly as a combination of assininity and owlishness. There was something subhuman, diabolic, in his eyes. Philemon despaired of making a successful portrait of him.

Oaxus was now standing in water to the waist. They had chosen a section of the shore near the promontory where the Countess' villa stood, to be quite sure that the prisoner would not hit one of the sandbars to the north.

The shore was black with a mass of human beings, Thainians and Irenikis. Practically all the Thainians had turned out. Their chiefs were sitting with the judges, which included Laos and Aristotimus and Prince Andreyev.

It is healthier to spare the details. In the trial, Bowena and Emma-Emma were important witnesses. Poor Oaxus. Nobody loved him. Emma-Emma had gone to Laos and extracted a promise from him that the slow torture be spared, considering that he was not a Thainian; on that condition, she would testify against Oaxus about the rape. Oaxus was of course foredoomed. He could not make his own defense and had no one to plead his case. He was frightened, frightened as a wounded beast fearing for his life. After Bowena testified about the rape, even his wife, Clymene, dried her tears. She sat silently like a mute statue hearing the proceedings.

He was pronounced guilty. The fact was, the public, all keyed up to see the chase in the water, would have been sadly disappointed if the verdict had been different.

The chase began. All around him were Thainian swimmers waiting in boats, armed with long poles. Someone jumped in to grapple with him, and purposely let him get away. Oaxus fought back, like an animal at bay. He ducked and swam out for his life. The real excitement began. In order that the amusement might be prolonged, the condemned had not been bound or shackled; he was expected to give a good account of himself. But the best swimmer would have no chance against several dozen men waiting in boats to subdue him whenever he popped his head up above the water. Even if he did escape out into the ocean, he would be like a refugee from the Foreign Legion escaping into the Sahara Desert. Now his head came up. The swimmers went for him. He vanished under the water. He bobbed up elsewhere. There was a long, fascinating chase. The swimmers had to be good, too. Whenever he appeared within reach, they dealt him blows. It was the scientific, measured technique of exhausting the bull before the kill.

Eurydice was sick at heart. She had heard from Emma-Emma that the Thainians had agreed to Laos' proposal, that the water chase be allowed as a form of sport, which the public demanded, but that as soon as he was captured, he should be given a quick drowning. The delicate situation had been handled to the satisfaction of both parties.

Where was Alcibiades Wriggs? Nobody had seen him. He was not at the sandbars, not on this day.

She left the beach while the chase was still going on. She asked Philemon and everybody she met. Nobody knew.

When she came out of the woods, she saw Dr. Lysippus, limping along toward the beach.

"Have you seen Alcibiades Wriggs?"

"He not at the shores?"

"No."

"I saw him last night, in late afternoon. He went forth toward the Delian Heights. Thither he went."

"Was he alone?"

"Yea, all alone."

Eurydice started to run. The town was practically empty. She had a feminine inspiration. Of course, she knew. Mount Ida, of course. She knew the exact spot where he would go, where they had spent an hour together two nights ago. It was a good three miles' walk to the top, and she had to go up the ridge and down the valley again.

Reaching the ridge, she gazed up at Mount Ida. The bluish-gray crags stood in the morning sun, silhouetted against a cloudless sky. Every detail high up on the skyline could be seen clearly. She saw something moving. She was sure it was he.

She started to run. But it was a long stretch, and slow going when she started climbing the slope. While she was still far off, she spied him at the foot of the crags. He had evidently seen her coming. She waved and he waved back. She shouted, but he could not hear her. Then he started to run down toward her.

"Alie, I am not going. Because you are not. I am staying — with you," she said when they met.

Alcibiades' young face was shining when he said, "But you are making such a great sacrifice for me."

"It's no sacrifice at all, Alie. No sacrifice at all . . ."

Her voice was smothered in a passionate embrace.

"Let's go up. We get a splendid view of the water chase up there. I never want to watch it at close distance."

They turned their steps up toward the peak. Way down below, out in the sea, the chase was still going on.

"We are like Olympians," said Eurydice, her hands resting happily on his shoulders.

"Yes, we get a certain perspective, don't you think?"

They remained on the peak, forgetful of the people below. Alcibiades had brought sandwiches and some fruit with him. Later in the day, they saw Groucho's speedboat approaching the ship anchored offshore. Twenty minutes later, the steamer glided out toward the south, her white funnel gleaming in the sun, her stern kicking up foamy white lines behind, headed majestically and peacefully toward the world beyond.

A lethargic state hung about the island when the festivities were over. Routine activities of the shopkeepers and artisans and their wives were completely disrupted. The Institute of Comforters of Men's Souls was closed; the doctors of men's psychic ills needed a rest as much as the patients. It was noticed that husbands did not beat their wives quite so often during this period. It was human nature not to feign illness when there were no pretty nurses in the hospital. Apart from the announcement of a few engagements owing to the heightened amatory activities during the festival nights, nothing was being done. Wives refused to cook or do laundry; the men had to eat cold roasts and pastries until their stomachs were sick.

Giovanni's restaurant was doing a good business. Joanna was very, very busy. For days, the idle islanders sat and talked and speculated about the trial of Oaxus. Oaxus had been quickly drowned after three hours in the water. Elder colonists remembered a man who was found still floating and alive on the third morning, so far setting a record. Now that Oaxus was dead, the people at the tavern began to reopen the trial, an idle post-mortem reminiscent of historians. The audience was prejudiced, some held; the judges had simply sold out Oaxus' life to preserve peace with the Thainians. Pietro, violinist and tavern philosopher, began to examine the juridical problem whether, since drunkenness was not punishable during the holidays, a man should not also be absolved from the consequences of drunkenness. This discussion went on and on for days, and nobody was the wiser.

Something was being done, however, for Oaxus' widow and the two children. At the council, Laos proposed that the widow be honored by the Republic in view of her husband's contribution to the maintenance of peace on the island. He proposed, much to Thrasymachus' horror, that a brass medal, made very bright and beautifully engraved, be given to the wife, in honor of the man who was the first of the veterans to die for the Republic, and his children be given education free at the state's cost. Prince Andreyev was delighted with the suggestion. Some minutes were wasted in deciding on the name of the new order now to be created: should it be Legion of Honor, or Order of the Eagle, or Knights of St. Nicholas?

Thrasmychus demurred. "Oaxus did not voluntarily seek death for the winning of the peace."

Laos replied, "No hero on the battlefield ever did."

Laos concluded that in view of the fact that the inhabitants had been fortunately saved from a civil war by the sacrifice of one man, and the further fact that the spectacle of the water chase gave an outlet, in some mysterious way, to certain regressive, destructive tendencies in the human psyche, Oaxus had performed a useful service to the nation. In recognition of this service of the criminal in extinguishing his life by drowning, and after his death had been certified by the police authorities, Prince Andreyev, as the President of the Republic, pinned the medal on Clymene the widow at a ceremony with proper blowing of horns and trumpets. As a further expression of the nation's gratitude toward the one they had disposed of, his two orphans were given education free at the state's expense. The whole ceremony gave the community a satisfactory sense of law and order. The nation had honored its hero. Men and women gradually went back to work, and peace was restored on the island of Thainos.

INDEX

Index